JEWS IN SOVIET CULTURE

JEWS IN SOVIET CULTURE

Edited by
JACK MILLER

Published for
the Institute of Jewish Affairs, London

Transaction Books
New Brunswick (USA) and London (UK)

The Institute of Jewish Affairs gratefully acknowledges the assistance of the Memorial Foundation for Soviet Culture which made the preparation and publication of this volume possible.

Library of Congress Catalog Number: 83-17906
ISBN: 0-87855-495-5 (cloth)
Printed in the United States of America

Library of Congress Cataloging in Publication Data
Main entry under title:

Jews in Soviet Culture.

Includes index.
1. Jews—Soviet Union—Intellectual life—Addresses, essays, lectures. 2. Soviet Union—Civilization—Jewish influences—Addresses, essays, lectures. 3. Soviet Union—Ethnic relations—Addresses, essays, lectures. I. Miller, Jack, 1912- .
DS135.R92J468 1984 305.8'924'047 83-17906
ISBN 0-87855-495-5

Contents

Introduction
Jack Miller vii

1 The Position of Jews in Soviet Culture: A Historical Survey
Shmuel Ettinger 1

2 Jews in Soviet Art
Igor Golomstock 23

3 Jews in Soviet Music
Joachim Braun 65

4 A Structural Study of Jews in Russian Literary Criticism, 1917-32
Benzion Munitz 107

5 The Jewishness of Babel
Efraim Sicher 167

6 Ilya Ehrenburg
Anatol Goldberg 183

7 Jews in Soviet Philosophy
Yehoshua Yakhot 215

8 The Jewish Contribution to the Development of Oriental Studies in the USSR
Inessa Axelrod-Rubin 247

Contributors 317
Name Index 319

Introduction

The idea of a symposium on the subject of this volume was prompted in part by the fact that the Jewish emigration from the USSR in the 1970s included authorities on particular fields of Soviet culture. Their scholarly knowledge of the contribution made by Jews and the circumstances of that contribution was likely to be informed by direct knowledge of personalities and conditions. The opportunity to commission and publish authoritative papers in this field was regarded as an opportunity not only in the area of modern Jewish studies but also in the study of Soviet culture and in the more general phenomenon of ethnic minorities which come to play an important part in the culture of the host nation.

While the Jewish contribution to Soviet culture has been considerable it is not a subject on which much work has been done. To that extent this symposium has an exploratory character, for which some variety of approach and method is not inappropriate. Also, the topics treated depended upon the fields in which contributors were available. Five of the seven topic papers are on the arts. Thus two studies comprise comprehensive treatments of painting and music, and of the three studies on literature two are each on a single writer while the third deals with a whole section of the literary scene. The other topics treated are philosophy and Oriental studies. Some of the papers cover the whole Soviet period and others the relatively free and formative years up to the early 1930s. A historical survey by Dr Ettinger provides a strong framework for all the topic essays.

The papers covering painting, music, philosophy and Oriental studies are by recent emigré authorities, and are indeed informed with a personal as well as scholarly knowledge of these fields of Soviet artistic and intellectual life. Of the studies in literature, that on the post-Revolutionary schools of literary criticism is by an earlier emigré student of the immediate post-Revolutionary period. The late Anatol Goldberg, who contributed the essay on Ilya Ehrenburg, had a profound knowledge of the USSR which was appreciated by listeners there to his regular Russian broadcasts from London. Dr Efraim Sicher, author of the essay on Isaak Babel, is a young Western scholar.

The difference in approach between Mr Goldberg and Dr Sicher exemplifies the wide range possible in dealing with Jews in Soviet culture. Mr Goldberg treats Ehrenburg as a Russian writer who happened to be a Jew. He did add at the end a reference to a possible Jewish quality, but did so in response to an editorial suggestion. Dr Sicher systematically and sensitively seeks to trace elements of Jewish culture throughout Babel's work. This difference in treatment must reflect to some degree a difference in interests between the two contributors to the symposium, but it must also reflect some significant difference between Ehrenburg and Babel as individual vehicles of the Jewish cultural tradition behind them.

The extent to which a difference of this nature may depend upon factors such as personality and the degree to which the minority culture was received in youth is amongst the many questions of inter-cultural influence which lie beyond the brief of this symposium, though several of the essays, in addition to Dr Sicher's, provide material for its consideration.

Most of the essays deal more with the general than the biographical aspects, and these offer much material on the influx of Jews into Soviet cultural life. The broad picture is one of young Jews emerging, after the reforms of the 1860s-1870s, from the purely Jewish world of the Pale into the larger Russian world. In culture as in politics, Jews began to break the shackles of their own narrow national traditions by joining and promoting the innovatory movements of the host nation. After the Revolutions of 1917, which offered cultural opportunities on a new scale, and therewith opportunities and pressures for assimilation, the re-assertion of Russian nationalism and its traditional antisemitism created contradictions for the majority of Jews, who in some full or limited cultural sense had become Russians, and especially for that high proportion of them who had become active in almost all spheres of Russian cultural life. Thus the Jewish contribution to the Soviet arts, humanities and intellectual life generally, and the conditions in which it was made, constitute a subject of great but by no means unique complexity, since inter-cultural influences are one of the basic processes of the human condition.

It is hoped that, in addition to the contribution made by each paper to its topic, this symposium as a whole will help to clarify questions of the imprint of one culture upon another, in particular of Jews on many cultures of the diaspora as well as the Soviet Russian case.

Glasgow, 1983 *Jack Miller*

1

The Position of Jews in Soviet Culture: A Historical Survey

Shmuel Ettinger

In the course of their long history the Jews have been influenced by the modes of life and the cultures of the great civilizations with which they have come into contact or to which they have been subject, and in many cases they have also contributed to the spiritual creativity of those civilizations. Works by Jews in Greek, Arabic, Spanish and modern European languages reflect these interactions. However, works by Jews in the modern era are marked by characteristics which clearly distinguish them from those of the Middle Ages and the Ancient World. In modern times, within the compass of European Jewish history, not only did the Jews acquire a command of the language of their region, its mode of life, and its cultural and scientific concepts; they also came to identify to a great degree with its moral and social values, and to judge the events of the time according to standards derived from the non-Jewish environment. No longer were there works in Greek extolling the sublime character of Judaism and its religious and moral creativeness for the benefit of the enlightened Gentile, nor were there justification and glorification of Judaism in Arabic, in terms of Kalam and Aristotelianism; there was rather identification with the 'spirit' of Germany, of France, of Poland and of Russia. Hence, the modern enlightened Jew regarded himself, and wanted to be regarded by his environment, as an integral part of its spiritual and social essence. Even his perception of Judaism and the Jews was not infrequently determined by the attitude prevalent in his cultural environment. And since Judaism was perceived in Christian-European thinking as inferior to Christianity, or as a preliminary to it, much of this attitude penetrated the perception and spiritual achievements of European Jews.

A not inconsiderable degree of striking roots was required in order to bring the Jews to the point where they could play an active part in the cultural creativity of the modern European countries. In all the lands, this was preceded by a period of absorption, learning, and gradual integration: forming commercial and social ties, reading newspapers and books, studying in the state schools, etc. In general, the earlier the stage in the modernization process of a particular country at which groups among the Jews began to strike roots in the non-Jewish environment and in its modern creativity the greater was the Jewish contribution to the culture. Very few Jews played an important part in molding the spiritual life of the countries of Western Europe, but their contribution was greater in the Central European countries (this includes Germany and Austria), and even more outstanding in the countries of Eastern Europe. And this despite the fact that Marranos from the Iberian Peninsula had already reached the Low Countries, England and France in the sixteenth and seventeenth centuries.

Seemingly, such Jews should have been accepted with open arms by the European countries undergoing the modernization process, since Christian preachers and polemicists opposed to Judaism had, in all the ages, been demanding from its adherents that they abandon their 'isolation' and 'prejudices,' and join the 'true culture,' i.e. Christianity. But, in fact, in the countries in which Jews settled there were many fears, overt or masked, among the majority of the populace: that the Jews might injure their Christian character; that they would not be loyal to their new homelands; that they would introduce an 'alien spirit,' not necessarily Jewish, but a spirit different from the native tradition. In Germany, during the 'War of Liberation'—that is, in the years of the Napoleonic conquests—the Jews were accused of bringing into the country the 'Western Spirit' from the other side of the Rhine, the 'French Spirit.' In Russia of the middle and later nineteenth century, the Jews were also accused of bringing in 'Western' ideas—that is to say, of causing the penetration, as it were, of the 'Manchesterian' materialistic attitude of avarice, the attitude of formalistic legal pedantry which characterized Europe and which was destroying the inner harmony of the Russian nation and damaging its most precious element—the rural community. These contentions carried weight in Russia especially, because the fourth decade of the nineteenth century saw the beginning, in intellectual circles, of the development and growth of the ideological conflict between the Slavophiles and the 'Westerners.' The Slavophiles sought to preserve Russia's unique historical way of life and its traditional political and social structure, and they criticized the reforms of Peter who tried to instil quasi-Western ways in the state. Conversely, the Westerners hoped that Russia would be freed from its 'Asiatic' past and tread the path of progress, following the examples of the enlightened European countries. Jews took no part in this controversy, and it is doubtful whether even the enlightened among them were sufficiently aware of it—although to some writers, philosophers and journalists, the Jews served as the ultimate example of the danger threatening Russia from capitalist activity. The prominence of some Jews as financiers, bankers, railroad builders and merchants of agricultural products was not only not considered an accomplishment and a breakthrough to an esteemed position in society, as in some Western countries, but rather bestowed a negative quality on the financial activities of Jews in general and created for them the image of a pernicious and parasitic group. And this was in addition to the historical, religious, and cultural tradition relating to Jews, which was so negative that until the partition of Poland at the end of the eighteenth century there was an absolute ban on the entry of Jews into Russia, even on an individual basis.

Strangeness added to the hostility. The residents of Russia, even the intellectuals among them—except for those who lived in the formerly Polish regions—did not know the Jews; not their mode of life, and certainly not their religious and cultural mores. And among the Jews almost none were acquainted with the Russian culture. The *maskilim*, i.e. those who supported the ideas of the Enlightenment and sought to approach the culture of the non-Jewish environment, were a small minority which did not dare to raise its voice in public, and was tied, culturally speaking, to the center of the Enlightenment in Berlin (either directly or by way of the Galician *maskilim*). Until the seventh decade of the nineteenth century very few Jews were proficient in the Russian language, and the cultural language of the *maskilim* was German or Polish (and to a lesser degree, French) among those Jews who lived in Warsaw and ethnic Poland.

The change took place during the 'Period of Great Reforms', that is, the early years of the reign of Aleksandr II (1855-1881), who instituted a whole series of changes in the political and social order of the Empire. An important milestone was the Polish Revolt of 1863, whose suppression wrought changes in the legal status and social order of what had been known until then as the Kingdom of Poland. The liberation of the peasants from serfdom and the undermining of the position of the Polish landowners opened possibilities for the capitalist development of Russian Poland and the entire Empire, and cleared new routes for the activities of Jewish entrepreneurs. For a time Jews with appropriate education began to be accepted for government service, and to a greater degree, to enter the professions and to become integrated among the employees of the local, municipal and rural authorities (*zemstva*). These options opened the way for the speedy Russification of Jewish youth, their adoption of the language and culture of Russia, and the growth of Russian Jewish newspapers and literature (that is, publications in the Russian language aimed at Jewish readers or dealing with Jewish problems). In the 1860s and 1870s young Jews began to attend secondary schools and colleges in large numbers, and within a short time their proportions at these institutions exceeded their proportions in the general population (Jews constituted about 4 percent of the population of the Empire; in 1863 they made up 3.2 percent of the students at the secondary schools for boys; in 1873, 13.2 percent; in 1886, 10.2 percent; and in the same year, at the universities, 14.5 percent). The reformed military service law of 1874, which gave a number of important exemptions to those with higher education, served to increase this trend.

However, this trend in Jewish occupations and education encountered opposition, first and foremost from members of the Russian intelligentsia. It is difficult to judge how great a part was played here by the historical tradition of hostility to the Jews and the negative image of the Jew in Russian literature and publicistic writings, because there were also manifestations of a sympathetic attitude for the trend towards integrating Jews into Russian society, especially at the end of the 1850s and the beginning of the 1860s. However, in the mid-1870s a Jewish revolutionary complained that strong anti-Jewish views were prevalent and deep-rooted even among the revolutionaries. From the end of the 1860s and during the 1870s the negative attitude to the Jews increased continually in Russian publicistic writings and *belles-lettres*, both in the publications of the right-wing Slavophiles and in those of the left-wing *Narodniki*—and the image of the Jew was the stereotype of the ludicrous stranger who is not sufficiently conversant with the Russian language, whose accent is odd and whose appearance is showy and vulgar; a speculator on the stock exchange who bribes government officials, or an entrepreneur whose business is based on deceit; a dealer with a local liquor monopoly who destroys the people by drunkenness, or a money-lender at high interest who drains the blood of the poor and weak in the nation. Of this type are the Jews in a poem by N. Nekrasov (1821-1878), the stories of N. Leskov (1831-1895) the novels of A. Pisemsky (1821-1881), P. Boborykin (1836-1921) and V. Krestovsky (1840-1895), the sketches of F. Dostoevsky (1821-1881), and F. Reshetnikov (1841-1871). Allegations of the exploitation of the people by the Jews were also published in the newspapers of Moscow and St Petersburg, but they were especially vociferous in the newspapers appearing in the Pale of Settlement, such as the *Vilensky vestnik*, the *Kievlyanin*, and *Novorossiysky telegraf* (which appeared in Odessa). This reportage became frequent and more hostile after the outbreak of riots against the Jews in southern Russia at the beginning of the 1880s. The newspapers of the right and those of the radical left (including those of the revolutionary underground), and even a number of newspapers which belonged to the liberal camp, expressed themselves in the same manner: the pogroms were the revenge of the people against their exploiters. In the radical periodical *Otechestvennye zapiski*, one well-known publicist argued that the whole essence of the Jews was that they were a 'union for exploitation.' There were few among the Russian intelligentsia at that time who held other views. From the time of the shift to conservatism and antisemitism, which took place with the accession of Aleksandr III to the throne in March 1881, this view accorded with the view of those in the regime, especially the line taken by the new Minister of the Interior Ignatev. In the preceding years the negative attitude of the Russian intelligentsia to the Jews was more extreme than that of the government officials. It was almost universally agreed that Jewish solidarity helped Jewish individuals to succeed in their undertakings, and that those of any influence advanced their own people at the expense of others. Could this have reflected a fear on the part of the younger intelligentsia of non-aristocratic extraction (*raznochintsy*), uncertain of its power and position in the face of competition by young ambitious people who were increasingly becoming a part of the Russian culture and paving a way for themselves in a period of expanding opportunity?

The element of common ground between the Slavophiles and the radicals, despite their bitter political struggle with each other, and the negative, ridiculing attitude prevalent among most of the Russian intelligentsia towards the weak liberal center, sharpened the aversion to capitalist development and the Western-style democratic trend, and served as an accepted background to attacks on the Jews. It followed, therefore, that an enlightened Jew who wished to make a way for himself in Russian society had to stress his aversion to Judaism, either by religious conversion or by taking part in the criticism of Judaism for its 'deficiencies', even for the 'social harm' wrought by the Jews. This situation intensified greatly the opposition between the *maskilim* and the greater part of the Jewish public which remained true to its traditions—an opposition and hostility which had existed since the first signs of the Enlightenment had appeared among the Russian Jews. However, unlike the first generation of *maskilim* the majority of those in the time of Aleksandr II who did not convert to Christianity (except for the few who succeeded in becoming a part of the establishment) were not able to put their trust in the authorities. They could not hope for support from the right, and did not achieve the sympathy of the left. Therefore, only a few of them did not lose hope for integration. The rest, who had only recently left the Jewish traditional framework which, despite all the crises it had undergone in the nineteenth century, had not lost much of its stability, continued to be active within the confines of Jewish society. Indeed, they sought to adjust this framework to the conditions of the time and the spirit of advancement; but precisely for this reason it was important for them to work within Jewish society. The journalism and *belles-lettres* in Hebrew and Yiddish also served the trend to modernization without loss of social and cultural identity. The enlightened Jew who wished to advance and develop his own society had, therefore, an alternative: even when he had mastered the principles of Russian culture and been influenced by its great works, he could preserve his pride and his ties within the Jewish society, without joining in the attacks on 'Judaism' and the 'Jewish spirit', as did those in the radical circles.

The pogroms at the beginning of the 1880s served as a milestone in the development of the Russian Jewish intelligentsia. This was due in part to the shock at the positions taken by the outstanding representatives of the Russian intelligentsia (Turgenev and Tolstoy did not raise their voices to oppose the riots, even after they had been requested to do so), and in part to a loss of faith in the revolutionary way in general, when its success in assassinating the Tsar only made the regime much more reactionary and led to martial law. As a result many of the radical Jewish youth began to 'return to the people' but this time to their own people, and to take an interest in its conditions and problems. Some of them were completely discouraged as to the possibility of improvement in Russia, and they chose emigration.

At the same time, despite the limitations the regime began to set on the entry of Jews into higher education and the absolute closing-off of civil service and academic careers to Jews, and the obstacles to their entry into the professions (law, medicine, engineering, agronomy), there was a constant increase in the number of those considered part of the intelligentsia. They might well have had to emigrate – like the tens of thousands of Jewish workmen and unemployed who began at that time to leave for Central and Western Europe and overseas – though the chance that they would be able to practice abroad the professions they had so arduously acquired was remote, but in the meantime changes took place in Russia which opened new avenues for the integration of the Jewish intelligentsia. The Government, under the leadership of Witte, began to devise ways to accelerate industrialization. The stream of investments from outside Russia grew, and closer ties were established with financial institutions abroad. Even prior to this, financial activity aimed at exploiting the country's natural resources (iron, coal, forests, oil, precious metals) was intensified. New opportunities arose for Jewish professionals in private economic corporations. And the views of the public on the Jews began to change as the press laid the responsibility for the backwardness of which Russia was becoming acutely conscious on the Government. In intellectual circles those calling for the adoption of Western ways, whether liberal or Marxist, increased in number. In rejecting the ways of the Tsarist regime, they began to take exception to its political methods, including its antisemitism. The attitude towards the Jews became for them one of the problems of the position of the ethnic groups who lived and worked within the compass of the Russian Empire—Poles, Finns, the Baltic peoples, the Caucasians, the peoples of Asiatic Russia, etc. Russian educated society became divided between those who advocated equality for the Jews and those who opposed it, with Government circles and even the Court on the anti-Jewish side. Antisemitism and the general attitude towards the Jews became one of the important issues in the public controversy which raged in Russia in the last years of the nineteenth century and the early years of the twentieth. But let us not be misled into thinking that the left and center completely lost their hostility to the Jews in those years. There were still those who feared that Russian spiritual life could become exposed to predominant Jewish influence, and professed 'asemitism', that is, the neutralization of that influence. And there were those who saw as a condition for the equality and integration of the Jews their utter assimilation in the Russian environment, and therefore strongly opposed the nationalist trends among the Jews, and believed that 'the idea that there is such a thing as a Jewish nation is only the imaginary and morbid outcome of the abnormal legal conditions to which the Jews were subject in Russia', in the words of the liberal philosopher Peter Struve. But it was precisely this controversy that brought the problems of the Jews and their culture close to the intellectual Russian public. This interest grew to the point where during the years of the First World War the writers Maksim Gorky, Leonid Andreev and Fedor Sologub founded the Society for the Dissemination of Correct Information about the Jews.

This was also the period during which the Jews began to take up a notable position in the spiritual and cultural life of Russia. Some Jews became renowned in the professions, such as the lawyers Aleksandr Passover, Arnold Dumashevsky and Oskar Gruzenberg, and the ophthalmologist Maks Mandelstamm. The academic world was wholly under the control of the Ministry of Education, which was completely reactionary and antisemitic, and there was no place there for Jews who had not converted. Some Russian Jews, such as the mathematician Hermann Minkowski or the biologist Vladimir Haffkine, won acclaim outside the borders of Russia. A number of Russian Jewish writers, such as the poet Shimon Frug (1860-1916), were popular only with Jews, but others, such as Semen Yushkevich (1868-1927), David Ayzman (1869-1922) and Osip Dymov (1878-1959), also had non-Jewish readers. The poet Nikolay Minsky (Vilenkin) (1855-1937), who began to write for Jewish periodicals, became well-known to the general public; he is considered one of the first

Symbolist poets in Russian literature. The literary and theatrical critic Akim Volynsky (Flekser) (1863-1926) had a great deal to do with the transmission of Western influences into Russia—he was the spirit behind the leading literary periodical *Severny vestnik*. There was a shift away from the social-realist trend in literary criticism founded by V.Belinsky (1811-1848), N.Chernyshevsky (1828-1889) and N.Dobrolyubov (1836-1861), which had become prevalent in Russia in the latter half of the nineteenth century. The Symbolist trend and others similar to it, which brought to Russia the newer directions which were developing in the West, greatly influenced the molding of spiritual and cultural life at the beginning of the twentieth century. However, a Jewish literary scholar of Slavophile tendencies, such as Mikhail Gershenzon (1869-1925), also attained an honored position (even though he did not agree to change his religion in order to gain a university post, as did the literary historian Semen Vengerov (1855-1920)).

Despite the important contributions of all these people to Russian culture, they did not have any significant effect on it. Only in two disciplines can it be said that as early as the latter half of the nineteenth century the Jews had any influence on determining the forms of creativity therein—music and the plastic arts. Musical performance and education were largely molded by the activities of the brothers Rubinstein, Anton (1829-1894) and Nikolay (1835-1881), the founders of the Conservatories in St Petersburg and Moscow. Anton Rubinstein, the pianist, and Henryk Wieniawski (1834-1880), the violinist, as a result of their performances and their place in musical life were granted the title 'His Majesty's Soloist'. Leopold Auer (1845-1930) founded a school of violinists which produced the greatest of the twentieth century virtuosi, many of them Jews (Yasha Heifetz (1901-), Mischa Elman (1891-1967), Nathan Milstein (1904-), Efrem Zimbalist (1889-) and many more). Serge Koussevitzky (1874-1951) did much as a conductor and music publisher to advance modern Russian music. Less than this, but nonetheless important was Jewish influence in the fields of sculpture and painting. Mark Antokolsky (1843-1902) was among the important Russian sculptors, and Isaak Levitan (1860-1900) was considered the father of Russian landscape painting; however, a number of other sculptors and painters gained renown such as the sculptor Ilya Guenzburg (1859-1939) and the painter Leonid Pasternak (1862-1945). And at the beginning of attempts to break out of the limitations of Russian art and to become a part of trends accepted in the West, Leon Bakst (Rosenberg, 1866-1924), who excelled in the decorative arts, especially for the stage, played an important role in the *Mir iskusstva* group.

All the foregoing prepared the ground for the outstanding position filled by the Russian Jews in the artistic creativity and the spiritual life of Russia in the years of the Revolution and after it, especially during the 1920s. But this development could scarcely have taken place without the massive influx of Jews into public life at the beginning of the twentieth century. The public awakening of the 1890s brought about, as has been noted, changes in public thinking and the development of ties with the West, soon followed by the emergence of political parties which caused a ferment in Russian society and prepared the way for the outbreak of the Revolutions of 1905 and of 1917. Despite the stringency of the autocratic regime, which did not permit legal activities by political groups, the year 1897 saw the creation, out of Jewish Marxist groups in Vilna, Warsaw, Bialystok and other places, of the Bund, the General Alliance of Jewish Workers in Lithuania, Poland, and Russia, which played a primary part not only in the lives of the Jews in Russia, but also in revolutionary activities in the country as a whole. The Bund was at its most influential during the 1905 Revolution, since in many ways it was in the vanguard of the other Marxist groups in Russia. At the same time, the Zionist Federation, which was also being formed by the Russian Jews, stimulated the nationalist trends among them already manifested in the *Hibbat Tsiyon* groups as early as the 1880s. These two groupings included a number of factions, some of which ultimately became parties which held socialist ideas, or demanded the granting of wide-reaching autonomy to the Jews in Russia in matters of culture and communal life, or combined the two principles. Thus, the Socialist Zionist Party demanded that a Jewish society, socialist in principle, be established in a special territory to be set aside for the Jews; the 'Jewish Socialist party', the 'Seymists', demanded a superior leadership institution, 'Seym', for every one of the nations which would belong to the Federation of the Nations of Russia; the 'People's Party' (*Folkspartey*), led by the historian Simon Dubnov, demanded a large measure of autonomy for the Jews within the framework of the Russian State in the areas of culture, laws of marriage and the family, days of rest, and social welfare.

However, in addition to political and ideological activities within a Jewish framework, many Jews also played a part in organizing the general Russian political parties. The Bund was an important component in Russian Social Democracy (founded in 1898), although many of the Social Democrats who criticized it for its 'separatism' (that is, its demand that there be a separate organization for Jewish workers) were also Jews. When the Russian Social Democratic Labor Party split into two factions —Bolsheviks and Mensheviks—both factions had many Jews in their leaderships (such as Boris Akselrod, Yuly Martov, Lev Trotsky, Grigory Zinoviev and Lev Kamenev) and among their most active members. Many

Jews also played a part in the foundation and leadership of the party, which represented the interests of the peasantry and continued the political tradition of the *Narodniki*—the Socialist Revolutionary Party (SR): for example, Mikhail Gots was one of the Party's main theoreticians and Grigory Gershuni was the leader of its fighting organization, which carried out terrorist acts against the Tsarist regime. In the leadership of the party of the liberal center—the Constitutional Democrats (KD), which like the SRs was organized in the early years of the twentieth century—there were a number of Jews (such as Maksim Vinaver, Iosif Gessen and Mikhail Gertsenshteyn). These activities, along with their professional, publicistic and cultural activities, transformed the enlightened Jews into one of the leading elements in Russian society in the years before the Revolution. However, the official and public antisemitism, that of the Court and that of the militant right whose influence grew in the years of reaction (1907-1917), prevented them from becoming a part of the educational institutions, scientific institutes, artistic groups, etc.

This situation changed totally when the March 1917 Revolution broke out. Not only were the laws discriminating against Jews repealed, but the great majority of the public, including the rightist publications, welcomed this development. The way to the scientific and cultural institutions was opened. However, the Bolshevik Revolution had a greater impact, due to the changes in the spiritual life which it caused. The greater part of the old hands among the Russian intelligentsia (including many Jews) were hostile to the Bolshevik regime on account of its violent character, its repression of freedom of expression, its interference in cultural and spiritual matters, and because it conferred great authority on simple folk, some of them completely ignorant. Many of those who expressed opposition to the new regime were arrested, even executed; others emigrated or were exiled. Many refused to serve the Bolsheviks in the positions they had formerly occupied or even to cooperate with them. In all these ways Russia lost a significant part of its intelligentsia, which was small in numbers but high in quality, and which had developed over a long period. This weakened the academic and artistic establishment and left the way open for the entry of young, ambitious and talented people, along with many of little or no education, who took advantage of the new opportunities which had arisen. In the new conditions, with the arbitrariness of the commissars adding to elements of anarchy, there was room for all sorts of experimentation, for the absorption of unripened ideas which had been brought in from the West, and for bringing members of different classes into the process of artistic creation. Because of the important role assigned by the new regime to propaganda, and its willingness to allot resources for this purpose, new channels were opened for the expressive arts—posters, caricature, popular drama, experimental theater, and improvizations of various kinds. Opportunities arose for local initiatives and for the appointment of talented people as commissars in the various areas of the arts. The regime laid great emphasis on the indoctrination of the masses and therefore provided funds for education, including art education.

Amongst the literary and artistic trends and groups which came into existence, some were a continuation of groups which had existed before the Revolution (Acmeism, Imaginism, Futurism, Suprematism), and some arose out of the new ideas which spread during the Revolution and after it (Proletkult, Lef, Constructivism), or in reaction to them (Serapion Brothers). The controversies and struggles among the groups and trends had a positive aspect and activated cultural life. This gave momentum to the development of a mass culture and to the inclusion of popular elements in art.

This change had an especially strong influence on Jewish artistic life, which had not ventured much beyond the limits of the traditional folk culture (*Purim-shpil*). Even the new-style theater founded by Abraham Goldfaden (1840-1908) did not leave the framework of the didactic play and melodrama. The overwhelming influence of the Revolution on the lives of the Jews in the Pale of Settlement was felt in this area too. Jewish youth from the cities and towns of the Pale of Settlement was caught up by radicalism: as a result of the extreme antisemitism of the 'Whites' and the various nationalist groups, and because of the removal of the barriers against leaving the Pale of Settlement and entering educational institutions, government service and the Party apparatus, most of the Jewish youth sided with the Bolsheviks. The Jews, who made up less than 2 percent of the population of the Soviet Union, constituted in 1927 about 4.5 percent of the Party members and 13 percent of the students in institutions of higher education. The diversion of tens of thousands of Jewish families to agricultural settlements (in 1930 more than 10 percent of the Jews in the Soviet Union made their living by agriculture) also wrought a basic change in the traditional Jewish mode of life. Together with this, the regime did not take into consideration the special conditions of Jewish communal life which existed in Tsarist Russia, and viewed those in the lower middle class among the Jews—the small tradesmen, the various middle-men, the independent craftsmen, the religious teachers—as people of 'bourgeois social origin'. In the Soviet State in its early stages these were officially defined as second class citizens, and at times became *lishentsy*, i.e. deprived of the right to vote or to enter the institutions of the regime, which meant deprived of basic rights, such as housing, medical services, and, at times, schooling for their children, etc.

In addition, the economic changes resulting from the destruction of industry and communications during the Civil War undermined the traditional role of the Jewish small town (*shtetl*) as the intermediary between the city and the countryside. The destruction of the *shtetls* was hastened by the policies of the regime, as enumerated above, towards most of their inhabitants. A comprehensive and hurried migration ensued from the *shtetls* to the cities, and from the Pale of Settlement to the heart of Russia, primarily to the large urban centers such as Moscow and Leningrad. The acclimatization of those newly arrived in the big city and the new culture, despite partial successes, created many problems, including the opposition of the existing residents in the form of antisemitic outbursts. The Jew was not only a competitor for jobs in the conditions of unemployment which were prevalent in the Russian cities of the 1920s, but he was *par excellence* the 'Nepman', that is, one who adapted quickly to the opportunities for private economic initiative which the regime allowed in its 'New Economic Policy' of the 1920s to encourage the revival of the economy, and which was decisively suppressed at the close of that decade. Thus, the Jews became a symbol of 'bourgeois' exploitation. However, in this manner there was also created the infra-structure for the resurgence, now in the new Jewish population concentrations as well as in the towns in the Pale of Settlement, of a Yiddish culture—literature, theater and plastic arts with Jewish motifs.

The new state educational system included schools using Yiddish at the elementary and higher levels, as well as a number of institutions for research into 'proletarian culture'. These created a basis for cultural activities in Yiddish, which the regime viewed as a means of indoctrination and of struggle against the traditional and secular Hebrew culture which had been suppressed. The encouragement of Yiddish cultural institutions was part of the attempt to encourage creativity in the communist spirit in the national languages, an attitude prevalent then towards all the smaller nationalities. It was also an attempt to exploit the 'Jewish question' in order to encourage large Jewish organizations and Jewish intellectual circles abroad to cooperate with the Soviet state. Opportunities arose for other experiments as well: the Habima Hebrew theater was established. The theater adopted what was then considered an important theatrical achievement, the method of the noted Russian director, Konstantin Stanislavsky (1863-1938). But it did not gain a firm foothold in Moscow because of the negative attitude to the Hebrew language; it did not return to Russia after a foreign tour, and finally settled in Tel Aviv. The Jewish State Theater, which began its activities under the direction of a man far from the Jewish mode of life, Aleksandr Granovsky (Avraham Azarkh, 1890-1937), sought to institute modern theatrical methods in the framework of the Jewish popular theater. Under the direction of Solomon

Mikhoels (Vofsi, 1890-1948), this theater, which served as an example to Jewish theaters in the Ukraine and White Russia, became one of the most important Jewish cultural institutions in the Soviet Union. The belief that it was possible to exploit the great opportunities of government support for Jewish culture in Yiddish not only attracted many young talents from the *shtetls* to literary and cultural activities, but also brought about the return to the Soviet Union of a number of noted writers who had emigrated from Russia at the outbreak of the Revolution, and even some who had not been there before, such as David Bergelson (1884-1952), Perets Markish (1895-1952), Der Nister (Pinkhes Kahanovich) (1884-1950), David Hofstein (1889-1952), Meir Wiener (1893-1941) and Max Erik (1898-1937). For a period, the Soviet Union, and especially Moscow, became a most important center of Yiddish creativity.

Together with this upsurge of Jewish secular culture, but to a much greater degree, went the process of the integration of Jews into the spiritual and cultural life of Russia and, to a lesser extent, of the other nations comprising the Soviet Union. It is worth noting that, despite the fact that until the Holocaust the great majority of the Jews in the Soviet Union lived in the Ukrainian and Byelorussian Republics, the position of the Jews in cultural life there was relatively modest, even though the writer Zmytrok Byadula (Shmuel Plavnik, 1886-1941) was considered one of the founders of Byelorussian literature, and there were a number of writers and poets of Jewish extraction who wrote in Ukrainian—Leonid Pervomaysky, I. Stivun-Katsenelson, Natan Rybak, etc. It would appear that this was the result of the attitude of most of the Jews who considered these cultures as inferior to Russian culture and possibly also the result of the long historical hostility to the Jews which existed in the Ukraine.

In contrast, the influence and singularity of the group of writers of Jewish descent originating in south-western Russia, and especially Odessa, was felt as early as the 1920s. From the 1860s onwards Odessa was the center of activities of the Jewish Enlightenment. The Jewish press in the Russian language—*Razsvet, Sion*—developed there (as did the Hebrew periodical *Ha-melits* and the Yiddish *Kol Mevaser*), and at the end of the 1860s, *Den*. At the end of the century a circle of enlightened Jews and Hebrew writers was active there—Mendele Mokher Sforim (Sh. Abramovich), Ahad Ha-am (A. Ginsberg), M. L. Lilienblum, H.N. Bialik, J. Klausner, the historian S. Dubnov—and these activities left their mark on the life and culture of the city. In Odessa V. Zhabotinsky, S. Yushkevich and D. Ayzman began their literary and journalistic work. A Russian literary style in which southern and Jewish elements played an important role was created. To the group of writers active after the Revolution belonged the poets Eduard Bagritsky (Dzyubin, 1895-1934) and Ilya

Selvinsky (1899-1968), the writers Lev Nikulin, (1891-), Lev Slavin, Ilya Ilf (Faynzilberg, 1897-1937), and others. Outstanding among them was Isaak Babel (1894-1941), in whose works Jewish life in Odessa occupies a primary position. However, writers of Jewish descent also played an important part in other literary groups: for example, Lev Lunts (1901-1924) and Venyamin Kaverin (Zilberg, 1902-) in the circle of the Serapion Brothers.

Two major changes in the Soviet Union, which began at the end of the 1920s and to a great degree determined the subsequent character of that country, had a decisive influence on the integration of the Jews into the surrounding society and on their place in its creativity. These were the Five Year Plans and the stringent control of the regime over all aspects of life. Many Jews, who in the interim had begun in great numbers to complete their higher education, joined this gigantic new establishment, which ranged from the fields of education, medicine and economic planning to those of the army and secret police. This changed the socio-economic structure of the Jewish community in the Soviet Union; it also tied many Jews firmly to the various agencies of the regime, and made them dependent on its trends. Even when Stalin began his process of rapprochement with Nazi Germany in the late 1930s, and at the same time began to eliminate Jews from key political positions, Jews continued to stream into the ranks of the establishment. The majority of Jews in the arts worked in accordance with the wishes of the regime, in literature, in poetry, the theater, music, painting and sculpture, and architecture. There is no doubt that some did so out of political conviction, but not a few put their talents at the service of the regime out of fear or simply careerism. Even those who were less dependent on the regime such as scientists and artists, did not behave otherwise. These included the most important of the scientists such as the physicists Lev Landau, Abraham Ioffe, Leonid Mandelshtam, the chemist Aleksandr Frumkin and others.

All the more worthy of note are those Jews—and they are among the greatest figures in Russian art of the twentieth century—who, after they had discerned the true character of the regime, refused to serve it, and paid the price of refusal; they include Isaak Babel, Osip Mandelshtam (1891-1938), and Boris Pasternak (1890-1960). The Jewish element played a primary role in the works of Babel; Pasternak showed great interest in Jewish matters in his youth, but even his sharp polemic against Judaism in his last years reveals its importance for him. Mandelshtam retained some traits of Jewish influence despite his later animosity and even aversion to everything Jewish.

The 1930s were a time when culture and art in the official style flourished. In order to ensure Party control in this area, groupings in the arts were banned, Modernist experimentation was suppressed, and unified organizations of writers, theater people, painters, composers, etc. were created, their appointed leaders being put in charge of safeguarding ideological purity and 'Socialist Realism'. In the years of the terrible famine and the terror of the 1930s, novels were written on the 'victory of socialism', poets praised the land 'where a man so freely breathes', portraits were painted of the leaders and of harvest festivals in the collective farms, and cantatas to Stalin were composed. At the same time, the regime invested large sums in art displays and in supporting talent. As a result, the classical ballet in Russia reached remarkable heights, a new generation of musicians and virtuosi arose, and impressive films were made. In all this Jews played a large part: the Messerers, Asaf (1903-) and Sulamith (1908-) and Maya Plisetskaya (1925-) in choreography and ballet; the violinists Nathan Milstein, David Oistrakh (1908-1974), and Leonid Kogan (1924-1982), all of them students of Peter Stolyarsky of Odessa; the pianist Emil Gilels (1916-); and many actors and singers. The relatively new art of the film blossomed, and among the outstanding directors were Sergey Eisenstein (1898-1948), Dziga Vertov (Denis Kaufman) (1897-), Mikhail Romm (1905-1971), Iosif Heyfits (1905-) and Aleksandr Zarkhi (1908-).

Many Jews were included in creating a popular culture in the new mode, and some of them were notorious in imposing the Party line in the various cultural areas, e.g. Leopold Averbakh (1903-1938), the theoretician of 'proletarian literature' in the late 1920s-early 1930s; Isaak Brodsky (1884-1939) and Evgeny Katsman (1890-), who nurtured the Socialist Realist approach in painting; and Boris Iofan (1891-), who helped impose the neo-classical style in architecture in the 1930s. Jewish prominence in both respects led to friction and even to expressions of antisemitism, but mainly served as justification after a number of years for the anti-cosmopolitan campaign of the 1940s as well as for the outbreak of intellectual antisemitism in the years after Stalin.

The demonstrative identification of many Jews with the Soviet regime was put to a stringent test when Nazi Germany attacked the Soviet Union. It was in the republics of heaviest Jewish population—the Ukraine, Lithuania and Soviet Moldavia—that there were so many collaborators with the Nazis and many took an active part in the destruction of the Jews. Stalin himself took an antisemitic line—for example, in his talks with the Polish General Anders—and antisemitism was widespread in the higher echelons of the Government (Central Committee Secretary Shcherbakov was outstanding in this regard). As so frequently at times of crisis, the popular antisemitism erupted in full strength: it was claimed that the Jews were exploiting the wartime suffering by 'fighting in Tashkent.' This sentiment was felt strongly in the partisan units fighting behind the German lines. On the other hand, in those difficult days of retreats and military defeats, the Government seized on the idea of Jewish solidarity and tried to exploit it for its own benefit. That self-same Government which denied the existence of a Jewish nation supported the Jewish Anti-Fascist Committee, whose chief goal was to enlist the support of world Jewry and especially US Jewry in the struggle against the Nazis. The principal effort to turn the Committee, which included well known Soviet Jews, into a Jewish representative organization was made by the refugees from Poland and the areas annexed to the Soviet Union in 1939-40, to whom the idea of self-organization came naturally.

The Holocaust and the establishment of the Jewish Anti-Fascist Committee left their mark on the consciousness of veteran Soviet Jews too, even those who had become completely assimilated, especially after the fate of the Jews in the areas captured by the Germans became publicly known. The sufferings of the Jews were mentioned more than once in the reports of Ilya Ehrenburg (1891-1967) to the army newspapers. Poems and stories about the ghettos in Nazi-occupied areas appeared. Ehrenburg and Vassily Grossman (1905-1964) worked on the publication of a 'Black Book' of Soviet Jewry, which was to serve as witness to the Holocaust and to the bravery of the Soviet Jews in war. (Publication of the book was ultimately banned by the Government.) Pavel Antokolsky (1896-1981), a poet far from Jewish interests, wrote poems on the 'Incinerated Shulamith' and exclaimed 'all the universe cries "Hear, O Israel!" '. Many assimilated Jews began to ponder on the reason for the terrible fate of their people.

We cannot be certain of the reason for the antisemitic campaign in which the authorities engaged soon after the end of the war. There were the morbid suspicions of the ageing Stalin, whose inner circle began to make use of his increasingly antisemitic tendencies as a factor in the struggle for succession. There was apprehension in the face of expressions of national Jewish identity by some of the Jewish intelligentsia who, because of the trauma of the Holocaust, sought a solution in Jewish statehood within the USSR. At the same time, survivors of the Holocaust in the Ukraine and Byelorussia began to make their way in a number of organized groups to the Autonomous Jewish Region of Birobidzhan, and there were those who spoke of finding a 'Jewish Territory' in European Russia, for instance in the Crimea. There was official displeasure towards many Jews who revealed their sympathy for the struggle of the Jews in Palestine for political independence, at a time when the Soviet Government supported it in 1947. Perhaps, the fear that Soviet soldiers returning from the heart of Europe might prefer the mode of life of the 'corrupt West' and demand democratic reforms made any group having natural contacts abroad seem a potential risk.

Be that as it may, the first signs of suppression of any manifestation of Jewish national attitudes became apparent in 1947, and a full-scale 'anti-cosmopolitan' campaign began early in 1949 with an attack on the theater critics. They were accused of belittling the greatness of the Russian people and its accomplishments and of kowtowing to the West. The campaign widened and was aimed at writers, painters, musicians, and people involved in the theater and films who deviated from the socialist realist line 'under Western influence'. The campaign also struck at scientists in various fields; it was made clear that all the important scientific discoveries and technological achievements had taken place in Russia, beginning in the seventeenth century ('the priority of Russian science'). As a result, the Jewish Anti-Fascist Committee and all Jewish cultural institutions were closed and all publications in Yiddish ceased. Tens of thousands were arrested, especially those active in Yiddish culture, and in August 1952 some of them were executed on charges of 'a conspiracy to sever the Crimea from the Soviet Union'. Many Jewish artists were excluded from the writers', painters', and composers' unions, and many scientists were dismissed from their positions, the attacks on them being of a clearly antisemitic nature. Individual Jews were attacked in the streets and on public transport. The antisemitic campaign spread to the People's Democratic Republics in Eastern Europe; in the trial of the Czechoslovak Communist Party Secretary Rudolf Slánský in November 1952, Zionism and Israel were presented as the inner circle of an imperialist plot. In an official declaration made public on 13 January 1953, prominent doctors in Moscow were accused of murdering Soviet leaders by criminal medical methods, at the behest of the American intelligence services and through the instrumentality of Israel and the main Jewish relief organization, the 'Joint'. There is evidence that a general expulsion of the Jews from European Russia was planned, just as during the war years other national groups had been sent to various Asiatic regions. Only Stalin's death, it seems, prevented this program from being carried out.

Under Khrushchev, Yiddish culture failed to be rehabilitated and the struggle against 'reactionary Judaism' occupied an important place in the anti-religious campaigns (as a result, of several hundred synagogues which existed after the war, less than one hundred remained). Every sign of Jewish national identity was suppressed. The role of the Jews in history was obscured, as was their part in the revolutionary movement, and even their suffering and struggle during the Second World War. However, a number of the victims of the 'anti-cosmopolitan' campaign were restored to their former positions and others found a place in the devastated Soviet western republics and in the republics in Asia which had commenced technological and cultural development during the war. Institutions of higher education were once again opened to Jewish youth, as were managerial positions—although care was taken not to admit them into 'sensitive' departments which prepared workers for the Party apparatus, the intelligence services, the diplomatic service, etc. The academization of the Soviet Jews continued at an accelerated pace in those years; the percentage of Jews among the occupational category defined as 'scientific workers' was more than ten times their percentage in the population (after the Holocaust, the Jews made up only about one percent of the population), but their representation in government—even at the low level of the local soviets—was relatively smaller. The lack of confidence of the authorities in the Jews remained.

Nonetheless, many Jews hoped that the campaign against Stalin's crimes on which Khrushchev had embarked, as well as the ambitious goals set by him to outstrip America materially and technologically, would augment the demand for professional workers and strengthen ties with the West. Thus, it was hoped, the Soviet Union would follow the path of liberalization and anti-Jewish discrimination would be abolished. These hopes proved futile.

The years of Khrushchev's 'liberal' rule ended with a harsh antisemitic outbreak. This was manifested in the controversy which arose over the need to erect a monument to the Jewish victims of the Nazis at Baby Yar in Kiev, and in the emphasis placed on the Jewish names of those found guilty of 'economic crimes'. Khrushchev himself argued that there were Nazi collaborators among the Jews, as there were among other nations. He also attacked outstanding members of the Jewish intelligentsia—the writer Ilya Ehrenburg, the poet Boris Slutsky, the sculptor Ernst Neizvestny—for ideological deviations. This approach was intensified under Khrushchev's successors. Thus, at the time of the suppression of the 'Prague Spring' in 1968, the Soviets resorted to antisemitic slogans; even in the closed circle of the Party leaders antisemitic remarks were directed against Frantisek Kriegel, who was of Polish Jewish descent. During the campaign against the liberal intelligentsia in Poland in 1968, Soviet periodicals copied antisemitic articles published in Poland, and this was repeated during the struggle against Solidarity in 1980-81.

Even in this period cause and effect are difficult to distinguish. There is no doubt that the large number of Jews in the protest movements in the Soviet Union in the 1960s and 1970s strengthened the ire of the authorities against the Jews, while the discrimination which ensued served to nourish the protests. In any event, manifestations of overt Jewish activity—cultural and social—appeared as early as the 1960s among Soviet Jews. The reasons for this were the desire to perpetuate the memory of the victims of the Holocaust as Jews; to preserve Jewish cultural values, tradition and folklore; and to preserve ties with the State of Israel, including emigration there. Israel's victory in the Six Day War only intensified this desire. On the other hand, the indifference of the Soviet public to the Soviet invasion of Czechoslovakia in 1968 demonstrated to many in the protest movements the futility of hoping for liberalization in Russia, and many 'democrats' among the Jews turned to nationalistic Jewish activity.

Jewish protest activities in the Soviet Union in the late 1960s and the success of Israel and Western Jewry in making the plight of the Soviet Jews a topic of concern throughout the world—even an important issue in inter-bloc relations—led to a breach in the gates of the Soviet State. In 1971 an unprecedented Jewish exodus from the Soviet Union commenced, rising within a few years to an annual emigration of tens of thousands of Jews. In the ten years to 1980 over 250 thousand Jews left the Soviet Union.

This emigration has far-reaching political, demographic, social and cultural implications. There is no doubt that the emigration, the biological slump (according to the 1970 census, about one quarter of the Jews in the RSFSR were aged sixty-five and over) and cultural assimilation all serve to reduce quickly the number of Jews in the Soviet Union. However, this has not reduced the seriousness of the problem of the position of the Jews as a national entity in that country, and therewith the problem of Jewish cultural creativity and the Jews' contribution to the culture of the surrounding society. It is worth noting that the numerical diminution of the Jews and the development of new scientific and cultural forces, both Russian and in the national republics, able to replace the Jews in cultural and professional life, served as factors both for increasing discrimination and for easing emigration. Since Stalin, Jews have not usually been dismissed from positions in the scientific and cultural areas, but the way has been barred to new Jewish appointments.

Discrimination by the authorities, rejection by significant parts of the public, fear of the 'Judaizing' of Russia widespread among intellectual circles and reflected in official periodicals, *samizdat* publications, and even in emigré circles—all these have stirred new interest among the Jews—especially among the young and the educated—in the history of their people. Alongside the official organ for Yiddish writers, *Sovetish Heymland*, and the theater companies, unofficial classes for the study of Hebrew and seminars for the study of Judaism and Jewish history have arisen. Despite persecution by the authorities, these increased in number in the 1970s. However, the most prominent sign of the creation of an independent Jewish culture was the *samizdat* publications in the Russian language, which concentrated around the periodical *Evrei v SSSR* (Jews in the USSR) and several other publications. Thus was created a literature whose central theme was the Jewish identity, historical and sociological research, and *belles-lettres* dedicated to the problems of Soviet Jewry and of the Jewish people generally. It can be stated that the independent culture of the Jews of the Soviet Union is an accomplished fact.

There are still many Jews in important positions in the economy of the Soviet Union, in technology, the sciences, and the cultural and artistic areas, but their number is diminishing fast, in view of the ageing of the Jews as a group, in the wake of the emigration, and because the way is barred to young talented Jews who wish to enter the universities and to be appointed to important positions. In contrast, Jews have begun to play an important role in the unofficial scientific and cultural creativity which emerged and developed in the 1960s and 1970s. Some of these innovators emphasize their attachment to Russia and reject any attachment to Judaism; there are those who have converted to Christianity; but among most of them are definite signs of wrestling with their roots and with their Jewish fate.

Boris Pasternak became the focal point of the struggle for independent literary work by the publication abroad of his novel *Dr Zhivago*. A similar fate befell the militant satirical writings of Yuly Daniel and Andrey Sinyavsky (the latter is, indeed, a Russian and a believing Christian, but he nevertheless chose for himself a distinctly Jewish literary *nom-de-plume*—Abram Tertz—and the position of the Jews in Soviet society occupies an important place in his works). One of the important Russian poets of the period immediately after Stalin—and possibly the most important of them—is Iosif Brodsky (1940-). The militant ballads of Aleksandr Galich (1919-77) and Vladimir Vysotsky (died 1980) are outstanding.

Jewish influence is great in the artistic avant-garde. Ties with artistic trends in the West were severed in the 1930s. And the works of painters in which Jewish themes appeared, such as Anatoly Kaplan (1902-80), Robert Falk (1886-1958) and Aleksandr Tyshler (1898-1980), also did not reach the attention of the younger generation. Nevertheless, in the 1960s a new generation of artists arose which turned to new artistic experimentation and partly also to the Jewish experience. The principal artist of this generation was Oskar Rabin (1928-), but Jewish links were to be found in the Leningrad group calling itself 'Alef'. The works of Ernst Neizvestny received prominence because of Khrushchev's attack on them. Some of the new artists have emigrated from the Soviet Union; others continue to struggle from within. There is, however, no doubt that the influence of Jews is great in the new trends in literature and art and that this connection is intensified by their position as members of an oppressed minority in the Soviet Union.

Precisely for this reason, the Jewish element was very important in the spiritual struggle within the Soviet Union in the 1970s, a struggle which is still continuing today. There is a tendency in Russian intellectual circles to view the Bolshevik Revolution as an essentially non-Russian phenomenon, which took place under the influence of the minority nations in the Russian empire, chiefly the Jews. There are those who regard the political terror as a phenomenon connected mainly with the Jews (this element is to be found in, or inferred from, Aleksandr Solzhenitsyn, the oppositionist, and Valentin Kataev, the official writer). Such an attitude is also behind militant antisemitism, both in publicistic writings and in *belles-lettres*, portraying the Jews as plotters who, since Peter the Great, have sought to harm Russia and are now corrupting Soviet society. In this manner anti-Jewish pogroms and measures in the past are presented as protests against exploitation (this line is maintained by the writers Valentin Pikul and Ivan Shevtsov, and the journalists Lev Korneev and Vladimir Begun). Even writings which are considered, more or less, historical or literary research works posit a need for defense against the 'baneful influence of Judaism'. Consequently, liberal artists and scholars who oppose the nationalistic distortion of Russian history are described as 'helpers and defenders of the Jews'. Antisemitism is becoming increasingly the mark of those who have roots and are loyal to the national tradition. This controversy extends beyond the borders of the Soviet Union and is conducted to varying degrees in emigré publications. The role of the Jews in Russian life and Russian culture has ceased to be a topic for objective historical research and is becoming one of the main problems of the political struggle in the Soviet Union, as it was at the end of the nineteenth century and the beginning of the twentieth. Despite both the decrease in the number of Jews in Soviet Russia and discrimination, 'the Jewish question' remains a burning issue in the Soviet Union.

2

Jews in Soviet Art

Igor Golomstock

Pre-Revolutionary period

When we speak of Russian, French or, say, Indian art, we have in mind some quality of the artist's inner world superimposed on the object depicted. Thus, a Russian landscape painted in Russia by a French painter would have an 'accent' of the French tradition and we would recognize in it particular features depending on when it was painted—Poussin's classicism, Barbizon's school of painting, Impressionism and so on. But is it possible to speak in similar terms of some Jewish cultural element which imparts a national character to art created by Jews in various countries? A reply to this question can hardly be simple.

The national character of any work of art (music, painting, literature, etc.) depends on the presence of at least two essential features.

First, it depends on the specific way in which the world is seen, felt, grasped: that is, what constitutes the concept of cultural-national character.

Secondly, it depends on the presence at the given historical moment of specific stylistic forms in which that sense of the world—or that national character—has already revealed itself. By the beginning of our century the Jewish stylistic tradition had revealed itself in full in some of the arts, but the field of pictorial art presents more difficulty.

The point is that historically the Jews had no figurative tradition. Certain commandments of the Old Testament (the Torah) had been interpreted by the Jews as prohibiting any images. Biblical archaeology in the territory of Palestine shows only weak sources of figurative culture. During the two thousand years of Diaspora the Jews enriched literature, music, the sciences and philosophy of the countries of their dispersion, but painting and sculpture remained untouched by their influence until quite recently.

Insofar as the existence of the Jews had any effect on the visual art of mediaeval Europe, it was only on the depiction of religious subjects, as betrayers or torturers of Christ, counterposed to him as evil is to good, as the false religion is to the true religion. Only during the epoch of the Reformation, with the awakening of a deep interest in the Old Testament, do characters of the Jewish ghetto begin to be portrayed as conveyers of the true biblical morality, mores and ideas, in the art of individual painters (mainly Rembrandt and his school). However, up to a certain point in the history of European art there are almost no names of outstanding Jewish painters.

The situation changes sharply from the second half of the nineteenth century. In some countries painters who were Jews by origin— but still not many in number—began to appear in the ranks of first-class national masters. Moreover, Joseph Israels in Holland (who exercised a great influence upon the formation of the young van Gogh's creative work), Max Liebermann in Germany, Camille Pissarro in France, become the greatest exponents of the national culture and life of those countries. In Russia a similar place came to be occupied by I.I. Levitan. His landscapes, according to generally accepted opinion, not only reflect the democratic tendencies of that period but are the most 'Russian' in spirit; in the whole history of Russian landscape painting they express Russian nature the most fully and subtly.

An analysis of the causes of and conditions for the emergence of Jewish painters in that period as the clearest exponents of the spirit of an alien national culture, so different from theirs, would take us too far into the little-explored territory of historical psychology, of the national and historical-cultural sense of things. Let us then merely note the fact and turn to our immediate theme.

In the peculiar conditions of Tsarist Russia, it was more difficult than in other countries for Jews to enter the world of 'official' art. The part they played was insignificant until a split appeared in Russian art, when the more progressive painters made a stand against the conservatism of academic education and when they began a struggle to create a democratic art which would reflect the actual social conditions of people's lives. As this opposition strengthened, an increasing number of gifted young Jews joined the struggle against the official art; they came from the small towns of the Pale and somehow, by avoiding police registration laws, settled in St Petersburg and Moscow.

The beginning of this movement dates back to 1863, when a group of young painters left the official St Petersburg Academy of the Arts and a few years later formed a fellowship for peripatetic or 'wandering' art exhibitions. With them begins the epoch of nonconformism, the emergence of many associations, trends and groupings. The interrelation between them and their common struggle against the prevailing tastes define the real history of Russian art right up to the Revolution of 1917. From the founding of that movement, democratic and oppositional in character, begins the part played by Jewish painters in Russian art, which grew in step with the spread of the movement, whose forms took an increasingly revolutionary coloring.

We have already spoken of I.I. Levitan (1860-1900). He became a member of the fellowship of 'Wanderers' in 1891. His fate is typical of a Jewish painter in pre-Revolutionary Russia. Arriving in Moscow from the remote small township of Kiberta (in the territory of the present Lithuanian Republic), his brilliant talent enabled him to enter the Moscow School of Painting, Sculpture and Architecture. As a student he lived a semi-legal beggar's existence, but he soon became one of the greatest Russian masters. By 1898 he was in charge of teaching landscape painting in the same school from which he had graduated 10 years earlier. He died at the age of 40 of tuberculosis. He was and still is 'the most typical, complete and important painter of "expressive landscape", making on his contemporaries an immense impression unequalled by anything either before or since'.[1]

If in painting Levitan stands alongside such masters as Repin or Serov, then in the sculpture of the time M.M. Antokolsky (1843-1902) unquestionably occupies the premier position. Antokolsky began his work with genre-reliefs portraying Jewish artisans at work—tailors and shoemakers—as if transferring the descriptive realism of the 'Wanderers' to the language of sculpture. In the 1870s and 1880s this product of the Jewish ghetto in Vilnius, who wrote Russian with difficulty, became the portrayer of Russian history and perhaps the most popular sculptor of his time. In his vast 'Peter I' and 'Ivan the Terrible', as in his domestic genre-reliefs, the attention of his contemporaries was attracted by the psychological realism, the democratic purposefulness and the high professional execution. His pupils, above all I.Ya. Ginsburg (1859-1939), developed the naturalistic genre tendency of their teacher right up to the beginning of the Soviet period.

The revolutionary character of the 'Wanderers' was limited. Their differences with the Academy and the offical art was of a thematic kind; it did not affect the underlying stylistic and philosophical character of their art. They continued to develop the method of descriptive realism which had developed, long before their time, within academism. They only added to it a democratic and critical social coloring. Therefore, when new artistic trends appeared in Russia, differences between the 'Wanderers' and the Academy were overcome by their united front as keepers of the tradition of realism. Amongst all the outstanding 'Wanderers' only Levitan (apart from V. Serov) understood the artistic limitations of their method, and in his later works he went over to the creation of an epic, philosophical-symbolic landscape in the style of the early 'World of Art' (*Mir iskusstva*)—a trend which superseded the 'Wanderers'. Only his early death prevented him from changing his creative method more radically.

The 'World of Art' movement (chronologically and stylistically close to the international *Art Nouveau*) appeared in the late 1890s as a result of a general dissatisfaction with the state of Russian art as a whole: its provincialism, its aesthetic conservatism (both the academicians and 'Wanderers'), its claim to express the 'advanced ideas of the time', as essentially inexpressible in the visual medium at any level above mere illustration. This new movement captured all that was best in Russian art and constituted a whole epoch in its brief history, at the turn of the century. From the new movement's first steps, directed towards the 'Europeanization' of the country's culture, it took Russian art beyond a purely national framework and revealed to it the spiritual wealth of other countries, epochs and styles. While in the fields of painting and graphic arts its leading exponents, such as A. Benua, N. Rerikh, M. Vrubel, K. Somov and M. Dobuzhinsky, are amongst the great masters of this style, in the field of stage design Russia was far superior to the West. Russian art is indebted primarily to L. Bakst for this.

Lev Samoylovich Bakst (real name Rosenberg, 1866-1924) was the true reformer of the art of stage design. Previously this element of theater provided only a neutral, most often a naturalistic, background to the performance, but with Bakst it gained equality and became an organic part of a theatrical production. His sketches for costumes and back-drops are staggering in their wealth of imagery, precise knowledge of styles and masterly graphic craftsmanship. They are not only independent works of art. Produced, as a rule, for individual actors, they suggested to the actor the image he was to create. The organic fusion of color, music, draughtsmanship and motion made the performances breathtaking spectacles. In 1909 the Russian Ballet of Diaghilev, with the staging by Bakst and other outstanding Russian artists, set out on its triumphal tour of the capitals of Europe. But neither his world fame nor his connection with the highest cultural circles of Russia as one of the creators of the 'World of Art' society could prevent his deportation in 1909 from Petersburg because as a Jew he had no right to live in the capital. In that year Bakst, together with Diaghilev's ballet, left for Paris and never returned to his native country.

Thus Levitan, Antokolsky and Bakst held key positions in various fields of Russian art at the end of the nineteenth and beginning of the twentieth centuries. Their contribution to it was recognized, their influence on it unquestionable. Like all Jewish painters of that time—without exception—they arrived in the capital from small provincial towns, in high reverence for Russian art and culture, aspiring to assimilate from it all that they saw as best progressive and revolutionary. For many of them art, imbued at the time with the spirit of safeguarding the rights of the multi-national Russian people, of which they themselves were part, was a means of struggle against the official imperial ideology. However, their art developed entirely within the Russian tradition. But only a few were able to overcome the barriers put in their way to culture, and to occupy by right their place amongst the Russian painters. The situation changes at the beginning of the second decade of our century: a growing stream poured in from the outlying areas to the capitals, through the breaches in the official ideology made by the first Jewish painters, and the new generation brought with it not only themes unusual in Russian art but a basically new attitude to life and culture.

In 1911, on the outskirts of Paris, in a large building with adjoining wooden barracks which became known as 'La Ruche des Artes', there worked, side by side with bohemians of many nations, five painters who had been thrown into the limitless Parisian ocean by the whim of Russian Jewish fate: N. Altman from Vinnitsa, M. Chagall from Vitebsk, D. Shterenberg from Zhitomir, Osip Zadkin from Smolensk and Chaim Soutine from Minsk. Zadkin and Soutine remained in Paris and acquired world fame outside their motherland. Altman and Shterenberg were to play a paramount part in the history of Soviet art. Chagall was already becoming known both in Russia and France.

Marc Chagall was born in 1887 in Vitebsk. In his autobiography he writes with surprise: 'How could I have been born here? And in general, how is it possible for any one to be born in such a godforsaken hole?'[2] And in the very same book Chagall speaks warmly about that 'godforsaken hole' where his first 20 years were spent: 'Here I am, here are my pictures, here are my roots.'[3]

All around, the life of our turbulent century was coming to the boil. Technical, social and aesthetic revolutions were imminent. But in the crooked little streets of Vitebsk, in the hovels of the Jewish poor, everything is as it was 200 or 300 years ago. The days pass by between shop and synagogue, each year at Passover the doors of the houses are left open in expectation of the Messiah's imminent arrival, and the biblical prophets seem more real than the Russian Tsar or the German Emperor. The combination of times and epochs marked the lives of these Jewish people with a certain unreality, a sense of illusion. Chagall came to art not through artistic ideas and bookish notions, but he learned from life itself as it unrolled before his eyes. And the sharp sensation of the unreality of that life has determined the character of his work up to the present.

Chagall's first works, in 1908-09, were pictures of Vitebsk, its old ramshackle huts, boarded fences, bearded Jews in the streets. But in the world of these pictures logical connections are replaced by ties of fantasy and poetic metaphor: the body of a dead man lies surrounded by funeral candles in the middle of a street, a fiddler seated on a roof plays a funeral melody over him, a green horse floats by, and in the womb of a blue cow we perceive an unborn lamb.

In 1907 Chagall arrived in Petersburg and entered Lev Bakst's art school. In three years his talent and other circumstances brought him to Paris, where he worked from 1910 to 1913. The 'Art Capital of the World' he accepted, in his own words, 'as my second Vitebsk'. The subjects of his pictures have not changed: the same little old churches on hillocks, the same crooked huts, the same lovers, although now painted with the Eiffel Tower as background. In Paris he discovered a new style of art, new for him, but he did not eulogize it: it endowed Chagall only with technical possibilities for expressing his visionary world, but it did not basically affect those visions.

Within the artistic life of France as well as Russia, which was undergoing a profound revolution at the time, the distinctive art of Chagall was not regarded as too exotic. As in all revolutions, the aesthetic revolution at the end of the nineteenth and beginning of the twentieth centuries, which destroyed the old art system dating back to the Renaissance, called new forces into play. Rejuvenation of the senescent culture was in progress throughout Europe. Let us remember that the three greatest post-impressionists—Cézanne, Van Gogh and Gauguin—settled in the world's art capital from different outlying parts of Europe, and that the bearers of the outlandish, almost barbaric elements were for Paris Picasso, and for Munich Kandinsky and Klee. Russia went through the same process. Her artistic centers absorbed healthy currents from the provinces. An overwhelming majority of the renovators of Russian art (M. Larionov, K. Malevich, V. Tatlin, the brothers V. and D. Burlyuk, P. Konchalovsky, I. Mashkov, M. Saryan, K. Petrov-Vodkin, B. Kustodiev and many more) arrived in Moscow and Petersburg from distant parts of the Russian Empire. In this process of renewal there was a strong Jewish current, at the basis of which was Chagall's work.

It is difficult to over-estimate Chagall's importance for world (not only Russian) art. He was the first who, from a starting point in his national feel of the world, found a 'plastic' means of expressing it and created that cultural-stylistic element which can impart a national spirit to art. The distinguishing features of his style were developed by many Jewish painters who worked in Russia, now abandonning them, now returning to them (N. Altman, L. Lisitsky, A. Tyshler and others). But there is something else of importance: the irrationality and phantasmagoria of Jewish life in outlying parts of Russia, which Chagall 'cast' in his own style, proved harmonious with the general world-view of twentieth-century man, for whom the universe appeared less and less a cosy place for his daily existence and increasingly open to processes and powers beyond the category of common sense. The age-old perception by the Jewish people of their 'alienism' in this world, their hopeless yearning to join the world and a certain feeling of nostalgia for the lost biblical paradise on earth (in prose Kafka expresses it most powerfully, and in some poems O. Mandelshtam)—all this has become a general mood of contemporary European culture, assuming form at the beginning of our century. That is why Chagall's style conveys not only the Jewish-national content, but a content common to all men. From 1911 the materialized metaphor stepping down from Chagall's pictures began, according to André Breton, its march through contemporary painting.[4] Chagall was a decade ahead of surrealism in many features, and it is possible to say that the cosmic phantasmagoria of this trend had its beginning in seeds thrown onto Jewish soil.

Thus, the part played by Jewish painters in Russian pre-Revolutionary art may be summed up in the following way:

(a) They developed the chief tendencies of the Russian art culture assimilated by them, and acted as creators and bearers of its most precious values (Levitan, Antokolsky, Bakst);

(b) They enriched it with new stylistic forms—through the vehicle of the Jewish perception of the world (Chagall);

(c) By their oppositional energy they stimulated in it the more radical, revolutionary tendencies.

The last function gained ground particularly during the decade preceding the Revolution when art, obeying the logic of development, saw the necessity of creating a radically new system. Robert Rafailovich Falk (1886-1958), a contemplative, precise painter, was one of the first in Russia to follow Cézanne; he saw the constructive logic of form in Cézanne and in the French Cubists. In 1910 he was one of four founders (together with A. Lentulov, I. Mashkov and P. Konchalovsky) of the 'Knave of Diamonds' (Bubnovy valet)—an art association which formed the beginning of Russian Cubo-Futurism, under whose flag Russian art developed in the last pre-Revolutionary decade and (under another terminology) in the first post-Revolutionary years.[5] In these years of crisis, perhaps the most brilliant period in the history of Russian art, the 'Knave of Diamonds' became the focus of artistic life in Russia and a generator of radical artistic ideas and forms. In Petrograd a similar role was played by the 'Union of

Youth' (Soyuz molodezhi) of which N. Altman became a member.

This was the contribution of Jewish painters to the pre-Revolutionary culture: they occupied many positions in it, but their number was small. The Revolution, which reshaped the social structure of Russia, brought far-reaching changes into its national-cultural composition.

Soviet administration of art

Motives for a sharp increase in the Jewish element of the Revolutionary culture of the first Soviet years were the same as those which attracted Jews to the Revolution itself. On the one hand, they were in natural opposition to the social system and its official ideology which kept them in an inferior legal status amongst the people of Russia. Culture in the first decade of our century developed in all the leading countries of Europe, and not only in Russia, in a re-assessment of all values and had a revolutionary character. On the other hand, this general process of re-evaluating material and spiritual foundations weakened the system of social and national moral-religious interdictions which for centuries had chained the immense cultural potential of the Jewish people, its creative activities, its age-old longing for the spiritual in life.

It is difficult to estimate the exact proportion of Jewish participation in Soviet creative art during the first post-Revolutionary years. This would demand a study of many archives in the USSR, parts of which no longer exist. But a few published materials make an approximate estimate possible.

Here, for example, we have a list of painters whose pictures were planned in 1919 to be bought for the department of painting of the Museum of Fine Arts:[6] amongst 142 names at least 20 are Jewish, say 10-15 percent. Approximately that percentage is of Jewish extraction amongst the names in art exhibitions and in designing for Revolutionary celebrations from 1918 to the mid-1920s in Moscow and Petrograd, in which hundreds of painters, architects, designers and so on took part.[7] In comparison with the number of Jews in the population of Russia and their participation in the artistic life of the pre-Revolutionary period, this proportion is not small. However, a quantitative estimate can hardly help us to understand the essence of our theme: of many painters of that time, Jews and non-Jews, only names remain, on yellowing pages of old catalogues or old archives which impart little information to an art historian. Much more important was the actual part played by the work of particular painters in the development of Soviet art, its theory, and its organization.

Immediately after the Revolution begins the formation of the structure of Soviet art, or, in a wider sense, the artistic life of the country, which from then on exists at three main levels which interact with and influence each other. In the foreground there immediately appeared a system of state institutions which took upon itself the function of administrating art. There came a system of art ideology, either imposed from above or oppositional, originating from former times or arising spontaneously in the art of that time. And last, art as such, developing along its own immanent laws but in due course falling more and more under the harsh domination of the directing organizations and the ideology they proclaimed. Relations between these levels have changed over more than half a century of Soviet art, but the general outlines of the structure remain the same up to the present day. In order to understand the part played by a social or national group, it is necessary to follow it along each of these levels.

In November 1917, a few days after the proclamation of Soviet power, the intelligentsia of Petrograd were invited to the Smolny Palace to discuss problems of collaboration between cultural figures and the new Government. Only five responded to the call: the poets V. Mayakovsky, A. Blok and R. Ivnev; the producer M. Meyerhold; and one of the painters, Natan Isaevich Altman (1889-1970). This indicates that the Revolution was accepted only by a few of the intelligentsia—namely, those who accepted it as a revolution of the spirit, as a liberation of creative work from all norms and traditions. In practice, they were the followers of the extreme left currents which even before the Revolution had attracted most of the Jewish painters. It was not surprising that on 22 May 1918, a new supreme directing institution was set up—the 'IZO' (visual arts) department of Narkompros (Commissariat for Enlightenment). Its head was the leftist painter D.P. Shterenberg (1881-1948), close in his ideology to the futurists, of whom the Commissar Lunacharsky said: 'My old friend, the left Bundist, an outstanding painter and an honest man'.[8] Altman was immediately included in the Collegium of IZO, and in 1921 succeeded Shterenberg as its head. Both of them had joined the Revolution because of their leftist position as artists, and Shterenberg also as a result of his revolutionary Bundist activities. These two great masters, men of broad outlook and culture, sincerely convinced (up to a certain time) of the correctness of their artistic and political positions, were to play a decisive part in the first stage of Soviet art.

Relative creative freedom

As the official history of Soviet art frankly informs us, 'Already during the first years after the Revolution, Soviet power did everything possible . . . to subordinate art to the interests of the Soviet State'.[9] The interests of the State at that time required it first of all to attract the creative intellectuals to its side, to establish control over their artistic work and transform it into a means of propagating communist ideas. However, between the implementation of the first and last of these points in the Leninist program, there were to be ten years of intensive struggle between various art ideologies, a period of triumphs and defeats, which finally gave rise to two opposed phenomena: an art of the Revolutionary avant-garde and Socialist Realism.

In the first five years (1917-1922) after the Revolution, during the years of Civil War, famine and general devastation, the new power had no time for art. Besides, it was self-evident that the Revolution opened to the people vast vistas for every kind of creativity, that all artistic and social groups, having hitherto borne 'the yoke of the Tsarist regime', found in the Revolution their defender and protector. Therefore, during the first stage of the Revolution there existed a relative freedom in creative art—relative because it was allowed only within the limits of proletarian and Revolutionary ideology. Activities of organizations not accepting it were stopped immediately after the Revolution, and artists who came into conflict with it—at once or later—left the country during the first decade or were deprived of any possibility of work.[10] But it was some sort of freedom because, for the purpose of expressing this ideology, various forms and methods were permitted, even those formed in pre-Revolutionary times. In practice, all this gave rise during the first years of Soviet power to a multiplicity of groupings in art.

Their origin was dictated not so much by the creative need of individual painters as by economics: with IZO of Narkompros as their sole client and customer, artists could sell their wares only by offering them in acceptable ideological packaging. Individual production had to be included in the stream of collective efforts to solve by means of art the main political problems, which were: to create a proletarian culture, to build a socialist state, to struggle against bourgeois ideology, and so on. These tasks became the uniform and compulsory ideological range on offer of any artistic grouping and were reflected in the texts of every aesthetic program, declaration or manifesto; they were, so to speak, the compulsory collective recipe of loyalty to the Revolution, the proletariat and Soviet power. But the fulfilment of these tasks assumed at the time a wide variety of methods and forms. For some artists, such aims arose naturally from their artistic posture and political outlook; for others, the bombastic political phraseology served as a camouflage concealing their aesthetic aspirations, but often their purely material self-preserving interests. Soviet power endeavored to place under its control this motley conglomeration of aesthetic ideas, artistic trends and personal interests, handing it over to IZO of Narkompros. The bitter struggle between all these elements set the direction and character of Soviet art in the first stage of its existence.

Futurism

Soviet art developed in this period under the symbol of Futurism. In Russia Futurism originated as a purely negative phenomenon. It anticipated the subsequent ideas of the French and German 'Dadaists' more than it followed the Italian founders of Futurist ideology, and aimed first and foremost at the destruction of each and every kind of cultural tradition. However, in the sixth year of its existence Futurism reached a critical point. The changes in its ideology were first noted by David Burlyuk. 'Now to rave, to preach, to punch the head of one's listener, is to force an open door. We have found acceptance, agreement and a willing audience, the time has come to create', he wrote in 1915.[11] At the end of the same year Mayakovsky predicted the future of Futurism: 'The first part of our program of destruction we consider accomplished. Therefore, don't be surprised if today instead of a jester's rattle you see in our hands an architect's designs. Futurism has seized Russia in a death grip.'[12] This was prophetic: Futurism gained absolute supremacy in the art and artistic life of Russia immediately after the Revolution. Not only because the Futurists were the most revolutionary-minded people in the arts. More important was the fact that the ideology of Futurism seemed at first amazingly in harmony with the revolutionary destructive-constructive spirit: what Marxism preached (in the negative and positive parts of its program) in the sphere of social life, Futurism translated into reality in the life of art — destruction of the old social order (or — for Futurism — bourgeois culture) and the creation of a new social order (or proletarian culture).

In 1917 the poets V. Mayakovsky, V. Kamensky and D. Burlyuk began to publish a Futurist paper under the slogan 'Revolution of the Spirit'. In this paper the terms 'Futurism' and 'Communism' were almost identical. In January 1919 a 'Communist-Futurist' group ('Comfut') was formed under the Vyborg District Committee of the Communist Party. The paper *Iskusstvo kommuny* (Art of the Commune), which became the voice of their ideas, gave an account of the event: 'Comrade Kushner was elected Chairman and Chief Secretary of Comfut and Comrade Natanson Secretary.'[13]

Mayakovsky proclaimed the idea of Futurism after the Revolution. Its theorist was Osip Brik — professional revolutionary, writer and publicist, and a close friend of Mayakovsky.

The significance of Futurism was not limited to one specific group. It came to express the most creative constructive-destructive spirit of the Revolution, being accepted by the intelligentsia as the 'revolution of the spirit'. As such it became the ideological nucleus and in its way a ferment stimulating and directing the development of aesthetic ideas during the first post-Revolutionary years, on the basis of which arose collectives of masters and the activities of artistic groupings. (It is not without reason that the word 'Futurism' came to be used of all leftist revolutionary trends in the field of culture.)

With the serious shortage of competent people who favored the Revolution, the theory and ideology of the new art were formulated at that time by a small group of people. Along with N. Puni and V. Arvatov, those who immediately made a decisive contribution in this sphere (apart from N. Altman and D. Shterenberg) were Osip Brik, Boris Kushner, Nikolay Chuzhak and, somewhat later, David Arkin. In the first post-Revolutionary years they occupied key positions in the system of state institutions which covered a wide range of the ideology, scholarship and education of Soviet art as well as its theory and practice. Works by Moisey Yakovlevich Ginzburg ('Epoch and Style', published in 1924) and I. Ioffe ('A Synthetic History of Art', 1929) are still considered classics of the sociological method, which at that time was predominant in the study of art. They were all close to Futurism, contributed to its ideology and practice, and later developed its ideas in new directions to meet practical problems—both of art and State policy concerning it—in subsequent stages of development.

Constructivism

The main line of development in the ideas of the Soviet artistic avant-garde is fairly clear. Still in the pre-Revolutionary period, in the depths of Cubo-Futurism there was formed a conception and practice of a 'non-figurative' art, crowned with Malevich's Suprematism and his 'White Square on White Background' in 1919, which was, in effect, a rejection of the very nature of painting. 'In Suprematism one cannot even speak of painting, painting has long been outlived, and the painter himself is a prejudice of the past'[14]—this is the summing up by the painter of what he had already reached in practice. The idea that easel painting would die away during the epoch of the proletarian dictatorship became central for the Futurists and associated trends. 'The easel picture is not only not needed by contemporary culture, but it is one of the most powerful obstacles to its development',[15] wrote O. Brik. No epithets were too abusive to be hurled by the avant-garde at the supporters of easel art, right up to accusing them of being bourgeois and counter-revolutionary by nature. Hence the logical conclusion:

> The main distinguishing feature of the present times we consider to be *the triumph of the Constructive method.* We see it in the new economy, in the

> development of industry, in the psychology of our contemporaries and in art. We stand for constructive art, not for art which makes life more beautiful, *but one that organizes it.*[16]

On the basis of this ideology arose Constructivism, which determined the style of Soviet art and architecture in the first half of the 1920s. Characteristic of the sociological and aesthetic arts of Constructivism were the theoretical work 'Epoch and Style' by M. Ya. Ginsburg and 'And Yet it Revolves', a book by Ilya Ehrenburg. Its printed organ became the journal *Veshch* (Thing), which Ehrenburg and Lisitsky began to publish in Berlin. In 1919, its supporters united in the Society of Young Painters (OBMOKhU) in which the brothers V.A. and G.A. Sternberg were active, together with A. Rodchenko and G.B. Yakulov. The largest architectural group of that time—the Association of New Architects (ASNOVA)—was formed in 1923 on analogous ideas: its first chairman was the engineer A.F. Loleyt.

Productivism

But even Constructivism was not the sum total crowning the ideas of Soviet avant-gardism. From its theory of organizing life by means of art, there was only one step to the idea of abolishing art altogether, of turning it into work for organizing life (the so-called theory of life-building) and transforming the painter into a creator of utilitarian instead of aesthetic objects. This step was taken in the theory of 'Production Art' or 'Productivism', which became the second current, parallel to Constructivism, in the mainstream of the avant-garde in the 1920s. Its manifesto was a symposium of articles *Iskusstvo i proizvodstvo* (Art and Production) published in 1921. In the introductory article D. Shterenberg wrote: 'In order to be convinced that a chair or table can become an artistic object, of equal value to some Madonna and suchlike fetishes of painting and sculpture . . . , mountains of evidence are needed. The task of the symposium is to provide this evidence.'[17] The evidence was assembled to prove that art divided into 'high' and 'low', 'pure' and 'applied', etc., was only a survival of the bourgeois outlook.

> The bourgeoisie divided people into creators and creatures according to their occupations. We do not act like that . . . we maintain that architects, sculptors, painters, are as much workers as engineers, metal-workers, textile-workers, wood-workers and so on . . . for us a factory is a means of collective creation. We must show the artist that production is an inexhaustible source of creation and persuade him to direct all his creative forces to it.[18]

The merging of painter, engineer and manual worker into a 'life-builder', and his work in creating things for use—chairs, clothes, houses, machines, etc.—was proclaimed the prime task and the high road of development for proletarian culture. 'Contemporary times affirm production art as the basic tendency of depictive culture. The latter thus proves to be in close connection with the culture of production, the culture of machine industry, as determining all the creativity of material forms made by man'.[19] The originators and champions of this conception were, together with Arvatov, O. Brik, B. Kushner and D. Arkin. The idea of Constructivism and Productivism as a guide for the practical activity of an artist was supported by D. Shterenberg and N. Altman and became, in effect, the offical ideology of IZO, and through it of the largest scholarly and educational institutions.

Ideological guidance

In May 1920, the 'Institute of Art Culture' (INKhUK)—a scholarly and theoretical center—was established under IZO, to formulate ideology for the whole of Soviet art. Its first president was Vasily Vasilevich Kandinsky. He provided a program for all the work of the Institute. An artist of world fame, the founder of Abstractionism and an outstanding theorist whose book 'On the Spiritual in Art' had been translated into many European languages, Kandinsky oriented his program towards a composite study of the influence of art forms on the perception and creation of a synthetic art in which painting, sculpture and architecture would merge into one whole. However, in the bitter struggle for the leading role in artistic life, the effectual means of which was political demagogy, his theories were soon declared idealist, bourgeois and 'harmful to the proletariat'. Kandinsky was forced to leave the Institute and soon left Soviet Russia. A new orientation to the work of INKhUK was given by its new chairman O. Brik, who was also a member of the IZO Collegium.

> A significant moment . . . in the creative activities of INKhUK was 24 November [1921], a day of undoubtedly great historical importance. On this day Brik delivered an address in which he invited the painters who had left easel work to get down to real, practical work in production. The basic principle of the new proposition was accepted in its entirety by INKhUK. Twenty-five of the foremost artists acknowledged that their work as nothing more than painters had been aimless.[20]

Thus did INKhUK's own account of its work assess the role of its chairman and the significance of his activity. N. Altman and member of the INKhUK board B. Kushner were active in helping to implement these ideas through the organs of state power (the Supreme Council of National Economy, the Central Council of Trade Unions, etc.).

The members of IZO and INKhUK made the decisions regarding the basic professorial staff in the art education institutions of that time, thus introducing there the ideas of Constructivism and Productivism. In September 1918, out of the Academy of Art, the Moscow School of Art, Sculpture and Architecture and the Stroganoff College, which had been abolished by a decree issued by Lenin, the State Free Art Workshops (GSKhM) were created; they were directed by Commissars for Art Affairs who were appointed by the IZO Department of the the Narkompros. In 1919 O. Brik became one of these commissars and in 1920 Shkolnik. E. Ya. Shtalberg, N. Altman, Yakob Moisevich Guminer, I. Ioffe and others were appointed Professors in the Workshops. Later the Workshops were merged with the State Higher Art-Technical Workshops (VKhUTEMAS) which had been set up in 1920; these became the largest center not only of education but also of the artistic life of the country, the generator of the most advanced ideas in art of the Soviet avant-garde of the 1920s.

Thus ideological guidance in the sphere of art, during the first years of the Soviet State, was carried out almost solely by IZO and institutions depending on it. IZO had the political and economic means of fulfilling this function: being the highest State organ in this sphere, it was the only allocator in the entire country of orders, work premises, rations, rates of pay and other material blessings on which, in those hungry years, depended not only the creativeness but also the physical existence of individual painters and groups. Management, ideology, education, artistic practice and theory were at the time in the hands of, in effect, one group of people, amongst whom the proportion of Jews and the real part they played were very high indeed. This situation can be explained not only by the talent and higher revolutionary commitment of the Jews, but also by certain peculiarities of the general political circumstances of the time. The young proletarian power found it easier to uproot the remains of old Russian 'bourgeois' culture with the hands of strangers, of newcomers, 'to destroy', as Lunacharsky wrote at the time 'the remains of the institutions that were Tsarist by their very nature, the Academy of Art, for example . . . to free education of men with established reputations?'[21]

As to the practitioners of art summoned to build on the ruins of the old culture a culture of the future, the main line of the Soviet vanguard of the 1920s was defined by Constructivism, with its rejection of 'easelism' and its aim to provide a new material environment for man by means of artistic creativeness. These ideas gave birth to a new type of painter, changing his functions in the spheres of art and social life.

The painter refuses to depict, he wants to build—as purposively as the work-

> man makes things; the painter rejects narrowly specific aesthetic materials (oil, gouache, pastel)—he wants to use the ordinary materials of daily life: he goes for charcoal, enamel, paper, varnish, etc. Moreover, his very methods of work change. Now he does not make drawings in the traditional sense but technical drawings, . . . does not prepare sketches but precise plans. The artist has embarked on the road of the engineer.[22]

This was written in 1924 by B. Arvatov about Natan Altman. However, this universal definition of an avant-garde painter is to a much greater degree applicable to the initiators of Russian Constructivism—Malevich, Tatlin and Lisitsky.

L.M. Lisitsky

Lazar Markovich Lisitsky (El Lissitzky) (1890-1941) made an important contribution to the Jewish fine arts tradition as a young man. He illustrated sixteen Yiddish and Hebrew books, and it is easy to detect Chagall's strong influence in his drawing style. He was also involved in the design of synagogues in the Ukraine and Byelorussia. However, it is his continuation of Malevich's and Tatlin's ideas, that made him a figure in the history of Rusian art, as a major representative of Russian Constructivism. He wrote in 1920: 'In this chaos [i.e. war, which turned technology from creation to destruction] originated Suprematism, which extolled the square as the source of creative expressiveness. And then arrived communism, which extolled labour as the true source for the beating of the human heart'.[23] Thus the social revolution was for Lisitsky the final link in the spiritual evolution of humanity, and he remained faithful to this idea until his last days. His significance for the development of Russian Constructivism lies in the fact that he translated the Suprematist style of Malevich into the language of spatial forms, creating in 1919-24 his own 'Prouns'—an acronym from 'projects of assertion of the new'—which he defined as 'bridges between painting and architecture'. 'Prouns' were long series of abstract compositions, in which the painter experimented with spatial relationships of geometrical planes. At the same time he expressed these ideas in material form, and created spatial compositions serving as bases for architectural projects. A classical example for the Soviet avant-garde was to be his project of the 'Leninist tribune' intended for the delivery of speeches by the leaders of the Revolution to great masses of the people. This project, however, like all the architectural projects of Lisitsky, remained on paper. But his formal discoveries were implemented in other artistic spheres.

Living abroad from 1921 to 1925, where he published with Ehrenburg the journal *Veshch* and through Georg Grosz initiated links between the Soviet avant-garde and revolutionary-minded German artists, Lisitsky managed to mount all the largest Soviet exhibitions in Germany and to create on the basis of his 'Prouns' a completely new and innovatory style of exhibition design.

Another sphere in which the formal experiments of his 'Prouns' were realized, and in which he appeared as a true innovator, was graphics: the political poster, book design, emblems, etc. He tried to reduce the chaos of the collapsing world to the simplest order of elementary forms, on the basis of which it might have been possible to build the world of the future: 'Shapes which are not ambiguous and which can be recognized at once must be geometrical. No one can confuse a square with a circle and a circle with a triangle'.[24] And in his posters, such as 'The Machines are Awaiting You' or 'Smash the White with a Red Wedge' (given in all histories of art as exemplary political posters and—in official works on Soviet art written since the early 1930s—as examples of 'senseless formalism'), Lisitsky by the conjunction of these geometrical shapes gave simplicity and the utmost clarity to the political idea. If Malevich called his 'Suprematist' compositions 'semaphores of cosmic space', Lisitsky's posters created on the 'Proun' principle could be called 'semaphores of social space': stuck on the fences of houses or on the walls of antediluvian factories, all the posters were symbols, signs, landmarks, semaphores, pointing the way towards a bright world of the future in which reign the order, harmony and simplicity so lacking in the world of the present. In the language of geometrical shapes he told the children entire stories of how, for example, the dark planet of exploitation was liberated by the red forces of the laboring proletariat.[25] Lisitsky was a true reformer of typography and book design, on which he worked to the end of his life. He was the most striking type of 'engineer-artist' born of Constructivism who moved away from artistic creativity to the creation of a 'second nature'—man's actual environment.

N. Altman

D. Shterenberg and N. Altman were not as radical in their direct creations as the founders of Constructivism. As painters, they were both widely known before the Revolution. Shterenberg worked mainly abroad at that time. He arrived in Russia in 1917, already a mature master with a style of his own of somewhat two-dimensional pictorial images.

In his youth Altman, like Lisitsky, worked on Jewish subjects, and in particular, was interested in Jewish ornamentation. On his return to Russia from Paris in 1911, he immediately became immersed in the artistic life of St Petersburg which was then seething with new ideas. He became a member of the Futurist 'Union of Youth' group, joining the pick of the Russian avant-garde of those years (members of which included M.

Larionov, N. Goncharova, K. Malevich, the Burlyuk brothers, V. Tatlin, A. Ekster, P. Filonov, L. Popova, Vladimir Mayakovsky). The search for new directions in art had already led a number of its masters to a radical rejection of traditional forms and methods in figurative art and to a transition to 'non-subjectivism' (the Suprematism of Malevich, the 'Ray-ism' of Larionov, the 'Pictorial reliefs' of Tatlin, etc). But, despite common aesthetic ideas, Altman still remained within the limits of the figurative language of painting, enriching it with the newest trends and improving its technique. His brilliant talent, sharp intellect and human qualities opened to him the doors of all the Petersburg literary-artistic salons. In addition to his colleagues in the 'Union of Youth' he was well acquainted with Gorky, Esenin, Mandelshtam, Khlebnikov, Blok and Shalyapin, and was a particular friend of Anna Akhmatova. His 1914 portrait of Akhmatova (the best of all portraits of the great poetess), in which Cubist deformations serve only as a means of psychological characterization, is a brilliant example of his style of the pre-Revolutionary period.

In the post-Revolutionary years Altman concluded that the easel picture was no longer part of social life and almost ceased to work in this medium (he returned to it later during his Paris period). He devoted all his energy to what were then called mass forms of art. He became the leader of Lenin's plan for monumental propaganda, by which the towns were to be decorated by monuments of outstanding revolutionaries, scientists and cultural figures; he was in charge of design for the revolutionary festivals—at that time the most effective form of artistic propaganda. To celebrate the first anniversary of the October Revolution he, together with Shterenberg, decorated the central square of the Revolutionary capital. The front of the Winter Palace and the pedestal of the Aleksandr I. Column were draped by immense Cubist panels and constructions, to 'create a colorful mood of joy, celebration, by means of colored, figured surfaces, the main colors of which were orange, green and red'.[26] 20,000 arshins (14,000 metres) of canvas alone (in that time of poverty) were allocated by the Soviet Government for this self-advertisement, which may have exceeded in scale anything of the kind previously done anywhere. In 1920 during the same festival Altman staged the capture of the Winter Palace. Against his gigantic Cubist stage sets thousands of participants, including armed detachments of the Red Guards, re-enacted with realistic precision this symbolic act of establishing Soviet power. To Altman belong the first sketches of the Soviet flag, the State emblem, the postage stamps, the seals and other emblems. Also, he was one of the few painters permitted to paint Lenin from life. In 1920 he spent many hours in Lenin's study in Smolny, observing the Soviet leader at work and making sketches of him. These keen and by no means idealized sketches reproducing the live appearance of Lenin stand at the source of a many-branched, elaborate iconography of the leader, which in official art criticism is given a central place in the history of Soviet art.

A. Pevsner and N. Gabo

Outstanding personalities in the art of the twentieth century were the brothers Anton Pevsner (1886-1962) and Naum Gabo (1890-1977), although in the development of the Soviet avant-garde they did not play as important a part as Lisitsky or Tatlin. Both of them began before the Revolution with Cubist sculpture, both joined the Constructivists in the first post-Revolutionary years, creating their own version of that trend. In 1920 they published their 'Realistic Manifesto' in which, while sharing the general conception of Constructivism on creating a new reality by means of art, they understood the character of this reality in their own way. The product of a painter's work, in their view, must have nothing in common with utilitarian objects. A painter deals with such abstract categories of reality as time and space and—translating them into the language of harmonious shapes—constructs pure rhythms of the universe. What is not a reality for the perception of man becomes that in the work of art. Also in 1920 N. Gabo created the first ever 'kinetic model'. These moving constructions of his, either freely hanging in the air or set in motion by a small motor, initiated a long line in the development of contemporary sculpture, leading directly to the 'mobiles' of A. Calder and to the creativity of the (unofficial) group of Moscow 'Kineticists' active in our days. However, their ideas of pure art not connected with practical utilitarian tasks contradicted the general spirit of materialism and utilitarianism of the Soviet avant-garde of the 1920s and found no support. In 1922 Pevsner and Gabo left Soviet Russia. They received world recognition outside their native country.

M. Chagall

The personal and artistic fates of Marc Chagall were similar during those stormy years in the history of Soviet art. Chagall was far from political struggle. As he wrote in his autobiography: 'My first feeling after the Revolution was: now I shall have nothing more to do with residence registrations'[27] . . . and further that the social revolution had something in common with the revolution that Chagall himself accomplished in art: 'Lenin turned Russia head over heels—the same way as I do with my pictures.'[28] (Much later, in 1937, he painted the picture 'Revolution' in which he portrayed Lenin as a clown standing on one hand in a crowd of Chagallite people. But then Chagall had not yet got over his illusions.) In

1918 he was appointed Commissar of Arts in his native Vitebsk, where immediately on his arrival he founded a School of Arts, inviting as teachers K. Malevich, L. Lisitsky and I. Puni. Once, on the first anniversary of the Revolution, the streets of Vitebsk were decorated with—instead of portraits of Lenin and Marx and Cubist slogans—green horses and blue cows of Chagall's pupils, enlarged to the size of the banners. The communist leaders viewed this idea with disfavor. Indeed, Chagall's fantastic realism, like the 'pure' creativeness of Pevsner and Gabo, proved at variance with the spirit of the Revolutionary avant-garde. At the same time, the conditions of intolerance, of Revolutionary slogans, and the worship of material progress, were deeply alien to his nature as a free poetic-painter. 'Where are we going? What is this epoch that composes hymns to technical art and makes a god of formalism?'[29]—were questions that disturbed Chagall. The end result was a mutiny against him in the school of which he was director, and his removal from official posts. Chagall moved to starving Moscow and, with nothing else available, started work in the studio of Granovsky, out of which eventually grew the Jewish Theater.

Granovsky's studio was at the time the center for the activities of Jewish painters. It was here that A. Tyshler and I. Rabinovich began; N. Altman, R. Falk and others worked there. But the theater acquired a style of its own with the arrival of Chagall. His scenic designs gave a new direction to the theater, changing it from the realism of everyday life in the Sholem Aleichem manner to a metaphysical realism, from a superficial image of the national life to an expression of its age-old, innermost meaning. They had the strongest influence not only on the paintings of the artists working there (even Altman, in the pictures he produced not long before his death, returned to these deeply national, illusory-fantastic images), but the acting was affected too. The great Jewish actor Mikhoels said that acquaintance with Chagall's sketches changed all his own creative individuality, the rhythmic quality of his body, of his speech and movements.

Intensification of ideological conformity

The departure at that time of the greatest 'Leftist' painters (Chagall, Pevsner and Gabo, Kandinsky, Ekster and others) was the result of changed conditions in the country. The Soviet State, having totally vanquished the counter-revolution, could now take up art in earnest and start to implement the last point of its cultural program—the transformation of art into means of propagating communist ideas. In this the primary problem came to be the artistic language, one necessarily comprehensible to the masses. The Commissar for Enlightenment, Lunacharsky, responsive to the moods of the leaders, changed course sharply in 1922 and advanced the slogan 'Back to the Wanderers'. The new policy in art needed new executants: Shterenberg and Altman left the leadership of IZO department of the Narkompros. A highly charged struggle that was to last ten years began for a mass realistic art 'comprehensible to the broad masses of the people', reflecting the great deeds and achievements of the Revolution and recreating the images of its leaders. This was a period of the uprooting of all leftist, 'Formalistic' tendencies, a period crowned by the victory and absolute supremacy of Socialist Realism. In this movement backwards, although the Jews had not the same importance as in the development of avant-garde ideas, their part was not insignificant.

The first reaction to the extremes of avant-gardism which had gone so far as to reject easel pictures (the Constructivists) and art in general (by the Productivists) was the formation in 1921 of NOZh (New Society of Painters). It comprised new graduates of VKhUTEMAS: S. Ya. Adlivankin, A.M. Gluskin, A.M. Nyurenberg, M.S. Perutsky, G.G. Ryzhsky and others. Their Declaration stated:

> We, former Leftists in art, were the first to sense the utter groundlessness of further analytical-scholastic gropings . . . A painting must have a subject and realism . . . Considering that painting has in the process of laboratory researches torn itself away from life, that its language has thereby become alien and incomprehensible to the masses, we have taken from tradition the least modernized and aesthetic forms and thus the least dangerous.[30]

The NOZh group performed creative rather than political tasks, so it did not play a decisive role in the struggle against Formalism and for domination in the world of art—the framework in which the subsequent period of Soviet art was to develop. In this the initiative was taken by the Association of Artists of Revolutionary Russia (AKhRR, shortened to AKhR in 1928).

As has already been observed, the attitude of the artistic intelligentsia to the new regime was not uniform in the first stage of the Revolution. In official works on Soviet art the following is usually said about this: 'Many people in the arts waited for the outcome of the struggle between the working people and the exploiter classes, not openly taking sides with either the new power or the counter-revolutionaries.'[31] But it has never been disclosed who were those who 'waited'. A quite cursory acquaintance with the biographies of the most substantial cultural figures of AKhR—the future pillars of Socialist Realism—is sufficient to see that the waiting position was taken by those who, five years later, when Soviet power had become stabilized and clearly required not creators of new form but glorifiers, took on themselves the functions of defenders of popular, realist and socialist art. And when their first, timid voices were heard against the dominance of Futurism, N. Altman was able to declare quite justifiably: 'Why was a whole year of proletarian power and revolution, which gripped half the world, needed for "the silent to start talking"? Why did only revolutionary Futurism march in step with the October Revolution? . . . Only Futurist art is now the art of the proletariat.'[32]

In 1922 'the silent started talking' at the top of their voices. In that year the Society of Wanderers renewed their activities by their 47th exhibition, having lived through their crisis in the 1890s and since then having played no noticeable part in the development of Russian art. During the debate which accompanied the opening of the exhibition, and which expressed ideas half a century old to the effect that art's chief function was to reflect people's lives, an association of painters studying the revolutionary way of life was conceived. It was this that soon developed into AKhR. Its initiators were the landscape painter Wanderer P. Radimov, A. Grigorev—a painter who had spent several years in Party work—and a young portrait-painter Evgeny Aleksandrovich Katsman. Soon V.N. Perelman, who with Katsman was to become one of the most active figures in this organization, entered its leadership. Amongst the AKhR artists the central figure for a long time was a pupil of I. Repin, Isaak Izrailevich Brodsky.

The first declaration of AKhR, which E. Katsman helped to draw up, was notable for the aggressive character of its high-flown political terminology:

> Our social duty to mankind is to impress by artistic documentation the greatest moment of history in its revolutionary impulse. We will depict the present: the daily life of the Red Army, of workers, peasants, leading Revolutionaries and heroes of labor. We will give a true picture of events and some abstract fabrications which discredit our Revolution in the eyes of the world's proletariat.[33]

In subsequent documents the position of AKhR was clarified even further:

> In the eleventh year of the October Revolution, on the front of figurative art two main camps have formed sufficiently clearly: on the one side AKhR, working in the ranks of the proletariat and laboring peasantry, under the slogan of active participation in the class struggle and the building of socialism, working under the slogan 'art to the masses' and being on the verge of creating the foundations of a proletarian art, and on the other side the camp of all the other groups—pursuing petty bourgeois ideology under the guise of Formalist tasks, hampering the forward march of socialist construction.[34]

Thus AKhR counterposed itself to the rest of Soviet art and saw one of its main tasks as struggle against 'the occupation of the commanding posts of figurative art in governmental and other public bodies by anti-AKhR people'.[35] This was a frank struggle for power, directed first of all against the IZO Department of Narkompros, and the organizations INKhUK and VKhUTEIN (Higher Artistic-Technical Institute) where exponents of Left art still held positions.

AKhR had, in practice, two main guiding principles: (1) the creation of a thematic picture reflecting socialist reality in its forward development and (2) appealing to the masses in a simple and comprehensible language. The first enabled them to reach the higher Party and Governmental people whom they portrayed and glorified in their pictures. The second principle made it possible to discredit in the eyes of these people—who were ignorant of art but well versed in politics—the leaders of their opponents, accusing them of non-intelligibility (and thus of being against the masses) and other mortal sins. It was by this recipe that the AKhR-ites produced genre scenes, landscapes, portraits, painted in the style and with the technique of the Wanderers and passed off as creations of the new revolutionary and heroic Realism.

Isaak Izrailovich Brodsky (1884-1939) is generally considered the creator of the thematic revolutionary picture in Soviet art. In 1919 he began work on an immense composition—'Triumphal Opening of the Second Congress of The Comintern'—which was displayed with much pomp at the AKhR exhibition in 1924. After that came 'The Execution of the 26 Baku Commissars' (1925)—a classic of Soviet Socialist Realism, 'Lenin in Smolny' (1930), and other pictures based on Lenin, in which Brodsky was the pioneer. In his work on thematic pictures he freely used photographic material (he became a pioneer in that too), transferring mechanically onto his canvas not only details of photographs but whole scenes. He was accused of naturalism and plagiarism; his name became a synonym for naturalistic art ('Brodskyism'—a term originating in the 1920s to describe that kind of art). There was a court case and he was expelled from membership of AKhR. But Brodsky continued to paint portraits of those revolutionary leaders who were in power—Kirov, Voroshilov, Frunze, Menzhinsky, Stalin and others— and his position in Soviet art became increasingly assured. He may be the only Soviet painter whose home (in Leningrad) has been made into a museum.

Evgeny Aleksandrovich Katsman (born 1890) had not the same creative scope as Brodsky. Most of his energy went into administrative work. He was the most active ideologist and organizer of AKhR, an exponent of the most aggressive attitude towards anything that deviated in any way from the criteria of narrowly understood Realism, i.e. from the line which, having gained support at the political summit, won absolute supremacy from the 1930s. As a painter he made his name by painting portraits of Party leaders (Kalinin, Voroshilov and others). He painted genre scenes in soft pink and blue pastel shades on the lives of workers and peasants; he created 'heroic images of the revolutionary proletariat' as alike as two peas to the salon products of the end of the last century. Very similar, if not in technique then in result, were the paintings of the majority of other members of AKhR, both of Jews—whose proportion in AKhR was much smaller than in the Left groups—and of non-Jews.

During the second half of the 1920s the position of AKhR as the center group in Soviet art became increasingly firm; its ideas spread through the top political levels and its activities began to threaten the existence of all other trends in art. In order to resist AKhR and preserve the remnants of creative freedom, artists of the other trends began to create their own associations. They all now recognized easel art and subscribed to the struggle to create thematic pictures reflecting the conquests of the Revolution. But within these limits they endeavored to preserve freedom of stylistic exploration and solutions. The largest of these many associations were two groupings: the 'Easel Society' (OST) founded in 1925, whose chairman was D. Shterenberg; and 'October', which in 1928 brought together leading painters, architects, art critics and film artists (such as A. Deyneka, A.A. and V.A. Vesnin and S.M. Eisenstein); M. Ya. Ginsburg, L.M. Lisitsky and the leading book illustrator Solomon Benediktovich Telingater were active in it. In 1926 a number of artistic groups requested in a letter addressed to the Central Committee of the Party

> an end to the situation in which one artistic group is marked out from the rest by all possible signs of goodwill, expressed not only in making material provision for this group but—much more important—opening for it a moral credit in wide circles of Soviet society that cannot be justified by the cultural-artistic achievements of this group alone.[36]

This communication was signed by leading Soviet painters D. Shterenberg, Yu. Pimenov, A. Goncharova, I. Grabar and S. Gerasimov. There were repeated references in resolutions of the Arts Sector of Narkompros and even in Party documents to 'the unsatisfactory nature of AKhR productions both as to ideological and artistic quality'[37], 'the petty-bourgeois character of its leadership (Katsman, Perelman)', 'undue flexibility in the understanding of class ideology, adapted to the requirements of petty-bourgeois tastes . . . , its claims to leadership in contemporary art—discredited by insignificant results in artistic practice'.[38] But while the painters and men of culture exchanged their written and verbal high words, Brodsky, Katsman and, later, Aleksandr Gerasimov painted portraits of Stalin, Voroshilov, Kirov and Menzhinsky, showing them taking a walk or making a report against the background of gigantic buildings and enthusiastic masses of workers, quietly chatting with Gorky or passionately orating. It was just such art, devoid of quality, that was needed by the Party bureaucrats who at the time were coming to power and whom it was easy to convince that anything else was only intrigues by the enemies of the Soviet regime. AKhR, in effect, left the domain of cultural-artistic institutions and placed its fate in the hands of the higher political elite.

With such support AKhR could no longer be satisfied with the status of one group, even one in every way encouraged by the Government; the aim of its leaders was to control all Soviet art. This aim was soon attained. On 23 April 1932 came a decree from the Central Committee of the Party, 'On the Reconstruction of Literary-Artistic Organizations', which abolished all artistic groups in the country and replaced them by creative unions. In the field of figurative art the Union of Soviet Painters assumed such a place. The main controlling positions in it were taken by former AKhR men. I.I. Brodsky became the president of the newly-formed Academy of Arts of the RSFSR.

At this point the history of Russian art finishes and the history of Socialist Realism begins.

Socialist Realism

'In effect the history of Soviet art is nothing more than the history of the formation, confirmation and development of Socialist Realism'.[39] This statement by the 'General of Aesthetics' V. V. Vantslav (the present head of the Department of Theory at the Institute of Art History, USSR Academy of Arts) defines exactly the official set-up in the mid-1930s. It not only determined the subsequent development of Soviet art but several times obliged its entire preceding history to be rewritten and reconstructed, divesting Soviet art of everything that had constituted its living body and emphasizing phenomena which were then without significance.

The essence of Socialist Realism was formulated in 1934 at the First All-Union Congress of Soviet Writers: 'Socialist Realism requires of the artist a truthful, historically concrete depiction of reality in its revolutionary development. At the same time, the truthfulness and historical concreteness of the artistic representation of reality must be equal to the task of remaking the ideas of the working people and educating them in the spirit of socialism.'[40] The history of Socialist Realism in the following three decades is the consistent eradication of everything that does not accord with 'remaking the ideas of the working people' and implementing the last point of Lenin's aesthetic program (not set down in writing but arising from the spirit of all his statements and measures in this sphere), i.e. transforming art into a means of agitation and propaganda. The actual development of Socialist Realism has been defined by the changing official conception of what, at the given stage, must be advocated and for what purpose propaganda must be conducted. Thus the history of Soviet art is, in the main, a history of the succession of the themes and objects depicted, which have changed in accordance with changes in Party slogans and the individuals proclaiming them, and likewise the history of successive simplifications of the language of art in which these slogans are expressed and these individuals portrayed. From the end of the 1920s the main subject of paintings in Socialist Realism was the labor feats of the Soviet people and their increasing well-being. The more violent the famine which was killing millions of villagers, while millions of other peasants, workers and members of the intelligentsia were flung into prisons and concentration camps, the brighter became the colors, the more lavish the food piled on *kolkhoz* tables in the pictures, and the happier the smiles on the faces of the working people when meeting Party and Government leaders on the canvases of the 'truthful portrayers of reality in its revolutionary development'. The other main theme was 'the images of the leaders of the toiling masses', but in step with the purges of particular leaders their images were removed from the canvas by the Socialist Realists and replaced by their successors. (Perhaps the first picture subjected to such an operation was I. I. Brodsky's 'Triumphal Opening of the Second Congress of the Comintern'.) Of primary importance during the war was the theme of the people's struggle at the fronts and in the rear, and in the post-war period the whole country was covered by images of the 'Leader and Teacher' in plaster, marble, bronze, oils or granite. With the ending of the Cult of Personality, they were replaced by images of Lenin made of the same materials. As for the artistic language of the Socialist Realists, it evolved from the simplified monumental heroic forms in the 1930s, passionately asserting strength, struggle, labor and spiritual well-being in the style of Italian art of that period, to the detailed naturalism of the 1940s and early 1950s in the German manner. Description of this process and the exposure and study of the parts played in it by various artists, art critics and theorists is a subject for a sociologist interested in Sovietology or Kremlinology rather than for an art historian.

We can observe only that the proportion of Jews who participated in this destruction of culture, and in its replacement by Socialist Realist pseudo-culture, was noticeably lower than in activities of the first post-Revolutionary years. At the helm of artistic life the mediocrities moved into position, men who were not notable for extreme revolutionary views either in aesthetics or in politics, but who quietly waited for those useless discussions on art to end and attention to turn to more practical and material matters, such as sharing out the 'state cake'. The role of the painter Aleksandr Gerasimov, and of others like him, grows; gradually he became the all powerful dictator in Soviet art and in 1947 he officially secured this position by becoming head of the new Academy of Arts of the USSR. Coming in most cases from the better-off sections of the pre-Revolutionary peasantry, these artists brought with them to the new sphere of activity their peasant practicality, their lack of ideals and narrow-minded tastelessness. These qualities permitted them not only to attain power, but also to remain for many years at its pinnacle, from which the more principled and intellectual comrades were cast out wholesale during those years, direct to Kolyma and other camps. It is natural that Jews, because of their peculiar position in Russia, belonged not to those attaining power but rather to the outcasts. Besides, their access to top positions in official artistic life was hampered by genuine Russian anti-intellectualism, with its shade of antisemitism, which was carried by people who now became the new rulers in Soviet art and which, with time, colored official Soviet ideology. The culmination came with a wide-ranging official antisemitic campaign during 1948-53 under the guise of 'struggle against cosmopolitanism'. In any case, amongst the first ten official Socialist Realist prize-winning portrait painters of Soviet leaders, who occupied all the key positions,[41] we do not find a single Jewish painter. Only in the sphere of political cartoons, which came to equal posters as the leading genre of Soviet graphic art, there was, with the Kukryniksy, Boris Efimov—who in the late 1940s became notorious for his explicitly anti-semitic drawings in the magazine *Krokodil.*

This does not mean that the percentage of Jews in Soviet art decreased in those years. The 'Short Encyclopaedia of Art', perhaps the most objective source of official information, gives about 30 Jewish names amongst 300 important artists of the Soviet years—some ten percent.[42] However, their position in the pecking order declined: in the official sphere only second and third levels are left to the Jews. In official histories of Soviet art the names of the leading lights of Socialist Realism—A. Gerasimov, B. Ioganson, N. Tomsky and others—are followed by E. Katsman, G. Shegal, V. Ingal, I. Chaykov, L. Kerbel and a few others, and behind these stand a mass of almost nameless artists who are prevented from reaching a higher level not so much by lack of ability as by the presence of Jewish nationality in their biographical questionnaire.It is hardly worth while describing here these suppliers of the mass-products of Socialist Realism, as they differ from each other mainly by genre and technique. They are defined only by the quantity, not the quality, of their output.

Pioneers of the Soviet avant-garde and painters of great talent who do not fit into the narrow frame of the new requirements and tasks were obliged to lead a semi-underground existence in these long years.

Lazar Lisitsky, who kept up his faith in communist ideals to the end, earned his living by designing for the journal *USSR in Construction*, published for propaganda abroad, while he made drawings of vast projects of palaces and whole new city regions which remained in the drawers of his desk.

The name of David Shterenberg became synonymous with Formalism, a term used to frighten students of art schools. In the early 1930s he designed children's books and illustrated Isaak Babel's 'Odessa Stories' but soon, evidently, fell silent, up to his death in 1948; in any case Soviet official sources mention no works of his last ten years.

Natan Altman left in 1928 for Paris, where he returned to painting. However, the life of a half-emigré (he kept his Soviet citizenship and continued to consider himself as belonging to Soviet culture), proved unbearable: too much tied him to the revolutionary past. In 1935 he returned to the Soviet Union but the only professional corner available turned out to be the theater. To the end of his days Altman spent most of his time staging plays in various Leningrad theaters. In his last works the images of his childhood seemed to return—the Chagall-like fantastic everyday life of the Jewish *shtetl*—from which he had escaped when young but the memories of which could not be destroyed by all the troubles of his stormy life as a commissar.

Only recently there emerged, out of complete obscurity, the name of a Leningrad graphic artist, Anatoly Lvovich Kaplan (1902-1980), although he began intensive work in the 1930s. Kaplan's drawings are almost exclusively on Jewish themes. He made many illustrations for Sholem Aleichem; no one has re-created better the warmth, humor and humanity of the writer's characters, engraved sometimes in his lithographs with the authenticity of an old daguerreotype.

In those years the name of Aleksandr Grigorevich Tyshler (1898-1980)—one of the most brilliant and talented Jewish artists of our time—was almost completely forgotten.[43] The main field of his official activities, as in Altman's case in the last years, was stage design, but at the same time, throughout his life, he painted, drew and sculpted. Tyshler created a specific national artistic style which, while distinct from Chagall's, transformed the exotic characters of Jewish life into fantastic harmonious forms; his images, whether Shakespearean characters or portraits of contemporaries, bear the seal of an almost biblical spirituality and seriousness. However, Tyshler's works began to be exhibited only at the end of the 1950s.

Almost equally unnoticed in these years were the works of many talented Soviet masters—the theater artist Isaak Moiseevich Rabinovich (1894-1961), the outstanding book illustrators Solomon Benediktovich Telingater (1903-69) and Solomon Borisovich Yudovin (1892-1954), the sculptress Sarra Dmitrevna Lebedeva (1892-1967), and others.

More tragic was the fate of Aleksandr (Rudolf) Davidovich Drevin (1889-1938?), who in the 1920s emerged as one of the founders of the Soviet avant-garde, but in the late 1930s disappeared in Stalin's camps.

None of these artists, the list of whom could be extended, escaped accusations of Formalism in their time, although by no means all of them continued with the former avant-garde ideas. The persecution, or at best, the silence they suffered, had other reasons. An example of this is the fate of the great Soviet painter Robert Rafailovich Falk, who was mentioned early in this article.

Falk was what is called a 'pure painter'. He did not, like Lisitsky or Chagall, set new trends. He had no inclination, as many of his brothers in the avant-garde had, to underpin his art by lengthy theoretical treatises or widely publicized manifestos. Nevertheless, his personality and his works are memorable in Russian art of the twentieth century.

In 1918 Falk became a Professor of Painting at VKhUTEMAS and later the Dean of its Department of Painting. He taught his students to transform nature in a new way by means of art, but found himself between two fires: the ultra-revolutionary Futurists accused him of bourgeois traditionalism, while the future Socialist Realists accused him of bourgeois Formalism. For a painter who wished simply to work in art without the flag of any ideology, it was becoming increasingly difficult to exist in Soviet Russia.

In 1928 Falk managed to visit Paris, and it is understandable that his visit there lasted a long time—ten years. One would think that having arrived at the center of contemporary art, at the very focus of all its Leftist currents and free to follow any of them, the painter could not but submit to their influence and make new experiments. But Falk's reactions were the opposite. In Paris his Realist manner came to fruition, and he continued to perfect it even after his return to the USSR in 1938. Falk's evolution is in some ways similar to that of Pasternak who, from his youthful enthusiasm for the formal aspect of words, moved to the deep spirituality of his late poems. A small bunch of flowers in a window, the corner of a room, a few objects on a table—the still lives of Falk express a whole world of emotions, thoughts and associations.

It would seem that in his late works Falk attained the highest level of Realism. However, those on whom the fate of Soviet art depended saw things differently. The official history of Soviet art says of Falk simply that:

'Of all the representatives of this trend, the least [from the point of view of Realism] was achieved by Falk'.[44] Under the 'representatives of this trend' are meant his former comrades in the 'Knave of Diamonds': Konchalovsky, Mashkov and Lentulov. Of them only Konchalovsky fitted in with the official masters, since he used his outstanding talent to paint still lives of luxuriant lilacs and rich food good enough to adorn the walls of the most fashionable restaurants. The name of Falk—the most talented of the four—became a synonym for the still undestroyed bourgeois Formalism.

What was the reason for this hostility towards one of the greatest Soviet Realists? The following story was current: once, sometime in 1905, in the dining hall of the Moscow School of Painting, Sculpture and Architecture, a student was speaking loudly on an antisemitic theme. Another student slapped him on the face. The first student was Aleksandr Gerasimov, future President of the USSR Academy of Arts, the second was Falk. The legend rings true. And indeed, in time, the voice of antisemitism did become increasingly discernible amongst the persecutors of art. However, that is only partly an answer to the question. Another wholly factual story, from more recent times, throws more direct light on the problem.

It is the year 1962, the culmination of the so-called Khrushchev liberalism. In the Manezh building an exhibition of Moscow painters was opened—the most Left exhibition in the past quarter of a century. The new President of the Academy of Arts, Vladimir Serov, guided Khrushchev round the halls. His aim was to show the Party leader how Soviet art had declined in the conditions of liberalization. The first painting shown to Khrushchev by Serov was the beautiful 'Nude' by Falk, painted in 1922—still in the tradition of the 'Knave of Diamonds'. Khrushchev's reaction was understandable: he could see nothing but pornography and outrage against Soviet womanhood, and the subsequent newspaper campaign against Formalism directed its principal attacks on the name of Falk.

It is not difficult to understand why the current President of the Academy needed to show an old painting of the deceased painter as an example of the most recent Formalism. The point is that during the three decades of absolute domination by Socialist Realism a pervasive cultural vacuum was formed. Suffice it to say that in all those years there was neither a single exhibition nor a single book on modern art. In 1947 the Museum of Modern Western Art in Moscow had been abolished and its building taken over by the newly formed USSR Academy of Arts. In 1949 the State Museum of Fine Art was closed, at the height of the struggle against Cosmopolitanism. The State Museum housed the only collection of classical Western paintings in Moscow. Its premises were used for a permanent exhibition of gifts to Comrade Stalin. The items shown at the Tretyakov Gallery in Moscow and the Museum of Russian Art in Leningrad, ended with the 'Wanderers', and even Levitan began to arouse suspicions of an alleged tendency towards Impressionism. All this inevitably led to a sharp decline in artistic taste, creative potential and the level of professionalism, a decline considerably aggravated by the notorious dogma of Socialist Realism that the artist must be understood by the masses, who usually understand nothing about art. The output of Socialist Realism degenerated to the level of badly painted photographs; its producers understood that their wares looked like crude imitations alongside genuine art. To prove their worth, it was necessary to avoid comparison. Thus the struggle against Formalism turned logically into a struggle against all movements in art as such, whether Abstractionism or Realism. The victims of this struggle turned out to be the most gifted artists, including those we have noted here.

Soviet unofficial art

The cultural vacuum reached its culmination in the last years of Stalin. Then came the reaction, which gave birth to the phenomenon known at present in the USSR as 'unofficial' or 'underground' art.

It is scarcely possible to speak of the existence of an 'unofficial' or 'underground' art in Stalin's time. The 'supply' did exist: work went on in those years by artists of the former generation who had not accepted the new creed. However, the breach between this ideology and twentieth century world culture was so great, the level of cultural consciousness in the country had fallen so much, that not only the paintings of Lisitsky or Shterenberg, but also those of Vrubel or Renoir came to be, in the eyes of the overwhelming majority of the public, indistinguishable from the dabs on a canvas made by the tail of a donkey—the same donkey's tail that was used to describe the person responsible for any art which departed from the customary criteria of Socialist Realism. The Soviet fine arts, having finished by the middle of the 1940s with all the remaining 'Formalism', advanced as united and closed ranks of unswerving champions who put up a fight for the same piece of the 'state cake'. All other kinds of art—almost totally lacking an audience—did not and could not find any place in public life. This happened later—during the so-called Khrushchev liberalism, when there was some lifting of the iron curtain which had firmly divided the country from the rest of the world—in space (from contemporary culture) and in time (from all the cultural past)—and the cultural vacuum began powerfully to suck in the atmosphere from the other side of the curtain.

The first and strongest stimulus in this process was an immense exhibition mounted in Moscow during the 6th World Youth Festival in 1957, at which over 4,500 works by young painters from 52 countries were shown. Here Soviet painters, as well as the public, saw for the first time in twenty-five years the living art of the twentieth century and breathed the fresh atmosphere of free experimentation and innovation. They not only saw: some even had the opportunity to work side by side with their Western colleagues for several days in studios provided for the purpose. There followed other exhibitions in the late 1950s and early 1960s: Picasso, Léger, Modern English painting, French, American and others.

The former 'Stalin's eagles' in art, fearing (not without foundation) retribution for sins of their dark past, remained in the shadows for a time. Their places on editorial staffs, in publishing houses, exhibition committees and other art organizations were occupied by younger and more liberally-minded people. The best fruits of this general process appeared in literature (the journal *Novy mir* under Tvardovsky, the emergence of Solzhenitsyn and other anti-Stalinist writers). In art this process was not so intensive, but some articles on contemporary art appeared from time to time; although semi-critical they gave a certain amount of objective information and attempts were made to 'rehabilitate' some of the Soviet avant-garde and painters of the past whose work was considered 'reactionary' (El Greco, for example). The culmination of this process was in 1962, when at the Moscow exhibition noted above, which celebrated the 30th anniversary of the Moscow Union of Artists, the general public were for the first time introduced to the works of some avant-garde masters (Falk, Drevin, Tyshler and others) and also some young painters who by then had moved away from the strict canons of Socialist Realism. But this was also the end of liberalization. As mentioned above, the leadership of the USSR Academy of Arts used the occasion to prove to Khrushchev the ideological danger of departing from the old principles. Persecution of the new Leftist art began, together with a systematic advance of reaction, which continued and has intensified up to the present. It is sufficient to say that from 1968 the Presidency of the USSR Academy of Arts has been occupied by N. Tomsky—the former court portrait painter of Stalin, who filled the country at that time with sculptures of Stalin. With him other champions of Socialist Realism, who had eradicated everything that differed from it, returned to their posts. However, the relaxation in the late 1950s and early 1960s had most serious after-effects: it introduced a split in the hitherto orderly ranks of Soviet art.

As to the participation of Jews in this opposition movement, here we can repeat, in slightly different form, the paragraph at the beginning of this article which describes the situation in Russia at the end of last century: the part they have played has grown sharply from the moment the split in Soviet art appeared, when the best painters came out against the routine of academic education and the rules of official Socialist Realism, and began to struggle for the right to free exploration of new forms and free expression of aesthetic ideas. Their oppositional activity is determined, as it was almost a hundred years ago, by two main factors: the deprived position of Jews amongst other peoples of Soviet Russia who also suffer substantial deprivation, and their refusal to accept this situation.

The first to be drawn into this process were those who most keenly felt the cultural vacuum, those who were the primary targets of the values (anti-values) of Socialist Realist culture (anti-culture). (Socialist Realism can be called 'anti-culture' in every sense, for it has long existed not by creating new values but—to put it mildly—by criticizing all existing values.) It is not difficult to guess who these people were, two or three years after the nation-wide 'anti-cosmopolitan campaign' conducted by Stalin and the entire apparatus of the CPSU and KGB, a campaign celebrated in the verse and prose, and by the brush and chisel of the Socialist Realists. In the unhappy years following the anti-cosmopolitan campaign (and, to a considerable extent, at the present time too), in order to preserve one's position in the field of culture a Jewish artist, art critic or art historian not only had to express acceptance of the ideology—which is what, say, a Russian had to do—but also to prove his loyalty in practice, his devotion to the official ideas; he had to distance himself from those who wavered and to denounce the enemy; he had to prove this on 'the forward line of the ideological front', as did, for example, Boris Efimov in his antisemitic caricatures, Evgeny Katsman in his political demagogy, the literary critic Aleksandr Dymshits in his pogrom-type attacks, and many others. It is natural that in the new situation where artists could choose to reject the official art ideology (in the sense that now deviation was not followed by immediate arrest) many artists of the new generation rejected the official alternative. This lies behind the extremely high proportion of Jewish artists in the unofficial art movement.[45]

From the very beginning of the post-Stalin epoch of re-appraisal of values in Soviet art, two tendencies became clear. On the one hand, many understood that to take up the reconstruction of society, to preach political ideas in an artistic form or to demonstrate socialist achievements, was by no means the most important thing for a painter or sculptor. Rejecting in this way the most basic imperatives of the so-called Marxist-Leninist aesthetics, they automatically excluded themselves from official artistic life and formed what is called at present unofficial or underground art.

Other painters obeyed the basic imperative to a certain degree. As a rule, they were those who had begun to study directly after the war, often before they had time to remove their uniforms. Their creative work began in the manner of Soviet art, but they tried to contrast the trivial realism of the Gerasimovs and Tomskys with truly revolutionary art, the ideal of which they saw in the Soviet avant-garde of the 1920s. They spoke openly against the official ideology, contrasting it with their own wider conception of Socialist and Realist art. They formed a fairly strong Leftist wing within the Union of Artists, which remained influential up to 1962.

Perhaps the most active and consistent champion of the new ideas from the very beginning was Ernst Neizvestny. In his book on Neizvestny the English critic John Berger cites Neizvestny's words about himself: 'My war started in my early childhood; it is not finished yet.' It may be that in this self-appraisal the artist provides the key to his personality and works. In 1942, when he was sixteen years old, Ernst Neizvestny joined the army as a volunteer. He commanded a platoon in a landing party and was seriously wounded. As a student he chose monumental sculpture as his profession—one of the most massive, active and social types of art. In the post-Stalin years he entered the struggle against the old methods of guiding artistic life, against the deathly atmosphere of fear and conformist adaptability which destroyed everything alive in Soviet art. At the time of the ill-starred visit by Khrushchev to the Manezh exhibition, sculptures by Neizvestny were shown to him together with Falk's pictures as examples of the degradation of Soviet ideology. The infuriated Khrushchev abused the sculptor to his face, almost accusing him of criminal actions, and only tremendous self-control and personal courage allowed Neizvestny to defend his principles and right to creativity.

The passion of struggle is carried over by this sculptor into his art. His style is nearest to Expressionism. His images are always, as it were, on the brink of life and death, destruction or survival, victory or defeat.

Apart from him, since the late 1950s several painters exhibiting under the name 'The Group of 8' have stood out as the strongest opposition group: N. Andronov, P. and M. Nikonov, M. Ivanov, K. Mordovin, N. Egorshina, B. Birger, and V. Veysberg. Their last joint exhibition was in May 1966. After it some of them were compelled to compromise in order to retain their position in Soviet art. The others continued to experiment and, in effect, left the sphere of official activities. Amongst the latter were the most gifted painters, in the first place Birger and Veysberg. They both began work within the mainstream of Soviet art but became more interested in problems of painting than ideology. They broadened their traditionalism, seeing themselves as successors not only of the 'Wanderers' and the founders of Socialist Realism, but also of the Soviet avant-garde of the 1920s and the Western masters of the late nineteenth and early twentieth centuries.

Boris Birger (born 1923) spent the whole war at the front, then graduated from the Surikov Moscow Art Institute and began to exhibit in 1953. His earlier paintings were in the spirit of the 'Knave of Diamonds' and other 'Leftist' currents; he experimented with color and form, introducing fresh currents of exploration and experiment into the post-Stalin stuffiness. He soon won renown and the Soviet press began to describe him as 'one of the leading young artists'. Only at a mature age, some time in the 1960s, did Birger find his own artistic path. Formal exploration changed to an aspiration to affirm his own vision of the world and to work out a technique of painting capable of embodying this vision. He turned to the Rembrandt tradition of light and shade, having developed a complex technique of multicolored strokes by which each millimeter of the canvas seems to consist of several color pigments. The most delicate play of colors within the limits of golden-brown or light-blue-olive tonalities create in his pictures an inspired, picturesque milieu, in which people live and 'breathe' and interact, as do objects of his still life pictures. (He works mainly in these two genres.) Thus Birger has developed from conventionality to realism (in this he is like Falk), and it is now difficult to name a painter in the Soviet Union who is a finer portraitist and who depicts more expressively the inner life of things. However, as soon as Birger reached a level far above the Soviet aesthetic standard he was accused of formalism and his pictures were no longer shown.

Vladimir Veysberg (born 1924) has limited himself to a sphere of purely painting problems. In his early portraits and still life pictures the influence of various masters—Cézanne, Modigliani, Seurat and Falk—is recognizable. For many years Veysberg was seriously interested in theories of perception of color and shape and evolved his own technique. His later works are simple shapes on a simple background—often white dishes on a white cloth, in which the painting uses objects only to affirm its own worth. Very few such perfectionists can be found, but he is not shown at Soviet exhibitions.

The fate of Vadim Sidura (born 1924) is similar. He is one of the most gifted sculptors in the Soviet Union. His search for plastic expressiveness led to generalized, almost non-figurative shapes, which has naturally closed for him the doors of official exhibition halls and state purchasing commissions.

It is these and similar artists who constitute Soviet non-official art. However, its nucleus derives from outside the Union of Artists: it arose as a reaction to the cultural vacuum in the country by artists who were only beginning their creative work in the mid-1950s.

During the short period of liberalization under Khrushchev, many young artists realized that to reach existing standards meant going beyond the boundaries of art. They avidly visited foreign exhibitions and devoured books, journals and reproductions. Contemporary Western painting, the art of the Soviet avant-garde of the 1920s, old Russian painting, foreign classical art—all that for many years had been carefully hidden from them turned out to be utterly unlike what they had been taught. They preferred the freedom of creation to the relative well-being of an official artist. They worked as loaders, orderlies, watchmen; in their tiny rooms they painted what their hearts and talents prompted, what the great old and new examples taught them. They formed small groups or circles and set no practical aims other than friendly contact and exchange of information.

One of these 'circles' formed in Moscow in the mid-1950s around the art critic Ilya Yogannovich Tsirlin. He had entered the artistic life of the capital directly after his war service and occupied a fairly important position (he was Chairman of the Criticism Section of the Moscow Society of Soviet Artists (MOSKh), head of a department in the largest art publishing house 'Iskusstvo', head of the Department of fine Arts in the Institute of Cinematography and author of many books and articles). The artists who visited his flat could not be called an organization or a group. Tsirlin simply spoke to them of modern art, showed twentieth century reproductions and assisted materially those in need. About 1960 he was 'exposed' as a 'secret Abstractionist' and therefore an enemy of Realism, removed from all his posts and hounded to his death: he died a year later of heart failure. But even this brief and completely innocent activity was, in those years, sufficient to assist and encourage several young artists who are now influential in non-official art.

Another group of artists and poets was formed at the time in the workmen's settlement of Lianozovo, not far from Moscow. The leader of the group was the painter Oskar Rabin (born 1928).

Painters in the Soviet Union have become involved in non-official art in various ways. Some of them negated their own experience of life and it was natural that sooner or later their experience should come into conflict with the false ideology of heartiness that was thrust upon them. They began to see the world with their own eyes, to search for a special language to express their vision and naturally dropped out of the sphere of official art. Such, for example was the path of Oskar Rabin. Real life for Rabin was the barracks in his native Lianozovo, an overcrowded working-class suburb of Moscow—slums round a railway station, where Rabin worked as a loader after his expulsion from the art institute for 'Leftism'. He began to paint what he saw: rickety houses, crooked, muddy little streets with tins, bottles and cats. This ramshackle, unobtrusive world of simple objects, a world which never aspires to anything great, is warmed in his pictures by the human presence: smoke rising from the chimneys and glimmering yellow lights in the little windows show to the world outside something of the cosy life within. Rabin uses exaggeration, the grotesque, to increase this feeling of organic unevenness, cosy asymmetry, the usual decay in human surroundings. But at the same time, he has a wonderful feeling for the material substance of things: his herring or bottle suddenly reveals a wealth of color and shape with all the brilliance of the old masters. Sometimes Rabin is called a social painter. However, his social character is very indirect. He simply prefers the Moscow of twisted little alleys—created for people—to the side avenues built for cars and parades. He prefers signboards to slogans, brick belfries to concrete tower blocks. In his views of London or Paris (painted from his imagination or from reproductions), the stained-glass windows of Notre Dame glimmer like the little windows of Moscow barracks and Big Ben leans like the top of an old Russian church.

The turning point for many other painters was their confrontation with the new Western currents and with their Russian predecessors. They did not imitate others. The confrontation had deeper consequences: they discovered their own creative potential, which had been stifled by the limitations of their Socialist Realist education and training.

At the beginning of the 1960s, there formed round the young painter Lev Nusberg an entire group which deal with the problem of creating a synthetic art combining color, light, shape, sound, movement and so on. They covered the search by the term 'scientific shape-formation' and design—with which the leaders of Soviet industry were then very concerned in order to raise the lamentable quality of products. This provided the group with an opportunity for a short semi-official existence and even to hold several exhibitions of a semi-closed type. But, in fact, they developed the ideas, by then forgotten, of A. Pevsner, N. Gabo and other avant-gardists. Naturally, their activities were soon brought to an end.

Ilya Kabakov and Vladimir Yankilevsky are close to the tendencies of contemporary Western pop art, although the irony and often the rousing brutality of their compositions put them in line with the Russian art derived from the Primitivism of Larionov. Vladimir Yakovlev expresses in his abstract and imitative compositions a lyrical attitude to the world. Eduard Shteynberg devotes himself to problems of painting.

Amongst this group there are not many painters of Jewish themes. Such themes appear in the graphic drawings of Yu. Kuperman; L. Shteynmets used biblical themes; the self-taught painter N. Fayngold uses Hebrew characters to create abstract compositions; Brusilovsky introduced them as a decorative element in his graphic fantasies; and there are various others.

I give here the names of painters known to me, mostly from Moscow, who seem the most interesting. This list could, of course, be considerably extended if we were to include names of painters working in various towns of the Soviet Union. Their work is very varied on account of their different cultural origins and individual styles. But they are all united by a common urge to follow art in their own ways, independent of the official artistic ideology coming from above.

Soviet unofficial (or underground) art, in the form it has taken in the past two decades, is a unique phenomenon, probably without parallel in the history of twentieth century art. Its uniqueness is by no means due to its being underground or unofficial. Our long-suffering century has known various forms of similar art, for wherever creative freedom is suppressed by a totalitarian regime a natural reaction against the suppressor sets in, embodied in art. Thus, in the 1930s and 1940s unofficial art appeared in Mussolini's Italy; it existed also in the territories occupied by the Nazis. It is sufficient to recall the names of the Germans Käthe Kollwitz, Hans and Lea Grundig, of the early French and Italian neo-Realists, Guttuso, Mucchi, Fougeron, Taslitzky and many others. They combined their art with political struggle thus expressing, in Aesopian language, their protest against totalitarianism and oppression.

But the initiators of Soviet underground art were painters far removed from political struggle and their work had no direct or indirect political allusions. If they carried on a struggle, it was a struggle for the right to be a painter working in the wide stream of the world's cultural tradition. In recent years, it has become more difficult to defend this right, perhaps especially so for Jewish painters.

This is, in my view, the main reason for the ever increasing emigration of painters from the USSR. They include the masters of book illustration L. Zbarsky and Yu. Krasny, who reformed the style and format of Soviet books in the 1960s; L. Shteynmets, who was scarcely ever exhibited in the USSR, and immediately on arrival in the West was awarded second prize at a European biennial exhibition; Yu. Kuperman, Yu. Grobman, and others. One would like to see their departure from the USSR not only as a loss. In the West, they have an opportunity to develop their talents and to become a source of creativity for the future painters of Russia, in the same way as the art of Chagall, Pevsner, Gabo and many others emigré painters, both Jews and non-Jews, was a source of creativity for them.

In the few years since this paper was concluded, there has occurred in Soviet art an essential move towards widening the rigid framework of classical Socialist Realism; at the same time, its ideology has turned slowly to Stalin's times. Among the official artistic upper stratum one hears more open talk about the necessity of reflecting not only the heroism of Soviet people but also the historical greatness of the Russian State in works of art, as well as about the continuation of the great national tradition, Russian patriotism and other subjects belonging to the thematic range well known from the not so distant past. All this does not, of course, improve the situation of the Jewish artist in the USSR. This is apparently why Jewish youth remains an important reserve from which Soviet unofficial art replenishes its strength.

During these years a young generation of artists has matured, developed new creative trends and began squeezing out the 'old men'. Correspondingly, official pressure on the artistic opposition has grown stronger, and this in turn has stimulated emigration from the USSR. Emigration began in the late 1960s and culminated in the mid-1970s, in particular, after the exhibition organized by Moscow artists on the outskirts of the capital was crushed by bulldozers and watering machines. But it came up against unsurmountable barriers erected by the authorities in the late 1970s and early 1980s. During the time, no less than 300 artists left the USSR, including Ernst Neizvestny, Oskar Rabin, Lev Nusberg and Natan Fayngold, who were discussed in our paper.

Notes

1 A. Efros, *Dva veka russkogo iskusstva* (Two Centuries of Russian Art) (Moscow 1969), 252.

2 Marc Chagall, *My Life* (London 1965), 10.

3 Ibid., 16.

4 *Le Surréalisme et la peinture* (New York 1945).

5 *Manifesty i programmy russkikh futuristov* (Manifestos and Programs of the Russian Futurists) (Munich 1967), 50.

6 The symposium *Sovetskoe iskusstvo za 15 let* (Soviet Art for Fifteen Years) (Moscow 1933), 125-6. This document seems to me the most indicative for the part played by Jews in the art of those years. First, the selection of pictures for purchase was done by a competent commission of INKhUK directed by V.V. Kandinsky and, secondly, the criterion was first and foremost quality—which was then often not the case in selecting works for exhibition, which were usually organized without a jury or the help of genuine professionals.

7 See *Agitatsionno-massovoe iskusstvo pervykh let Oktyabrya. Materialy i issledovaniya* (Agitational Mass Art in the First Days of October: Materials and Research) (Moscow 1971).

8 *Novy mir*, no. 9, 1966.

9 *Istoriya russkogo iskusstva* (History of Russian Art) (Moscow 1957), vol. 2, 11.

10 Here is a far from complete list of the masters who left Russia in the first decade of the Soviet regime: 1919: I. Puni; 1920: N. Rerikh, I. Bilibin, D Burlyuk;. 1921: V. Kandinsky, L. Pasternak; 1922: V. Falileyev, F. Malyavin, M. Chagall, A. Pevsner, N. Gabo; 1923: N. Feshin, K. Korovin, A. Ekster; 1924: Yu. Annenkov, Z. Serebryakova, K. Somov, S. Konenkov; 1925: V. Baranov-Rossin; 1926: A. Benua; 1928: S. Chekhonin, R. Falk, N. Altman. From the mid-1920s it became extremely difficult to leave Russia, and subsequently impossible.

11 D. Burlyuk: 'From now on I refuse to speak badly even of the work of fools'—1915. See *Manifesty . . .* , 155.
12 Ibid., 159-160.
13 *Iskusstvo kommuny* (Art of the Commune), no. 8, 26 January 1919.
14 K. Malevich, *Suprematizm* (Suprematism) (1920), 3.
15 O.M. Brik, 'Ot kartiny k sittsu' (From picture to calico), *LEF*, no. 2(6), 1924, 27.
16 L.M. Lisitsky, 'Blokada Rossii konchaetsya' (The blockade of Russia is ending), *Veshch*, (Berlin), nos. 1-2, 1922.
17 D. Shterenberg, 'Pora ponyat' (Time to understand), in the symposium *Iskusstvo i proizvodstvo* (Art and Production) (Moscow 1921).
18 O.M. Brik, 'V poryadke dnya' (The order of the day), ibid.
19 D. Arkin, 'Izobrazitelnoe iskusstvo i materialnaya kultura' (Depictive art and material culture), ibid.
20 *Sovetskoe iskusstvo za 15 let*, 143.
21 *Novy mir*, no. 9, 1966, 337-8.
22 B. Arvatov, *Natan Altman* (1924), 12-13.
23 Sophie Lissitzky-Küpper, *El. Lissitzky, Life, Letters, Texts* (London 1968), 327.
24 Ibid., 332.
25 *Pro dva kvadrata: kniga dlya detey* (About Two Squares: a Book for Children) (Berlin 1922).
26 *Severnaya kommuna* (The Northern Commune), no. 147, 3 November 1918.
27 Chagall, 133.
28 Ibid., 135.
29 Ibid., 109.
30 *Sovetskoe iskusstvo za 15 let*, 310-312.
31 *Istoriya russkogo iskusstva*, 12.
32 N. Altman, 'Futurizm i proletarskoe iskusstvo' (Futurism and proletarian art), *Iskusstvo kommuny*, no. 12, 15 December 1918.
33 *Sovetskoe iskusstvo za 15 let*, 345.
34 Ibid., 377-8.
35 Ibid., 350.
36 *Revolyutsiya i iskusstvo* (Revolution and Art), no. 6, 1928.
37 *Izvestiya Ts. K. VKP(b)*, no. 4(263), 15 February 1929.
38 *Sovetskoe iskusstvo za 15 let*, 427-8.
39 V.V. Vantslav, 'O sotsialisticheskom realizme' (On Socialist Realism), in *Sovetskoe izobrazitelnoe iskusstvo i zadachi borby s burzhuaznoy ideologiey* (Soviet Figurative Art and Tasks of the Struggle against Bourgeois Ideology) (Moscow 1969), 31.
40 *Istoriya russkogo iskusstva*, vol. 2, 181.
41 In the first rank of Soviet art at that time stood B. Yoganson, V. Efanov, D. Nalbandyan, V. Serov, A. Loktionov, A. Plastov, the sculptors N. Tomsky, E. Vuchetich, M. Manizer, S. Merkulov, and others.
42 *Kratkaya khudozhestvennaya entsiklopediya. Iskusstvo stran i narodov mira* (Short Encyclopedia of Art. Art of the Countries and Peoples of the World) (Moscow 1971), vol. 3, 636-757.
43 See I. Golomostock, 'Aleksandr Tyshler, 1898-1980', *Soviet Jewish Affairs*, vol. 11, no. 3, 1981, 15-23.
44 *Istoriya russkogo iskusstva*, vol. 2, 138.
45 Thus, for example, Yuri Kuperman writes in his article ' "No Places!": the Jewish

outsider in the Soviet Union' (*Soviet Jewish Affairs*, vol. 3, no. 2, 1973, no. 2, 19): '99 percent of the best artists in Moscow are Jewish.' This number is, of course, exaggerated. It is enough to name such unofficial non-Jewish artists as B. Sveshnikov, D. Plavinsky and A. Zverev, who are amongst the 'top ten', to realize the exaggerated nature of this percentage. It is not now possible to calculate the number of Jews in this movement: there is no published information and it is difficult to state qualitative criteria for selection. I think, however, that a figure of 50 percent would be too low rather than too high.

3

Jews in Soviet Music

Joachim Braun

The topic we are concerned with is a complex one, as are most problems in the history of Jewish spiritual life in the Diaspora. It involves numerous issues outside the realm of music and overlaps many adjacent fields. As well as the general, well-known difficulties faced by students of Jews in the Soviet Union, especially with regard to the arts, the researcher of the Jewish idiom in Soviet music is confronted with certain other problems arising from the specific nature of music, for example, the still obscure question of national, in particular Jewish, expression in European musical performance; the significance of the use of Jewish musical intonations in the works of non-Jewish composers; the diffusion of different national musical styles, etc. At the same time certain trends in the history of Soviet Jewry are seen more vividly and are more clearly expressed in music precisely because of that specific nature. The abstract nature of music made it possible for an aspiration towards Jewish self-expression to appear first in the field of music, even while Jewish culture was being suppressed—I refer to the Jewish folksong concerts given by N. Lifshits and other singers in the early 1950s when Jewish spiritual life had been silenced by the Soviet authorities.

Until now scholars have been concerned with two topics: Jews in the Soviet Union, with hardly any reference to music; and music in the Soviet Union, with no mention of the Jewish aspect. The few articles in Western books or journals on the subject are usually limited to the 1920s[1] or consider particular problems within the subject.[2] The only article concerned with the subject as a whole is unfortunately of dubious value, abounding in errors.[3] Soviet literature on music simply avoids the existence of Jewish musical values in Soviet music, for example the five-volume 'History of the Music of the Peoples of the USSR'[4] which gives information on Chuvash,

Yakut, Mari, Udmurt, Kabardin and Ossetian music, that is the music of peoples who number less than 500,000, but which makes no mention of the musical life of nearly three million Soviet Jews. Only one piece of research on Jewish music has been published during the fifty-seven years of Soviet rule.[5] The following table illustrates the point:

TABLE 1: MUSIC AND BOOKS ON MUSIC WITH A JEWISH SUBJECT PUBLISHED IN THE USSR, 1917-72[6]

	1917-22	1923-27	1928-32	1933-37	1938-42	1943-47	1948-52	1953-57	1958-62	1963-67	1967-72
Music	8	9	17	16	8	2	0	2	3	0	8
Books	0	1	1	3	0	0	0	0	0	0	

This table is even more eloquent if we bear in mind that, according to the third edition of the 'Great Soviet Encyclopaedia', vol. 10, pp. 60-62, in the entry 'Publishing' on p.662, the number of publications in the USSR just in the period 1940-71 increased by an average of some 400 percent, while the increase from 1917 can be estimated at about 600 percent.

It is possible to find reviews of Jewish folk song collections or other publications in Soviet periodicals, as well as some short articles on Jewish folk music. But in these cases the main purpose is always to prove that the 'idea of a distinct Jewish people is scientifically untenable, from a political point of view, reactionary'.[7] Reference books are the only sources for Jewish music in the Soviet Union. The 'Great Soviet Encyclopaedia', whose different editions were written according to the official policies prevailing at the time, shows an interesting development in treatment of our subject. The first edition of 1932 devotes three of the eighty-two pages of a general article on Jewish matters to Jewish music.[8] The one-page entry on Jews in the 1952 edition makes no reference to music. Information on music is also lacking in the 1972 edition, although a special entry is devoted to Jewish literature. The entry on Jewish music in the first edition of the only music reference book, the 'Encyclopaedic Dictionary of Music' (1959) merely gives a bibliography (M. Beregovsky, D. Magid, A. Idelson), without any text. The 1966 edition has three entries on Jewish music—'Ancient Hebrew Music', 'Jewish Music' and 'Israeli Music'—while other national musical styles come under one entry. This is evidently to demonstrate the thesis of the main Soviet reference book that 'Jews have no common culture'.[9] It is not without interest that the entry 'Jewish Music' in the Soviet encyclopaedia of music gives a reference to E. Müller von Azov's article, 'Das

Judentum in der Musik', published in the classic antisemitic book by Th. Fritsch, *Handbuch der Judenfrage* (Leipzig 1932).[10]

We can already see from these few examples that the history of Soviet Jewish music is the history of the contradiction between the suppression of Jewish musical life and the officially proclaimed right of every people in the Soviet Union to national development. On the one hand the existence of a common Jewish culture is denied and the very idea of a Jewish people is claimed to be reactionary, while on the other hand that culture exists, and a people sings and plays and has the right to express itself just like every other people.

What then are the general lines of development in the history of Soviet Jewish music and who are the central figures in this development?

The decades preceding the 1917 Revolution created a most favorable situation for the development of Jewish music. The establishment of national musical styles in Eastern Europe in the second half of the nineteenth century and the influential school of Russian national music, the emancipation of Jewish artists in Europe, activity in the field of folklore collecting and early examples of Jewish secular music—all this led logically to the idea of a Jewish national style of music. The idea of Jewish cultural revival crystallized especially in pre-Revolutionary Russia where famous figures such as N. Rimsky-Korsakov and V. Stasov were active and where there was a strong Jewish community. Jewish folk music first drew a large audience in the performance given by Y. Engel in November 1900 in the Moscow Polytechnic Museum. Rimsky-Korsakov expressed the general atmosphere when listening to 'A Romance on a Jewish Tune' by his student E. Shklyar: 'Why should you Jewish students imitate European and Russian composers? The Jews possess tremendous folk treasuries . . . Jewish music awaits its Glinka.'[11]

A group of Jewish musicians, many of whom were students of Rimsky-Korsakov, applied for permission to set up a Jewish Music Society. The Tsarist Government, represented by General Drachevsky, refused permission, but on 30 November 1908 did allow the Petersburg Society for Jewish Folk Music to be established.[12] It is interesting that the Tsarist Russian authorities were more or less willing to accept Jewish folk music activities but not art music, just as is the case in Soviet Russia.

We can see how promising the situation was from the activities of this Society. It had about 389 active members throughout Russia, held some 150 concerts and lectures a year and published a large amount of music (eighty-five items between 1909 and 1917;[13] seventy-three items between 1917 and 1972), and was active in collecting folk music. Some of its most famous and talented composers at that time were I. Akhron, S. Feynberg,

M. Gnesin, A. Krein, M. Milner, S. Rozovsky, L. Saminsky, E. Shklyar; Y. Engel was one of its writers on music, and concerts were given by I. Press, E. Tsimbalist, Y. Heifetz, F. Shalyapin, N. Milstein and others. We may add that famous schools of performance headed by Jewish musicians developed in pre-Revolutionary Russia, such as the L. Auer school of violin at the Petersburg Conservatory, the P. Stolyarsky school of violin in Odessa, and the K. Davidov school of cello in Petersburg. All these activities brought about a situation which in the history of music is always characteristic of a speedy development of a 'classical' period in the particular national style. The famous non-Jewish musicologist of the period, L. Sabanejev, expressed this very well in the conclusions drawn from his research on the school of Jewish national music:

> All preconditions for a further development of this spirit exist: musical talent, a number of Jewish musicians, the artistic temperament of the nation, suitability to musical activity, an interest in national art, the example of past musicians of genius—all this justifies the assumption that the Jewish people will enrich world music literature with a stream of fresh and original works . . . At the present moment, when an intellectual stratum is emerging from the masses, it [the Jewish people] can and must attain world significance. The historical perspective has not yet been revealed. But we can justifiably assume that the blossoming of the Jewish people's culture has announced itself.[14]

This natural development was violently disrupted by the October Revolution of 1917. Among the first practical results of the change in situation was the dissolution of the Petersburg Jewish Folk Song Society which was declared to be 'incompatible with the spirit of the time'.[15] The overall situation in musical life changed completely. Lenin's statement at a session of the Petrograd Soviet on 25 October 1917 was certainly equally true of music: 'From today began a new period in the history of Russia . . . we must now devote ourselves to building the proletarian socialist state.'[16] For music this meant, according to Lenin, that although 'every artist takes it as his right to create freely, according to his ideal, whether it is good or not', nevertheless, 'we are Communists. We must not . . . allow the chaos to ferment as it chooses. We must . . . guide this development and mold and determine the results.'[17] The entire development of Soviet music moves from the first thesis to the second, from free creation to strict determination of the results of creation. For the Jews, as already suggested, this meant the contradiction between the complete negation of a Jewish people and the limited acceptance of spiritual life and art, 'national in form and socialist in content', for every people.

The Revolution divided the Russian musical world, including Jewish musicians, into many parts according to attitude to the events. Many welcomed the Revolution with hope for the future. The main figure in the new national Jewish school, M. Gnesin (see below), wrote: 'I waited and yearned for the Revolution, I thirsted for activity, I wanted to see how the artistic life of the people would change'.[18] The famous Jewish pianist, Samuel Feynberg (1890-1962), greeted the Revolution with enthusiasm and spoke proudly of the opportunity to play for Lenin in January 1919 in Sokolniki.[19] It is interesting that the other pianist Lenin heard, Isay Dobroven (1894-1953), was also Jewish (these are the only two recorded instances of Lenin's listening to music after the Revolution). According to Maksim Gorky, Dobroven played the *Appassionata* at E. Peshkova's Moscow home in the presence of Lenin.[20]

Other musicians were more reserved in their reaction. The well-known Jewish ballet conductor, Yuri Fayer (b. 1890), who in those years was a violinist in the orchestra of the Moscow Bolshoy Theater, writes: 'November found us in inertia and obscurity. No performance. To whom the theatre belonged was incomprehensible, and it was not as if the authorities would be interested in opera or ballet. The new revolution was met with even more embarrassment than the one in February.'[21]Many figures in the world of music decided immediately or in the next few years to leave the socialist state forever. Let us mention only the names of the greatest artists both among Jews and in the whole world: the pianists Horovitz and Dobroven, the violinists Auer, Heifetz, Akhron, Tsimbalist, Milstein, the cellist Pyatigorsky, the musicologists Yasser and Slonimsky. Many of the active members of the Jewish Folk Song Society, the composers Saminsky, Rozovsky, Shklyar, the music critic Engel and many others, left Russia and so saved themselves for Jewish music.

The fate of the Jewish composers who stayed in the Soviet Union is extremely significant. Mikhail Gnesin (1883-1957) was one of the most promising figures in the modern Jewish Renaissance and later one of the most respected Soviet composers. Most of his works, and the best of them, are purely Jewish. Gnesin himself wrote: 'Elements of Jewish music captured my musical feelings and imagination to such an extent that even when I did not have the mission to look for a Jewish style, those elements appeared in my works'.[22] In 1966 this composer was described in Soviet reference sources as a 'Russian and Jewish composer'[23] but the new 'Encyclopedia of Music' (Moscow 1973) refers to him simply as a Soviet composer and in the 65-line article only one sentence mentions his place in Jewish music: 'Was a well-known master of Jewish music' (p. 1025).

Until the end of the 1920s Gnesin wrote music deeply rooted in Jewish tradition and over forty-five of his sixty or so works were written before 1930, that is before he was fifty years old. His most significant works were composed in the 1920s: the operas 'The Youth of Abraham' (1921-23) and 'The Maccabees' (1921), symphonic works 'Songs from the Old Country' (1919), 'The Jewish Orchestra at the Ball of the Town Bailiff' (1926), the song cycle 'Red-Headed Motele' (1926-29), the 'Quartet' (1929), 'Ten Jewish Songs' (1927), 'The Song of Songs' (1922), 'Songs of the Knight-Errant' (1927), etc. Although Gnesin had been connected with Jewish music from 1912-14, his work of the 1920s was the result of hope for the revival of Jewish culture in a socialist state. But to understand the direction his mind took, it is also important to remember that he twice visited Palestine, in 1914 and 1922, where he collected folk melodies, some of which he used in his later works (e.g. 'Variations on a Palestinian Melody', 'Galilean Songs'). During his second trip he worked at, and was closely connected with, the Tel-Aviv Conservatory, 'Shulamit', which was an important period both for the composer and for the Conservatory.[24]

In the 1930s the Jewish idiom does not appear so constantly in Gnesin's music, while in the 1940s there is usually no reference to this idiom in the titles of the music ('Elegy', 1940; 'Trio', 1943; 'Sonata-Fantasia', 1945, etc.). In the 1930s he started transcribing Azerbaydzhani, Armenian, Adygey, Mari, Circassian, Chuvash and other folk music. 'The immersion in Jewish folk music helped me to understand folk art in general', he wrote in a letter of 13 March 1945 to the American musicologist Rene B. Fisher.[25] One has to see this document and read between the lines to sense the wound in the composer's heart. The letter is a confession, not a mere reply to a colleague. From 1917 to 1945 there was not a word on Jewish music in his many published writings, including the 'Reminiscences', yet suddenly he answers a letter he had received over a year previously and then lost (?) in the VOKS.[26] 'Of course you no longer need my reply, nevertheless I should like to answer you.'[27] After a few autobiographical sentences, which also indicate the personal nature of the document, there follows an eight-page effusion on Jewish music in general and on the Jewishness of his own creative work.

Gnesin was also one of the most famous teachers of composition in the USSR. Among his pupils are A. Khachaturian, T. Khrennikov, B. Kluzner, G. Mushel, A. Leman, N. Namizamidze, A. Eshpay, Z. Khabibulin and many others. One of his most famous pupils, the Armenian Khachaturian, wrote:

> The strongest features of Gnesin the composer are the strikingly-expressed national character of his works, which are connected mainly with Jewish subjects. Gnesin reflected real Jewish folk intonations and characteristic psychological features with tremendous force and stylistic chastity. The feeling for folk intonations was so organic in Gnesin that he could create poetic songs in the style of folk improvizations such as 'On Her Tender Face', 'Songs

> of the Knight-Errant' and others, without using real melodies . . .M.F. [Gnesin] was one of the first to assert that the national character is one of the basic principles of musical creation . . . It is no accident that composers who subsequently occupied a significant place in the musical life of the national republics came precisely from M.F.'s class.[28]

The Music Institute in Moscow founded by the Gnesins in 1895—Mikhail and his sisters, the piano teachers Elena, Evgeniya and Mariya—was regarded as one of the leading music schools in the country for nearly half a century. (Since 1944 it has been called the Gnesin Music Pedagogical Institute.)

Gnesin's work is deeply Jewish, as the composer himself states and as is evident from his work. He took the advice of his teacher Rimsky-Korsakov ('Why should you Jewish students imitate European and Russian composers?'), and this was one of the reasons for his success. If Soviet musicology today tries to erase this from human memory, it can change nothing.[29] The active and highly successful period of his creativity coincided with the time when he was connected with the Jewish idiom, that is, until the early 1930s. Afterwards his work declined in both quantity and quality.

The fate of the Krein family reveals the same picture of simultaneous decline of Jewishness and creative spirit. Old Abraham Krein (1838-1921), a *klezmer* (Jewish folk musician), violinist and folk-tune collector, had seven sons, five of whom became musicians. His son Aleksandr (1883-1951) was one of the most talented Jewish composers. Like Gnesin he was already mature at the time of the Revolution. From 1918-20 he was Secretary for Modern Music in the Commission for Folklore and from 1922 a member of the editorial board of the State Publishing House. In 1934 he was awarded the title of Honored Artist. Before the Revolution he had written numerous chamber works and songs in which synagogue laments and modern Jewish folk tunes were combined. After 1917 Krein turned to theater music. He wrote more than ten incidental works for the Habimah, the Moscow, Byelorussian and Ukrainian Jewish State Theaters. The Jewish idiom appears in his later work too: he wrote a symphonic cantata 'Kaddish' (1922), 'Ornaments for Voice and Piano' (1924-27), 'Ten Jewish Folk Songs' (1937) and some others. It is significant that his only opera, *Zagbuk*, (1930) is based on a drama by A. Glebov concerning a revolutionary plot in ancient Babylon. This was a veiled expression of his yearning for the Jewish idiom. He wrote: 'As the plot takes place in ancient Babylon, in any case in the East, it demands some oriental coloring in the style of the opera as well as a specially chosen treatment of the orchestra and its colors. The music to *Zagbuk* must be the birth of a new musical orientalism.'[30] A. Lunacharsky also connected A. Krein's work on this libretto with his excellent knowledge of and skill in the field of Jewish music.[31]

But A. Krein had to turn to other subjects as well in order to please the authorities. We therefore find works with most curious titles, for example, a symphonic dithyramb called 'The USSR — The Shock Brigade of the World Proletariat' (1932). He also wrote a 'Funeral Ode for Lenin' (1926), a 'Tone Poem for Orchestra "Birobidzhan" ' (1935) and 'Songs of the Stalinist Falcon' for violin and piano. In the 1930s and 1940s he wrote a number of works, including a popular ballet, 'Laurentsia' (1937) in which he avoided Jewish intonations. Although the 'Encyclopedic Dictionary of Music' describes him as a 'Soviet Russian and Jewish composer', not one of his almost thirty Jewish works (out of a total of fifty-five works) is mentioned. Articles in *Sovetskaya muzyka* (Soviet Music), no. 12, 1943 pp.87-8 and *Muzykalnaya zhizn* (Musical Life), no. 17, 1963, p. 19, on the occasion of his seventieth and eightieth birthdays do not mention at all that he has any connection with Jewish music.

Aleksandr's brother, Grigory (1879-1955), was also a talented composer but he wrote only a few works with Jewish intonations and never found his own style of expression. Another brother, David (1869-1926), a violinist and, from 1918-26, professor at the Moscow Conservatory, was driven to suicide by antisemitism, according to eye-witness testimony.[32] Grigory's son, Yulian (b. 1913), a child prodigy who studied under P. Dukas from 1926-32, never touched the Jewish idiom. He and his wife, Nana Ivanovna Rogozhina, wrote a book about Aleksandr Krein, but mainly to prove his family's loyalty to the regime and to dissociate the Kreins from anything Jewish.[33] L. Sabaneev again sees the historical situation exactly: 'The three Kreins felt like national Jewish musicians, pioneers of national music. If they did not succeed it was not their fault but because ideological considerations of an extra-musical nature saw their national trend as superfluous, harmful and as one that shakes the system's foundations.'[34]

Perhaps the most Jewish of all these composers was Moses (Mikhail) Milner (1882-1953) who matured as a musician in the Jewish Folk Song Society. His fate was also the most tragic. He did not forsake Jewish music until the last days of his life. His music was not published, hardly performed, and today he has been expunged from Soviet historiography even though he was highly admired as a composer in the early 1920s and wrote the first opera in Yiddish to be performed in Russia ('The Heavens Aflame', first performance 6 May 1923 in the Leningrad State Opera). After the second performance the opera was 'forbidden even in concert form, by an order . . . because of its mystical quality'.[35] Later he wrote more than ten pieces of incidental theater music for Jewish theaters, voice and piano music, some orchestral works and two more operas, 'The New Way' (1932) and 'Josephus Flavius' (1935), all imbued with Jewish feeling and intonations. He was severly attacked for a second time after the performance of 'Josephus Flavius' which was declared 'reactionary'. A similar fate befell other Jewish composers: the choice between rejecting the Jewish idiom or sinking into oblivion. Most opted for the first, such as A. Veprik (1889-1958) who from 1930 was Professor and Head of the Department of Instrumentation at the Moscow Conservatory, or S. Feynberg (1890-1962), one of the most famous Soviet pianists and teachers, who from 1922 was Professor and Head of the Piano Department of the same institution. In the 1920s Veprik still wrote some Jewish dances for orchestra, and it is curious to see how in the 1930s Soviet musicology was already trying to purge him of his Jewishness. After the performance of his 'Five Dances for Orchestra, Opus 17', a review in the important journal *Sovetskaya muzyka* (no. 3, 1936, pp.100-1) stated: 'The composer never speaks of the dances as Jewish. And although the foreign press calls Veprik a "Soviet Jewish composer", justice demands that this definition be strictly limited . . . The composer himself is willing to speak of the Jewish-Ukrainian nature of his music.'

Although Jewish music *per se* declined during the late 1920s and 1930s and then vanished altogether, there was a large increase in the number of Jewish musicians in Soviet music at this time and in the following decades. The new status of the Jewish population after the Revolution made possible an influx of Jews into various fields of science, literature and the arts. This was especially the case in such fields of music as performance, teaching and musicology, in which the national idiom is not so evident. It was here that the concept 'Jewish brains and talent—yes, Jewish art and self-expression—no!' could be practised most successfully. In the 1920s-40s the Soviet regime unreservedly accepted the creative spirit of Jewish musicians so long as they did not display their Jewishness, at least on the surface of their art.

During the first years after the Revolution musical life in Soviet Russia was headed by the young, modern-minded Jewish composer Artur Lure (1892-1966) who is now considered one of the first dodecaphonists and a highly talented composer. Lunacharsky, the first Commissar of Education and the main Party spokesman on culture, chose Lure as his chief assistant in the field of music. In this capacity Lure was responsible for most of the administrative work in music in those first years of Soviet rule and for working out the new policy of proletarian music, e.g. the nationalization of theaters and conservatories, the closure of the Russian Music Society and, apparently, of the Jewish Folk Song Society, reforms in music education, organization of the Association of Contemporary Music (ASM), etc. But in

1923 Lure left the Soviet State. Perhaps none of the musicians involved in building up the new system of Soviet music from the first years after the Revolution to the present day is referred to in Soviet musicology with such hostility: 'An aesthete-decadent, a composer void of individuality, eclectic, with pretensions to innovation, Lure used his official position to advertize himself and to support musical adventurists like himself.'[36]

Jewish composers who were more or less Jewish in their art were among the most active and talented creative artists in the young Soviet State. For example, B. Asafev, the highest authority in Soviet music, names three composers as the leading musicians in the field of song, including A. Krein and S. Feynberg.[37] The new generation of composers was headed by Lev Knipper (b. 1898), Zinovy Kompaneets (b. 1902), Genrikh Litinsky (b. 1901) and Zara Levin (1906-76). The rise of the popular composers of 'mass songs', Isaak Dunaevsky and the brothers Daniil, Dmitry, and Samuil Pokrass, also occurred at this time (see below). None of these composers used the Jewish idiom as their main means of expression, and its appearance is somewhat fortuitous. Of course, future research into their life and work, and that of many other Jewish musicians, may reveal that their Jewishness had a deeper, indirect impact on their art or may suggest some deeper, hidden evidence of the Jewishness of their art.

Kompaneets was perhaps the only one who had an unexpressed urge for Jewish music throughout his life. In 1939 he wrote a 'Rhapsody on Jewish Themes' for symphony orchestra; he published a collection of folk songs in the 1940s and five original songs in 1960, and in 1970 he edited a collection of songs in Yiddish. This last collection included some of his own works, mostly based on the poetry of the officially approved Soviet Yiddish writer A. Vergelis. It is worth noting that the urge of Jewish composers to express themselves through their own native idiom is invariably interpreted by Soviet musicology as the interest of a Russian composer in a general Eastern or Oriental idiom.[38] Kompaneets wrote a number of instrumental works as well as popular 'mass songs' ('The Song of Bygone Marches', 'The Lace-Maker and the Blacksmith'). He and especially Knipper wrote numerous works based on the folk tunes of Eastern peoples. Thus, Knipper wrote suites on Tadzhik, Turkmen, Buryat, Iranian, Kazakh etc. themes, and even 'The Master Buddha's Stories'. He was very productive, writing eight operas, fourteen symphonies, numerous vocal and instrumental works and some well-known mass songs. In the 1930s he was regarded as one of the pioneers of modernism. He was attacked both by the authorities and by great artists: the first condemned him as a fruitless experimenter and his music as 'unemotional', diminishing the pathos of the Revolution;[39] while Shostakovich claimed that he could see in Knipper's music 'neither purity nor simplicity'.[40] Neither his 'Far Eastern Red Army

Symphony' and 'Poem of the Fighting Komsomol' (the popular song 'Polyushko' is from this work), nor his ten suites based on various (but not Jewish) folk tunes, and not even the article he wrote in 1951 under the eloquent title 'Against cosmopolitanism, for a Russian national style,'[41] helped him to gain highest official recognition (although he was twice awarded a Stalin Prize and the title of Honored Artist by two republics; the highest title for composers, the title of People's Artist; and a chair at a conservatory he did not deserve). Of greater concern is the fact that the work of a talented composer never reached its potential level and that today it is quite forgotten. Rimsky-Korsakov's question is still relevant: 'Why should you Jewish students . . . ?'

Zara Levin gained recognition mainly in the field of chamber song, especially children's songs. She wrote some music, for example, 'Poem for Violin and Piano' (1930), and some songs, in which a Jewish idiom appears. Her childhood in Simferopol where her father, an amateur violinist, or *klezmer*, played Jewish folk tunes at home, naturally left some trace on her art. But today she recalls only one episode from this period, according to her Jewish biographer Noemi Mikhaylovskaya: in 1914 the eight-year-old Zara wrote a waltz 'Salute to the Russian Warriors' for the recruits of the Tsar.[42] Her Jewishness finds no place in the entire book.

Even G. Litinsky, who was one of the talented Modernists in the 1930s, attacked for his non-conformity and lack of repentance[43], and who was one of the few to remain consistent in those times, turned some years later to the national styles of music in the Russian peripheries and to musical theory.

Lev Pulver (1883-?), a composer of an earlier generation but whose work is connected with the 1920s and 1930s, is also of interest. Until 1923 he was a violinist in the opera orchestra of the Bolshoy Theater. He then took over as musical adviser to the Jewish Theater in Moscow. During the years when the theater was active he wrote music for more than forty plays (e.g. *200,000, Tevye—the Milkman, Freylekhs, King Lear, The Vagabond Stars*). In 1925 he and L. Shteynberg wrote the music for the *Purimshpil* (traditional play for the festival of Purim) at the Kharkov Jewish Theater. From 1949, when Jewish culture in the USSR was completely destroyed and the theater was closed, Pulver was silent as a composer except for some song arrangements. His greatest productivity was in the 1930s when he worked with Mikhoels and other great Jewish actors and wrote most of his incidental theater music. At that period he was highly recognized as a conductor and composer of Jewish theater music, and in 1939 he was even awarded the title of People's Artist. It was mere chance that he did not share the tragic fate of most of that theater's artists.

It is enough to note that forty-five percent of the newly appointed teachers at the Leningrad and Moscow Conservatories in the 1920s were Jewish to demonstrate how great was the influx of Jewish musicians into Soviet music and how great their influence on it. The most famous of these were E. Volf-Israel, I. Eydlin, M. Polyakin, F. Zelikhman, I. Braudo, S. Ginzburg, M. Yudin, V. Sher in Leningrad; and M. Gnesin, F. Blumenfeld, S. Feynberg, L. Tseytlin, A. Yampolsky, A. Mogilevsky in Moscow.[44] At this time Jewish participation in instrumental performance was especially high. Many scholars speak of a Russian Jewish school of violin founded by Leopold Auer and then developed by the famous teachers L. Tseytlin, A. Yampolsky, D. Oistrakh, V. Sher, I. Eydlin, I. Yankelevich.

We can see the immense contribution of Jewish musicians to this field from the example of chamber music, in particular quartet music. One of the most famous and long-standing quartets in the Soviet Union was the A. Glazunov Quartet, which was founded in 1919. Three of its members—I. Lukashevsky, A. Rivkin and D. Zissermann—were Jewish. The V.I. Lenin Quartet was founded in the same year and included L. Tseytlin and G. Pyatigorsky. A. Mogilevsky played in the Stradivarius Quartet, founded in 1920, which later included A. Knorre and B. Simsky, V. Pakelman and G. Gamburg, and, after 1927, P. Bondarenko. All the time at least three of its members were Jewish. This last Quartet was so named because of the Stradivarius instruments given to the musicians by the Government from the State Collection of Rare and Old Musical Instruments which had just been founded. Lunacharsky took a direct part in organizing the Quartet and its concerts in the early 1920s. He called it 'one of the creations of the Revolution'[45], and it very soon received high recognition. On 16 March 1923 *Pravda* wrote that it 'is already one of the best ensembles in the world'. The Quartet was active until the beginning of the 1930s.

The Glière Quartet (I. Targonsky, A. Targonsky, M. Lutsky, K. Blok) was completely Jewish. It shared first place with the Stradivarius Quartet at the Quartet competition in Moscow in 1927. Another all-Jewish Quartet was the excellent Vuillaume Quartet (M. Simkin, A. Staroselsky, G. Pekker, I. Vaks) which was active from the early 1920s to the 1950s. In the Ukraine there was the famous Leontovich Quartet (S. Bruzhenitsky, M. Levin, E. Shor, I. Gelfanbeyn). This list of fine quartets which existed in the Soviet Union at this time, not only in the main centers but also in the peripheries, could be continued, and in each case the participation of Jewish musicians would be from fifty to one hundred percent.[46]

Today it is impossible to reconstruct the position in orchestras, but the high number of Jewish musicians, especially in the string instrument section, is well known. New ideas in orchestral playing, the result of a 'revolt against the tyranny of the conductor', were also the product of the Jewish spirit. The Persinfans (First Symphony Ensemble), an orchestra without conductor, was founded in 1922 and spiritually guided by the violinist L. Tseytlin. It existed until 1932. It gained international fame in its first years: 'With such an orchestra the technique of execution reaches its maximum.'[47] The Persinfans had several followers in the Soviet Union, but this practice was not fully recognized, even for chamber orchestras most of which are conducted. Nevertheless, this idea had far-reaching consequences in increasing the consciousness and creativity of the orchestral musician.

Historical and social conditions, still to be fully clarified, encouraged Jewish participation in the 1920s, 1930s and 1940s mainly in four fields: (1) popular music, (2) national music cultures, (3) instrumental performance, and (4) musicology. In general, the extent of the Jewish contribution to these four fields hardly changed in those decades. This is very different from the picture of creative activity in the field of Jewish music which is indirectly depicted in Table 1. The powerful momentum of the activities of the Russian Jewish national school and the Jewish Folk Song Society could be maintained during the 1920s and 1930s despite the blow Jewish culture received in 1917. Although Jewish music lost a large number of creative minds in the 1920s and had to adjust itself to the new interpretation of Jewishness, at certain times it had an illusion of equality and hopes for an overall solution to the national problem in a communist state. An official Jewish folk song tells us that after the years of destruction and Civil War the Jewish mother could lift her head and sing:

> All my children have become
> Teachers and engineers.[48]

It is true that this demanded a complete rejection of all traditions, and more besides:

> Who will lead you to the canopy, dear son?
> —The whole Komsomol, mother dear!
> Oh, who will bless you, dear son?
> —Oh, Stalin and Kalinin, mother dear!

The idea of Birobidzhan and Jewish collective farms also appeared in the permitted folk song as one of the illusions which blinded the people. Only a few musicians had a real sense of the destruction which was taking place, and even fewer could express it, and then, of course, only in personal documents as we can see from a letter written by I. Akhron's grandfather who was a cantor: 'Recently there has appeared Jewish literature which is not in the least Jewish, simply vile, you can't understand what's written there.'[49]

The Jews were permitted to have some Jewish music to nourish their national feelings at the given moment but they were not to develop their national idiom because, in any case, the future would dissolve the Jewish people into communist society. Thus Tsarist General Drachevsky's idea remained relevant: folk music—yes, serious music—no. Of the seventy-three items in Table 1 more than forty-five are connected with the transcription of folk music.

All this explains, too, the artistic, musical level of the composers active in this field. The names of R. Boyarskaya, I. Dobrushin, A. Yuditsky, L. Kogan, Sh. Kupershmid, who were active in the field of folk song transcription and publication, or the names of L. Yampolsky, I. Shaynin, B. Riskind, M. Shalit, I. Bakst etc., who were active in the field of popular songs or brass music, are neither known nor really important. The most significant musical work on a Jewish theme in the 1930s is the 'Overture on Jewish Themes for Sextet with Clarinet and Piano' written by S. Prokofiev in 1919 and transcribed for symphony orchestra in 1934, the time when some short-term hope for Jewish culture seemed to emerge.

Let us now turn to the main fields in which Jewish musicians were active.

The so-called mass song is a genre which arose in the Soviet Union and includes different groups of songs: patriotic and Revolutionary songs as well as work and love songs. The official requirement for these songs, however, remains ideological texts, in the Soviet sense, and simplified musical features. This genre originated from and absorbed various kinds of songs such as folk songs, prison and exile songs, urban folklore, and *blatnaya pesnya*—thieves' songs. The last two were especially widespread in south Russia, in the Jewish centers of the Ukraine and Moldavia. Transformed and mixed with Jewish folklore, these songs developed into a genre of popular music which at an early stage revealed itself in the work of Goldfaden and later formed a group of songs with catchy, declamatory intonations, elements of *Freylekhs*, and certain rhythmical patterns such as the march. These songs made up a large part of the Soviet mass song. It was Jewish professional and semi-professional composers, mainly from those areas of South Russia (M. Blanter was born near Mogilev, I. Dunaevsky—near Kharkov, the Pokrass brothers—in Kiev, O. Feltsman—in Odessa, A. Tsfasman—in Zaporozhe, F. Khayt—in Kiev, etc.), who, sensitive to the signs of the times as Jews in the Diaspora are, and responding to the demands of the mass music market, created most of the popular music in the 1920s-1940s. Some forty-five percent of the mass song composers mentioned by the 'Encyclopaedic Dictionary of Music' (Moscow 1966) are Jewish. Out of the seventeen most popular mass songs in the Soviet Union named by that same 'Encyclopaedia', eight are written by Jewish composers (p.297). Among the most officially recognized and also most popular mass song composers are Matvey Blanter (b. 1903), Isaak Dunaevsky (1900-55), Dmitry Pokrass (1899-?), Daniil Pokrass (1904-54), Samuil Pokrass (1897-1939), Oskar Feltsman (b. 1921), Aleksandr Tsfasman (b. 1906), Sigizmund Kats (b. 1908), Ilya Khayt (b. 1897), Lev Shvarts (b.1898), Zinovy Kompaneets, Venyamin Basner (b. 1925), Mark Fradkin (b. 1914), Yan Frenkel (b. 1920), David Pritsker (b. 1900), Eduard Kolmanovsky (b. 1923).

Dunaevsky, Blanter and Dmitry Pokrass laid the foundations of the Soviet mass song. They developed the pattern of the melodious and march-like Soviet patriotic song. Intonations of Jewish urban folk music appear frequently in their songs and had a great impact on their whole work. This is so obvious that it was recognized even by Soviet musicology: 'Jewish folk music, song and dance melodies became one of the intonational components' of these songs.[50] The intonations of *Freylekhs* appear in the songs of Dunaevsky, Pokrass, Feltsman, Kompaneets, Pritsker and others. D. Pokrass's song 'Those are Storm Clouds . . .' was so Jewish that the melody was popular in the Warsaw Ghetto resistance movement. We feel Jewish intonations in many of Dunaevsky's and Blanter's works, including their stage works (operettas). This feature of the mass song is not limited to the work of Jewish composers: Jewish intonations are frequent in the songs of N. Boguslavsky. They do not, of course, appear in pure form but are fused with other intonations from different national and social strata.

Songs by these composers which are most popular, and not only in the USSR, include the 'Song of the Fatherland', 'Kakhovka', 'The Captain's Song', 'March of the Enthusiasts', 'March of the Joyful Boys' by Dunaevsky, 'On the Way' and 'Katyusha' by Blanter, 'If There Is War Tomorrow' and 'Budenny's March' by the Pokrass brothers, 'I Believe' by Feltsman, 'The Song of the Dnieper' and 'Farewell' by Fradkin, 'The Song of Bygone Marches' by Kompaneets, 'On the Nameless Height' and 'What the Homeland Starts From' by Basner, 'Aviamarch' by Khayt, and others. In the 1940s and 1950s lyrical intonations increasingly dominate in this genre and Jewish ones are more difficult to discover.

The operettas, musicals and cinema music by these composers were as popular throughout the Soviet Union as the Viennese operetta. Dunaevsky himself wrote twelve operettas including 'The Free Wind' and music for the well-known films 'Circus' and 'Volga, Volga'.

Jewish mass song composers wrote many of the apologetic songs of the time which became widespread due to their talent and the popularity of their style. It is enough to recall the popularity of the Stalin songs written by Dunaevsky, Blanter and others to see this genre in general and the work of those composers in proper perspective. Here the sentimental intonations of the Russian urban romance and features of the bellicose Revolutionary songs are combined.

Part of the Soviet nationality policy was to cultivate professional national styles of art which had no genuine art music background in the European sense. Those cultures were designed to serve the new system from the first day of their creation. About twenty such cultures appeared in the space of some ten to twenty years, and in the early stages Jewish participation in their creation was considerable. Jewish musicians who had received an excellent education in the 1910s-30s at the Moscow and Leningrad Conservatories turned to this field for several reasons: it was a vacuum in which recognition could be speedily gained; work was carried out in the peripheries, away from the central authorities and was therefore somewhat freer; it was a fascinating field for the questing Jewish mind. All this is true, but it seems to us that there is another, most significant reason: the frustrated urge for their own national idiom whose expression had been violently disrupted and was under constant repression, sought and found satisfaction in the creation of other national styles—a kind of national sublimation. Future research will perhaps demonstrate this in detail. Meanwhile, it can probably be substantiated by pointing to the large contribution of Jewish composers to the creation of Central Asia's musical cultures—Kazakh, Kirgiz, Uzbek, Turkmen—which are related to the Middle Eastern idiom. We could quote a number of transcriptions of the folk tunes of various small Central Asian peoples used by Jewish composers and which are very close to the Jewish idiom, for example a Changrian[51] song by A. Veprik published in *Sovetskaya muzyka* (no. 10, 1936).

The older generation of Jewish composers—M. Gnesin, A. Krein, L. Kniper, M. Shteynberg, A. Veprik, etc—had been interested in the folklore of the Russian periphery and had written some works in the style of certain national musical cultures. M. Gnesin wrote transcriptions of Tadzhik, Mari, Chuvash and other folk tunes, and in the 1930s he wrote a 'String Quartet on Azerbaydzhani Melodies' and an 'Adygey Sextet'. M. Shteynberg (1883-1946), a pupil of Rimsky-Korsakov and himself a prominent Soviet composer and teacher (D. Shostakovich was one of his pupils at the Leningrad Conservatory), wrote a 'Turksib' symphony with Kazakh themes, an opera and symphony (No. 5) and some other works on Uzbek themes. He was the first to use the Uzbek and Kirgiz idiom in symphonic music. (His only work written with Jewish intonations is his Third Symphony.) Veprik wrote an opera 'Tantagul' based on Kirgiz folklore. Kniper wrote some of the first Tadzhik symphonic works ('Vankh' and 'Vakhio Bolo'). It is significant that it was Jewish composers who were most sympathetic to the needs of the national musical cultures. In 1928, for example, in response to a request from the Government of Turkmenistan, six Moscow composers wrote songs for Turkmen school-children; four of them—Z. Levin, Z. Kompaneets, B. Shekhter, V. Bely—were Jewish.[52]

This trend was greatly developed. Many Jewish composers not only visited these parts of Russia for some time in order to write their works but even settled there for longer periods. According to official Soviet sources about thirty to thirty-five Jewish composers have been awarded the titles of Honored Artist and People's Artist by the national governments of Soviet republics and autonomous republics.[53]

Among significant Jewish composers in national styles are Evgeny Brusilovsky (b. 1905), who in the 1930s wrote the first Kazakh operas ('Kiz Zhibek', 'Zhalbir', 'Er-Targin') and symphonic works (six symphonies, concertos, etc.); Mikhail Raukhverger (b. 1901), the composer of an early Kirgiz ballet and opera, written in 1942-43; Pavel Berlinsky (b. 1900), composer of the first Buryat musical drama ('Zhargal', 1941); Georgy Mushel (b. 1909), one of the creators of the Uzbek opera; Boris Shekhter (1900-61), a highly talented musician who wrote the first Turkmen symphony works ('The Turkmenia Suite', 1932) and the first opera ('Yusup and Akhmet', 1941); Boris Tseydman (b. 1908), composer of several Azerbaydzhani operas and symphonic works, who taught many well-known Azerbaydzhani and Uzbek composers at the Baku and Tashkent Conservatories; David Gershfeld (b. 1911), the author of the first Moldavian opera ('Grozovan', 1956); Genrikh Litinsky (b. 1901), one of the most prominent Soviet musicologists and composition teachers at the Gnesin Institute in Moscow, who wrote the first Yakut operas and ballets (1947), etc.

The third field to which Jews contributed and in which they achieved the highest world renown is musical performance. This is not only true of Russian-born and Russian-educated Jews but is a general historical phenomenon. Soviet Jewish instrumental performance in the last half-century has maintained the highest standards, although different trends and periods can be discerned. The success of the Soviet school of performance may be attributed to a combination of factors: the talent of Jewish musicians, the totalitarian system of education in which no expense is spared to gain a victory at a competition and the high tradition of musical performance in Russia.

Jews make up about forty-five percent of Soviet musical performers.[54] Many of them come from south Russia, like the mass song composers. Pre-Revolutionary conditions—the Jewish Pale of Settlement (this restriction was occasionally lifted for those studying music), limitations in the choice of profession (music and medicine were permitted)—provided the social basis for the influx of Jews on to the concert platform. The musical basis was the art of the *klezmers*; nearly every one of the great Soviet Jewish instrumentalists has links with this tradition. Their success was also based on the phenomenon of the Jewish child prodigy and the tradition of music education. Statistics show that for many years (until the mid-1960s) about fifty percent of candidates for professional music schools in the large cities were Jewish. Fifty to sixty percent of the prizes at Soviet and international competitions in the 1930s were awarded to Soviet Jewish musicians. Table 2 below, which gives the percentage of Jews in such competitions, indicates how the situation of Jews in the musical performing arts developed over the years. We must bear in mind that it is quite another question how far the Jewish heritage and their Jewish origin influenced the work of Jewish artists and how far we have the right to speak of Jewish features of musical performance. This question has not yet been thoroughly explored. We can, perhaps, point to such features of Soviet instrumental performance in the early period as a singing-declamatory sound quality, a distinctive melancholy tone, a strong subjective note in the interpretation, as ones that could be traced to Jewish tradition. And perhaps the contemporary formal-virtuoso style of Soviet performance is related to the social and national alienation of the Jews from the regime.

The largest group of Jewish performers is concentrated in the field of bow instrument and pianoforte music where the percentage of Jewish musicians is as high as sixty-five to seventy percent. For example, at the six Chopin Competitions in Poland from 1927 to 1960, fourteen of the twenty-one Soviet prize-winners were Jewish.[55] Seven of the eleven Soviet prize-winners at the Wieniawski Competition in the same country from 1935 to 1962 were Jewish.[56] Thirteen of the twenty Soviet violinists who won prizes in the Eugene Izai and Queen Elisabeth Competitions in Brussels from 1937 to 1964,[57] and five of the nine pianists, were Jewish.[58] At the Marguerite Long and Jacques Thibaud Violin Competitions from 1953-63, ten of the sixteen Soviet prize-winners were Jewish;[59] at the two Tchaikovsky Competitions in Moscow (1958-62), fourteen out of twenty-five.[60] Between 1920 and 1940 fifteen of the twenty-three holders of the chair of piano in the Moscow Conservatory were Jewish,[61] while seventeen of the twenty-five heads of the violin department from 1917 to 1966 were Jews.[62] The same source mentions that fourteen outstanding violinists graduated from the class of the most famous teacher, Professor A. Yampolsky, of whom eleven are Jewish.[63] We can add to this list the young Jewish musicians who have gained high recognition in international competitions and on the concert platform in recent years: the violinists Feliks Hirshhorn, Gidon Kremer, Oleg Kagan, Vladimir Lantsman, Vladimir Spivakov; the cellists David Geringas, Mikhail Maysky; pianists Vladimir Lyubimov and

B. Blokh.[64]

Chamber ensembles and orchestras reveal a similar picture. We have already mentioned the quartets in the 1920s and 1930s. We can now add the Jewish musicians in the Soviet Composers' Union Quartet: I. Targonsky, V. Vidrevich, I. Lipshits, L. Furer; in the Bolshoy Theater Quartet (the GABT): I. Zhuk, B. Veltman, M. Gurevich, S. Knesevitsky; in the Auer Quartet: I. Lesman, A. Pergament, L. Shifman, I. Livshits; and in the Tchaikovsky Quartet: I. Liber, V. Pikayzen, V. Tsiporin. The best Soviet quartet at the present time, the Borodin Quartet, includes V. Berlinsky (first violin) and R. Dubinsky (cello).[65] Most of the string instrument orchestras are founded and led by Jewish musicians. We have already referred to the Persinfans; the Moscow Chamber Orchestra was founded and is led by Rudolf Barshay, the Gnesin Institute Chamber Orchestra by A. Gotlib, a second Moscow Chamber Orchestra by L. Markiz, the Latvian Philharmonic Chamber Orchestra by T. Livshits, the Bolshoy Theater Violin Ensemble by I. Reentovich. About fifty percent of the musicians in these orchestras and the string sections of theater and symphony orchestras up to the 1960s were Jewish. We see, for example, from a 1964 description of the Bolshoy Theater Orchestra that about fifty of the one hundred musicians playing bow instruments are Jewish.[66]

However, the deciding factor in music is, of course, not quantity but quality. All the musicians named above are excellent pianists, violinists, cellists etc. which is clear from their success at international competitions or membership of first-class ensembles and orchestras. Nevertheless, we must emphasize that these artists include many top masters whose fame is worldwide and whose art has been a historical contribution to their field. The pianists Emil Gilels (b. 1916), and Grigory Ginzburg (1904-61), the violinists David Oistrakh (1908-1974) and Leonid Kogan (1924-1982), the cellists Svyatoslav Knusevitsky (1907-63) and Daniel Shafran (b. 1923) are among the greatest musicians of our century. Among the younger generation (born in the 1930s and 1940s) we find the top world names of pianists: Vladimir Ashkenazi, V. Lyubimov, violinists G. Kremer, O. Kagan, V. Pikayzen, I. Oistrakh, cellists T. Gutman, V. Feygon. It is unnecessary to quote the world musical press to prove the range of these artists since their names speak for themselves. While speaking of instrumentalists we must mention the curious fact that the best Soviet organists are also Jewish even though this instrument has not historically been connected with Jewish tradition. For instance, Isay Braudo (b. 1896), professor at the Leningrad Conservatory and author of studies on musical performance; Leonid Royzman (b. 1915), professor at the Moscow Conservatory; Maru Shakhin (b. 1917) and Gari Grodburg.

We must bear in mind that the highest level of artistry and world fame have not, in most cases, saved these people from being deprived of human and national dignity under the Soviet regime. We do not even speak of the performance by these Jewish musicians of Jewish music; their general repertoire is strictly confined within the framework of styles and composers accepted in the Soviet Union, and every move in their artistic and social life is controlled. The dying words of one of these great Soviet Jewish musicians are chilling: 'I have to die, it is impossible to live with this hatred in the heart.'[67]

These artists, for various reasons (mostly material), are taking the path of assimilation perhaps more so than the average Jew.[68] There has been no lack of anti-Israel declarations signed by D. Oistrakh, L. Kogan, E. Gilels and others, and some, such as I. Yankelevich, have written articles on the subject. However, the Jewish emigration movement in the Soviet Union affected these artists too, and some of them applied to go to Israel and left the Soviet Union (F. Hirshhorn, V. Lantsman, I Risin, M. Shmit, B. Goldshteyn, etc.).

The second largest group of Jewish performers are the conductors. The leading figures in this field in the Soviet Union are Samuil Samosud (1884-1964), who for many years was chief conductor of the Leningrad and the Moscow Bolshoy Theaters; Boris Haykin (b. 1904), professor and conductor at the same theaters; Karl Eliasberg (b. 1907), chief conductor of the Leningrad Great Radio Orchestra; Natan Rakhlin (b. 1906), chief conductor of the USSR State and Ukrainian State Symphony Orchestras; Yuri Fayer (b. 1890), chief ballet conductor at the Bolshoy Theater; Arye Pazovsky (1887-1953), chief conductor of the Bolshoy Theater; Maru Paverman (b. 1907), chief conductor of the Sverdlovsk Philharmonic Orchestra; Leo Ginzburg (b. 1907), head of the department of conducting of the Moscow Radio Symphony Orchestra. In all, Jewish conductors make up about thirty percent of the Soviet professionals in this field.[69] Among the first four graduate conductors from the Moscow Conservatory were A. Braginsky, L. Ginzburg and B. Haykin.[70] The last two became longstanding professors of that same institution.

It is evident from the top Soviet Jewish conductors listed above that most Jewish conductors worked in the field of theater music rather than symphonic music. Perhaps they were attracted by the theatrical element of music, endeavouring to find a synthesis of music and drama (a legacy from the Purim plays, perhaps?). Important features in their style of conducting are improvization (e.g. N. Rakhlin, I. Aronovich) and a full-blooded, temperamental artistry (e.g. S. Samosud, Y. Fayer, M. Paverman).

Jews are less numerous in the fields of vocal music and wind instrument performance. There are several top vocalists, such as Debora Pantofel-Nechetskaya (b. 1904), a *coloratura* soprano, and Mark Reyzen

(b. 1895), a bass, both of whom are among the stars of the Bolshoy Theater. About nine percent of wind-instrument players are Jewish,[71] among whom are some excellent musicians.

The last group of musicians we have to consider is the musicologists. One-third of Soviet musicologists is Jewish; Jewish composers and musicologists, according to 1968 data, make up eighteen percent of the powerful Composers' Union of the USSR (cf. Jews are about one percent of the Soviet population). Out of a total 360 musicologists who are members of the Union, some 130 are Jews.[72] These figures are even larger if we consider only musicologists from Moscow and Leningrad, that is, the leading members of the field: out of 187, eighty-five are Jewish. It is not only the number of Jews in Soviet musicology which is significant: they have produced important and fundamental works. The earliest musicological works published in the Soviet Union relating music history to Marxism-Leninism were written in the 1920s by Evgeny Braudo (1882-1939)[73] and Boris Shteynpress (b. 1908).[74] The theory of so-called integral musical analysis was created by Lev Mazel (b. 1907)[75] and Viktor Tsukerman (b. 1903).[76] Later, in the 1960s, Mazel made the first attempt to justify more progressive styles in Soviet music.[77] Viktor Berkov (b. 1907) and Genrikh Litinsky wrote basic works on musical theory; the first and only general history of music was written by Roman Gruber (1895-1962);[78] the first history of Soviet music by Semen Ginsburg (b. 1901);[79] the first history of Russian music published in the USSR by Mikhail Pekelis (b. 1899);[80] the first and still the main encyclopaedia of music, by Boris Shteynpress and Israel Yampolsky (b. 1905),[81] and so on. Among the top Soviet musicologists we also find Arnold Alshvang, Lev Barenboym, Mikhail Druskin, Lev Ginzburg, Yakov Milshteyn, Israel Nestev, Aleksandr Rabinovich, David Rabinovich, Iosif Rizhkin, Semen Shlifshteyn, Grigory Shneerson, Daniel Zhitomirsky, etc.

Although Jewish music scholars were highly gifted and well educated, Jewish topics are absent from Soviet musicology. What is more, under the pressure of Soviet conditions prominent Jewish musicologists have tried to avoid any mention of Jewish subjects even when directly relevant to their topic.[82] Only in the field of folk music were there a few publications, as mentioned above. The only musicologist in this field was Moisey Beregovsky (1892-1961), who devoted nearly his whole life to Jewish music. Although some elements of his work are controversial (he wrote in Yiddish but used Latin characters, he was often more concerned with pointing out the impact of Russian and Ukrainian folklore on Jewish folklore than with analysing features of the Jewish heritage, etc.)—a direct consequence of working in Soviet conditions—he nevertheless remains an important Jewish musicologist. He was educated at the Kiev and Leningrad Conservatories and from 1928 to 1936 was Head of the Musical Folklore Department of the Institute of Jewish Proletarian Culture at the Ukrainian Academy of Sciences in Kiev. He was then appointed to the Folklore Department of the Kiev Conservatory. From 1941-49 he was again at the Ukrainian Academy of Sciences, this time as Head of the Musical Folklore Section of the Institute of Literature's Department of Jewish Culture. In 1944 he received his doctor's degree in the subject 'Jewish Instrumental Folk Music'.

Beregovsky published a major work, *Jidiser muzik-folklor* (Jewish Musical Folklore), vol. 1 (Moscow 1934), and *Yidishe Instrumentale Folks-muzik* (Kiev 1937). The other volumes of the first work, which was planned to appear in five volumes, have never been published. He also published a collection of folk songs (*Yidishe Folks-lider* (Kiev 1938)), together with Itsik Fefer, and a second collection was published posthumously (*Evreyskie narodnye pesni*—Jewish Folk Songs) (Moscow 1962). About ten articles by him on Jewish folk music appeared in journals.

Beregovsky's devoted work at the Jewish Institute of the Ukrainian Academy of Sciences, the only institution in the Soviet Union at which research was carried out into Jewish culture, was very significant. This Institute was set up in the late 1920s and remained active until 1949.[83] It had a group of literary specialists (I. Dobrushin, M. Viner, Z. Skuditsky, A. Yuditsky), and, besides Beregovsky, M. Maydansky and R. Lerner worked there for some years in the field of music. In 1946 its archives contained about 7,000 records of musical folklore (in written music and tapes), most of which had been collected by Beregovsky. Only a small part of Beregovsky's work prepared at the Institute (the five-volume study of Jewish musical folklore, more than forty articles, etc.) has been published. He was very active during the war, as he himself has described:

> During the summer of 1944 we received from our correspondents a number of ghetto songs, labor-camp songs and Jewish partisan songs . . . We organized expeditions in 1944 in Chernovtsy . . . . in August 1945 in the Vinnitsa area . . . in 1946 we visited Vilnius and Kaunas where we collected material from the Vilnius and Kaunas Ghettos. We prepared for the publishing house the book 'Jewish Folklore in the Period of the Great Patriotic War.'[84]

After the destruction of Jewish culture in the USSR in 1949 Beregovsky had no opportunity to continue his work. Today he is not referred to in Soviet musical literature, and there is no mention of the Jewish musical folklore institutions in Kiev. Even the obituary to Beregovsky (*Sovetskaya muzyka*, no. 11, 1961, 160) speaks only of his general work on folklore, although it does mention that 'he wrote a number of articles and studies on Jewish, Ukrainian and Bashkir folklore'.[85] His life and work still await complete, objective treatment.

Another example of musicological research on Jewish musical folklore is an article by A. Vinkovetsky, 'Jewish musical folklore in Russia'. This was written as preface to an 'Anthology of Jewish Folk Song', whose publication was discussed in the late 1960s in the Leningrad Music Publishing House. Dmitry Shostakovich wrote to him about this planned publication: 'I have made the acquaintance of your 'Anthology of Jewish Folk Song' and I continue to do so every day. It is a very interesting work and I am very grateful to you for it.'[86] The preface gives a description and some analysis of the 244 songs in the 'Anthology'. This latter has yet to be published, but the preface was recently published in an underground Jewish magazine in the Soviet Union, 'Jews in the USSR'. We may draw from this the sad conclusion that the only Jewish musicology in the USSR today is underground.

When discussing the role Jews played in Soviet musicology, we must consider one more question. There were six Jews among the eleven musicologists who violently attacked modern music according to the Party line at the First Congress of the Soviet Composers' Union in 1948. There are also many Jewish names among the most vocal defenders of official Soviet musicology.[87] None the less, the work of many Jewish musicologists contains an important, creative element, showing a quest for real, objective values. There are many different reasons for this relatively strong creative trend among Jewish musicologists (as well as among Jewish scholars in other fields of the humanities), and they naturally involve such factors as the democratic traditions of the East European Jewish intelligentsia, international contacts, knowledge of languages, and such like. The popularization and analysis of progressive musical trends which the Soviet authorities condemned in 1938 and 1948 were to a large extent linked with Jewish names.[88] This could not pass unnoticed by Soviet officialdom.

The attack on the most talented composers and musicologists in 1948-49 is well known. Professor Boris Schwartz has accurately defined the events of those days as 'musicologists on trial'. The destruction of Jewish culture and the wave of open antisemitism which reached a peak at the same time are equally well known. Although as Schwartz points out, 'Whether, in view of the anti-Jewish campaign which began in late 1948, any antisemitism played a part in the purge of musicologists is difficult to determine,'[89] the matter seems clear enough.

In the totalitarian Soviet system both the violent suppression of human freedom and the antisemitic state policy are manifestations of one and the same idea. Not so apparent in the 1920s and 1930s, it surfaced openly in the late 1940s. In footnote 10 above, I quoted two similar statements on music from Nazi and Soviet sources. It is also no accident that we can give the following chronology of events from 7 to 13 January 1948:

7 January: Solomon Mikhoels, the great Jewish actor and head of the Soviet Jewish Anti-Fascist Committee, left Moscow for Minsk. At the railway station he told his relative, the composer Veynberg, with foreboding that Shostakovich, Prokofiev, Myasnovsky and some others had been summoned to the Party Central Committee.

10 January: Stalin's confidant, Zhdanov, who master-minded the ruin of modern music in the USSR, talked to the leading Soviet composers.

12 January: Mikhoels was killed in Minsk. This was the prelude to the subsequent arrests and murders of most Jewish artists and writers and the closure of all Jewish institutions.

13 January: A meeting of the Party Central Committee began at 1 o'clock at which the musicians were informed of the notorious resolution condemning 'Western modernism and homegrown formalism' in music. At 3 o'clock news of Mikhoels' death reached the musicians assembled in the Central Committee hall. In the evening Shostakovich said to his closest friends: 'This is a campaign which starts with the Jews and will end with the whole of the intelligentsia.'[90]

Thus the ideological struggle in music combined with the Jewish tragedy. Out of nineteen musicologists accused of 'anti-patriotic, harmful activity, aimed at undermining the ideological basis of Soviet music', denounced for 'cosmopolitan errors and groveling before Western music' and also for 'standing apart from current creative works',[91] fourteen were Jewish.

All this is no accident, neither an average case of antisemitism nor the usual case of a struggle between the old and the new in art. It was a definite trend which started in the Soviet Union in the 1930s and continues to the present and which is motivated by deep social, political and aesthetic factors. It is a struggle by the authorities against aesthetic principles which threaten the system or at least refuse to submit to its supervision. It is a struggle against a social-national community which does not fit into official policies. Not all the names in the Nazi and Soviet sources quoted above are Jewish: the social and national groups do not coincide exactly, but they do overlap by some seventy to eighty percent. The Soviet population supported the struggle against modern music because of the Jewish names the authorities constantly referred to. In Nazi Germany a number of non-Jewish musicians (Stravinsky, Hindemith, Stuckenschmidt) were attacked for their 'Jewish' art. In Soviet Russia the same people were attacked for 'anti-realistic, anti-social art'. The accent shifts from nationality to aesthetics and vice versa. The Jews are to be destroyed because of their corrupt musical aesthetics (according to Nazi theories), and hostile musical aesthetics are to be attacked via the Jews (in the Soviet version). Antisemitism based on musical aesthetics and musical aesthetics molded by antisemitism are curious features of twentieth-century totalitarian regimes.

When this pattern emerged in the Soviet Union, Jews and the Jewish idiom began to be ousted from Soviet music. A *numerus clausus* was introduced first by an oral order at the end of the 1950s and then by a secret order of the USSR Minister of Culture, E. Furtseva, in 1969.[92] The national cadres policy—the policy of employing members of the native nationality in the various republics in preference to other nationalities—which was officially introduced to further the development of local cultures, in fact became a racial policy which officially recognized privileged nationalities, i.e. the local nationality of the republic and, of course, the Russian nationality. There is no room for the Jews in this policy. Its results can be seen from Table 2.

TABLE 2: SOVIET JEWISH PRIZE-WINNERS AT MUSIC COMPETITIONS (IN PERCENTAGES)

1933	1938	1945	1957	1963	1969
54	60	25	23	12	9

(100% = number of Soviet prize-winners)

This is one of the reasons for the decline over the past fifteen years in the number of significant Soviet musicians who have been awarded first prize at major international competitions. The case of Leonid Kogan is well known in Soviet music circles. In 1951 he was not accepted by the Soviet Ministry of Culture to compete in the Queen Elisabeth Competition in Brussels. But after Stalin had written on the list of candidates 'Get the first prize', the list was changed and Kogan included. Since then Jews have been included among the Soviet competitors at such events only when the authorities are especially interested in ensuring that the Soviet Union win the main prizes. After the Jewish musician has performed this task he is often kept from the concert platform. This was the case with, for example, Gidon Kremer (first prize at the Tchaikovsky Competition), Natalya Gutman (second prize at the same competition), Feliks Hirshhorn (first prize at the Queen Elisabeth Competition), Mikhail Vayman (second prize at the same competition), Vladimir Lantsman (first prize at the Montreal Competition), and others. We must, of course, bear in mind that the question of access to the concert platform in the Soviet Union is a sophisticated system of incentive and punishment.

The percentage of doctoral dissertations written by Jewish musicologists and accepted at the Moscow and Leningrad Conservatories has changed as follows (100% = all dissertations accepted): [93]

TABLE 3: DOCTORAL DISSERTATIONS BY JEWS AT MOSCOW AND LENINGRAD CONSERVATORIES (IN PERCENTAGES)

1934-41	1942-52	1953-63	1964-74
50	23	13	10

For Jewish musicologists the path to the doctor's degree is strewn with innumerable petty, artificial obstacles so that in some cases they find it impossible to get the degree and in others the whole process is very much protracted. Thus, for example, the musicologist and composer Maks Goldin (b. 1917) struggled to be granted the doctor's degree for more than five years after he had completed his dissertation (on Latvian folk music). Goldin also devoted much time to research in the field of Jewish folklore, none of which has been published, and he wrote a number of instrumental pieces based on Jewish folk tunes. He was the author of the last publication of Jewish folk song transcriptions (*Evreyskie narodnye pesni* (Moscow 1972)).

The new situation and trends which emerged in Jewish cultural life after 1948-50 had far-reaching, often indirect and complex consequences. The Soviet authorities do not always insist that Jews be completely ousted from musical life. In certain cases and situations they are willing to accept the Jewish idiom for propaganda purposes. This was the case with the Jewish folk singer Nehama Lifshits (b. 1927), who was sponsored by the authorities in the early stage of her career. She was sent to concerts in Paris in 1961. By the late 1960s she was not permitted to perform more than two or three Jewish songs at her concerts in the Soviet Union and many concert halls were completely closed to her. In 1971 she emigrated to Israel.

Some rare publications of Jewish folk songs are permitted for the same purpose of propaganda (see Table 1). The use of Jewish folk melodies in classical musical forms is much rarer and usually interpreted as an accidental deviation from the composer's main style (e.g. in Vaynberg, Basner). It is frequently condemned, as during the discussion of Vaynberg's Sinfonietta at the Composers' Union in 1948 when one of the leading musicologists was indignant that 'the music of *lapserdaks* and *peyses*' could be heard in Soviet music.[94] Yet a little later Tikhon Khrennikov, the General Secretary of the Composers' Union from 1948 onwards and Party spokesman for official music policy, decided to use this same Sinfonietta for propaganda and praised the composer as an example of 're-orientation' after the Resolutions on Music of 10 February 1948: 'We now have to check how our composers are liberating themselves from formalism, how they are fulfilling the Party's directives . . . how they are using the great treasures of folk art, how they are defending the national character of Soviet music against the reactionary idioms of bourgeois cosmopolitanism'.[95] During the antisemitic orgy of 1948-49, what could be better for world display than to give Vaynberg as an example? Khrennikov continues:

> As a composer he [Vaynberg] was strongly influenced by Modernistic music which badly mangled his undoubted talent. By turning to the sources of Jewish folk music, Vaynberg has created a bright, optimistic work dedicated to the theme of the shining, free working life of the Jewish people in the land of socialism. In this work Vaynberg has shown uncommon mastery and a wealth of creative imagination.[96]

After this dithyramb, extraordinary for the conditions of those times, the work was performed several times and then increasingly avoided. Today the Jewish idiom of the work is completely ignored and not even mentioned in articles about Vaynberg or in Soviet music history books.[97] Such are the complex, ambiguous destinies of a Jewish piece in Soviet music.

The authorities are more willing to accept Jewish musicians if they avoid their national idiom and contribute to Soviet music based on the idiom of the main nationalities of the USSR. Thus there emerged a new generation of talented Jewish composers who, unlike the older generation (Gnesin, Krein, etc.), turn to their Jewishness only occasionally and mainly work in the style of other national idioms or in a non-national, modern style which itself is not encouraged by Soviet ideology. This group includes musicians who are regarded as the most talented Soviet composers.

Yuri Levitin (b. 1912), a highly gifted composer, has written an opera, oratorios (Stalin Prize in 1952) and many works of symphonic and chamber music. He is active in the field of the Ukrainian and Russian mass song or writes in a modern, non-national style. However, he has often been accused of a 'dry and rational manner' or of 'a not sufficiently convincing interpretation of the heroic' in Soviet music,[98] while if he attempts a more Jewish idiom the reaction becomes sharper. Thus, the music for his song cycle 'Letters from Prison', based on Nazim Hikmet's texts, was criticized as 'not individual, with some [quite unexpected!] elements of Eastern song'.[99] By the mid-1960s Levitin was regarded as an established composer, conservative enough not to be dangerous and modern enough not to be entirely neglected by the younger generation. The authorities could rely on him, as we see from the policy article he wrote on the situation in Soviet music in the Party newspaper *Pravda* (20 June 1965).

Moisey Vaynberg (b. 1919), whom we have already mentioned, came to the Soviet Union to study in 1939 and, when the Germans entered his native Warsaw, remained there. He is considered to be one of the top Soviet composers and one of the close followers of Shostakovich. He was married to Mikhoels's daughter and was therefore a victim of the anti-Jewish persecution: he was arrested in January 1953 without charge and was released in March after Stalin's death. His work includes four operas, three ballets, eleven symphonies, twelve quartets, some instrumental concertos, numerous pieces of chamber music, about one hundred songs, film music, etc. It is mainly based on Moldavian, Russian, Byelorussian, Polish, Uzbek and Armenian folklore or else written with no connection with a particular national idiom. The Jewish idiom appears, as mentioned above, in the 'Sinfonietta' and also in a 'Trio' of 1943 and some songs of the 1940s based on poems by Y.L. Perets. Vaynberg is defined in the Soviet music encyclopaedia as 'one of the great Soviet symphonists',[100] but even so he has never received, in the Soviet Union, full official recognition or wide recognition in music-listening circles. His fate is characterized by the 'contradiction between the high and deserved recognition of Vaynberg's talent in professional musical circles and his relatively small popularity in wider circles of listeners', as a musicologist wrote in *Sovetskaya muzyka*, going on to complain that concert organizers made no attempt to have Vaynberg's works played, and some of these had yet to be performed: 'No musicological article has been written about a composer who has composed such a vast number of works, while special articles or even brochures are written about composers who have only just graduated from the conservatory!'[101] This was written in 1960. Since then there has been no other article on Vaynberg. 'Why should you Jewish students . . .?'

Venyamin Basner (b. 1925) is well known both in the field of symphonic-chamber music, popular mass song, operetta and folk music. The love for music in the simple Jewish families of cobblers, the Basners, and, on his mother's side, the Greditors, had a strong impact on the young composer. He has remembered some of the Jewish melodies he heard from his father and grandfather and used them in his works, for example, in the 'Third Quartet'.[102] This was written in 1960 and is recognized as one of his best works, and the 'Scherzo' of the 'Quartet' in which the Jewish element appears is the most significant movement of the work. Here the Jewish heart of the composer opened in impetuous joy and suppressed pain. Most of his works, however, have no connection with his Jewishness, neither in title nor in content.

The group of Soviet 'Modernists', insofar as this term is applied to composers who use some dodecaphonic or aleatoric elements, includes the Moscow Jewish composers Alfred Shnitke (b. 1934), who has written a number of vocal-instrumental and pure instrumental works, and Romuald Grinblat (b. 1930), until 1972 in Riga and now in Leningrad, who has composed two ballets, five symphonies, chamber and film music. Both of these composers have often been criticized. Their works are not officially banned but are none the less ignored by philharmonic organizations.[103] They are regarded in professional circles as talented composers. There are other composers of Jewish origin in this group, such as Yuri Falik and Lazar Feygin.

We have no right to end an account of Soviet composers connected with the Jewish people or the Jewish idiom without mentioning the greatest and most famous Soviet musician, Dmitry Shostakovich. The tragic personality of this man is a subject to be discussed elsewhere. What concerns us here is his position on the Jewish question. Let us set aside his personal, unpublished pronouncements and sympathies:[104] he belongs to that section of the Soviet Russian intelligentsia whose views are often controversial, which sees in the Soviet Jewish situation a human tragedy and which, in its sympathy towards the Jews, expresses a kind of protest against the regime. The publication of collections of Jewish folk songs over the past ten years has usually been carried out under D. Shostakovich's supervision (e.g. the above-mentioned publication by Z. Kompaneets in 1970). But when we turn to his work, a mere list of the compositions in which he uses Jewish melodies, intonations or subjects is sufficiently eloquent:

Trio, Op. 67, 1944, written in memory of his close friend, the musicologist I. Sollertinsky, who was denounced by the Soviet authorities, at a time when the Russian intelligentsia became aware of the real dimensions of the Holocaust.

Concerto for Violin and Orchestra, Op. 77; Vocal Cycle 'From Jewish Folk Poetry', Op. 79, both written in 1948 during the Soviet Jewish tragedy. Both works were first performed only in 1955. The choice of texts for vocal cycle is significant: eight of the eleven songs are tragic and some have clear connotations, such as the songs 'Warning', 'Lament on a Dead Infant', 'The Abandoned Father', 'The Song of a Girl'.

Quartet No. 4, Op. 83, 1949, written in the year of the mass arrests of Jews and first performed only in 1953.

Quartet, No. 8, Op. 110, 1960, an autobiographical work with the use of the DSCH theme,[105] a symbol of personal identification.

Symphony No. 13, Op. 113, 1962, inspired by Evtushenko's poem 'Baby Yar', which had been attacked by Khrushchev. Shostakovich first wrote a symphonic poem 'Baby Yar' and then turned it into the first movement of the Thirteenth Symphony, adding some other poems by Evtushenko.

In the 1950s and 1960s a new movement for Jewish national renaissance emerged in the Soviet Union as the result of various internal social and external political events: the suppression of Jewish spiritual life in the Soviet Union, the Soviet authorities' antisemitic actions, the establishment of the State of Israel and Soviet hostility to this State, the suppression of freedom in the Soviet Union and short periods of limited liberalization, certain cultural contacts between East and West, etc. Just as antisemitism was combined with political dictatorship and artistic conformity, so the Jewish renaissance of this period was linked with the Russian democratic (civil rights) movement and progressive tendencies in art. Both the act of self-expression in art by Jews and the act of solidarity by non-Jewish musicians became, in Soviet conditions, a symbol of humanism and resistance. National self-expression and self-determination were equal to human resistance. We have mentioned the creative work of D. Shostakovich. Another example is the Jewish song.

A new development in the field of Jewish song emerged in the late 1950s. Ruth Rubin is only partly right when she says that the 'Soviet-Yiddish folk songs of the Second World War were the close of Yiddish folk song in the USSR' and that 'with the tragic destruction of Yiddish cultural institutions and of many prominent Jewish men of letters during the years 1948-53 this phase of Yiddish song may also have been brought to an abrupt end'.[106] It was only a phase which had come to an end. In the late 1950s the Yiddish song received fresh impetus, new life and new development. Jews started to hum and whistle the song 'Yankele—You Have to Learn Khumesh'. In the early 1960s 'The Song of Baby Yar' and later 'Next Year in Jerusalem' or 'Pharaoh, Let My People Go'[107] were being sung by Jews in groups and private meetings, at home and at Holocaust memorial places (Baby Yar near Kiev, Rumbula near Riga, Paneri near Vilnius, Devyaty Fort near Kaunas), as well as outside the Moscow Synagogue on Arkhipov Street.

The Jewish song is one of the most exciting developments in the history of Soviet Jewry: after the complete destruction of Jewish cultural life in the Soviet Union, when there was a ban on Jewish language and art, there suddenly emerged in the mid-1950s a spiritual safety-valve, born by the creative instinct of the people. A number of amateur and semi-professional singers and reciters, not always sufficiently educated or artistically perfect, began to perform Jewish folk songs at concerts, first in various club-houses at amateur evenings and in amateur groups, then on more professional stages, and finally in philharmonic halls.

Amateur choirs were organized in Riga and Vilnius in club-houses.[108] They were active intermittently until finally closed in the mid-1960s. The first Jewish folk song concert after more than ten years of silence took place on 1 August 1955 and was given by Saul Lyubimov who had returned home after exile under Stalin. The concert hall was packed and the success, despite a fairly modest artistic level, was tremendous.[109] Lyubimov performed his programme of Jewish songs in many cities (Kiev, Kharkov, Chelyabinsk, Ufa, Omsk, etc.). A number of other folk singers appeared: Mariana Gordon, Rozalia Golubeva, Loyter Yakubovich, Emil Gorovets. The popular Soviet vaudeville actress and singer Anna Guzik (b. 1908), daughter of the well-known Jewish actor Yakov Guzik, included some Jewish folk songs in nearly every concert. She relates how frequently she would hear only one thing from a somewhat frightened Jewish member of the audience: 'Thank you'.[110]

The repertoire of all these singers was based on the Yiddish folk song of middle and south Russia of the nineteenth century and they dared not overstep this limit: those 'old Jewish songs', as we are told, 'some with a hint of sadness, some . . . with a sad smile, others humorous and lively' all have one function: 'to recreate scenes of the past',[111] and so to show that the Jewish song and Jewish culture in general are a matter of the sad past in Tsarist Russia. Nevertheless, these concerts were enormously successful.

Some years later, at the end of the 1950s and the beginning of the 1960s, Jewish songs were being performed throughout the country, and in 1957 the number of people attending these concerts reached three million.[112] The Jewish song received new impetus when artists of a high level appeared in this genre. Mikhail Aleksandrovich (b. 1914), a cantor in Latvia before the Second World War, an excellent singer of the Italian school, became famous in the Soviet Union during the war and was regarded as one of the top Soviet singers. He was awarded the title of Honored Artist in 1947 and received a Stalin Prize in 1948. His participation in concerts at the front during the war brought him this recognition. In an order issued by the Leningrad Philharmonic Society we read; 'Deserving of special mention is the courageous and patriotic attitude of Mikhail Aleksandrovich . . . which was splendidly manifested during the Leningrad blockade when his concerts took place under sustained enemy fire.'[113] From the late 1950s he often included Jewish songs in his concert programmes. He would usually perform these songs as encores after the end of the programme. The Jewish audience knew of this habit and would wait impatiently for these songs to acclaim the artist not only as a singer but also as a Jew. And if for various reasons (frequently on the 'advice' of 'responsible workers of the Ministry of Culture') which were unknown to the audience he did not sing Jewish songs, the audience would go home disappointed and distressed despite his excellent performance of arias and Neapolitan songs.[114]

In the early 1960s Aleksandrovich's insistence on performing Jewish songs increased along with the opposition of the authorities. The Ukrainian and Byelorussian SSR were closed to him because he performed some Jewish songs at a concert in Kiev after the Philharmonic authorities had removed them from his programme. In 1945, at the first Jewish New Year after the war, he had sung as cantor at the Moscow Synagogue at the invitation of the Moscow Party and city authorities. His singing of the 'Prayer for the Dead' was arranged as a big propaganda show to which diplomats, television, radio and the press were invited. But now, in the early 1960s, he was told that he could not be entrusted with the education of a Soviet audience as he was a cantor. However, after two years' battle he was eventually permitted not only to include some Jewish songs in his programme but also to devote an entire part of the concert to them. None the less he never managed to obtain permission for a whole concert of Jewish songs. Aleksandrovich included in his repertoire not only arrangements by Milner, Kogan, Likhtenshteyn and Yampolsky, and folk songs, but also the 'Kaddish' (Prayer for the Dead) by Ravel, the 'Joseph Aria' from Méhul's opera 'Joseph in Egypt' and other classical works on Jewish themes. But the artist received the greatest satisfaction when he managed to perform, under a folk song title, a song such as '*Dos Yidishe Lid*' by Sinkop and could feel that the significance of the song for the present day was understood by the audience (*Men ruft im ben melakh/A yakhsn, a gvir/Un yedes land farmakht far im di tir*—He is called a King's son/A man of note of wealth/And every country shuts the door to him).

At the beginning of 1970 Mikhail Aleksandrovich applied to emigrate to Israel, and after a struggle of nearly two years (hunger strikes, petitions, demonstrations) without work or income, he received permission. Since then his name has been removed from Soviet reference books,[115] his records have been withdrawn from use on the radio, from music shops and libraries.

At the All-Union Competition of Variety Performers in 1958 the Vilna-born singer Nehama Lifshits (b. 1927), was awarded the first prize. From an early age she had listened to Jewish songs and sung them by herself. When her teacher at the Vilna Conservatory, N. Karnaviciane, first heard her sing a Jewish song she said: 'This is your mission'. Her success at a concert in December 1956 when she performed a Jewish song for the first time in public was decisive for her future. Some years later her performance was praised as high art:

> The great skill of the singer (N. Lifshits) is a veritable aesthetic synthesis of music and word. She brings to the listeners not only every intonation of the melody but also every detail of the text. Each song of the artist is a story in music, a complete genre scene or romantic novella, a three-minute story of human fate, or a humorous episode. Lifshits performs with so much sympathy and heart that we can no longer call it singing: she lives the feelings of her heroes . . . We cannot find another explanation for this except the shortest and, very likely, the only one: talent!

Thus writes the Soviet journal *Sovetskaya muzyka*, not overly generous with compliments.[116]

We have already mentioned the propagandist function her concerts were meant to perform in the Soviet Union and even more so abroad (Paris, Brussels, Vienna). Nevertheless her art spread throughout the country and hundreds of thousands listened to her Jewish songs. In nearly every Soviet city Jewish composers, both amateur (M. Gebirtik, E. Berdichever, B. Broder) and professional (I. Rozenfeld, D. Pokrass, G. Bruk, L. Kogan and the non-Jewish A. Barkauskas, etc.), started working in the field of the Jewish song and wrote specially for her. From 1961 she often sang at her concerts the song by D. Pokrass 'Hot Lands' ('Hot lands, how am I to find the road to you, how am I not to mistake the road?'). This song is from a play with a Soviet Revolutionary theme and therefore acceptable to the censor, but the sensitive Jewish audiences would interpret the words in their own way. People listened, hummed the songs with her and started to think. The effect of the Jewish song concerts became increasingly ambiguous: the audience's reaction was no longer one of pure musical enjoyment: 'Tears flowed down the joyous faces of the men and women in the audience, young and old people . . . they cried openly and unashamedly', relates one witness.[117] I myself remember some of Lifshits's concerts in Riga: a strange excitement imbued the halls of the Latvian Philharmonic Society. Simply attending a concert at which some ninety-five percent of the audience was Jewish was exciting: there was no place where Jews could meet except at the Jewish song concerts. And then the songs. Even if the performance was not always on the highest artistic level, every sound, every word was seized upon, overflowed with emotion and associations, was interpreted in every heart and mind in a hundred ways. This was the rebirth of national feelings and aspirations, of national consciousness and pride. The storm of applause which thundered through the hall and the pride contained in this applause expressed the pride of a people.

In the mid- and especially the late 1960s the situation became more difficult. Several concert halls were closed to Lifshits and to Jewish songs in general. These concerts had to take place in clubs or suburban halls. By the end of the 1960s she could perform only in her native republic of Lithuania where she was still employed as soloist of the Philharmonic Society. The pressure on Jewish songs and culture grew every day along with the anti-Israel and anti-Jewish campaign in the Soviet media and the systematic expulsion of Jews from Soviet musical life. With this development the Jewish song changed its social status from being the Jewish folk song officially accepted and used for propaganda to being the persecuted Jewish resistance and underground song.

These songs were composed or emerged spontaneously in collective creative spirit, as is the case with folk music. They were born in the Nazi ghettoes, changed their function and turned into resistance songs, were composed by Jewish partisans in the Second World War, and now were sung in new conditions. They were composed in secret in forests and Soviet labor camps, transmitted orally and preserved in the people's memory. They are sung in the family or at private gatherings, at memorial places outside the towns, at cemeteries or outside synagogues. They are sung during the arrest of Jewish emigration activists. These songs often have weak texts and melodies borrowed from other songs, or weak melodies and somewhat altered, borrowed texts. They are sung in Russian, Yiddish and occasionally Hebrew or with all these languages combined in one song, like the spoken language of Soviet Jews. They are lyrical, fiery, heroic or full of gentle humor. One feature alone unites them and secured their popularity: they are imbued with a people's aspiration to national self-expression and self-determination. Some of the songs have been brought to the West secretly and edited by folk music specialists in the USA. An excellent example is the record by Theodore Bikel and Issachar Miron, 'Silent No More' (Star Record Co.), which includes the best Soviet Jewish underground songs. The song 'Pharaoh—Let My People Go', based on Soviet marching-song intonations, appeals to historical analogies and so seemed to be less dangerous although its subject is perhaps the sharpest. It was frequently sung during the arrests of groups of Jews protesting at the Party Central Committee or Supreme Soviet in Moscow:

Oh Pharaoh, Pharaoh, I tell you—Let my people go!
Let the Jewish people go to their proper homeland,
I shall never tire of repeating: Let my people go!
At your peril, at your peril do not keep my people.
To the Lord's own country let my people go.

A gypsy melody and changed text is used in the song 'O My Clumsy Heart':

So often in my dreams a wondrous land appears;
A land of blue skies and a red sea.[118]

We hear Jewish intonations in the song 'Our People Lives':

Our beautiful bright star will
Wondrously light our way.
Let them know, let them hear
Our song which says: We are alive!

Military motifs appear in a song similar to a Soviet mass song:

We are marching into dawn patrol;
The third wind blows out of the Sinai Desert.

Full of humor mixed with patriotic feelings is a song based on the old Russian song 'Once Again', half in Yiddish and half in Russian:

Outside there is a frost,
A real Russian snowstorm.
May our enemies perish—
I can hardly believe it could happen.

General Moshe Dayan—
He the angry one—[119]
Will not let the Jews
Be thrown out of Israel

Though they deliver more new MiGs
And new Katiusha rockets,
Yet the Fascist still will perish,
We will rock him fast asleep.

Frequently, as already mentioned, well-known Soviet mass songs were sung with a certain concealed meaning, a new interpretation of the words. This is the case with the song by I. Frenkel with the text of K. Vanshenkin:

It happened so that I am now far away
From our city,
Between us is an endless way
Which only in dreams is short.
The taiga is whispering above the snow-covered valley . . .

This song was sung in memory of the 'Prisoners of Zion' in Soviet labor camps.

The Soviet Jewish underground song is a new historical phenomenon, not older than the early 1970s, but it is a most important subject of musical folklore which deserves careful analysis in the future. These songs are a new contribution of Soviet Jewry to Jewish and Soviet music.

We may formulate the situation of the Jews and the Jewish idiom in Soviet music at the present time as follows: a narrow margin of official Jewish musical culture is permitted for the purpose of propaganda; a somewhat broader participation of Jews in different fields of music is possible if they neglect their Jewish heritage. The policy of the authorities is moving towards the complete assimilation of Jews and Jewish music. As a result, a movement of Jewish national renaissance was born and Jewish underground music and musicology are now developing, historically linked to the Soviet liberal dissident movement.

The chapter of Jewish music in the Soviet Union and of the Jews in Soviet music is not yet closed, for a people's spirit—the Jewish people's spirit—cannot be destroyed.

Notes

1 J. Heskes and A. Wolfson, *The Historical Contribution of Russian Jewry to Jewish Music* (National Jewish Music Council, 1967).
2 E.G. Mlotek, 'Jewish Soviet life as reflected in the Jewish folk song', *The Workman's Circle Call*, January 1963, 13-16.
3 Gershon Svet, 'Evrei v russkoy muzykalnoy kulture v sovetskom periode' (Jews in Russian musical culture in the Soviet period), in *Kniga o russkom evreystve: (1917-67)* (Book on Russian Jewry) (New York 1968), 248-65.
4 *Istoriya muzyki narodov SSSR* (History of the Music of the Peoples of the USSR), vols. 1-5 (Moscow 1970-74).
5 We refer to the work by M. Beregovsky (see below in the text).
6 This table is based on Soviet and Western sources and the personal archive of the author. It is possible that some items were unavailable to the author, but this in no way alters the general picture.
7 *Sovetskaya muzyka*, no. 8, 1970, 104.

The typescript of this article was completed in 1974. Circumstances have prevented re-writing or up-dating the information to reflect developments since then. In 1977 a version of this article was published by the Soviet and East European Research Centre of the Hebrew University of Jerusalem (Research Paper no. 22, mimeographed). Additional findings are reflected in Joachim Braun's Jews and Jewish Elements in Soviet Music *(Tel Aviv 1978); 'The Jewish national school in Russia', in* Proceedings of the World Congress on Jewish Music: Jerusalem 1978, *ed. J. Cohen (Tel Aviv 1982), 198-204; 'The double-meaning of Jewish elements in the music of Dmitry Shostakovich', paper at the 13th Congress of the International Musicological Society (Strasbourg 1982).*

8 The anonymous entry on Jewish music seems to be written by M. Gnesin, as emerges from comparing it with some of his other writings.
9 *Bolshaya sovetskaya entsiklopediya* (Moscow 1952), 'Jews'.
10 *Entsiklopedichesky muzykalny slovar* (Encyclopaedic Dictionary of Music) (henceforth *EMS*) (Moscow 1966), 172. Soviet reference books give only officially approved bibliography. In this connection it is interesting to quote two sources: 'In music . . . more and more forces emeged which destroyed harmony and melody and excluded all content from music. We now have music without logic, but which demands high virtuosity from the performers. This begins with the Jew Mahler; Schoenberg is their apostle . . . Among the young composers are Ksenek, Berg, Hindemith, Stravinsky . . . Their aim is the destruction of the Western tone system . . . through dissonance' (Müller von Azov, see Th. Fritsch, *Handbuch der Judenfrage*, 329). 'The characteristic of this music is the negation of classical music, the propagation of atonality, dissonance . . . negation of melody and logic, passion for chaos. This music . . . ruins the art of music.' 'What was started in the school of Arnold Schoenberg and in the expressionism of Alban Berg and Anton Webern, was developed by Ksenek and Hindemith and finished by Messiaen, Menotti and Britten . . . ' (Resolution of the Central Committee of the CPSU of 10 February 1948, and paper by B. Asafev at the First Congress of Soviet Composers, Stenographic Report (Moscow 1948), 16).
11 A. Soltes, 'The Hebrew Folk Song Society of Petersburg', in Heskes and Wolfson, *The Historical Contribution* . . .M. Glinka (1804-57) is the founder of Russian national music.
12 See A. Weisser, *The Modern Renaissance of Jewish Music* (New York 1954), 45.
13 Weisser, ibid., gives a complete list of its publications on pp.67-9.
14 L. Sabanejev, *Die nationale jüdische Schule in der Musik* (Vienna 1927), 24-5.
15 J. Yasser, 'The Hebrew Folk Song Society', in Heskes and Wolfson, *The Historical Contribution* . . .41. This is the only statement so far by an eyewitness of the events. No records from Soviet sources are available. We may assume that a certain element of self-dissolution was also present.
16 V.I. Lenin, *Polnoe sobranie sochineniy* (Complete Works), vol. 35, 2.
17 Klara Zetkin quoted in Louis Fisher, *The Life of Lenin* (New York 1967), 490.
18 M.F. Gnesin, *Stati, vospominaniya, materialy* (Articles, Reminiscences, Materials) (Moscow 1961), 7.
19 S.E. Feynberg, *Pianizm kak iskusstvo* (Piano-playing as Art) (Moscow 1969), 5-6.
20 A.V. Lunacharsky, *V mire muzyki* (In the World of Music) (Moscow 1958), 552.
21 Yuri Fayer, *O sebe, o muzyke, o balete* (About Myself, Music and Ballet) (Moscow 1970), 96.
22 Gnesin, 202.
23 *EMS*, 120.
24 Archive of I. Akhron, Jewish Music Institute, The Hebrew University, Jerusalem, Mus 12, j 13, Letter from M. Norenko to I. Akhron, 14 August 1933.
25 Gnesin, 202.
26 USSR Society for Cultural Relations with Foreign Countries—a secret department of the KGB, like every institution of this kind in the USSR.

27 Gnesin, op. cit., 196.
28 A. Khachaturian, 'Slovo o moem pervom uchitele' (A word about my first teacher), ibid., 231-2.
29 An article for the nineteenth anniversary of the composer's birth in *Sovetskaya muzyka,* no. 3, 1973, 138, makes one reference to Gnesin's connection with Jewish art: 'Gnesin successfully used in his works Russian, Ukrainian, Azerbaydzhani, Armenian, Chuvash, Jewish, Latvian, Mari, Morodovian, Kazakh and Adygey melodies.'
30 A. Krein, 'O muzyke k *Zagbuku* (On the music to *Zagbuk*) in A. Glebov, *Zagbuk*, 17.
31 Ibid., 3.
32 The well-known cellist and composer Yoakhim Stuchevsky told this to the author.
33 Y. Krein and N. Rogozhina, *Aleksandr Krein* (Moscow 1964).
34 Article in *Novoe russkoe slovo* quoted in *Kniga o russkom evreystve . . .*, 262.
35 Weisser, 95.
36 *Istoriya muzyki narodov SSSR*, vol. 1, 57.
37 I. Glebov, 'Perspektivy russkoy muzyki' (Prospects for Russian music), *Zhizn iskusstva*, no. 1, 1926.
38 *Istoriya muzyki narodov SSSR*, vol. 1, 207.
39 Ibid., vol. 2, 163-4.
40 *Sovetskaya muzyka*, no. 5, 1935, 32.
41 Ibid., no. 2, 1951. During the 1950-52 'anti-cosmopolitan campaign' the word 'cosmopolitan' was synonymous with 'Jew'.
42 N. Mikhaylovskaya, *Zara Levin* (Moscow 1969), 5.
43 *Sovetskaya muzyka*, no. 5, 1936.
44 (i) *100 let Leningradskoy konservatorii* (100 Years of the Leningrad Conservatory) (Leningrad 1962); (ii) *Moskovskaya konservatoriya (1866-1966) (The Moscow Conservatory, 1866-1966)* (Moscow 1966). The overall number of Jewish teachers in the Leningrad Conservatory from 1917 to the mid-1960s was about 160, i.e. about twenty percent of the entire teaching staff (see (i), 219-85), and at the Moscow Conservatory about 150 ((ii), 642-88), that is, about fifteen percent. This and other figures on the origin and nationality of the musicians are given somewhat approximately. As complete information cannot be obtained from Soviet sources, this calculation is based on name studies, indirect evidence, and the author's personal sources. In any case, the small degree of uncertainty cannot change the general picture.
45 *Izvestiya*, 15 March 1923.
46 See L. Raaben, *Mastera Gliretskogo kamerno-instrumentalnogo ansamblya* (Masters of the Glière Chamber-Instrumental Ensemble) (Leningrad 1964).
47 Quoted from B. Schwartz, *Music and Musical Life in Soviet Russia, 1917-1970* (New York 1970), 47.
48 All folk songs are quoted in the translation by Ruth Rubin, *Voices of a People* (New York/London 1963), 405, 407.
49 Letter from M. Morgalin to his grandson, Iosif Akhron, Leningrad, 3 May 1926, The National and Hebrew University Library, Jerusalem, Mus 12, j 1.
50 *Sovetskaya muzyka*, no. 8, 1970, 105.
51 Changri is in Turkey.
52 *Istoriya muzyki narodov SSSR*, vol. 1, 359.
53 *EMS: Soyuz kompozitorov SSSR* (Moscow 1968). We have not considered

republics with long musical traditions (the Ukraine, Byelorussia, Latvia, Lithuania, Estonia, Armenia and Georgia). Cf. some forty Russian composers awarded titles in the areas under consideration.

54 This and some following statements are based on an analysis of Soviet sources: *Sovetskaya muzyka*, newspapers, music, encyclopaedias, the book *Muzykalnye konkursy v proshlom i nastoyashchem* (Music Competitions in the Past and Present) (Moscow 1966), and the books referred to above on the Moscow and Leningrad Conservatories.

55 In 1927—G. Ginzburg; 1932—A. Lufer, L. Segalov, T. Gutman, E. Grossman; 1937—:I. Zak, R. Tamarkina, T. Goldfarb; 1949—B. Davidovich, V. Merzhanov; 1955—V. Ashkenazi, N. Shtarkman, D. Paperno; 1960—I. Zaritskaya.

56 In 1935—D. Oistrakh, B. Goldshteyn; 1952—I. Oistrakh, I. Sitnovetsky; 1957—R. Fayn, M. Komisarov; 1962—M. Rusin.

57 In 1937—D. Oistrakh, E. Gilels, B. Goldshteyn, M. Fikhtengolts; 1951—L. Kogan, M. Vayman; 1955—I. Sitnovetsky, V. Pikayzen, I. Politkovsky; 1959—A. Markov, R. Sobolevsky; 1963—A. Mikhlin, S. Snitkovsky.

58 In 1938—E. Gilels, I. Flier; 1956—V. Ashkenazi, L. Berman; 1964—E. Mogilevsky.

59 In 1953—N. Shkolnikova, R. Sobolevsky; 1955—E. Grach; 1957—B. Gutnikov, V. Pikayzen, I. Politkovsky; 1961—V. Zhuk; 1963—V. Lantsman, R. Nodel, N. Beylina.

60 In 1958—violin: V. Pikayzen, M. Lubotsky, V. Liberman, V. Zhuk; piano: N. Shtarkman, E. Myansarov; 1962—cello: V. Feygin, N. Gutman, M. Khomitser; violin: B. Gutnikov, N. Beylina, A. Markov, E. Grach; piano: V. Ashkenazi.

61 *Moskovskaya konservatoriya . . .* , 412; F. Blumenfeld, S. Feynberg, M. Nemenova-Lunts, A. Shatskes, G. Ginzburg, E. Gilels, I. Flier, I. Zak, T. Gutman, E. Grossman, A. Yokheles, L. Levinson, I. Milshteyn, B. Berlin, V. Natanson.

62 Ibid., 446-62; M. Press, D. Krein, A. Mogilevsky, L. Tseytlin, B. Sibor, A. Yampolsky, B. Belensky, D. Oistrakh, I. Oistrakh, P. Bondarenko, I. Bezrodny, I. Yankelevich, L. Kogan, I. Rabinovich, M. Pitkus, M. Polyakin, N. Blinder.

63 Ibid., 450; I. Rabinovich, L. Kogan, I. Bezrodny, P. Bondarenko, A. Amiton, I. Yankelevich, Y. Targonsky, M. Pitkus, I. Sitnovetsky, N. Beylina, M. Lubotsky.

64 Some of the violinists, pianists and cellists I have named are *de facto* Jewish although not according to their Soviet passports, e.g. G. Kremer, I. Oistrakh, F. Hirshhorn. Some have left the USSR: F. Hirshhorn, V. Lantsman, M. Maysky, I. Zaritskaya, B. Goldshteyn are in Israel.

65 See L.Raaben, *Mastera . . .*

66 *Teatr*, no. 2, 1964, 187.

67 This was told to the author by the musician's widow, and for obvious reasons the name cannot yet be disclosed.

68 The following is a clear example of both the assimilation and the self-determination trends. When fourteen-year-old Oleg Kagan applied in 1961 for a place in the violin class of the Moscow Conservatory, the late Professor Isay Yankelevich wrote a letter to the boy's parents suggesting that since he was changing his native city of Riga for Moscow it would be the right moment to

change his nationality, too, from Jewish to Russian. In this case he would accept the new pupil. The boy's father refused and he entered the class of Professor B. Kuznetsov. This story is known to the author since he was then Kagan's violin teacher.

69 The reference book *Sovremennye dirizhery* (Contemporary Conductors), edited by L. Grigorev and I. Platek (Moscow 1969), names ninety-six Soviet conductors of whom twenty-eight are Jewish. As of 1 January 1969, nine out of twenty-nine theater orchestras are headed by Jewish conductors, and thirteen out of thirty-seven symphony orchestras (pp. 318-23).

70 *Moskovskaya konservatoriya . . . ,* 489.

71 S. Bolotin, *Biografichesky slovar muzykantov-ispolniteley na dukhovykh instrumentakh* (Biographical Dictionary of Musical Performers on Wind Instruments) (Leningrad 1969).

72 *Soyuz kompozitorov SSSR. Spravochnik na 1968 god* (USSR Union of Composers: Handbook for 1968) (Moscow 1968). A musicologist is accepted as a member of this union only if he has 'published works which are a contribution to Soviet musicology' (from the statutes of the Union).

73 *Osnovy materialnoy kultury v muzyke* (The Bases of Material Culture in Music) (Moscow 1924).

74 *Voprosy materialnoy kultury v muzyke* (Problems of Material Culture in Music) (Moscow 1931).

75 *Fantaziya f-moll Shopena. Opyt analiza* (Chopin's Fantasia in F Minor. An Attempt at Analysis) (Moscow 1937); *Stroenie muzykalnogo proizvedeniya* (The Construction of a Work of Music) (Moscow 1960).

76 *'Kamarinskaya' Glinki* (Glinka's *Kamarinskaya* (Moscow 1957)); *Muzykalnye zhanry i osnovy muzykalnykh form* (Musical Genres and the Bases of Musical Forms) (Moscow 1964); *Tselostny analiz muzykalnykh proizvedeniy i ego metodika* (Integral Analysis of Works of Music and its Methods), *Intonatsiya i muzykalny obraz* (Intonation and the Musical Image) (Moscow 1969).

77 L. Mazel, 'O putyakh razvitiya sovremmenoy muzyki' (On the paths of development of modern music). *Sovetskaya muzyka*, nos. 6, 7, 8, 1965.

78 *Vseobshchaya istoriya muzyki* (General History of Music), vol. I (Moscow 1956); *Istoriya muzykalnoy kultury* (History of Musical Culture), vols. I, 2 (Moscow 1941-59).

79 *Muzykalnye literatury narodov SSSR* (Musical Literatures of the Peoples of the USSR) (Leningrad 1963).

80 *Istoriya russkoy muzyki* (History of Russian Music), vols. 1-2 (Moscow 1940).

81 *Muzykalnaya entsiklopediya.*

82 We can quote as an example an article by I. Yampolsky (*Sovetskaya muzyka*, no. 10, 1959, 134) on the great Jewish musician Iosif Guzikov.

83 It was planned to open a similar institution in the same year at the Byelorussian Academy of Sciences, but the plan was not realized.

84 From the M. Beregovsky Archive at the Leningrad Institute for Theater, Music and Film. Quoted from A. Vinkovetsky, 'Evreysky muzykalny folklor v Rossii' (Jewish musical folklore in Russia) in the Soviet underground publication *Jews in the USSR* (in English: New York, September 1973, 91). The book Beregovsky refers to did not appear.

85 Not one of the Soviet reference books (*Muzykalnaya entsiklopediya,* vol. 1 (Moscow 1973)), 419; T. Bernandt and I. Yampolsky, *Kto pisal o muzyke* (Who Wrote about Music), vol. 1 (Moscow 1973), 87), can name an article by

Beregovsky on Ukrainian or Bashkir musical folklore.

86 Letter of D. Shostakovich of 3 November 1970, quoted by Vinkovetsky, 79.

87 G. Shneerson, K. Rozenshild, A. Sokhor and I. Nestev especially distinguished themselves in this field.

88 Books and articles by L. Mazel, I. Nestev, I. Belza, S. Sheyfshteyn, I. Vaynkop, D. Zhitomirsky, G. Kogan, V. Berkov, S. Ginzburg, R. Gruber, I. Rizhkin, A. Rabinovich.

89 Schwartz, 251.

90 These facts are known to the author from some of the participants in the events whose names cannot yet be revealed.

91 *Sovetskaya muzyka*, no. 2, 1949, 36.

92 The author knows of the oral order from the Deputy Minister of Culture of the Latvian SSR, who confirmed it during an audience at his office. I had the opportunity to read the 1969 order in the office of the Director of the Special Music School in Riga.

93 The figures in Tables 2 and 3 are based on Soviet sources mentioned previously. Information for recent years is approximate as the official sources are not always available.

94 Related by a composer who attended the meeting.

95 T. Khrennikov in *Sovetskaya muzyka*, no. 1, 1949, 21.

96 Ibid., 27.

97 Ibid., no. 1, 1960, 40-7; *Istoriya muzyki narodov SSSR*, vol. 4, 23.

98 *Istoriya muzyki narodov SSSR*, vol. 4, 188, 264.

99 Ibid., 294.

100 *Muzykalnaya entsiklopediya*, vol. 1, 649.

101 *Sovetskaya muzyka*, no. 1, 1960, 46-7.

102 I. Beletsky, *Venyamin Basner* (Leningrad-Moscow 1972), 7.

103 See *Sovetskaya muzyka*, no. 1, 1968, 24-5 for A. Shnitke's case. R. Grinblat's music was prohibited by the Director of the Philharmonic Society in Riga, F. Shveynik, a Jewish Party spokesman who became notorious throughout the Soviet Union for his hatred of any progressive movement in art as well as his hostility to Jewish musicians. His words to a group of Philharmonic Society workers and musicians when he was told that Nehama Lifshits was leaving for Israel are well known: 'I only hope that the first Arab bullet, which really is ours, will get her' (reported by L. Makhinson and other witnesses). Shveynik was also the one who provoked the arrest of several young Jews when he called for army units to come to the concert of Israeli singer Geulah Gil in Riga in 1966.

104 We have mentioned some of them: the letter to A. Vinkovetsky, his words after the death of Mikhoels, his friendship with M. Vaynberg.

105 DSCH are the first letters of Dmitry Shostakovich's name which the composer used for a musical theme: D = Re, S = Mi^{b}, C = Do, H = Si.

106 Rubin, (see footnote 48 above), 240.

107 The texts of the songs are published in Mlotek, (see footnote 2 above), 13, and the songs themselves recorded by Th. Bikel and J. Miron, *Silent No More* (Star Record Co., New York 1971).

108 See David Garber, 'Choir and drama in Riga' in *Soviet Jewish Affairs*, vol.4, no. 1, 1974, 39-44.

109 S. Schwartz, *Evrei v Sovetskom Soyuze* (Jews in the Soviet Union) (New York 1966), 283.

110 From conversations the author had with A. Guzik, Tel-Aviv, May 1974. A. Guzik and many other Jewish song performers (N. Lifshits, M. Aleksandrovich, E. Gorovets) left for Israel in the 1970s.
111 From the annotation to the record 'Recital by N. Lifshitsaite', D08341-42, *Mezhdunarodnaya kniga.*
112 S. Schwartz, 406.
113 N. Mikhaylovskaya (ed.), *Mikhail Aleksandrovich* (Moscow 1964), 2.
114 This and some other facts on Aleksandrovich's activities are known to the author from conversations with him in Tel-Aviv, February 1974, and from the personal reminiscences of the author.
115 The 1966 edition of the 'Encyclopaedia of Music' has an entry on him; the 1973 'Encyclopaedia', which is five times larger, has none.
116 *Sovetskaya muzyka*, no. 12, 1963, 88-90.
117 From M. Kolb's diary quoted in Mlotek, 14.
118 The English translations are from the record *'Silent No More'.*
119 The translation of this line has been changed to keep close to the original.

4

A Structural Study of Jews in Russian Literary Criticism, 1917-32

Benzion Munitz

The Soviet period of Modernism (1917-32)

The revolution as a stimulus of Modernism

The Revolution dealt a shattering blow to the surface of art. The pattern in the artistic kaleidoscope changed. Many of the avant-gardists who considered themselves revolutionaries in art accepted the Revolution as an actual social embodiment of their ideas. They became Bolsheviks. Others saw in the Revolution a retrogressive phenomenon.

In spite of the blow, the Revolution did not change or suppress the main artistic phenomenon which existed before the Revolution—the wide spectrum of artistic opinion and expression and of aesthetic views. On the contrary, it stimulated an even greater variety of artistic expression. The period of 1917-32 is therefore very special because it allowed the variety to exist, allowed different aesthetic schools to co-exist, allowed Modernism to flourish under the guise of Revolutionary art. Many pioneering ideas were initiated during that period.

The period was of a turbulent nature: continuous sharp debates, active struggle for or against use of the arts in the achievement of social ideals, and an intense preoccupation with the masses. On the whole, it was a predominantly Westernizing period and as such it was of great interest and importance to the Jews. They took a very active part in the artistic life of post-Revolutionary Russia and made a distinct Jewish contribution to it.

Because of such distinctiveness, the Jewish aspect of the period is of interest to the historian of Soviet literature as well as to the student of Jewish influences in host cultures.

The Revolutionary impetus brought Formalism into a prominent position in Russian artistic life during the period under consideration. The existence of Formalism makes it the most interesting period in the whole of Russian literature. It was a period of co-existence of two aesthetic schools, Formalism and the Sociological school. Formalism was part of a wider international artistic and cultural phenomenon, the second phase of modernism called avant-gardism. Formalism in its different manifestations was a cultural phenomenon of a period of internationalism when the Soviet Union, although a communist state, did not turn its back on the world. In such an open atmosphere Formalism could thrive in parallel with Western cultural-artistic developments, and its theoretical and artistic achievements were of an international standard.

In addition to internationalist aspirations, the other peculiarity of post-Revolutionary Russian Formalism was the involvement of some of its sections in the domestic, the specific Soviet political scene. This gave Russian Formalism a specific flavor and made it distinct from Western Formalism. Formalism could exist as long as Russia maintained its internationalist posture coupled with high intellectualism in cultural and artistic life. The lowering of standards to the level of the masses after 1932 resulted in the disappearance of Formalism. Formalism could not exist in a culture geared to the man-in-the-street: it was too intellectual for that. It had to give way to the monolithic Sociological method.

The other school of criticism which was forced out of existence much earlier, in 1922, was the Religious-Philosophical one. This happened through expulsion to the West of its main representatives, the emigration of others and intimidation into silence of the rest. The Soviet authorities were then behaving strictly in accordance with Marxist theory, and to them the religious writers, not the experimenters, were the enemy. But in the first years after the Revolution all the three major schools of Russian criticism which had emerged before the Revolution continued their activity.

The Revolution was a great stimulus of variety of opinion, and this resulted in the proliferation of artistic groups. The 1917-32 period was indeed a period of groups, most of them brought to life by the Revolution, and some continuing from the pre-Revolutionary era with certain adaptational modifications. The many groups were in conflict with each other. They were at odds in their attitudes to the nature of literature, its function and that of the creative writer in society, the relationship between art and reality. The group structure of literary life, the group orientation of creativity, was the dominant literary feature of the period. 'Almost all Soviet writers of the first years of the Revolution were members of one or another group. And if somebody was not a member, he was "affiliated", was close to, was drifting towards some group.'[1] The importance of literature as an ideological weapon in an atmosphere of tense class struggle was responsible for the fact that the varying aesthetic views of the groups were not the exclusive affair of the literary circles but a nationwide controversy, the cause of a debate which attracted the attention of a great part of the population and involved the Government and Party apparatus. As Russian society was steadily moving towards a monolithic, conformist, dogmatic political ideology, the apparent discrepancy of the existence of pluralism in aesthetics made the debate as much political as it was literary.

Due to the combination of aesthetics with politics, the views expressed by various groups require to be considered not only in their academic, artistic, professional context but also in their political context. The adoption of a certain political stand sometimes gave undeserved importance to the aesthetic views of a group. The groups had different interests, and politics was just one of the weapons they used to achieve their aims. Not every writer or critic was active in debate. Some of the groups were indeed engaged in a struggle for power and literary hegemony, in an attempt to silence and eliminate their opponents; some were advocating free creative competition, did not seek any privileges and did not intend to monopolize the literary scene; still others were on the defensive and went about their work silently, although holding on to their particular aesthetic views.

The variety of groups was characteristic of the fact that after a sudden change towards a new economic and political reality, nobody really knew what the new, communist art should be. Experiments were necessary, and the aesthetic platform of each group was in fact a theory on an experimental basis. That is why this was a period of a multitude of artistic declarations and manifestos.

Classification of the groups

The variety of the groups and the complexity of the debate conducted on several levels makes it difficult to map out the situation without some danger of schematism, but some attempt at systematization needs to be made. Our first task is thus to establish the positions of the groups on the literary battlefield. Each group occupied two basic positions: artistic and political. We shall consider them separately, although the groups usually presented a combined artistic-political front.

Jewish writers and critics were present in almost every literary group of the period. Table 1 gives a list of all groups in which Jews participated, classifies them according to method, and indicates their additional characteristics. The few groups which did not have Jewish members were not important enough to make any changes in, or add a new dimension to, the picture of the literary structure of the period as presented in Table 1.

During the group craze, numerous little groups were springing up all over the country, lasting for a short while, usually a few months, and then disappearing without trace. It would be impossible to make up a list of such little groups, but these were unimportant anyway. In addition to the groups listed below, there was also a group called Krug (The Circle) which was essentially Sociological and included a number of important Jewish writers. However, this group was too short-lived and indistinct to merit consideration here. The VOKP (All-Union Association of Peasant Writers) naturally did not have Jewish members as there was no Jewish peasantry.

Methodologically, the groups divide between the two schools of criticism which existed throughout the discussed period. Thus groups were either Sociological or Formalist.

Unavoidably, the labelling in Table 1 is in a number of cases arguable. The division is largely schematic because in reality there was not such a clear-cut distinction between the groups. The difficulty arises from the fact that the majority of the groups were methodologically eclectic, i.e. the work of their members presented a mixture of the Sociological and the Formal methods. The eclecticism was due to a number of reasons.

—The experimental nature of the groups. Some writers on social topics were experimenting with Formalist techniques, some Formalist groups had a political aspect which involved them in the sphere of the Sociological method.

—A literary group is a loose organization. It is not like a political party which is subject to discipline. It is in the nature of the creative process to search for the unknown embodiment of an idea, and the result of such a search is often a surprise to the author himself. Therefore it is not unusual that some writers unintentionally deviated from the theoretical principles of the manifestos of their groups—theories to which they consciously subscribed. (Critics were more consistent in the sphere of theory than were creative writers.)

—Some groups at the time were themselves not aware of the method to which they belonged, or of any necessity to adopt a particular method. They were continuously in a state of polemics and struggle. The ideas which inspired the groups were tentative, experimental, and this often involved indiscriminate borrowing from a variety of sources and from both literary schools.

—After the Revolution, the groups had to contend with the specific politicized intellectual climate in the country. They had to consider the pressure of the Party and the new ideology. Such pressure worked against the Formalist groups, making them more political and thus increasing the degree of their eclecticism.

For these reasons the allocation of a group with an indistinct S/F or

TABLE 1: METHODOLOGICAL DIVISION OF THE GROUPS
(see pp. 164-5 for explanation of acronyms)

Group	Duration	1917	1918	1919	1920	1921	1922	1923	1924	1925	1926	1927	1928	1929	1930	1931	1932	A or P	G or E
The Sociological groups																			
Proletkult	1917-22	●	●	●	●	●	●											P	E
Poets' Collective	1920-?[a]				●													A	E
Kuznitsa	1920-30				●	●	●	●	●	●	●	●	●	●	●			P	G
VAPP	1920-28				●	●	●	●	●	●	●	●	●					P	G
Serapion Brothers	1921-34					●	●	●	●	●	●	●	●	●	●	●	●	A	E
Pereval	1923-32							●	●	●	●	●	●	●	●	●	●	P	E
RAPP	1925-32									●	●	●	●	●	●	●	●	P	G
VOAPP	1928-32												●	●	●	●	●	P	G
LOKAF	1930-34														●	●	●	P	G
Litfront	Aug-Nov 1930														●			P	G
The Formalist groups																			
Acmeists	1912-22	●	●	●	●	●	●											A	E
Tsentrifuga	1914-22	●	●	●	●	●	●											A	E
Moscow Linguistic Circle[b]	1915-21	●	●	●	●	●												A	G
OPOYAZ	1916-23	●	●	●	●	●	●	●										A	G
Imaginists	1919-24			●	●	●	●	●	●									A	E
Nichevoki	1920-23				●	●	●	●										A	E
Tvorchestvo	1920-22				●	●	●											P	E
Constructivists	1923-30							●	●	●	●	●	●	●	●			P	E
LEF	1923-28							●	●	●	●	●	●					P	E
REF	1929-30													●	●			P	E

a Year of dissolution unknown.
b Year of dissolution assumed.
Abbreviations: A – academic; P – polemical; G – genuine; E – eclectic.

F/S ratio to a particular method is a difficult task. It involves weighing up different aspects of a group, it requires deciding which of the methods used by a group is the prevailing one, which is the group's dominant characteristic. If a group was mainly preoccupied with social phenomena and Formalism was used only in an auxiliary role, then it is allocated to the Sociological school; if the other way round, it is allocated to the Formal school.

Perhaps, for greater precision, it would have been better to have four divisions instead of two: Pure Sociological, Eclectic Sociological, Pure Formal and Eclectic Formal. However, we decided not to go into such great detail, in order to avoid making the material too complex.

In addition to allocating groups to a method, Table 1 also distinguishes groups according to whether they were academic or polemical. The question of whether they were traditional or innovatory does not arise because all groups were innovatory. Traditional writers did not belong to any group. The division of the groups into polemical or academic was made according to whether (a) a group's first priority was pursuing an active policy of asserting its literary theory in its criticism directed against other theories, while its creative writing was playing a comparatively secondary role, or (b) a group's first preoccupation was literary scholarship, both theoretical and practical-analytical, in the classical sense, as well as a high standard of creative writing while polemics and power politics were of little or no interest.

The Sociological groups

Of the Sociological groups, those of the so-called 'proletarian' writers—Kuznitsa, RAPP, VAPP, VOAPP, LOKAF and Litfront—were purely Sociological in their method. The only exception was Proletkult. Those groups were devoted to the creation and propagation of special 'proletarian' art with the help of Marxism. They were doctrinaire in their approach to literature. All the remaining Sociological groups were eclectic.

Proletkult differed from the rest of the proletarian groups in that it was eclectic, incorporating elements of Formalism. The main theoretician of Proletkult, Bogdanov, had a theory of class exclusivity. According to him, each class creates its own culture, casting away all the past. Proletkult also followed the theories of the Austrian philosopher Ernst Mach (1838-1916), whose denial of the independent existence of all but sensations was severely criticized by Lenin. In creative writing, Proletkult propagated the theory of 'machinism', the imitation of machines in poetry. The latter was a purely Formalist device, more precisely—a Futurist device. Proletkult also shared with the Futurists an ardent desire to destroy the past.

Pereval was another eclectic group which most Western critics rate as the most significant within the Sociological method. The oddity of this group was in that although it was Marxist and supported the Party, it also stood up for artistic sincerity, for an 'organic union between the ideological and emotional vision of reality'.[2] The critics of this group 'tried to reconcile the group's desire to follow the Party line and its defense of the writer's individuality'.[3] The principal theoretician of the group was A.K. Voronsky, the editor of the most important literary magazine *Krasnaya nov* (Red Virgin Soil).[4] That is why Peveral is also known as 'the Voronsky group'.

Voronsky, a Marxist, subscribed to Trotsky's thesis that proletarian art was impossible. Because of that, he was severely attacked by the RAPP critics. Voronsky shared some of the philosophy of Henri Bergson, the intuitivist, specifically his theory of immediate impressions.

Kollektiv poetov (The Poets' Collective) is rather difficult to allocate because of its relative obscurity. According to some sources, it was a proletarian group. My information about it is that it was founded approximately in 1920 in Odessa by Lev Slavin, Ilya Ilf, Eduard Bagritsky and Yury Olesha. As the above writers were predominantly associated with the Sociological method, although not without certain flirtations with Formalism, the group appears to belong to the Sociological school.

The Serapion Brothers were artistically the most accomplished and the most durable of the Sociological groups. This was a group of experimental writers who were more devoted to the development of technical skills of writing than to social changes, although their writings did express an interest in social phenomena and included a social comment. Their ideal was art in its pure sense and their aim was to bring Russian writing up to the standards of Western writing. Although the principal theoretician of the group, Lev Lunts, was a pupil of the Formalists Shklovsky and Tynyanov, the group was not strictly Formalist. It was more of a Sociological group.

The Formalist groups

The list of Formalist groups in Table 1 can be divided into three sections: Futurist groups (Tsentrifuga, Tvorchestvo, Constructivists, LEF, REF), linguistics-orientated groups (Moscow Linguistic Circle, OPOYAZ), and style-orientated groups (Acmeists, Imaginists, Nichevoki).

Futurism was undoubtedly the most important Formalist trend. It influenced the creativity and the theoretical writings of the majority of Formalist groups. It consisted of a number of smaller factions which had certain theoretical differences with each other but which generally came under the heading of Futurism.

The distinctive feature of Futurist creativity was schematism. This schematism came into literary work from painting. Poems contained images of workers which resembled the schematic images on placards. Futurist art was preoccupied with the mass. The mass became the Futurist image of the Revolution.

The main thesis of post-Revolutionary Futurism was: the Revolution has brought new content and new content requires new form. The old forms, including the classical ones, represented an old content. That old content was unacceptable in a new era and had to be destroyed. Extreme Futurism advocated a total destruction of the past.

The participation of Jews in Futurist groups is significant. The destroy-the-past attitude appealed to the Jews more than to other nationalities, because of the strong assimilationist tendencies among the Russian Jewish intelligentsia.

Tsentrifuga (1914-22) was one of the earliest Futurist groups. In actual fact, it was a group which represented both neo-Symbolism and Futurism. The writings of the group's members contained pronounced Formalist elements. An important member of the group was Boris Pasternak who participated mainly as an expressionist poet.

Tvorchestvo (1920-22) was a markedly Futurist group which theoretically expounded LEF theories. It came into being in Vladivostok. Its main theoretician was N. Chuzhak. The group ceased its existence when most of its members moved to Moscow and joined the Futurist groups which were already in existence there.

Groups vary as to whether they are characterized mostly through their creative work or mostly through their theoretical writing. The LEF group (which in the beginning of 1929 became REF) was a group dominated by theory. It represented a blend of neo-Futurism, of the Formalist methodology, and Marxism. This blend found its expression on the pages of the *LEF* and *Novy LEF* magazines.

LEF differed from the linguistics-orientated groups in that the latter were true to the original theory of Formalism, i.e. were interested only in the literary form, while the former had a strong political and social awareness in addition to its commitment to the Formal method. The creative writings of the LEF members were modified versions of pre-Revolutionary Futurism. Original Futurism in the West was truly Formalist but Russian Futurism always had a social content and, in respect of subject-matter, was based in industry, in the activities of the industrial workers. Both leading members of LEF, Brik and Arvatov, were 'industrialists' in their attitudes to art. In spite of its politics, LEF was basically Formalist. It was one of the most important groups of the period, with great achievements in the theater and cinema. Meyerhold, Dziga Vertov, Esfir Shub and Eisenstein[5] were all LEFists. LEF served as a model for other critics who during the 1922-26 period produced many quasi-Formalist writings.

The Constructivists were another Futurist group, an offshoot of LEF. They were another version of the so-called 'leftist art' which combined industrialism with Formalism and 'industrial art' with political support for Bolshevism. 'Industrial art' implied imitation or copying of industrial processes in a work of art. The production of literary forms which were imitative of industrial processes was the basis of their creative writing and the main idea of their theoretical thinking. As industrialization was the main political preoccupation of the time, the Constructivists thought they were making a valuable contribution to the country's constructive effort. Their literature was very topical, politically in tune with the Party. Nevertheless, the Constructivist writers' interest in the literary form was greater than their interest in social phenomena.

The linguistics-orientated groups consisted of critics who represented original and genuine Formalism. There were only critics among them, not creative writers. They were the ones who created Russian Formalism. The authentic Russian Formalist movement was born in Moscow and Petersburg almost simultaneously, in 1915 and 1916 respectively, through the creation of two groups, the Moscow Linguistic Circle and OPOYAZ (Society for the Study of Poetic Language). The emergence of OPOYAZ criticism was due to a number of influencing factors, one of which was Futurism which came into being somewhat earlier. Here is how Erlich explains the motivation of the Formalist critics:

> To evolve a new poetics—to vindicate theoretically the Futurist revolution in Russian verse—was the task which called for the efforts of professional students of literature, conversant with, and sympathetic to, the new poetry. Such a critical movement had indeed come into being. Two parallel trends converged: if the poet needed the assistance of the literary scholar, the latter sought in his alliance with the literary avant-garde a way out of the impasse reached by the academic study of literature.[6]

The Acmeists appeared in 1912 as a splinter group of Symbolism. Their writing represented a marriage of Symbolism with Formalism, but their interest in the poetic form was greater than that of their predecessors, the Symbolists.

The Imaginists were a splinter group of Futurism. Initially, Imaginism consisted of only three poets: Shershenevich, Mariengof, and Esenin. The group was essentially Formalist. The characteristic interest of its poets was the word as a metaphor. Politically, Imaginism expounded individualist anarchism.

Nichevoki (Nothingers) was a group which imitated the Imaginists. There was nothing original about them. They had a number of Jews among their members.

Political classification of the groups

The question of whether a group was political or purely artistic (i.e. apolitical) is rooted in the basic controversy of Russian literature which started long before the establishment of the Soviet regime, at the beginnings of Russian statehood, during the time of Ivan the Terrible. This controversy, or perhaps conflict, has been a permanent feature of Russian history ever since, and reached its peak of sharpness under the Bolsheviks. Striving to create a strong nationalistic state, Ivan the Terrible in his letters to an exiled nobleman Kurbsky advanced the idea that the wellbeing of the state should be the first priority of any citizen, including a writer. Therefore, patriotic participation in a literature which is controlled by state interests and conscious manipulation of one's creative instinct in order to produce didactic writings, should be a writer's highest aim.

This idea started the continuous controversy, as it provoked the opposition of the advocates of independent art who sought for the artist an autonomous position in society, a position free from social obligations and dictates of the state, because, as some would say, an artist's work was not a conscious expression of the human will but a subconscious expression of Divine Truth, or, as others would say, a genuine artist's work was an expression of a total human truth which is achieved through free investigation and contemplation of man in *all* his relations to life, not limited by any particular ideology or interest.

Politically, i.e. in accordance with their attitude to the issue of the nature of the creative process of the artist in society, the groups divide as follows.

Political groups: Proletkult, Kuznitsa, RAPP, VAPP, VOAPP, LOKAF, Litfront, Pereval, LEF, REF, Tvorchestvo, Constructivists.

Apolitical groups: Acmeists, Tsentrifuga, Poets' Collective, Nichevoki, Imaginists, Serapion Brothers, OPOYAZ, Moscow Linguistic Circle.

Among the political groups, those of the proletarian variety were a natural attraction for committed Party members as those groups insistently claimed that only they were the true interpreters of Marxism in art. Nevertheless, all other political groups equally claimed true adherence to Marxism, at the same time disagreeing with the 'proletarians' in the artistic sphere.

One such opponent of the 'proletarians', the Pereval group, was an expression of Trotsky's views until he was 'unmasked'; after that this group amended its political standing. The proletarian groups and Pereval were composed mainly of writers of the new type, writers created by the Revolution. As for LEF, REF, Tvorchestvo, and the Constructivists, they were, in spite of their Bolshevik proclamations, less politically-minded than the other eight. They were essentially fellow-traveller groups consisting of radicalized representatives of the old intelligentsia.

The apolitical (artistic) groups tried to avoid politics as much as possible. If they did produce an occasional work on a political subject, this was a reluctant bow in the direction of the political realities, the result of the Party's pressure on writers. The artistic groups consisted either of fellow-travellers or of latent critics of the regime.

A list of Jewish Russian critics of the Soviet period of Modernism

Jewish literary critics and theoreticians of the 1917-32 period

The following is a list, as far as sources make possible, of Jews who participated in literary criticism during the period treated in this article, categorized by method (S = Sociological, F = Formal and R = Religious-Philosophical) and by academic or polemical bent. A dash (rather than a question mark) indicates that ascription to a school or a group could not be justified by the information at present available. Lack of information is the reason for the many question marks in the list.

The aim of this essay is to take a very preliminary step towards systematic study of Jewish participation in Soviet Russian literature, by providing raw material for one genre (literary criticism) during one period (1917-32). Nevertheless, in view of the limitations on sources even this step must be tentative and is made in the hope that further work will correct as well as develop it. Although in the late Tsarist and early Soviet conditions, groupings and labels are much more definable and natural than could be the case in the West, such ascription has often depended on a balance of the writer's judgement depending on available sources. Other researchers might well disagree, especially in the light of fuller information.

The problem of Jewish identification

Identification of Jews in a non-Jewish literature is always a problem. The difficulty in identifying Jews in Soviet Russian literature derives from the Soviet policy of classifying writers on the basis of their linguistic, not ethnic, belonging. Thus, if a Jew writes in any language other than Yiddish, he is described in the Soviet sources as a member of the nationality whose language he uses for writing. As a result, the majority of Jewish writers are classified as Russians.

My task in compiling the list of critics was to go through the sources indicated in the appended bibliography and select the names of those critics who for a number of reasons could be regarded as Jews. Of all the sources in the list, only one positively identifies all Soviet citizens of Jewish origin as such. That source is the Hebrew University's periodic publication *Jews and the Jewish People* which contains cuttings from Soviet periodicals on everything concerning Jews. The only snag with this source is that its publication started comparatively recently and therefore it is of limited use for the period of our consideration. The rest of the sources are of mixed value for identification purposes. Encyclopaedias are better than histories of Russian literature because they give the full name of an author, the real name of an author who uses a pen-name, the place and the date of birth,

TABLE 2: SOVIET JEWISH LITERARY CRITICS, 1917-1932

Name of Critic	Living*	Literary Debut	Method	Group or Movement	Political Involvement	Academic or Polemical
AKSELROD, Ida Isaakovna	early 1870s-1918	?	S	—	P	Acad
AKSELROD, Lyubov Isaakovna (pseud. Ortodoks)	1868-1946	1900	S	—	P	Acad
ALEKSANDROV, Vladimir Borisovich (real name Keller)	1898-1954	1918	S	?	P	Acad
ALTMAN, Iogann Lvovich	1900-1955	1920	S	?	P	Acad
ARONSHTAM, M.	?	?	?	?	?	?
ARVATOV, Boris Ignatevich	1896-1940	1912	F	Proletkult, LEF	P	Polem
ASMUS, Valentin Ferdinandovich	1894-	1924	F	Constructivist	P	Acad
AUSLENDER, Sergey Abramovich	1886-1943	?	F	—	NP	Acad
AVERBAKH, Leopold Leonidovich	1903-1938	?	S	VAPP	P	Polem
AYKHENVALD, Yuly Isaevich	1872-1928	1895	R	—	NP	Acad
AYZENSHTOK, Eremiya Yakovlevich	1900	1917	S	?	NP	Acad
BELENSON, Aleksandr Emmanuilovich	?	?	F	?	NP	Acad
BERKOV, Pavel Naumovich	1896	1925	S	?	NP	Acad
BERKOVSKY, Naum Yakovlevich	1901	1930(?)	S	?	NP	Acad
BERNSHTEYN, Sergey Ignatevich	1892	?	F	OPOYAZ	NP	Acad
BLEYMAN, M.	?	?	?	?	?	?
BLYUMFELD, L.G.	?	?	S	?	P	Acad
BONDI, Sergey Mikhaylovich	1891	1918	?	?	?	Acad
BORSHCHEVSKY, Solomon Samoylovich	1895-1962	1912	S	?	NP	Acad
BRAYNINA, Berta Yakovlevna	1902	1926	S	?	P	Acad
BREYTBURG, Semen Moiseevich	?	?	S	?	P	Polem
BRIK, Osip Maksimovich	1888-1945	1915	F	OPOYAZ, LEF	P	Acad
BRODSKY, Nikolay Leontevich	1881-1951	1904	S	?	NP	Acad
BROVMAN, Grigory Abramovich	1907	1931	S	?	?	?
BUKHSHTAB, Boris Yakovlevich	1904	1924	F	?	NP	?

BURLYUK, David Davidovich	1882-1967	1899	F	Futurist, Tvorchestvo	NP	Polem
BYALIK, Boris Aronovich	1911	1931	S	?	?	?
CHERNYAK, Yakov Zakharovich	1898-1955	1918	S	?	P	Acad
CHUZHAK, Nikolay Fedorovich (real name Nasimovich)	1876-1937	1916(?)	F	Tvorchestvo, LEF	P	Polem
DERMAN, Abram Borisovich	1880-1952	1903	S	—	NP	Acad
DEYCH, Aleksandr Iosifovich	1893	1911	?	?	?	?
DNEPROV, Vladimir Davidovich (real name Reznik)	1903	1920s	?	?	?	?
DOBIN, Efim Semenovich	1901	1929	?	RAPP	P	Polem
DOLININ, Arkady Semenovich (real name Iskoz)	1883	1905	S	—	NP	Acad
DREYDEN, Simon Davidovich	1905	1923	?	?	?	?
DYMSHITS, Aleksandr Lvovich	1910-1976	1928	?	?	?	?
EFREMIN, Aleksandr Aleksandrovich (real name Freyman)	1888	?	S	—	P	Acad
EFROS, Abram Markovich	1888-1954	1909	F	?	NP	Acad
EFROS, Nikolay Efimovich	1867-1923	1891	S	—	NP	Acad
EHRENBURG, Ilya Grigorevich	1891-1967	1910	F	Constructivist	NP	Acad
EISENSTEIN, Sergey Mikhaylovich	1898-1948	?	F	Proletkult, LEF	P	Acad
ELSBERG, Yakov Efimovich	1901	1920	S	RAPP	P	Polem
ENGELGARDT, Boris Mikhaylovich	1887-1942	1910s	F	?	NP	Acad
ERBERG, Konstantin (real name Konstantin Aleksandrovich Syunnerberg)	1871-1942	?	R	Skify, Volfila	P	Acad
ERDMAN, Nikolay Robertovich	1902-1970	1922	F	Imaginist	NP	Acad
EYDLIN, E.	?	?	?	?	?	?
EYKHENBAUM, Boris Mikhaylovich	1886-1959	1907	F	OPOYAZ	NP	Acad
EYKHENGOLTS, Mark Davidovich	1889-1953	1920s	F	?	NP	Acad
FEYNBERG, Ilya Lvovich (pseud. Samoylov)	1905	1928	S	—	NP	Acad
FRANK, Semen Lyudvigovich	1877-1950	?	R	—	?	Acad

* Single figure denotes date of birth.

Name of Critic	Lived*	Literary Debut	Method	Group or Movement	Political Involvement	Academic or Polemical
FREYDENBERG, Olga Mikhaylovna	1890-1955	1923(?)	F	?	NP	Acad
FRID, Yakov Vladimirovich	1903	1922	?	?	?	?
GALPERINA, Evgeniya Lvovna	1905	1929	S	—	NP	Acad
GELFAND, M.	1901	?	S	Litfront	P	Polem
GERSHENZON, Mikhail Osipovich	1869-1925	1894	R	—	NP	Acad
GEYMAN, Boris Yakovlevich	1899	?	?	?	?	?
GIMELFARB, Boris Venyaminovich	1880-1955	1906	S	—	NP	Acad
GINSBURG, Lidiya Yakovlevna	1902	?	F	—	NP	Acad
GOFFENSHEFER, Venyamin Tsezarevich	1905	1925	?	?	?	?
GOFMAN, V.	?	?	F	?	?	?
GORELOV, Anatoly Efimovich	1904	1926	S	RAPP	P	Polem
GORNFELD, Arkady Georgevich	1867-1941	?	F	—	NP	Acad
GRINBERG, Iosif Lvovich	1906	1931	S	—	NP	Acad
GROSSMAN, Leonid Petrovich	1888-1967	1903	S	—	NP	Acad
GROSSMAN-ROSHCHIN, Iuda Solomonovich	1883	?	S	RAPP	P	Polem
GUKOVSKY, Grigory Aleksandrovich	1902-1950	?	F	—	NP	Acad
GUREVICH, Lyubov Yakovlevna	1886-1940	1884	S	—	NP	Acad
GURSHTEYN, Aron Sheftelevich	1895-1941	1911	S	—	P	Acad
GURVICH, Abram Solomonovich	1897-1962	1925	S	—	P	Acad
GUS, Mikhail Semenovich	1900	1919	?	?	?	?
IOFFE, I.	?	?	?	?	?	?
ISBAKH, Aleksandr (real name Bakhrakh, Isaak Abramovich)	1904	1920	S	RAPP	P	Polem
IZGOEV, Aleksandr Solomonovich (real name Lande)	1872	?	R	—	P	Acad
KAMENEV, Lev Borisovich (real name Rozenfeld)	1883-1936	?	S	—	P	Polem

KATS	?	?	S	RAPP	P	Polem
KATSNELSON, S.M.	?	?	?	?	?	?
KAUFMAN, Isaak Mikhaylovich	1892	1927	S	—	NP	Acad
KAVERIN, Venyamin Aleksandrovich (real name Zilberg)	1902	1920	S	Serapion Brothers	NP	Acad
KHODASEVICH, Vladislav Felitsianovich	1886-1939	1905	F	—	NP	Acad
KIRSHON, Vladimir Mikhaylovich	1902-1938	1922	S	RAPP, VOAPP	P	Polem
KLEYNBORT, Lev Maksimovich	1875-1950	1902	S	—	P	Acad
KOGAN, Petr Semenovich	1872-1932	1895	S	—	P	Acad
KOVARSKY, Nikolay Aronovich	1904	1925	F	—	NP	Acad
KRANIKHFELD, Vladimir Borisovich	1865-1918	?	S	—	P	Acad
KUSHNER, Boris Anisimovich	1888-1939	1910s	F	OPOYAZ, LEF, Litfront	P	Polem
KUZMIN, Mikhail Alekseevich	1875-1936	1905	F	—	NP	Acad
LANN, Evgeny Lvovich (real name Lozman)	1896-1958	?	S	—	NP	Acad
LAVRETSKY, A. (real name Frenkel, Iosif Moiseevich)	1893-1964	1912	S	—	NP	Acad
LELEVICH, Grigory (real name Kalmanson, Labory Gilelevich	1901-1945	1917	S	VOAPP	P	Polem
LENOBL, Genrikh Morisovich	1906-1964	1931	S	—	P	Acad
LERNER, Nikolay Osipovich	1877-1934	?	S	—	NP	Acad
LEVIDOV, Mikhal Yulevich	1891-1924	1914	F	LEF	NP	Acad
LEVIN, Lev Ilich	1911	1930	?	—	?	?
LEVITSKY-TSEDERBAUM, V.O.	1883	?	S	—	P	Polem
LEYTES, Aleksandr Mikhaylovich	1899	1921	S	VUSSP	P	Acad
LEZHNEV, A. (real name Gorelik, Abram Zelikovich)	1893-1938	?	S	Pereval	P	Polem
LEZHNEV, I. (real name Altshuler, Isay Grigorevich)	1891-1955	?	S	—	P	Polem
LIBEDINSKY, Yury Nikolaevich	1898-1958	1922	S	RAPP	P	Polem

Name of Critic	Lived*	Literary Debut	Method	Group or Movement	Political Involvement	Academic or Polemical
LIFSHITS, Mikhail Aleksandrovich	1905	?	?	?	?	?
LIVSHITS, Benedikt Konstantinovich	1887-1939	1910	F	LEF	NP	Acad
LOKS, K.	?	?	?	?	?	?
LUNDBERG, Evgeny Germanovich	1897-1965	1901	R	Skify	P	Acad
LUNTS, Lev Natanovich	1901-1924	1922	?	Serapion Brothers	NP	Acad
LURYE, Solomon Yakovlevich	1891-1964	1917(?)	S	—	NP	Acad
MANDELSHTAM, Osip Emilevich	1891-1938	1910	F	Acmeist	NP	Acad
MANDELSHTAM, Roza Semenovna	1875-1953	1925	S	—	P	Acad
MARGOLINA, A.	?	?	?	?	?	?
MARIENGOF, Anatoly Borisovich	1897-1962	1918	F	Imaginist	NP	Polem
MASHBITS-VEROV, Iosif Markovich	1900	1924	S	RAPP	P	Polem
MAYZEL, Mikhail Gavrilovich	1899	?	S	RAPP, Litfront	P	Polem
MENDELSON, N.M.	?	?	?	?	?	?
MESSER, Raisa Davidovna	1905	1927	?	RAPP	P	Polem
MEYERHOLD, Vsevolod Emilevich	1874-1940	?	F	?	NP	Acad
MEYLAKH, Boris Solomonovich	1909	1930	?	?	?	?
MINTS, Sofiya Isaakovna	1899-1964	?	S	—	NP	Acad
MODZALEVSKY, Boris Lvovich	1874-1928	?	S	—	NP	Acad
MODZALEVSKY, Lev Borisovich	1902-1948	?	S	—	NP	Acad
MUNBLIT, Georgy Nikolaevich	1904	1925	?	?	?	?
MUSTANGOVA, Evgeniya Yakovlevna (real name Rabinovich)	1905	1925(?)	S	RAPP, Litfront	P	Polem
MYSHKOVSKAYA, Liya Moiseevna	1887-1959	1928	S	?	NP	Acad
NELS, Sofiya Markovna	1899	1929	?	?	?	?
NEYMAN, Boris Vladimirovich	1888	1912	?	?	?	Acad
NOVICH, Ioann Savelevich (real name Faynshteyn)	1906	1925	S	RAPP	P	Polem

NUSINOV, Isaak Markovich	1889-1950	1927	S	RAPP	P	Polem
OKSMAN, Yulian Grigorevich	1894-1970	1915	?	?	?	?
OTTEN, Nikolay Davidovich (real name Potashinsky)	1907	1924	?	?	?	?
PAKENTREYGER, Solomon Iosifovich	1891	?	S	Pereval	P	Polem
PASTERNAK, Boris Leonidovich	1890-1960	1913	F	Tsentrifuga, LEF	NP	Acad
PERTSOV, Viktor Osipovich	1898	1921	F	LEF	P	Acad
PESIS, Boris Aronovich	1901	1926	?	?	?	Acad
PINSKY, Leonid Efimovich	1906	1930	?	?	?	Acad
PLOTKIN, Lev Abramovich	1905	1930	?	?	?	?
POLYAK, Lidiya Moiseevna	1899	1925	S	?	P	Acad
POZNER, Vladimir Solomonovich	1905	?	S	Serapion Brothers	NP	Acad
PUMPYANSKY, Lev Vasilevich	1894-1940	?	?	?	?	Acad
RADEK, Karl Berngardovich (real name Sobelzon)	1885-1939	?	S	—	P	Polem
REYSER, Solomon Abramovich	1905	1926	?	?	?	?
REZNIK, Osip Sergeevich	1904	1930	?	?	?	?
RODOV, Semen Abramovich	1893-1968	1912	S	Proletkult, Kuznitsa, RAPP	P	Polem
ROZENBERG, V.A.	?	?	?	?	?	?
ROZENFELD, B.L.	?	?	?	?	?	?
RUDERMAN, Mikhail Isaakovich	1905	1920s	S	?	?	?
RYSKIN, Evsey Isaakovich	1903-1965	1926	?	?	?	?
SATS, Igor Aleksandrovich	1903	1923	S	—	P	Acad
SATS, Natalya Ilinichna	1903	1925	S	?	P	Acad
SELVINSKY, Ilya (Karl) Lvovich	1899-1968	?	F	Constructivist	P	Acad
SEREBRYANSKY, Mark Isaakovich	1900-1941	?	S	RAPP	P	Polem
SHABAD, A. Ya.	?	?	?	?	?	?
SHENGELI, Georgy Arkadevich	1894-1956	1909	F	Ego-Futurist, Acmeist	NP	Acad

Name of Critic	Lived*	Literary Debut	Method	Group or Movement	Political Involvement	Academic or Polemical
SHESTOV, Lev Isaakovich (real name Shvartsman)	1866-1939	?	R	—	NP	Acad
SHKLOVSKY, Viktor Borisovich	1893	1914	F	OPOYAZ	NP	Acad
SHNEERSON, M.	?	?	?	?	?	?
SHOR, R.O.	?	?	?	?	?	?
SHTEYNBERG, Aaron Zakharovich	1891-1975	?	R	Skify, Volfila	P	Acad
SILBER, V.	?	?	F	?	?	?
SLONIMSKY, Aleksandr Leonidovich	1881-1964	1904	S	—	NP	Acad
SLONIMSKY, Yury Iosifovich	1902	1919	?	?	?	?
SOSNOVSKY, Lev Semenovich	1886-1937	?	S	—	P	Polem
STEKLOV, Yury Mikhaylovich (real name Nekhamkis)	1873-1941	?	S	—	P	Polem
SUBOTSKY, Lev Matveevich	1900-1959	1921	S	—	P	Acad
TAGER, Evgeny Borisovich	1906	1927	S	?	P	Acad
TAIROV, Aleksandr Yakovlevich	1885-1950	?	?	?	?	?
TRAUBERG, Leonid Zakharovich	1902	1920s	F	?	?	?
TREGUB, S.	?	?	?	?	?	?
TRETYAKOV, Sergey Mikhaylovich	1892-1939	1913	F	Tvorchestvo, LEF	P	Polem
TRONSKAYA, Mariya Lazarevna	1896	1928	S	—	NP	Acad
TROTSKY, Lev Davidovich (real name Bronshteyn)	1879-1940	?	S	—	P	Polem
TSEKHNOVITSER, Orest Venyaminovich	1899-1941	1927(?)	?	?	?	?
TSEYTLIN, Aleksandr Grigorevich	1901-1962	1923	F	LEF	P	Polem
TYNYANOV, Yury Nikolaevich	1894-1943	1921	F	OPOYAZ	NP	Acad
VALBE, Boris Solomonovich	1889	1910	?	?	?	?
VEKSLER, Ivan Ivanovich	1885-1954	?	S	?	P	Acad
VENGEROV, Semen Afanasevich	1855-1920	?	S	—	NP	Acad
VENGEROVA, Zinaida Afanasevna	1867-1941	?	R	—	NP	Acad

VERTOV, Dziga (real name Kaufman, Denis Arkadevich)	1896-1954	?	F	LEF	P	Polem
VESHNEV, Vladimir Georgevich	1881	?	S	RAPP	P	Polem
VINOKUR, Georgy Osipovich	1896-1947	?	F	Moscow Linguistic Circle	NP	Acad
VOLFSON, Semen Yakovlevich	1894	?	S	—	P	Acad
VOLIN, Boris Mikhaylovich (real name Fradkin)	1886-1957	1923	S	RAPP	P	Polem
VOLKENSHTEYN, Vladimir Mikhaylovich	1883	1907	S	?	NP	Acad
VOLPE, Tsezar Samoylovich	1904-1941	1927	S	—	NP	Acad
VOLYNSKY, Akim Lvovich (real name Flekser)	1863-1926	?	R	—	NP	Acad
VOYTOLOVSKY, Lev Naumovich	1876	1901	S	—	P	Polem
VSEVOLODSKY, Vsevolod Nikolaevich (real name Gerngross)	1882	?	?	?	?	?
VYGOTSKY, Lev Semenovich	1896-1934	1915	F	—	NP	Acad
YAKOBSON, Roman Osipovich (in the West: Jakobson)	1896	?	F	Moscow Linguistic Circle	NP	Acad
YAKUBINSKY, Lev Petrovich	1892-1945	1916(?)	F	OPOYAZ	NP	Acad
YAKUBOVSKY, Georgy Vasilevich	1891-1930	?	S	Kuznitsa	P	Polem
YAMPOLSKY, Isaak Grigorevich	1902	1922	?	?	?	?
YARKHO, Boris Isaakovich	1889-1942	1913(?)	F	—	NP	Acad
YUZOVSKY, Iosif Ilich	1902-1964	1925	S	—	NP	Acad
ZARKHI, Natan Abramovich	1900-1935	?	F	?	P	Acad
ZASLAVSKY, David Iosifovich	1880-1965	1904	S	?	P	Polem
ZHIRMUNSKY, Viktor Maksimovich	1891-1970	1914	F	OPOYAZ	NP	Acad
ZILBERSHTEYN, Ilya Samoylovich	1905	1921	?	?	NP	Acad
ZINOVEV, Grigory Evseevich (real name Radomyslsky)	1883-1936	?	S	—	P	Polem
ZIVELCHINSKAYA, L.	?	?	?	?	?	?
ZONIN, A.	?	?	S	Litfront	P	Polem
ZUNDELOVICH, Ya. O.	?	?	?	?	?	?

information about relatives and other data which enable one to make a judgement. In some cases, entries are supplied with a photograph, which can be a very helpful means of identification. Some names of Jewish critics, absent from encyclopaedias, were discovered in other sources: bibliographies, books and articles on Russian literature, writers' memoirs and even advertisements.

The religious-ethnical side of the problem, the question of who is a Jew, is tackled as follows: the list includes not only those officially known as Jews but also those known as half-Jews or converts, as well as those who descended from converts. In an artistic context, it is a person's *involvement* with Jews, i.e. his or her positive or negative attitude to Jews, that matters. Converts and half-Jews may have 'Russian' written in their passports, but the very fact of conversion (in many cases, escape) or, in the case of a half-Jew, the need to show preference for the identity of one of the parents, means some involvement with the Jewish problem. Such involvement may well have a bearing on one's creativity.

The method of identification consists of an assumption of a person being a Jew on the basis of his name and the immediately available data; this, whenever possible, is followed by a verification of the assumption through examination of other sources. The assumption is not pure guesswork but a method of socio-linguistic analysis. Jews in Russia have characteristic names (given names, patronymics, and surnames) and these are the most natural signs of identification. In the ideal case, all the three elements of a name are Jewish. In most cases it is not so, and the onus of guessing shifts from the name to additional information. Naturally, the less there is of certainty in relevant elements, the greater the probability of an error. Doubtful names are identified through an examination of all available biographical data in a cultural-historical context. Such an examination often enables one to associate a person with Jews due to a discovery of specific Jewish characteristics.[7] Alternatively, it can enable us to eliminate doubts and make a positive identification of a person as a non-Jew.

Of course, in this kind of work mistakes are inevitable, but it is not my intention to present the list as an absolutely correct one: it is only material for further study and the first of its kind.

Structural aspects of the list

The list is made out in the form of a seven-column table. Such a presentation serves a dual purpose: (a) to give an overall picture of the Jewish critics of the period (the left-hand column), and (b) to attach detailed information to names, to put the critics into categories, to classify them (all other columns).

The critics formed a motley phenomenon as far as their understanding of a critic's function, their attitude to literature and their idea of the aim of literary criticism were concerned. Professionally, some of them were political commentators, some literary theoreticians, original thinkers, creators of new theories, and some philosophers who used literature as illustrative material. The categories into which the critics are selected indicate only the prevailing characteristic of a critic. Nobody in the humanities can be 100 per cent this, that or the other. Thus the categories are by necessity stretched. This is especially true of the eclectic critics who pose specific difficulties of allocation to a method (S, F, or R). The detailed information in the list can give only a rudimentary idea about the actual writings of the critics.

Due to lack of information, it was impossible to indicate the group affiliation of all the critics. When a group is not indicated, the column has either a question mark or a dash. The question mark means that the critic might have belonged to a group but the actual name of the group is unknown; the dash means that the critic is assumed not to have belonged to a group. Among the polemicists nearly all belonged to groups; among the 'academic' critics some did and some did not.

The indication NP (non-political) and P (Political) are generalized characteristics of an author's involvement with politics, of the relative importance of politics in his work. One cannot be fully precise in such definitions, and in a number of cases the indication is only a guess on the basis of an indirect deduction, a conclusion based on an insufficient amount of factual material.

The terms 'academic' and 'polemical' are also wide-ranging. Each term includes critics with varying characteristics such as degree of scholarship, political orientation and professional aim. The academics were literary scholars (literary historians and theoreticians) who were mostly concerned with literature, Russian and foreign, on the basis of theoretical analysis. The polemicists were critics who were mostly concerned with the immediate problems of Soviet Russian literature. They engaged in polemics because they were concerned with the social image of literature; they were not so much concerned with abstract theories as with trying to make society accept their particular literary ideal. They were interested in forming literary tastes and in propagating sets of values and methods of appreciation of art.

The classification of critics as academic or polemical, just as their classification as political or non-political, is not a customary one, it is my own. It became necessary as a result of my study of the primary sources, specifically the Soviet encyclopaedias. In those encyclopaedias the political element (the author's political awareness, his participation in politics) plays as important a role as his academic creative achievements.

Sometimes a critic's political position and his participation in the literary debate were the only data one could get about him. In such cases, if one were to ignore such data, one would be left with no information to characterize a critic and we would have nothing but his name.

The list does not reflect a value judgement of the critics; there is no column 'important or unimportant'. Importance requires a criterion of estimation. If the criterion is popularity, or volume of output, or depth of thought, then in most cases such an estimation could be attempted. But the main purpose of this paper is to make a first step in studying the spectrum of Jewish assimilationist creativity in the field of Russian Soviet literary criticism. Therefore each critic is equally important for our purpose.

The term 'critic' used in the context of this paper is a combination of two Russian terms: *literaturoved* and *kritik*. Both these terms are vague. *Literaturoved* can mean a literary historian, a literary theoretician, or anybody writing anything evaluative on a literary subject. *Kritik* usually means a critic of modern literature.

The list is not at all complete. Many names of less known Jewish critics who contributed to the literary press of the period have not been included. In certain cases, when no information about a critic could be found, only his name is mentioned, while the missing information is indicated by question marks. Question marks also indicate all cases where serious doubt exists.

Some of the critics in the list are generally known as emigrés but if they have spent certain lengths of time under Soviet rule and took part in Soviet literary life, they are included in the list.

Jews in Russian conservative and non-Marxist revolutionary movements

Before the Revolution there were three schools of Russian literary criticism – the Sociological, the Formalist and the Religious-Philosophical. The first two continued until 1932, but the latter ceased to exist in 1922 and therefore is generally ignored as a phenomenon of Soviet literary life. A neglectful attitude to this school exists not only in Soviet but also in Western specialist literature, the only exception being the works of Russian emigrés connected with the Russian Orthodox Church and concerned with the history of Russian spiritual life, scholars like Dr N.M. Zernov and Professor N.P. Poltoratsky. The trend is to classify a Religious-Philosophical critic according to a secondary characteristic of his writing (e.g. political motivation, choice of subjects), without acknowledging the main aspect of his work – his membership of a distinct school of criticism.

The Religious-Philosophical school has its origin in the ideological schism which divided the Russian intelligentsia at the end of the nineteenth century and the beginning of the twentieth century. Since the 1840s the Russian intelligentsia had largely supported the radicals—Positivists, Populists or Marxists. The religious renaissance of the beginning of the twentieth century manifested itself in the sharp turn by a considerable part of the intelligentsia from Positivism and Marxism towards philosophical idealism and neo-Slavophilism. Disappointment in the Positivist and Marxist ideas was expressed in various ways. Some individuals renounced the socialist revolution as a false idol and advocated a return to Orthodox Christianity and spiritual regeneration. Others remained socialist revolutionaries but began to see the Revolution in religious and idealist terms, in terms of mysticism and messianism. The first group tended to consist of former Marxists, people like Berdyaev, Bulgakov, Frank, Struve and others, who became ideologically associated with the Kadet Party. The second tended to consist of former Populists or crypto-Populists, people like Merezhkovsky, Vyacheslav Ivanov, Minsky and Lundberg. The change in this outlook initially found expression in the literary movement of religious Symbolism, the aesthetics of which contained many Populist tenets. Later, after passing through a series of transformations and augmented by newcomers to Symbolism, as well as radical idealists the second group found its final expression in the Left SR Party.

Apart from these two groups, there was a group of individuals who as critics belonged to the Religious-Philosophical school but who were either apolitical or stood apart from any political movement, i.e. were politically isolated or indistinct. These three groups were the component parts of the Religious-Philosophical school.

The label 'conservative' could be applied, with reservations, only to those who rejected the idea of a violent revolution, i.e. the Orthodox critics close to the Kadets. The Left SRs were not conservative, they were simply non-Marxist. To the former, the solution to the ills of mankind lay in the spiritual development and inner transformation of man—a process similar to their personal experiences. The Marxists saw such views as a betrayal of the people and of all the noble causes the intelligentsia had traditionally fought for. The Marxists were concerned with practical and material issues of here and now; anything which did not lead towards a political and economic change was seen as conservative and reactionary. The views of the Orthodox critics were seen as lacking in concern for the destiny of the people, as being indifferent to suffering and injustice, and as sanctioning the status quo.

The Religious-Philosophical school was able to exist only during the first five years of Soviet rule, and during this time, works by the founders of the school continued to appear, espousing the same ideas as before the

Revolution. In 1922, under Trotsky's directive, 120 leading scholars, writers and scientists—adherents of religious and idealist philosophy who were either close to the Kadets or politically indistinct—were expelled from the country.[8] In the same year the Left SRs were crushed as a result of their political rivalry with the Bolsheviks and their leaders were compelled to leave the country. The expulsion and the emigration of the leaders forced the remaining religious critics into silence. The school was liquidated partly because of the regime's ideological atheism but, more importantly, because of the association of the members of the school with political opposition. The authorities were looking for political supporters, and to them the religious writers, not the Formalists and the experimenters, were the enemy. The Formalists were atheists and were not in political opposition to the regime (in fact, a number of them were active members of the Communist Party), and they were allowed to develop their theories 'for the benefit of the Revolution' and to enjoy considerable prominence for a number of years. A few works of a Religious-Philosophical nature did appear in Russia at random after 1922, but those were the last convulsions, echoes of the past. As an intellectual trend, the school was practically eradicated on Soviet territory. However, this did not mean the end of the school because it successfully continued its work abroad and in the 1960s was revived in the Soviet Union in *samizdat* publications. The above revival of Religious-Philosophical criticism in Russia means that the school represents a permanent and basic element of Russian intellectual life.

Emigré Religious-Philosophical criticism may be regarded as a bridge between 1922 and the 1960s. Among the Religious-Philosophical critics who lived and worked in the West since 1922 were a number of Jews: S.L. Frank , A.S. Izgoev, I.I. Fundaminsky-Bunakov, L.I. Shestov, Z.A. Vengerova, N.M. Minsky, Yu. I. Aykhenvald, A.Z. Shteynberg, G.D. Gurvich, S.I. Gessen and others.

The transcendental idealists

These were a group of Religious-Philosophical critics among whom Jews were comparatively most numerous. They were politically indistinct, their main preoccupation being purely scholarly matters. Their main characteristic was philosophical, rather than religious, idealism. The critics of this group did not belong to the same organization. They were individuals who had in common a devotion to philosophical idealism, namely the acceptance of transcendental reality and the primacy of spirit over matter. This principle did not require adherence to any specific religion and enabled Jews to remain Jews if they wished to, and to discuss religious matters in a purely philosophical context. The group included critics of two kinds: philosopher-critics who concerned themselves mostly with philosophy and occasionally with philosophical problems in works of literature, and literary critics proper who concerned themselves essentially with literature and art while viewing these through the prism of philosophical idealism.

Most of the philosopher-critics were neo-Kantians who wrote for the *Logos* magazine—the Russian branch of the international philosophical magazine of that name. The Russian *Logos* was founded in 1910 by former philosophy students at the Universities of Marburg and Freiburg, the two centres of neo-Kantianism; Lossky calls these philosopher-critics 'representatives of transcendental-logical idealism'.[9] Among them were Sergey Iosifovich Gessen (1887-1950), Georgy Davidovich Gurvich (b. 1894), Leonid Evgenevich Gabrilovich (b. 1878), M. Rubinshteyn and D.M. Koygen. Separately from them stood Lev Shestov. All these philosopher-critics left Russia after the Revolution and continued work abroad. *Logos* continued to appear in Prague till 1928. The critics proper of this group were A.L. Volynsky (Flekser), L.Ya. Gurevich, Z.A. Vengerova and Yu.I. Aykhenvald. Under the broad umbrella of idealism they differed widely in specific ways.

Aykhenvald was an impressionistic critic. He repudiated history of literature as a discipline and wrote his historical articles in the spirit of lyrical essays. His appreciation of literature manifested itself in subjective impressions, in his particular aesthetic feelings. This original critic was both praised and criticized in the early Bolshevik press. He could not be forgiven, however, for his criticism of Belinsky, the idol of the atheistic revolutionary intelligentsia. He was exiled in 1922.

Volynsky was also an impressionistic critic. Before the Revolution he was principal critic of the *Severny vestnik* magazine (published by L. Gurevich), in which he expressed his religious mystical views on literature and his metaphysical philosophy in his polemics with the Populists and Marxists. He was often the target of violent abuse by the Russian press of all political shades. After the closure of the magazine in 1898 he had nowhere to publish his articles, so he concentrated on writing books, becoming his own publisher. After the Revolution, he adapted himself to Bolshevik rule by changing the subject of his criticism. He became a ballet critic, working for the *Teatr* magazine.

Gurevich was the daughter of a well-known pedagogue. While still a student, she became very keen on the Modernist ideas which appeared in Russia at the end of the nineteenth century, ideas directed against materialism and positivism and their aesthetic and artistic equivalents. Striving to give her idealism a practical expression as well as to provide an outlet for the native Modernistic talent, she became in 1891 the publisher of *Severny vestnik* which, under her direction, became the first Russian

Modernist magazine. This was a brave venture, considering her lack of funds. With hard work, sheer perseverance and idealism, she managed to keep the magazine afloat for seven years, till bankruptcy forced it out of existence in 1898. She also wrote articles and reviews for the magazine herself. Her critical views were very close to those of Volynsky, whom she held in high esteem. In 1904 she published a book of short stories. She accepted the Revolution and took Blok's side when most of his former friends became antagonized by his article 'The intelligentsia and the Revolution' (1918), which was an appeal to the intelligentsia to support the Revolution. After the Revolution, she became a theatrical critic and an art historian. However, her main contribution to Russian literature, for which she is remembered, is as the publisher of *Severny vestnik*.

Vengerova was the sister of Semen Afanasevich Vengerov, the famous Populist critic and literary historian. Unlike her brother, she was a Modernist and wrote for *Severny vestnik, Novy put* and *Voprosy zhizni*, as well as a number of foreign magazines. She spent several years studying in Paris and London and was fluent in the principal European languages. Together with Volynsky and Minsky, she was among the earliest harbingers of Modernism in Russia, popularizing the work of foreign Modernists in her articles and translations. Her translations of foreign prose were in great demand. She was well known in Modernist circles, attending Merezhkovsky's 'Religious-Philosophical Gatherings' (1901-1903) and Vyacheslav Ivanov's 'Wednesdays' (1905-1907). In 1922 she emigrated to Paris where she became the wife of the poet and critic Nikolay Maksimovich Minsky.[10]

Lev Shestov is, of course, the most famous name in the group. Chiefly known as an irrationalist and existentialist, his main works as a literary critic concern Dostoevsky. He emigrated voluntarily to Paris in 1920.

There were a number of other critics, generally known as Formalists or Sociologists who at one time or another belonged to the transcendental idealists. Among such critics one could mention A. Lezhnev, S. Pakentreyger, V. Meyerhold and V. Khodasevich. Some philosophers who during the Soviet period were known as Marxists began as idealist critics. Such critics included Yakov Aleksandrovich Berman (b. 1868), and Pavel Solomonovich Yushkevich (b. 1873), the younger brother of the novelist Semen Solomonovich Yushkevich. All these Marxists went through a stage of adherence to the neo-Positivist views of Mach and Avenarius.

The critics of the Left SR Party (Shteynberg, Erberg, Lundberg)

The Left SR Party, a party of agrarian socialists, emerged after the Revolution. It split off from the main Party in autumn 1917 and became an ally of the Bolsheviks. It was distinct from the right wing of the SR Party, which supported the Whites, and from the vacillating center. The Left SRs took part in a coalition government with the Bolsheviks but also clashed with them, as a result of which the Party was banned in 1922. Until 1922 the party was vigorously active, with its own publishing houses and propaganda centers. One of the spiritual sources of the Left SRs as a neo-Populist group was nineteenth century Populist ideology, namely identification with 'the people' i.e. the peasantry, and the need to fight for 'the people' who were seen as the only basis of Russia's future socialist order. The other spiritual source of the Party was the Religious-Philosophical renaissance of the beginning of the twentieth century when many intellectuals were influenced by mystical anarchism. In 1917 this idea found its material implementation in the form of the Left SR Party, members of which saw a political significance in religion and a religious significance in politics. From this perspective, the Left SRs saw the religious peasantry and the village commune as opposed to the irreligious proletariat and the individualism of the city of the Bolsheviks.

Part of the messianism of the Left SRs was their maximalism. Maximalism was always inherent in Russian religious thought calling for the unification of all mankind on the basis of the teachings of the Christian Gospels. At the beginning of the twentieth century maximalism became part of Vladimir Solovev's legacy to the religious Symbolists, who awaited the millenium, and began the apocalyptic trend in Russian literature. Politically, maximalism was undemocratic but, in any case, the Left SRs were not committed to democracy in the Western sense of the term. Left SR politics contained elements from Bakunin (e.g. the liquidation of the state) and Dostoevsky (soil-bound mysticism of the Slavophile type). This ideology, combined with the use of individual terrorism as a weapon in revolutionary struggle, made outsiders see little difference between the maximalism of the Left SRs and anarchism. The Left SR Party was widely regarded as semi-anarchistic.

It is important to note to which section of the intelligentsia the Left SRs appealed. First of all, they attracted a considerable number of former religious Symbolists who after 1910 disintegrated as a literary movement. The Revolution enabled a 'second coming' of the religious Symbolists but this time more in the political than in the literary sphere. They joined the Left SRs because they were believers, and wanted to preserve religion, especially among the peasantry. The most important ex-Symbolists in the ranks of the Left SRs were Aleksandr Blok, who responded to the Revolution with his two famous poems 'The Scythians' and 'The Twelve', and Andrey Bely, whose politics were motivated by a fear of the destruction of the patriarchal way of life in Russian villages as a result of the Revolution. Secondly, the Party attracted idealistic radicals (neo-Populists) who were not necessarily Orthodox believers. The most important personality among them was the critic and sociologist R.V. Ivanov-Razumnik. Thirdly, the party attracted a group of peasant poets (neo-Slavophiles), the most significant of whom were Nikolay Klyuev and Sergey Esenin. The peasant poets allied themselves with the Left SRs because the Party expressed the interests of the conservative part of the peasantry which were purely Russian orientated, nationalistic and Slavophile, and concerned with preserving the old traditions to which a mystical significance was attached. The Symbolists initially hoped to create a neo-Symbolist group, but instead, the Left SRs formed several literary organizations to propagate their views and to publish their works.

The first such organization was 'Skify' (The Scythians) named after Blok's poem. At the head of the group stood R.V. Ivanov-Razumnik, one of the Left SR leaders. The other participants included Blok, Bely, Shteynberg, Erberg, Lundberg, Klyuev and Esenin. The general characteristic of the group was its positive attitude to the Revolution (which was welcomed as a mystical phenomenon) and a belief in Russia's messianism. In literary terms, however, the group was heterogeneous, and was dominated by the ex-Symbolists seeking to revive Symbolism; therefore, the 'Scythians' could be partly viewed as a neo-Symbolist movement. However, the Symbolists were often criticized by Ivanov-Razumnik, and the peasant poets also stood apart from the Symbolists. Klyuev and Esenin could better express the soul of the Russian peasant than the Symbolists who were town-dwellers. The 'Scythians' had a publishing house in Petrograd where they published *Skify* during 1917-18. In 1920 the publishing house moved to Berlin.

The 'Scythians' had a special academic offshoot called 'Volfila' (*Volnaya filosofskaya assotsiatsiya*). It was organized by Bely in January 1919, with the close participation of Shteynberg and Ivanov-Razumnik; the aim was to acquaint the masses with the social and philosophical problems of artistic culture. Originally, it was to be called *Skifskaya akademiya* (Scythian Academy) or *Volnaya filosofskaya akademiya* (Free Philosophical Academy) but because of official objections the word 'akademiya' had to be dropped. 'Volfila' also functioned as a publishing house.

Another publishing house closely associated with the Left SRs was 'Alkonost'. It functioned in Petrograd from 1918 to 1923 as a private enterprise of S.M. Alyansky. Alyansky was an idealistic young man, a bookseller and a book-lover, especially keen on the Symbolists and their associates. Publishing their works became his main activity. In five years he published almost all the post-Revolutionary works of Blok, as well as books by Bely, Vyacheslav Ivanov, Akhmatova, Zinoveva-Annibal, Remizov,

Ivanov-Razumnik, Erberg, Beketova and others. He also published the magazine *Zapiski mechtateley* (Notes of Dreamers) from 1919 till 1922. The editor of the magazine was Blok, and chairman of the editorial board was Bely. Among the contributors to the magazine were, in addition to Blok and Bely, Vyacheslav Ivanov, Remizov, Meyerhold, Ivanov-Razumnik, Erberg, Radlov, Margarita Sabashnikova and Gershenzon.

In addition to the organizations they initiated, the Left SRs were also active in a number of other organizations. Among these were the Moscow branch of 'Proletkult', the Theoretical Department of the People's Commissariat for Education (TeONKP) in Moscow and the Moscow Palace of Arts.

For a number of reasons, the Left SR Party proved attractive to a certain section of middle-class Jews. The political reasons for this were the benevolence of the SRs towards national minorities and the provision of equality of all people and self-determination for minorities in the Party's programme. Jewish self-determination, according to the SR programme, meant not only the retention of the *kahal* as a body of a self-governing community but also its reorganization on democratic principles. (The *kahal* was regarded as similar to the Russian village community.) The ideological reasons for the attraction were Populism and messianism. There was a well-established tradition of Populism among Russian Jews, dating back to the middle of the nineteenth century. Many Jews believed in the saintly qualities of the Russian peasantry and desired to serve it altruistically. One great Russian Jewish Populist was the writer Ansky, later a Left SR. The messianism of the Left SRs had a certain affinity with Jewish messianism. Generally speaking, the religious element of the Party was not so much Orthodox Christian as mystical, and therefore it could accommodate members of different religions. The above characteristics attracted to the Left SRs Erberg and Lundberg, who came to the party via Populism and Symbolism, and Shteynberg, who came via philosophy and politics.

Aaron Zakharovich Shteynberg was born in 1891 in Dvinsk, Latvia, into a middle-class family with a strong Jewish Orthodox tradition. The family were descendants of Rashi, the famous eleventh century Jewish religious scholar who lived in France. Naturally, Judaism played a decisive part in his life and in the life of his elder brother Isaak, preventing them from assimilating the religious aspect of Russian culture. Aaron Shteynberg studied law at Heidelberg, graduating as Doctor of Law in 1913. The same year he published his thesis 'The Two Chambers System in Russia'. Later he became professor of philosophy at St Petersburg University. In 1917, together with his brother, he joined the newly formed Left Socialist Revolutionary Party. His brother, also a lawyer, was a politician by nature and became a leader of the new Party. During the brief honeymoon between the Bolsheviks and the Left SRs in 1917-18 Isaak was in the government as People's Commissar of Justice. Aaron, inclined to literary criticism, was active in the literary organizations of the Party. Together with Blok, Ivanov-Razumnik, Bely and other Left SRs, he was among the founding members of 'Skify' and 'Volfila', becoming secretary of the latter from 1918 to 1923. He was active in the work of the association, which organized literary meetings and lectures, and was also engaged in editorial work in the publishing house of the association. In 1920 his brother wrote a play *Put krestny* (The Road of the Cross). The collaboration between the Left SRs and the Bolsheviks was a stormy one. In 1919, accused of plotting an uprising, many Left SRs were arrested, among them Blok, Ivanov-Razumnik, Erberg, Shteynberg and Petrov-Vodkin. In 1921 Aaron Shteynberg contributed an article 'Development and decay in modern art' to the miscellany *Iskusstvo staroe i novoe* (Old and New Art) edited by K. Erberg. In this article he made a number of anti-Marxist statements and attributed to the work of art an extra-historical significance. In 1922 the Left SRs were finally crushed by the Bolsheviks and their leaders tried. Many fled the country, among them the Shteynberg brothers. They settled in Berlin, where Lundberg had earlier organized the 'Skify' publishing house. There, in 1923, Aaron Shteynberg published his most important critical and philosophical work, *Sistema svobody F.M. Dostoevskogo* (Dostoevsky's System of Freedom). His brother also published there his book *Ot fevralya po oktyabr 1917 goda* (From February till October 1917). Shteynberg's subsequent work was in the field of Jewish history. From 1934 he lived in England. His latest publication in the sphere of literary criticism was his book *Dostoevsky* (1966).

Erberg was the literary pseudonym of Konstantin Aleksandrovich Syunnerberg. He began his literary career as a poet at the beginning of the century and was close to the Symbolists. In St Petersburg he was friendly with Vyacheslav Ivanov and Blok and contributed critical articles to Modernist magazines, in which he appeared as a subjective idealist. His first publication in book form appeared in 1913. It was a philosophical treatise *Tsel tvorchestva* (The Purpose of Creativity), in which he propounded his theory of 'innormism', which advocated fighting against the necessity of having norms. This was an anarchistic theory: his formula for social relations was *homo homini leo*, the lion being the symbol of pride. His theory also included elements of Prometheism ('human creative spirit is Prometheus', a force 'which can defeat the laws of natural necessity'). He dreamed about a new nature—*Natura naturanda*—that which has to be created. With such a philosophy it was natural for him to join in 1917 the Left SRs, just as many other Symbolists did. His most productive creative period began after the Revolution, when almost all his works were published: in 1918 — a collection of poems *Plen* (Captivity), in 1919 — the second edition of *Tsel tvorchestva*, in 1923 (in 'Skify', Berlin) — a collection of articles *Krasota i svoboda* (Beauty and Freedom) in which he elaborated on the theory of his previous book. In 1921 he edited a collection of articles, *Iskusstvo staroe i novoe* (Art Old and New) to which he contributed the leading article, 'O dogmatakh i eresyakh v iskusstve' (On dogmas and heresies in art). In this article he saw the new Revolutionary art as a vindication of his theory of innormism — the breaking of the old norms. This was in keeping with the Left SR views on politics and art. His fate after 1922 cannot be ascertained.

Lundberg had more in common with Erberg than with Shteynberg: both were associated with the religious Symbolists. He was born in Taurage, Lithuania, and started out as a Leftist Populist. There was a definite religious dimension in his outlook which was perhaps more Christian than Jewish. In 1903 he took part in the Religious-Philosophical Gatherings of Merezhkovsky's circle.[11] At the beginning of the century he wrote critical articles on philosophical and religious aspects of modern literature. He published short stories and poems in the *Novy put* and *Voprosy zhizni* magazines of the religious Symbolists. In 1917, like Erberg and other Symbolist-minded critics, he joined the Left SRs, accepting the Revolution in messianic terms and did literary work in the framework of 'Skify'. In 1920, due to the fact that Germany was a country of cheap currency for foreigners, he went to Berlin, where he opened the 'Skify' publishing house, transferring the business of the St Petersburg 'Skify' to Berlin. Lundberg was apparently not a political emigré, he maintained links with the Soviet Government and opened for the latter the Berlin branches of the publishing firms 'Gosizdat' and 'Gostekhizdat'. In 1924, as a sympathizer of the Revolution, he returned to Russia. In 1930 he published the book *Zapiski pisatelya* (A Writer's Notes), in which he admitted to political errors and lashed out at the Russian emigration.

In addition to the above-mentioned personalities, there were a number of critics who ideologically did not belong to the Left SRs but cooperated with them. Among such critics were Meyerhold and Gershenzon, who had earlier been associated with the Symbolists. They contributed to *Zapiski mechtateley*. However, Meyerhold became absorbed after the Revolution in his own original (Formalist) theories, and Gershenzon was closer to the Kadets than to the Left SRs.

The Kadet critics of the Vekhi group (Frank, Izgoev, Gershenzon)

If the transcendental idealists were politically indistinct and religiously uncommitted, and if the Left SRs were basically pantheistic messianists, the Kadets of the 'Vekhi' group were distinguished by their Christian orientation. If we take adherence to Christianity as a measure, then we have to consider also Jewish critics who did not take part in 'Vekhi': Pasternak, Mandelshtam, Kuzmin and Auslender. However, our main consideration is literary criticism, and as critics these four were Formalists rather than anything else. We therefore discuss them in these terms. Frank, Izgoev and Gershenzon, on the other hand, belong to the Religious-Philosophical critics because of their preoccupation with philosophical ideas expressed in literary works and literary movements. All the above-mentioned critics were, without exception, Jews deeply assimilated in Russian culture, in most cases ignorant about Jewish culture and sometimes with prejudices against Judaism and distorted ideas about it. Frank, Pasternak, Izgoev and Kuzmin were converts or descendants of converts, Auslender presumably a convert, Gershenzon and Mandelshtam did not convert but were in fact, close to Christianity. Perhaps Shteynberg was the only observant Jew among all the Religious-Philosophical critics.

Frank was born a Jew, the grandson of a rabbi, and as a child went to synagogue and learnt Hebrew.[12] However, during his school years he drifted away from Judaism; he first embraced Marxism and later Christianity (in 1912). His pre-Revolutionary activities were marked by a close association with P.B. Struve, a former leader of the 'legal Marxists'. Frank's contribution to the 'Vekhi' miscellany was entitled 'The Ethics of Nihilism'. In this work he accused the Russian intelligentsia of being an order of monks of the 'nihilist religion'. He regarded their rejection of Christ as unethical. In 1922 he was exiled by the authorities.

Izgoev (real name Lande) was another contributor to *Vekhi*. As a sociologist, he wrote about the moral degradation of Russian students. The students were the principal social stratum which formed the ranks of the intelligentsia. In the 1890s Izgoev was a 'legal Marxist' and one of the closest associates of P.B. Struve. He later became a member of the 'League of Liberation' and ended up as a member of the right wing of the Kadet Party. Izgoev retained his Kadet views after the Revolution. When in 1921 the *Smena vekh* (Change of Landmarks—a miscellany whose authors argued for a revision of the *Vehki* ideology and urged the intelligentsia to support the Revolution), was published, Izgoev came out in defense of the old *Vekhi* in an article contributed to the Kadet miscellany *O smene vekh* (Concerning the Change of Landmarks) published in 1922 by 'Logos' in Petrograd. Izgoev, like Frank, was exiled in 1922.

Gershenzon was a critic of classical Russian literature and a historian of social ideas. In his approach to literature he was an idealist. He was close to Christianity and shared the philosophy of Kireevsky who was a leading Slavophile. Politically, before the Revolution, he stood closest to the Kadets, which is testified by his participation in the 'Vekhi'. The Revolution made a strong impact on Gershenzon. In the summer of 1920 he exchanged six letters with Vyacheslav Ivanov in which he disputed the attitude one should adopt towards the cultural heritage of the world in a post-revolutionary era. A year later the letters were published as 'Correspondence From Two Corners', a polemical brochure which became world-famous and was translated into many languages. Although Gershenzon retained his metaphysical outlook, he became sceptical about personal immortality and a personal God. In the atmosphere of general change and reorganization, he declared that he rejected the old culture which, forming the basis of European civilization was totally useless and harmful, and proposed to begin everything from scratch. (Ivanov defended the old culture). This desire to destroy the past was obviously an anarchistic streak in Gershenzon which made him come closer to the Left SRs and contribute to their magazine *Zapiski mechtateley*. It was also a desire he shared with many Jewish writers of the Sociological and Formalist schools, e.g. the Proletarian writers, the Futurists, and others. In 1922 Gershenzon published *Klyuch very* (The Key of Faith), another religious-philosophical work.

The Sociological critics

The non-political academic critics

The non-political academic Sociological critics differ from their political counterparts in that they had a prevailing interest in the purely professional side of their work (i.e. in the analysis of artistic merits), trying to keep unrelated subjects such as politics and economics out of their writings. Consequently, all of them were dealing with subjects other than Soviet literature. Avoiding Soviet literature meant avoiding the expression of political views, i.e. personal attitudes to, and positive involvement in, current events. They were realistic critics who sought no political aims through their professional activities although in their approach to literature they considered social factors as having a direct effect on a work of literature. Among such social factors were an author's class, ethnic and cultural background, his psychological makeup and the historical conditions in which he lived.

Having spent their formative years in pre-Revolutionary educational establishments, i.e. in conditions of comparative intellectual freedom, these critics were real professionals, on a par with their colleagues in Western countries. They did not experience the impediment of censorship on the import of foreign books and so were familiar with the world's latest achievements in their professional field. In the relatively liberal atmosphere of the period (as far as the arts were concerned), these critics were able to pursue their professional interests without much official interference. During the period of consolidation of power, the regime was more sympathetic to political neutrals than to political deviationists. A characteristic feature of these critics is lesser interest in theorizing and greater interest in practical analysis.

The following critics can be classed as non-political academic: Ayzenshtok; Berkov; Berkovsky; Borshchevsky; Brodsky; Derman; Dolinin; Efros, Nikolay; Feynberg; Galperina; Gimelfarb; Grossman; Kaufman; Kaverin; Lann; Lavretsky; Lerner; Lunts; Lurye; Mints; Modzalevsky, Boris; Modzalevsky, Lev; Myshkovskaya; Pozner; Slonimsky, Aleksandr; Tronskaya; Vengerov; Volkenshteyn; Volpe; Yuzovsky; Zilbershteyn.

The greatest number of the non-political academic critics were traditional analysts of classical Russian literature. Of those in the list such critics were Berkov, Borshchevsky, Brodsky, Derman, Feynberg, Dolinin, Lerner, Myshkovskaya, Slonimsky, Vengerov, Volpe, Zilbershteyn.

Zilbershteyn was one of the founders and editors of the important *Literaturnoe nasledstvo* series which began in 1931. Ayzenshtok and the Modzalevskys were engaged in textological work. The Modzalevskys as well as Kaufman were also noted bibliographers.

Berkovsky, Galperina, Gimelfarb, Grossman, Lann, Lavretsky and Tronskaya specialized in foreign literatures.

Lavretsky and Grossman were also theoreticians of literature. Mints was an expert on Russian folklore.

Derman, Efros, Grossman, Volkenshteyn and Yuzovsky were critics of drama. Lurye specialized in classical Greek literature.

A number of the Sociological non-political academic critics could be considered eclectic because of their partial use of the Formalist method. Such critics were primarily those of the Serapion Brothers group, Lunts, Kaverin and Pozner.

Lunts was interested in the theories of the Formalists but did not go to the extreme of adopting a complete Formalist approach to literature. He tried to bring the analytical sharpness of the Formalists into the creative sphere of the Sociological writers, especially the dramatists. Like the Formalists, he was against the boredom of psychologism in drama. His death at the age of twenty-four did not allow him to develop his theories in full.

Lunts's theories were continued by Kaverin who was his close friend. Kaverin advocated a neo-Formalist method of the 'literary mode of life' (*literaturny byt*). This method was criticized by the Marxists because it did not enable one to find out the laws of successive literary development.

Little is known about Pozner's work because he emigrated to France shortly after the Revolution. He is therefore not mentioned in Soviet sources. He is also largely ignored in emigré sources because in emigration he abandoned the Russian language and became a writer in French.

There are also a number of eclectic critics who come close to those mentioned above but because of their greater involvement with Formalist criticism merit more the label 'Formalist'. Such critics were Arvatov, Gornfeld, Gukovsky, Levidov and Tseytlin. They are dealt with in the chapter on Formalist critics.

The political academic critics

The political academic critics were first of all Marxists (Menshevik and Bolshevik) as well as critics representing various other shades of the socialist spectrum (Populist, Socialist Revolutionary, Bundist, etc.). These critics differed from the non-political ones in that they included both members of the old intelligentsia who before the Revolution became politically attracted to Marxist theory and were applying it in their literary analyses, and a smaller contingent of post-Revolutionary newcomers who were academically inclined and at the same time were following Party instructions. It was the criticism of the political academics which, with the addition of certain aspects of the criticism of the political polemicists, developed into, and formed the mainstream of, what Erlich calls 'Soviet neo-academism, misnamed Socialist Realism'.[13]

The political academics represented a combination of professionalism and ideological bias. The professionalism of most of them stemmed from their education under the Tsar which made them adhere to universal scholarly values and principles such as respect for culture, scientific integrity and diligence, the use of logic in argumentation, and substantiation of arguments with verifiable facts. In other words, they believed in the intellectual method of presenting a view instead of appealing to readers' emotions through slogans. In this respect they differed from the political polemicists who often resorted to sloganeering and vituperations against opponents as an argument in their critical writings.

Their ideological bias was not uniform. It was directed towards various brands of socialism represented by various political parties. In many respects they continued to develop the kind of Marxist criticism which started before the Revolution. In a work of art they were looking for a 'progressive ideology'. Artistic form interested them very little, or not at all. Many of them seemed 'to confound', in Shklovsky's phrase, 'the history of Russian literature with the history of Russian liberalism'.[14] Literary facts were not looked at for their own sake, but for the sake of providing a literary parallel for a Marxist philosophical or political thesis. As a result, they were using literature as a medium of political propaganda. Some critics, in their attempts to give a Marxist interpretation of literature, fell into the pit of 'vulgar sociologism'.

On the whole, the political academics show a much greater interest in Soviet literature and contemporary 'progressive' artistic developments than the non-political ones. In this respect, they came close to the political polemicists. Among the political academics one can distinguish the old-style academics and the Soviet-style academics. The latter were more prone than the former to compromise with fact to suit a political dogma. They were also more likely to choose Soviet literature as their subject.

The following critics can be classed as political academic: Akselrod, Ida; Akselrod, Lyubov; Aleksandrov; Altman; Blyumfeld; Braynina; Chernyak; Efremin; Grinberg; Gurshteyn; Gurvich; Kleynbort; Kogan; Kranikhfeld; Leytes; Lenobl; Lundberg; Mandelshtam, Roza; Polyak; Sats, Igor; Sats, Natalya; Subotsky; Tager; Veksler; Volfson.

According to their specialization, these critics divide as follows:

Marxist aesthetics: Akselrod, Ida; Akselrod, Lyubov; Kleynbort; Kranikhfeld.
Classical Russian literature: Aleksandrov; Akselrod, Lyubov; Kogan.
Drama: Altman; Gurvich; Sats, Natalya.
Foreign literatures: Aleksandrov; Blyumfeld; Kogan.
Soviet Russian literature: Braynina; Efremin; Grinberg; Gurshteyn; Polyak; Sats, Igor; Subotsky; Tager.
Yiddish literature: Gurshteyn.
Bibliography: Mandelshtam, Roza.
Philosophical and political problems of 20th-century Russian literature: Lundberg.[15]
Classics of Marxism about literature: Lenobl.

Lyubov and Ida Akselrod were sisters, daughters of a Vilno rabbi. There is almost no information about Ida, except that she and Lyubov were in the same field of activity. Lyubov was the elder sister and the more famous one. Early in her life she became a Marxist revolutionary who opposed the Tsarist regime and suffered as a result. She was predominantly a philosopher, writing under the pseudonym 'Ortodoks'. The Soviet press does not speak very favorably about her because she was a Menshevik. As an aesthetician, she was mainly preoccupied with methodology, continuing the kind of Marxist art criticism which was initiated in Russia by Plekhanov. Her literary tastes revealed a personality which justified her pseudonym. She was totally opposed to the Symbolists and other Modernists. As a literary critic, her main interest was Leo Tolstoy. Under the Soviet regime, she lectured at the Institute of Red Professorship (1921-23), the Institute of Scientific Philosophy and the State Academy of Arts. She was criticized in the Party resolution of 25 January 1931 for mechanistic revision of Marxist philosophy and her opposition to the Bolsheviks and to Lenin's philosophical views. Kranikhfeld was a Populist and an early Marxist critic who theorized on the subject of an artist's ties with his social milieu, as well as on the role of the intelligentsia in the social struggle. Kleynbort was a critic as well as a political pamphleteer. As a critic, his special interest was the origin and development of proletarian literature and press, predominantly the self-taught proletarian writers. He worked for the legal Marxist and Menshevik press and therefore it is not surprising that the *LE* refers to his works as 'politically and methodologically unsatisfactory'.

Aleksandrov (real name Keller) was a critic of great erudition, the son of Academician B.A. Keller. In the initial stage of his career, he was a 'vulgar sociologist', but in the late 1920s he was, according to *LE*, 'striving to overcome the vulgar sociological view of art'. Kogan was the famous author of histories of West European and Russian literatures. He was a strict Marxist in his approach to literature, a critic totally devoted to the Sociological method of art criticism who on principle did not pay attention to literary form. He did a lot to bring the old intelligentsia onto the side of the Bolsheviks, for which he was praised. He enjoyed a good standing with the authorities.

In the field of drama, the political academics were either historians of drama (Altman), or theoreticians of drama and theatrical critics (Gurvich, Altman, Sats). Altman was interested in Aristotle's theory of drama, in Lessing, as well as in Soviet playwrights. Gurvich examined the aesthetic characteristics of an actor's craft. Naturally, they judged plays and theater in terms of their 'progressiveness'. In a somewhat different category was Natalya Sats, the daughter of the composer I.A. Sats. In 1921, as an 18-year-old girl, she was offered the opportunity to organize a theater for children. As a result, without experience but with formidable drive, she became the initiator of the famous *Teatr yunogo zritelya* (Theater of the Young Spectator) in Moscow. Her work as a critic concerns the specifics of writing plays for children, the educational and political aspects of the latter, as well as the performance of such plays on stage.

As specialists in Western literatures, Kogan and Aleksandrov demonstrated the same qualities as in their criticism concerning Russian literature. Blyumfeld was on the editorial board of the *LE*, editing the Western Literatures section.

Soviet literature was a special subject and demanded criticism of a special kind. This kind of criticism was dispensed by the 'academic critics—Soviet style'. They were interested in the reflection of 'socialist reality' in an author's work, whatever that might be. They were all concerned with various specific problems of Soviet literature. Igor Sats was the literary secretary of A.V. Lunacharsky, the Commissar of Enlightenment, between 1917 and 1929, at the same time working at the Institute of Philosophy of the Communist Academy. Subotsky was a member of the editorial board of *Literaturnaya gazeta*, a fact which clearly characterizes his political line in literary criticism. Polyak was a university lecturer in the history of twentieth century Russian literature and Soviet literature. She and Tager were co-authors of *Sovremennaya literatura* (Contemporary Literature), the textbook on Soviet literature for the Russian high schools which became popular and has been re-issued many times over a number of years. Efremin studied Demyan Bedny. The *LE* does not tell us much about him except that he had an incorrect approach to Bedny's style. The *KLE* does not mention Efremin at all.

Gurshteyn was a typical Jewish Marxist who wrote in Yiddish and Russian on political literary subjects such as 'Lenin in literature', 'Socialist Realism' and other political aspects of Soviet literature. He also wrote numerous works on Yiddish literature and the Yiddish theater.

Roza Mandelshtam was the author of bibliographies on various Marxist aspects of literature of the pre-Revolutionary period.

The political academics brought to life a special brand of literary criticism called 'Classics of Marxism about literature'. One of such critics was Lenobl. He was born in London in 1906 and then came to live in Russia where in 1931 he graduated from the Moscow State University. The same year saw his first publication: 'Plekhanov and Lenin on Tolstoy'.

The political polemical critics

While the academics, even the political ones, were a phenomenon theoretically conceivable in pre-Revolutionary Russia or in a Western society because they were operating as professionals within the framework of their profession, the political polemicists were a phenomenon which was conceivable only in the Soviet Union. They were created by the specific Soviet conditions and typified the new Soviet mentality, especially the mentality of the new Soviet intelligentsia which regarded ideology as more important than any professionalism. If professionalism was subordinate to ideology, then it was positive; without an ideological bias it was 'creeping empiricism'. In this respect the political polemicists differed from the political academics: the latter were literary men with political aims, the former were politicians working in the field of literature.

The political polemicists were a section among Soviet critics in which Jews happened to excel more than anywhere else. It is quite possible that this section contained the greatest percentage of Jewish critics. Taking into consideration their socio-economic and cultural background and degree of assimilation, these critics were the most Jewish of the lot. Perhaps this fact had something to do with their excessive zeal as critics. Another factor to consider is their home background. Quite a number of them lacked proper education. To join the ranks of political polemicists was natural to them because such politicized Jews, to use Erlich's phrase 'lacked both the intellectual equipment and the frame of mind necessary for the exacting tasks of scientific analysis'.[16]

As a result, their articles remind one of a commissar, not an independent-minded intellectual. This was especially the case with 'vulgar sociologists', who examined reality and its reflection in art in terms of the division of society into classes and class struggle, attaching political labels to everything. While the academics' attitude to art was artistic appreciation, the attitude of the political polemicists was political appreciation. Political zeal led to extremism and over-simplification of Marxism. This was called 'vulgar sociologism'.

Because of their involvement with politics, the Party kept a close watch on them. Not surprisingly, many of them ended their careers by execution or imprisonment, far more than in the case of the academics. They also comprise the greatest percentage of those in literature who are still not 'posthumously rehabilitated'.

The following critics can be classed as political polemicists: Averbakh; Breytburg; Dobin; Elsberg; Gelfand; Gorelov; Grossman-Roshchin; Isbakh; Kamenev; Kats; Kirshon; Lelevich; Levitsky-Tsederbaum; Lezhnev, A; Lezhnev, I.; Libedinsky; Mashbits-Verov; Mayzel; Messer; Mustangova; Novich; Nusinov; Pakentreyger; Radek; Rodov; Serebryansky; Sosnovsky; Steklov; Trotsky; Veshnev; Volin; Voytolovsky; Yakubovsky; Zaslavsky; Zinovev; Zonin.

According to specialization, the political polemical critics divided as following:

Problems of 'proletarian literature' (vulgar sociological criticism): Averbakh; Breytburg; Dobin; Elsberg; Gelfand; Gorelov; Grossman-Roshchin; Isbakh; Kats; Kirshon; Lelevich; Libedinsky; Mashbits-Verov; Mayzel; Messer; Mustangova; Novich; Nusinov; Rodov; Serebryansky; Veshnev; Volin; Yakubovsky; Zonin.

Drama (vulgar sociological criticism): Kirshon.

Theoretical Party interpretation of literature: Kamenev; Radek; Steklov; Trotsky; Zinovev.

Political pamphleteering: Levitsky-Tsederbaum; Lezhnev, I.; Sosnovsky.

Classical Russian literature: Voytolovsky; Zaslavsky.

Yiddish literature: Nusinov.

Western literatures: Nusinov.

Pereval criticism (anti-RAPP): Lezhnev, A.; Pakentreyger.

The term 'vulgar sociologism' is mostly associated with the so-called 'proletarian' writers. They belonged to a number of groups and contributed to the publications of their groups. The critics divide group-wise as following:

Proletkult: Rodov.
Kuznitsa: Yakubovsky; Rodov.
VAPP: Averbakh; Kirshon; Lelevich; Libedinsky; Rodov.
RAPP:[17] Averbakh; Dobin; Elsberg; Gorelov; Grossman-Roshchin; Isbakh; Kats; Kirshon; Lelevich; Libedinsky; Mashbits-Verov; Mayzel; Messer; Mustangova; Novich; Nusinov, Rodov; Serebryansky; Veshnev; Volin.
VOAPP: Kirshon; Lelevich.
LOKAF: Libedinsky.
Litfront: Gelfand; Mayzel; Mustangova; Zonin.

The 'vulgar sociological' groups published the following magazines:

VAPP: *Na postu* (On Guard), *Oktyabr* (October) and *Molodaya gvardiya* (Young Guard).
RAPP: *Na literaturnom postu* (On the Literary Guard).
LOKAF: *LOKAF* (see 'Acronyms and Abbreviations').
Litfront: *Pechat i revolyutsiya* (The Press and the Revolution).

Rodov started his career in Proletkult, then after a spell in Kuznitsa he became a member of RAPP. He was the Acting Secretary of MAPP and the editor of *Na postu*. He also wrote for *Oktyabr*. He was better known as a poet and he did some poetic translations from Yiddish. Rodov represented 'left-wing On-guardism' (*levoe napostovstvo*). He was criticized later for sectarianism and vulgarizing tendencies.

Averbakh was one of the most active and most influential critics. He was editor of the *Molodaya gvardiya* magazine, member of the editorial board of *Na postu* and one of the founders of VAPP. When VAPP split as a result of internal disagreements, Averbakh headed the new group, RAPP, and became editor-in-chief of *Na literaturnom postu*. He was a controversial figure in the polemics on proletarian literature.

Kirshon was one of the top men in VAPP, RAPP and VOAPP. He was the creator of the Soviet revolutionary drama and a playwright of great talent. His critical writings concerned the problems of proletarian drama. He took part in the debate on proletarian art.

Lelevich was called 'the left comrade' for his extreme leftist views. He was also a poet and was interested in methodology. He mostly contributed to the *Oktyabr* and the *Na postu* magazines.

Libedinsky was a significant prose writer and critic. He was associated with the *Oktyabr* and the *Na postu* magazines when in VAPP, and later joined Averbakh in RAPP after the split in VAPP.

Gorelov was active in RAPP. From 1929 to 1937 he was editor of the *Rezets* (The Cutter) magazine.

Grossman-Roshchin was an anarchist before the Revolution. After the Revolution he became a RAPP critic. He contributed to the *Na literaturnom postu* and the *Oktyabr* magazines, polemicizing with the adversaries of RAPP—members of LEF, the Voronsky group, and others. According to the *LE*, his 'Marxist method was not always correct'.

Mashbits-Verov wrote the book *Pisateli i sovremennost* (Writers and the Present) (1931) which contained literary portraits of Soviet writers. Serebryansky was a critic and a poet, a member of RAPP. In 1932, together with Kirshon, he published a book of polemical articles *Za bolshevistskoe iskusstvo* (For Bolshevik Art).

Novich was an active RAPP critic. Volin together with Lelevich founded the *Na postu* magazine. Veshnev worked for the *Oktyabr*, the *Molodaya gvardiya* and the *Na literaturnom postu* magazines.

Nusinov's first works were in Yiddish. He was a member of the Bund. Later he joined RAPP and switched to Russian, participating in debates with Pereverzev, Lukács, Livshits, the LEF, and Litfront. He was known for his polemical sharpness. In the late 1920s he became a member of the editorial board of the *Literaturnaya entsiklopediya*. As a literary critic, he wrote numerous articles on Yiddish literature and was criticized for erroneous assessment of 'petty-bourgeois nationalistic writers'. He also wrote about Victor Hugo, Anatole France, Tolstoy, Gorky and Chekhov.

Zonin and Gelfand were disciples of Pereverzev and Friche. In 1929 they became editors of the *Pechat i revolyutsiya* magazine. In the squabbles within VAPP they represented the left-wing On-guardist minority. They were joined by Mayzel and Mustangova, both active members of LAPP. In 1930 they organized the Litfront, a left-wing splinter group of RAPP. The group existed only three months and was liquidated for political reasons. The members of the group were criticized for their political mistakes.

Of the five names associated with theoretical Party interpretation of literature, only Steklov is now mentionable (posthumously rehabilitated). The others are discarded as members of the 'opposition block'. Nevertheless, they all contributed articles on literary problems and these were given prominence in *Pravda, Izvestiya* and other Party publications. The most famous work which came out of this group is Trotsky's 'Literature and Revolution' (1924), a collection of articles in which he repudiated the idea of the class structure of art. Steklov was also an important critic. He wrote about Chernyshevsky and Bakunin and was the editor of Bakunin's work and correspondence.

Levitsky-Tsederbaum was a Menshevik political pamphleteer and a professional revolutionary. During the Civil War he fought against the Soviet regime for which he was tried by the Soviets but released, and he worked as a literary critic.

Isay Lezhnev was abroad from 1926 to 1930. In fact, he was expelled for his political errors. During the Civil War, he was with the Red Army, working for the Information Department of *Izvestiya* and for the Red Army press. From 1922 to 1926 he was editor of the periodical *Novaya Rossiya*, the political orientation of which was *smenovekhovstvo*, an ideological trend named after the publication *Smena vekh* which was criticized by the Party. This was probably the reason for his expulsion. In 1930 he was allowed to return and in 1933 he joined the Communist Party.

Sosnovsky was a political pamphleteer siding with the 'Trotskyist-Zinovevist opposition'. He took part in the polemics on literary problems and wrote critical essays on Mayakovsky, Gorky, Bedny, Esenin. In 1927 he was expelled from the Party and later repressed but posthumously rehabilitated.

Voytolovsky was a veteran Marxist pamphleteer (born 1876, first critical publication 1904). In 1927-28 he published 'A History of Russian Literature' in which 'vulgarizing tendencies' were detected.

Zaslavsky was a social democrat, a Menshevik. Later he joined the Bund. As a Bundist, he was opposed to the Bolsheviks, but in 1919 he 'acknowledged his mistakes'. His critical works were concerned with Saltykov-Shchedrin, Dostoevsky, and the relation of classical writers to modern times. From 1924 he worked as a feuilletonist, from 1928 in *Pravda*.

The distinctive position of the Pereval among the political polemical groups has already been discussed above. The critics of that group were Marxists, they were politically-minded and they polemicized about their ideas, but their ideas were such as to make them very distinctive among the Sociological political polemicists. They certainly did not fit that group. Next to Voronsky and Gorbov, Abram Lezhnev and Solomon Pakentreyger were the principal critics of the group. Lezhnev was close to the social democratic Mensheviks politically; as a critic, he emphasized the importance of 'psychological factors in literary style'.[18] Pakentreyger was less of a politician than Lezhnev. He was against the interference of human reason and ideology in artistic creativity, more specifically—against political influence on art.

The Formalist critics

The non-political critics, academic and polemical

As Formalism was a new method and as such had to fight its way into the literary establishment, the academic writings of the Formalist critics mostly included a polemical element as well. Therefore there were almost no purely academic or purely polemical Formalist critics. In any case, it would have been very difficult to make such a distinction. As a result, the distinction in this chapter is made on the political basis only.

The following critics can be classed as non-political Formalists: Auslender; Belenson; Bernshteyn; Bukhshtab; Burlyuk; Efros, Abram; Engelgardt; Erdman; Eykhenbaum; Eykhengolts; Freydenberg; Ginzburg; Gofman; Gornfeld; Gukovsky; Khodasevich; Kovarsky; Kuzmin; Levidov; Livshits; Mandelshtam; Mariengof; Pasternak; Shengeli; Shklovsky; Tynyanov; Vinokur; Vygotsky; Yakobson; Yakubinsky; Yarkho; Zhirmunsky.

The non-political Formalists are here classed according to group or trend and, when such information is unavailable, according to subject.

OPOYAZ criticism: Bernshteyn; Eykhenbaum; Shklovsky; Tynyanov; Yakubinsky.
Moscow Linguistic Circle criticism: Vinokur; Yakobson.
Structuralist criticism: Freydenberg; Vinokur; Yakobson.
Modified OPOYAZ criticism: Gukovsky; Levidov; Zhirmunsky.
Psychological Formalism: Gornfeld; Vygotsky.
Futurist criticism: Belenson; Burlyuk; Livshits, Pasternak.
Acmeist or Acmeist-like criticism: Auslender; Khodasevich; Kuzmin; Mandelshtam; Shengeli.
Imaginist criticism: Erdman; Mariengof.
Drama and the visual arts: Efros, Abram.
Romance literatures and theatre: Eykhengolts.
Folklore and medieval literatures: Yarkho.
Classical Russian literature: Bukhshtab; Engelgardt; Ginzburg.
Modern literature: Gofman.
Theory of literature: Kovarsky, Yarkho.

Bernshteyn, Eykhenbaum, Shklovsky, Tynyanov and Yakubinsky were the original founders of OPOYAZ. Eykhenbaum was an intuitivist before he became a Formalist. The others were younger than him and Formalism was their first independent critical venture. Shklovsky emerged as the principal theoretician of the group. He is reported as considering that fiction develops according to its special laws which do not depend on social life and class struggle in society; fiction is a *making*—with the help of a plot and word-linguistic combinations; the study of this is the main task of scientific literary criticism.

The Moscow Linguistic Circle started a year earlier than the Petersburg-based OPOYAZ. It differed from OPOYAZ in that its Formalist theories were more concerned with linguistics while OPOYAZ was more concerned with literature. Yakobson and Vinokur were students of Potebnya and were affected by the theories of the psychological ('idealist') philosophers of language Wilhelm Dilthey and Gustav Shpet. After 1920, Yakobson lived in Prague where he helped to organize the Prague Linguistic Circle with which he became involved. There he, together with some others, founded the structuralist branch of Formalist criticism. However, he did not sever his ties with the Russian Formalist movement and continued to contribute to Russian publications. He was working on theoretical problems of prosody. In 1938 Yakobson left Czechoslovakia and in 1941 settled in the USA. Freydenberg worked independently of Yakobson and Vinokur. She specialized in classical literature and collaborated with the language theorist N. Ya. Marr.

OPOYAZ gained followers in a wider literary field, i.e. among writers and critics who accepted its theory with certain reservations and modifications. Zhirmunsky was a member of OPOYAZ but disagreed with the extreme elements of Formalism. Gukovsky started out as a non-political Formalist critic and remained such until the late 1920s, when he defected from Formalism and fully embraced the Sociological method. However, even during the 1920s he was troubled by his Sociological leanings. Although his main academic interest was eighteenth century Russian literature (he was the first Soviet critic to turn to this subject), he also contributed polemical articles on the problems of the Formalist-Marxist debate, defending the Formalist theory and the position of LEF. A follower of Arvatov, he supported the latter's theory of Formal-Sociological criticism. His turn towards the Sociological method was presumably prompted by the concentrated attacks on Formalism by the Marxist critics. Levidov started his literary career in 1914. After the Revolution, he was a foreign correspondent of ROSTA, and was stationed in Reval (Tallinn), London and The Hague. In 1924 he published *Vse ob Anglii* (Everything About England). He combined his journalistic career with an active participation in the literary debate on behalf of the Formalists and LEF, and, like Gukovsky, propagated the Formal-Sociological method. For this he was disliked by the 'proletarian' critics. The *LE* charged him with 'petty bourgeois liberalism', with representing 'members of the intelligentsia and the petty bourgeois reader' and with being 'remote from Marxism'. He turned towards the Sociological method at about the same time and for the same reasons as Gukovsky.

Gornfeld was a student of Potebnya, the founder of the psychological trend in Russian linguistics and one of the forerunners of Russian Formalism. The psychological school was 'an aesthetic reflection of the second stage of Positivism, when the sociological approach to social phenomena was replaced by the psychological one.'[19] For this reason, the psychological school was eclectic; partly Sociological, partly Formalist. Gornfeld derived his critical approach from his tutor. In the 1890s he wrote for magazines with Populist connections. In 1906 he published an important theoretical work, *Muki slova* (The Torments of the Word), which received great critical acclaim. The style of Gornfeld's criticism was poetic, while his main sphere of interest was the creative process. He considered art as one of the forms of knowing reality, and therefore was branded an 'idealist' by the Marxists. After the Revolution, which he accepted, he worked as an editor of original Russian as well as translated literary texts and also appeared as a critic. A friend of Blok's, he was perhaps fairly close to the Left SR Party. Vygotsky was more a psychologist than a literary critic. In 1923 he published an important book *Psikhologiya iskusstva* (The Psychology of Art) which, among other things, examined the relationship between Freudian psychoanalysis and artistic creativity, and which was highly praised by Western scholars. The book was re-issued in Moscow in 1968.

Futurist criticism began before the Revolution, with Burlyuk being initially the main exponent of it and the principal figure behind the Cubo-Futurist manifestos. He expressed his theory academically, although in an extravagant form designed to shock, and polemicized about it in the press and as a lecturer. He was sympathetic towards the Revolution and advocated an alliance of Futurism with Bolshevism. In 1918 he went to Vladivostok where he became a member of the Tvorchestvo group. His participation in the debate between Formalists and Sociologists was short because in 1920 he emigrated to Japan. From there, in 1922, he emigrated to the USA where he continued to support Bolshevik causes. In spite of his political extravaganzas, he was basically a non-political academic and that is why he is included in this section. Livshits was a close associate of Burlyuk before the Revolution and also a signatory of Futurist manifestos and a writer of theoretical articles on Futurism. After the Revolution he joined LEF. Belenson was mainly a poet, but he wrote some criticism. He was the publisher of the Futurist miscellany *Strelets* (Archer), vols. 1-3 (Petrograd 1915-23). Pasternak contined his pre-Revolutionary involvement with Futurism. When the Futurist group Tsentrifuga of which he was a member was dissolved in 1922, he joined LEF, writing for the *LEF* magazine edited by Mayakovsky.[20]

The Revolution quickened the disappearance of Acmeism as a movement. After 1922 it practically ceased to exist, with Mandelshtam remaining the last defiant representative of Acmeism, a non-existent movement. His critical writings continued to express Acmeist aesthetics, which attached importance to the word as the thing-name. During the polemics between the Formalists and the Marxists, Mandelshtam took an independent stand, keeping away from the group struggle. During the existence of Acmeism, there were a number of modernist critics who were close to Acmeism but nevertheless were not pure Acmeists: they had certain leanings towards Futurism, the other great avant-gardist movement. One of such critics was Shengeli. Khodasevich, a Symbolist-turned-Acmeist, was on the contrary an arch-enemy of Futurism. Auslender was associated with the Symbolists and the Acmeists mainly as a prose writer and a dramatist, but he also wrote poems and criticism.[21] Another famous Symbolist-turned-Acmeist was Kuzmin. The Jewish connection of Kuzmin is difficult to establish but on the portrait painted by Somov he looks like a typical Jew. He is also known to be Auslender's uncle.[22]

Mariengof was one of the three stalwarts of Imaginism (together with Shershenevich and Esenin). His father was a Jew who converted to Christianity, a famous doctor in his town.[23] Erdman was also one of the theoreticians of the Imaginist movement, but not as important as Mariengof and Shershenevich. Imaginist aesthetics stressed the primary importance of the image as such, concentrating on the word-metaphor.

Efros was primarily concerned with the visual arts and to a lesser extent with drama. The first edition of the 'Great Soviet Encyclopedia' charges him with being subject to 'right-wing fellow-traveller influences' and with 'subjectivism and Formalism in art criticism'.

Eykhengolts was a historian of Romance literatures and theater who worked in France and Italy. In his critical approach to his subject, he was a Formalist. In the beginning of the 1930s he turned Marxist, like Gukovsky, Levidov, Kaverin, and many other Formalists and semi-Formalists.

Gofman was interested in the language of poetry. In 1936 he published a book *Yazyk literatury* (The Language of Literature) which consisted of sketches and studies of the linguistic properties of various poets. An important article in that book was 'The Linguistic Skill of Khlebnikov' which examined Khlebnikov's *zaum* (trans-rational language).

The political critics, academic and polemical

The non-political Formalists were critics primarily interested in their profession. Politics played a secondary role in their professional lives; they did not try to combine their innovatory critical method with the new political reality. The political critics, on the contrary, did make a direct connection between Formalism and leftist politics. All the political Formalists belonged to Formalist literary groups with a leftist political bias.

The following critics can be classed as political Formalists: Arvatov; Asmus; Brik; Chuzhak; Ehrenburg; Eisenstein; Kushner; Meyerhold; Pertsov; Selvinsky; Tairov; Trauberg; Tretyakov; Tseytlin; Vertov; Zarkhi.

The political Formalists can be classed according to trend or branch of art:

LEF criticism: Brik; Chuzhak; Eisenstein; Gukovsky; Kushner; Levidov; Pertsov; Tretyakov; Vertov; Zarkhi.
Constructivist criticism: Asmus; Ehrenburg; Selvinsky.
Formal-Sociological criticism: Arvatov; Tseytlin.
Cinema: Eisenstein; Trauberg; Vertov; Zarkhi.
Theater: Tairov.

Brik was the principal theoretician of LEF. He was a former member of OPOYAZ and one of its founders. During the Revolution, he became politically involved on the side of the Bolsheviks. In 1918 he became editor of the *Iskusstvo kommuny* (The Art of the Commune) newspaper. He did not abandon his Formalist aesthetic views. In January 1919 the group of Communists-Futurists ('Com-Fut') was organized in Petrograd under the auspices of the Vyborg Regional Committee of the Bolshevik Party. The leaders of the group were B. Kushner and O. Brik. Formation of the LEF group offered an opportunity to combine Formalism with Marxism. During 1923-25 Brik wrote for the *LEF* magazine (editor Mayakovsky) and during 1927-28 for the *Novy LEF* magazine. LEF had different associations with different groups: with some groups for political and ideological reasons, with others for aesthetic and artistic reasons. As a Marxist, Brik advocated 'literature of the social command' (i.e. written at the behest of society); as a Formalist, he advocated 'literature of the fact'. He was a literary critic with a strong linguistic bias, a structure-minded Marxist. LEF was formed in 1923, immediately after the dissolution of OPOYAZ. However, of the former members of OPOYAZ it was only Brik who became a member of LEF, for its Marxist appeal and also due to his friendship with Mayakovsky. Shklovsky became associated with LEF but not a member. His association with Brik was on the academic, not political, level. Here is what Shklovsky had to say about Brik the academic: 'His idea about the connection between rhythm and syntax is not only important but one cannot move without it in literary criticism.'[24]

Kushner was one of the founders of OPOYAZ but did not become very prominent in the group as a critic. He later became a Cubo-Futurist, a member of Tsentrifuga (1913-16), Com-Futs (1919-?), LEF (1923-25), Novy LEF (1927-28) and Litfront (1928-30). He was not only a literary critic but also an art critic; he was a strong advocate of his political views in his criticism. Pertsov joined LEF much later than Brik and Kushner. His first publication, which appeared in 1929, was entitled *Literatura zavtrashnego dnya* (The Literature of Tomorrow) and dealt with problems of Soviet literature on a Futurist basis. Chuzhak and Tretyakov joined LEF in 1922, after the dissolution of the Tvorchestvo group in Vladivostok, of which they were both leading members.

Not all members of LEF held identical aesthetic views. If Brik, Kushner, Pertsov, Chuzhak and Tretyakov were Marxists politically and Formalists aesthetically, Arvatov and Tseytlin were Marxists politically and Formal-Sociological critics aesthetically. The theory of the 'Formal-Sociological method'—a blend of the two methods—was created by Arvatov and was shared by Tseytlin, as well as the non-political Formalists Gukovsky and Levidov. Arvatov attempted to sociologize the Formal method and criticized OPOYAZ for its lack of social interest. He was not only a literary critic but an art critic too. He examined the development of art in connection with the history of material culture. Starting in the Soviet period as a theoretician of Proletkult, he was an accomplished 'vulgar sociologist'. His spell with the Proletkult had something to do with the creation of his theory and with his interest in 'industrial art'. He later joined the LEF group. His works of that time were concerned with the analysis of poetic form while retaining an interest in the social aspect. In 1923 he published 'Mayakovsky's Syntax. An Attempt at the Formal-Sociological Analysis of the Poem "War and Peace" '.His other important articles were 'Counter-Revolutionary Forms' (1923), 'Art and Classes' (1923), 'Art and Production' (1926), 'Sociological Poetics' (1928), 'Agitational and Productive Art' (1930). At the end of the 1920s Arvatov's literary career ceased as a result of mental illness. Tseytlin was an active participant in the debate between the Formalists and the Sociologists. He was interested in the problems of Soviet literature and wrote an important article on Arvatov's theory entitled 'The Marxists and the Formal Method' published in *LEF*, 3, 1923.

In the post-Revolutionary period, the former left trends in Futurism developed into two groups, the LEF and the Constructivists. Because constructivism was also the name of an artistic method which both groups shared, the term 'Constructivist' has a wider connotation than mere membership of the Constructivist group. It is often confusing when literature and art historians apply the label 'Constructivist' to a member of the LEF group. The essential difference between the two groups was not in the field of artistic practice but in the field of aesthetics, in the field of appreciation of art. The LEFists (especially Mayakovsky) stood closer to the notion of art as a social activity than the Constructivist group, some members of which stood for the naked form, the naked idolization of technology, restricting themselves to formal innovations only. But this was not true of all members of the Constructivist group, many of whom polemized with LEF while in fact sharing most of its ideas. In general, members of LEF were more prone to apply social and political criteria to their art; theoretically, they were more of a socially-conscious group. However, they suffered from a contradiction between theory and practice. In practical terms, there was very little difference between the two groups.

Most of the Constructivists were involved not in literary works but in the visual arts—painting, architecture, theater and cinema—where the strength and essence of Constructivism lay. The literary Constructivists were members of the LTsK (*Literaturny tsentr konstruktivistov*). The graphic artists and theatrical and cinema producers who used Constructivism as a method were mostly members of LEF: they were motivated in their work by left-wing political ideas. This fact should be borne in mind when reading about Eisenstein, Vertov, Meyerhold and Tairov as Constructivists. In order to avoid confusing method with group, I propose the use of the terms 'LEFist' and 'member of the Constructivist group' when speaking of group affiliation, and of the term 'Constructivist' when speaking of artistic method.

Among the members of the LTsK were Asmus, Ehrenburg and Selvinsky. Asmus was a leading Constructivist critic and theoretician who in 1932, like Kornely Zelinsky, Selvinsky, Ehrenburg and many other members of the group, recanted his sins and joined the approved trend. Selvinsky was more active as a poet than a critic. Ehrenburg was an enthusiastic Constructivist from the very beginning. In 1922 he and El Lissitzky, the famous graphic designer, edited the trilingual magazine *Veshch/Gegenstand/Objet* in Berlin. Ehrenburg also wrote a Constructivist manifesto. Also in Berlin, in 1922, Ehrenburg published a book of Constructivist criticism, *A vse-taki ona vertitsya* (But It Does Move). His novels *The Extraordinary Adventures of Julio Jurenito* and *Trust D.E.* were also written in the Constructivist style.

Of the LEFists-Constructivists among the theoreticians of the cinema, Eisenstein and Vertov are names of worldwide fame. The fullest description of Eisenstein's life and work is in the book by Mary Seton in which his Jewish origin is indicated.[25] Eisenstein began his career in the Constructivist theater of the Proletkult. He also worked as an artistic designer in Meyerhold's productions. Later, he switched to film directing and joined LEF. His early films were given over entirely to Constructivist ideas; his later films were made according to his original theories.

Seton's book attempts to explain Eisenstein's theories but it is not a comprehensive study of his theoretical heritage. She writes in the 'Preface':

> Eisenstein was not only a film director. He was a scientist searching for the roots of artistic expression. This led him to the development of a body of theory relating to the creative process and film aesthetics... A great part of his research and theoretical work is still unpublished... When all the unpublished work is assembled it is possible that posterity will rank Eisenstein the scientist and philosopher as high and even higher than Eisenstein the film director. Indeed, he may be generally recognized as a universal genius.[26]

Although Eisenstein was remote from Jewish life, he suffered from antisemitism. In 1942 he broadcasted to foreign Jews on behalf of the Soviet Jewish Anti-Fascist Committee,[27] and appeared together with Ehrenburg, Mikhoels and others in the Committee's film *To the Jews of the World.*[28]

Dziga Vertov was a film director and a theorist of the Soviet cinema. He started out before the Revolution as a Futurist noise composer; after the Revolution he progressed into film-making. His *agitprop* documentaries during the Civil War supporting the Red Army made him popular. Like Eisenstein he was a Constructivist, but his method was more radical than Eisenstein's. The latter produced films from scripts but Vertov did not believe in the portrayal of imaginary life and therefore concentrated on the documentary. He had no need for the psychologism of drama ('theatrical productions') in films, nor for scripts. In his view, 'everything can be included in the new concept of the newsreel film', even Dostoevsky. He was a proponent of 'factual cinema' (*kino fakta*). In 1922-1925, Vertov made a series of documentaries under the title 'Kino-Pravda'. His most famous films were *Kino-glaz* (1925), 'One Sixth of the World' (1926) and 'Stride, Soviet' (1926). He contributed articles to *LEF* and *Novy LEF* magazines. Vertov's theoretical works and hypotheses were published in Moscow in 1966 under the title *Stati, dnevniki, zamysly* (Articles, Diaries and Plans). He had a number of foreign imitators and successors.

Zarkhi was an innovating theorist of cinema and film script writing. He was also a playwright and a pedagogue. In the 1920s and early 1930s he published numerous articles on the cinema. His career as scriptwriter is linked most closely with the film director Pudovkin, who made the films 'Mother' (1926, based on Gorky's novel) and 'The End of St Petersburg' (1927), from Zarkhi's scripts. Zarkhi also collaborated with Eisenstein. He travelled a great deal both in the USSR and abroad. After visiting England, he wrote the play *Ulitsa radosti* (The Street of Joy) about the class struggle in England. It is most likely that Zarkhi began as an experimenter and was a member of LEF for some time before adopting realistic art. He was 'one of the first among the writers to enter the film industry'.[29] As a critic and theoretician, he was the first to fight for the recognition of script writing as an independent branch of literature. This was the subject of his report to the First All-Union Congress of Soviet Writers (1934) at which he was a delegate.

Vsevolod Meyerhold was born Karl Meyergold, the youngest son of a German emigré who converted from Judaism to Lutheranism. 'At the age of twenty-one Karl changed his name to Vsevolod (after the writer Garshin) Emilevich (patronymic) Meyerhold (changing the Jewish-sounding "g" to "h").'[30] 'Karl had grown very proud of his Russian nationality and consequently felt there was a fundamental difference between himself and his German father.'[31] A pupil of Stanislavsky, Meyerhold began his original career as a theatrical director with Symbolist productions, and he was designated 'by certain Petersburg Symbolist poets as the titular head of the Symbolist movement in the theater.'[32] After the Revolution, he became a leading Constructivist, developing a Constructivist theory of 'Biomechanics', with the emphasis on the use of gesture and grotesque. He was among the boldest experimenters of the avant-garde in the theater, implementing his natural tendency towards 'exaggeration' and continuously moving his theater further away from literature. His theater of the grotesque was based on the idea that acting is the 'apotheosis of the mask' every actor wears. He collaborated with LEF and was keen on implementing the ideas of the Revolution in the theater, but together with Tairov and other Formalists, he was a constant target of attacks by the RAPP group. He was eventually compelled to change his style and in the 1930s his importance declined.

Aleksandr Yakovlevich Tairov was another famous theatrical Modernist who, in 1914, founded the Kamerny Theater in Moscow. He was a fellow-comrade of Meyerhold in revolutionary art in the 1920s. As a director, he developed his original ideas moving from Futurism to Constructivism. The theater was for him 'part of everyday life, dealing with everyday problems in everyday language, in an everyday surrounding, where the distance between actors and the audience was practically removed.'[33] He also created the 'system of the "Synthetic Theater" in which the set, costume, actor and gesture were to be integrated to form a dynamic whole'.[34] The theoretical principles of his method were expressed in his *Zapiski rezhissera* (Notes of a Director) (Moscow 1921) and *Das entfesselte Theater. Aufzeichnungen eines Regisseurs* (2nd ed., Potsdam, 1927). A fellow Constructivist, Ilya Ehrenburg, wrote about Tairov:

> The sin of the Moscow Kamerny Theater is aestheticism expressed in various ways (attenuating circumstances: the nurse is Salome, Tairov likes everything beautiful, the theater is visited by poets, etc.) Nevertheless, it is a new theater. Instead of anarchy and 'mood-conditioned' actors or actors who 'condition others into a mood', there is a system, an organization, instead of harem canvasses there are three-dimensional mathematical forms of contemporaneity. But here also are the same reasons, the same impossibilities. The

> general a-theatrical rhythm of the environment slows down the movement as if into a dissonance but in reality it is for the sake of a rich rhyme. An ascetic mystery play appears. Tairov retreats behind the limelight but the lights are dim. He is not guilty.[35]

As in the case of most experimental directors, we know very little about Tairov's life and work, apart from a few random notes.

Notes

1 L.M. Farber, *Sovetskaya literatura pervykh let revolyutsii, 1917-1920* (Soviet Literature of the First Years of the Revolution, 1917-1920) (Moscow 1966), 135.
2 M. Slonim, *Soviet Russian Literature* (New York 1967), 104.
3 Ibid.
4 See R. Maguire, *Red Virgin Soil* (Princeton 1968).
5 Eisenstein is mostly described as a German. About his Jewishness and Jewish activities see below.
6 Erlich, *Russian Formalism* (The Hague), 32.
7 For more details, see my article 'Identifying Jewish names in Russia', *Soviet Jewish Affairs*, no. 3 (London 1972), 66-75.
8 N.P. Poltoratsky (ed.), *Russkaya religiozno-filosofskaya mysl XX veka* (Russian Religious-Philosophical Thoughts of the 20th Century) (Pittsburg 1975), 277.
9 N.O. Lossky, *History of Russian Philosophy* (New York 1952), 318.
10 Minsky is not included in the list because he emigrated in 1905: because of his association with the Bolsheviks, he was in trouble with the authorities and had to emigrate. He did not return after the Revolution, but nevertheless remained sympathetic towards the Bolsheviks and the Soviet regime and even worked in Soviet institutions abroad. Ideologically, at least, he belongs among the Soviet critics of the initial decade. His exclusion from the list is thus the result of a pure accident of a geographical, not ideological, nature.
11 See Poltoratsky (ed.), 293.
12 About Frank in greater detail see N.M. Zernov, *The Russian Religious Renaissance of the Twentieth Century* (London 1963), 159-64.
13 Erlich, 122.
14 Ibid., 5.
15 Although in this work Lundberg is classed as a Religious-philosophical critic, it should be said that after his return to the Soviet Union in 1924 he could no longer be viewed as such. His post-emigration articles were written in the Marxist vein.
16 Erlich, 32.
17 We consider here only the Moscow and the Leningrad branches of RAPP: MAPP and LAPP. Most of the RAPP critics listed here were members of MAPP with the exception of Dobin, Gorelov, Mustangova, Messer and Mayzel who were in LAPP.
18 E.J. Brown, *Russian Literature Since the Revolution* (New York 1963), 197.
19 'Psikhologicheskaya shkola' (The Psychological School), *KLE*, vol. 6, 66.
20 See B. Pasternak, *Ya pomnyu* (an autobiographical sketch).
21 See V. Ivanov, *Sobranie sochineniy* (Collected Works), vol. 2 (Brussels), 799; also K. Bjornager, comp., *Russkaya literatura XX veka. Vospominaniya* (Rus-

sian Literature of the 20th Century: Reminiscences) (Arhus 1972), 123.
22 See Ivanov, vol. 2, 799.
23 See M. Royzman, *Vse, chto pomnyu o Esenine* (Everything I Remember about Esenin) (Moscow 1973), 195.
24 V. Shklovksky, 'V kvartire "Lefa" ' (In the Quarters of Lef), in Bjornager, comp., 375.
25 M. Seton, *Sergey M. Eisenstein. A Biography* (London 1952), 18.
26 Ibid., 15.
27 L. Kochan, ed., *The Jews in Soviet Russia Since 1917* (London 1970), 272.
28 See M. Seton, 428-9.
29 I. Shtok, 'Nathan Zarkhi. (K 20-letiyu so dnya smerti)' (Nathan Zarkhi. (On the twentieth anniversary of his death)), *Teatr*, no. 10 (Moscow 1955), 154.
30 J.M. Symons, *Meyerhold's Theater of the Grotesque* (Cambridge 1973), 21.
31 Ibid., 23.
32 Ibid., 25.
33 C. Gray, *The Russian Experiment in Art, 1863-1922* (London 1962), 265-8.
34 Ibid., 200.
35 I. Ehrenburg, *A vse-taki ona vertitsya* (But It Does Move) (Moscow-Berlin 1922), 24.

Bibliography

Encyclopedias and reference books

Beletsky, A.I. *et al. Novoeyshaya russkaya literatura, kritika, teatr metodologiya. Temy, bibliografiya* (Modern Russian Literature, Criticism, Theater and Methodology: Themes and Bibliography) (Moscow 1927).

Bolshaya sovetskaya entsiklopediya (Great Soviet Enclyopedia). 1st ed., vols. 1-65 (Moscow 1926-47).

Bolshaya sovetskaya entsiklopediya (Great Soviet Enclycopedia). 2nd. ed., vols. 1-51 (Moscow 1950-58).

Bolshaya sovetskaya entsiklopediya (Great Soviet Encyclopedia). 3rd ed., vols. 1-30 (Moscow 1970-78).

Encyclopedia Judaica. Vols. 1-16 (Jerusalem 1971-72).

Ensiklopedichesky slovar (Encyclopedic Dictionary) (Brokgauz and Efron) 1-82 + appendices 1-6 (Petersburg 1890-1907).

Jewish Encyclopedia. Vols. 1-12 (New York 1901-06).

Kilimnik, O. and **Petrovsky**, O. (compilers). *Pysmenniki radyanskoy Ukraini* (Writers of Soviet Ukraine) (Kiev 1970).

Kratkaya literaturnaya entsiklopediya (Short Literary Encyclopedia). Vols. 1-8 (Moscow 1962-75).

Literaturnaya entsiklopediya (Literary Encyclopedia). Vols. 1-9, 11 (Moscow 1929-39).

Lvov-Rogachevsky, V. *Russko-evreyskaya literatura. Bibliografichesky i kritichesky obzor evreyskoy poezii, nachinaya s 1803g. do nastoyashchikh dney* (Russian Jewish Literature. A Bibliographical and Critical Survey of Jewish Poetry from 1803 to the Present) (Moscow 1922).

Evreyskaya entsiklopediya (Jewish Encyclopedia). Vols. 1-16 (Petersburg 1908-13).

Malaya sovetskaya entsiklopediya (Small Soviet Encyclopedia) 2nd ed., vols. 1-11 (Moscow 1935-47).

Marxism. Communism and Western Society. A Comparative Encyclopedia. Vols. 1-8 (New York 1972-73).

Roth, C. and **Wigoder**, G. (eds). *The New Standard Jewish Encyclopedia* (London 1970).

Russkie pisateli. Bibliografichesky slovar (Russian Writers: A Bibliographical Dictionary) (Moscow 1971).

Serebryanaya, E.I. (ed). *Istoriya russkoy filosofii: ukazatel literatury izdannoy v SSSR na russkom yazyke za 1917-1967 gg.* (History of Russian Philosophy: An Index of Literature Published in the USSR in Russian in 1917-1967) (Moscow 1975) 3 vols.

Slovnik spisovatelu narodu SSSR (Dictionary of Writers of the Peoples of the USSR) (Prague 1966).

Sovetskaya istoricheskaya entsiklopediya (Soviet Historical Encyclopedia). 1- (Moscow 1961-).

Soyuz pisateley SSSR. Spravochnik (The USSR Writers' Union: A Handbook) (Moscow 1961).

Soyuz pisateley SSSR. Spravochnik (The USSR Writers' Union: A Handbook) (Moscow 1966).

Teatralnaya entsiklopediya (Encyclopedia of the Theater). Vols. 1-6 + appendix (Moscow 1961-69).

Universal Jewish Encyclopedia. Vols. 1-10 (New York 1939-43).

Vitman, A.M. *et al. Vosem let russkoy khudozhestvennoy literatury (1917-1925)* (Eight Years of Russian Literature (1917-1925)) (Moscow-Leningrad 1926).

Wininger, S. *Grosse jüdische National-Biographie.* Vols. 1-7 (Czernowitz 1925-36).

Who's Who in World Jewry (New York 1965).

Who Was Who in the USSR (New Jersey 1972).

In addition, extensive bibliographical material can be found in:

Anderson, T. *Russian Political Thought* (New York 1967); **Billington**, J.H. *The Icon and the Axe* (New York 1970); **Utechin**, S.V. *Russian Political Thought* (London 1963); and **Zernov**, N.M. *The Russian Religious Renaissance of the Twentieth Century* (London 1963).

Memoirs and biographical material

Bjornager, K. (compiler). *Russkaya literatura XX veka. Vospominaniya* (Russian Literature of the 20th Century: Reminiscences) (Arhus 1972).

Charny, M. *Napravlenie talanta* (The Direction of Talent) (Moscow 1964).

Charny, M. *Ushedshie gody* (The Past Years) (Moscow 1967).

Khodasevich, V. *Literaturnye stati i vospominaniya* (Literary Articles and Reminiscences) (New York 1954).

Lidin, V. (ed). *Pisateli* (Writers) (Moscow 1928).

Mandelshtam, N. *Hope Against Hope* (London 1971).

Mandelshtam, N. *Hope Abandoned* (London 1973).

Royzman, M. *Vse, chto pomnyu o Esenine* (Everything I Remember about Esenin) (Moscow 1973).

Shklovsky, V. *Mayakovsky and His Circle* (New York 1972).

Shklovsky, V. *Sentimental Journey. Memoirs, 1917-1922* (New York 1970).

Histories of literature and art, and other historical material

Aleksandrova, V. *A History of Soviet Literature, 1917-1964. From Gorky to Solzhenitsyn* (New York 1970).

Anderson, T. *Russian Political Thought* (New York 1967).

Aronson, M. and **Reiser**, S. *Literaturnye kruzhki i salony* (Literary Circles and Salons) (Leningrad 1929).

Bely, A. **Ivanov-Razumnik**, R.J. and **Shteynberg**, A.Z. *Pamyati Aleksandra Bloka* (In Memory of Aleksandr Blok) (Petrograd 1922).

Billington, J.H. *The Icon and the Axe* (New York 1970).

Blok, A. *Sobranie sochineniy* (Collected Works). 8 vols (Moscow-Leningrad 1960-63).

Blok, A. *Zapisnye knizhki* (Notebooks) (Moscow 1965).

Bowra, C.M. *The Creative Experiment* (London 1949).

Brodsky, N.L., **Lvov-Rogachevsky,** V. and **Sidorov**, N.P. *Literaturnye manifesty* (Literary Manifestos) (Moscow 1929).

Brown, E.J. *Russian Literature Since the Revolution* (New York 1963).

Brown, E.J. *The Proletarian Episode in Russian Literature. 1928-1932* (New York 1953).

Buznik, V.V. *Russkaya sovetskaya proza dvadtsatykh godov* (Soviet Russian Prose of the 1920s) (Leningrad 1975).

Byalik, B.A. (ed). *Literaturno-esteticheskie kontseptsii v Rossii kontsa XIX-nachala XX veka* (Literary and Aesthetic Concepts in Russia of the End of the 19th-Beginning of the 20th Centuries) (Moscow 1975).

Elagin, Yu. *Ukroshcheniye iskusstv* (The Taming of the Arts) (New York 1952).

Erberg, K. (ed). *Iskusstvo staroe i novoe* (Old and New Art) (St Petersburg 1921).

Erlich, V. *Russian Formalism. History-Doctrine* (The Hague 1955).

Farber, L.M. *Sovetskaya literatura pervykh let revolyutsii, 1917-1920 gg.* (Soviet Literature of the First Years of the Revolution, 1917-1920) (Moscow 1966).

Frankel, T. *The Russian Artist* (New York 1972).

Friedberg, M. 'Jewish contribution to Soviet literature', *Bulletin on Soviet and East European Jewish Affairs*, no. 3 (London 1969).

Gibian, G. and **Tjalsma**, H.W. (eds). *Russian Modernism. Culture and the*

Avant-Garde, 1900-1930 (New York 1976).

Glazov, Yu. *Tesnye vrata* (Narrow Gates) (London 1973).

Gorev, B. 'Russkaya literatura i evrei' (Russian literature and the Jews) in **Lvov-Rogachevsky, V.** *Russko-evreyskaya literatura* (Russian Jewish Literature) (Moscow 1922).

Gray, C. *The Russian Experiment in Art, 1863-1922* (London 1962).

Hayward, M. 'Some observations on Jews in post-Stalin Soviet literature' *Bulletin on Soviet and East European Jewish Affairs*, no. 4 (London 1969).

Hayward, M. and **Crowley**, E.L. (eds). *Soviet Literature in the Sixties* (London 1965).

Holthusen, J. *Twentieth-Century Russian Literature* (New York 1972).

Ivanov, Vasily. *Formirovanie ideynogo edinstva sovetskoy literatury, 1917-1932* (The Forming of the Ideological Unity of Soviet Literature, 1917-1932) (Moscow 1960).

Ivanov, Vasily. *Iz istorii borby za vysokuyu ideynost sovetskoy literatury, 1917-1932* (From the History of the Struggle for the High Ideological Content of Soviet Literature, 1917-1932) (Moscow 1953).

Ivanov, Vyacheslav. *Sobraniye sochineniy* (Collected Works). Vol. 2 (Brussels 1974).

Ivanov, V. and **Gershenzon**, M.O. *Perepiska iz dvukh uglov* (Correspondence from Two Corners) (Petersburg 1921).

Ivich, M. *Trends in Linguistics* (The Hague 1965).

Kochan, L. (ed). *The Jews in Soviet Russia since 1917* (London 1970).

Kunitz, J. *Russian Literature and the Jew* (New York 1929).

London, K. *The Seven Soviet Arts* (London 1937).

Lossky, N.O. *History of Russian Philosophy* (London 1952).

Lvov-Rogachevky, V. *Noveyshaya russkaya literatura* (Modern Russian Literature) (Moscow 1925).

Magidoff, R. *A Guide to Russian Literature* (New York 1964).

Maguire, R. *Red Virgin Soil* (Princeton 1968).

Markov, V. *Russian Futurism: A History* (London 1969).

McVay, G. *Yesenin: A Life* (London 1976).

Metchenko, A.I. *et al.* (eds). *Istoriya russkoy sovetskoy literatury* (History of Russian Soviet Literature). Vol. 1 (Moscow 1958).

Mirsky, D.S. *A History of Russian Literature* (London 1968).

Moore, H.T. and **Parry**, A. *Twentieth-Century Russian Literature* (London 1974).

Munitz, B. 'Identifying Russian Jewish names' in, *Soviet Jewish Affairs*, vol. 2, no. 3 (London 1972).

Nash, J.M. *Cubism, Futurism and Constructivism* (London 1974).

Novozhilova, L.I. *Sotsiologiya iskusstva (Iz istorii sovetskoy estetiki 20-kh godov)* (Sociology of Art (From the History of Soviet Aesthetics of the 1920s)) (Moscow 1968).

Paul, E. and **Paul**, C. *The Proletkult* (Proletarian Culture) (New York 1921).

Poltoratsky, N.P. (ed). *Russkaya religiozno-filosofskaya mysl XX veka* (Russian Religious-Philosophical Thought of the 20th Century) (Pittsburg 1975).

Rothenberg, J. 'The Mandelshtam memoir and the Russian Jewish intelligentsia' in *Soviet Jewish Affairs*, vol. 2, no. 3 (London 1972).

Ruhle, J. *Literature and Revolution* (London 1969).

Sayanov, V. *Ocherki po istorii russkoy poezii XX veka* (Essays on the History of Russian Poetry of the 20th Century) (Leningrad 1929).

Sayanov, V. *Sovremennye literaturnye gruppirovki* (Present-day Literary Groups) (Leningrad 1929) (2nd edition: 1930).

Scott, W. *Five Approaches to Literary Criticism* (London 1962).

Sergeev, V.A. *Borba kommunisticheskoy partii protiv burzhuaznosti v iskusstve, 1917-1932 gg.* (The Struggle of the Communist Party against the Bourgeois Spirit in Art, 1917-1932) (Leningrad 1976).

Seton, M. *Sergey M. Eisenstein. A Biography* (London 1952).

Simmons, E.J. (ed). *Through the Glass of Soviet Literature* (New York 1953).

Slonim, M. 'Pisateli-evrei v sovetskoy literature' (Jewish writers in Soviet literature) in *Evreysky sbornik* (Jewish Miscellany), 2 (New York 1944), 146-65.

Slonim, M. *Soviet Russian Literature. Writers and Problems, 1917-1967* (New York 1967).

Slutsky, Y. 'Jews at the First Congress of Soviet Writers' in *Soviet Jewish Affairs*, vol. 2, no. 2 (London 1972).

Stacy, R.H. *Russian Literary Criticism. A Short History* (New York 1974).

Struve, G. *Russian Literature under Lenin and Stalin*, 1917-1953 (London 1972).

Struve, G. *Soviet Russian Literature, 1917-1950* (Oklahoma 1951).

Symons, J.M. *Meyerhold's Theatre of the Grotesque* (Cambridge 1973).

Tartakover, A. and **Kolitz**, Z. (eds). *Jewish Culture in the Soviet Union* (Jerusalem 1973).

Thomson, B. *The Premature Revolution* (London 1972).

Utechin, S.V. *Russian Political Thought* (London 1963).

Vekhi. Sbornik statey (Landmarks. A Collection of Essays) (St Petersburg 1909).

Vengerov, S.A. (ed). *Russkaya literatura XX veka* (Russian Literature of the 20th Century) 3 vols. (Moscow 1914-18).

Weiss, E. *Johannes R. Becher und die sowjetische Literaturentwicklung (1917-1933)* (Berlin 1971).

Wellek, R. 'Preface' to **Erlich**, V. *Russian Formalism* (The Hague 1955).

Zavalishin, V. *Early Soviet Writers* (New York 1958).

Zelinsky, K.L. *Na rubezhe dvukh epokh* (Between Two Eras) (Moscow 1962).

Zenkovsky, V.V. *Istoriya russkoy filosofii* (A History of Russian Philosophy) 2 vols. (Paris 1948, 1950).

Zernov, N.M. *The Russian Religious Renaissance of the Twentieth Century* (London 1963).

Periodicals

Adam. International Review, nos. 394-396 (London 1976).

Bulletin on Soviet and East European Jewish Affairs (London 1968-1970).

Jews and the Jewish People. Evrei i evreysky narod (Collected materials from the Soviet daily and periodical press) (Jerusalem 1961-).

Screen. A magazine published by the Society for Education in Film and Television (London) vol. 12, no. 4, winter 1971/72. (On the representatives and the theories of the 'leftist arts' in the USSR.)

Slavic Review (Illinois).

Soviet Jewish Affairs (London 1971-).

Acronyms and abbreviations

Com-Futs (Komfuty)	Kommunisty-futuristy	Communist Futurists
Gosizdat	Gosudarstvennoe izdatelstvo	State Publishing House
Gostekhizdat	Gosudarstvennoe tekhniche-skoe izdatelstvo	State Publishing House for Technical Literature
Kadets	Konstitutsionnye demokraty	Constitutional Democrats
KLE	*Kratkaya literaturnaya entsiklopediya*	Short Literary Encyclopedia
LAPP	Leningradskaya assotsiatsiya proletarskikh pisateley	Leningrad Association of Proletarian Writers
LE	*Literaturnaya entsiklopediya*	Literary Encyclopedia
LEF	Levy front iskusstv	Left Front of the Arts
Litfront	Literaturny front	Literary Front
LOKAF	Literaturnoe obedinenie Krasnoy Armii i Flota	Literary Organization of the Red Army and Navy
LTsK	Literaturny tsentr konstruktivistov	Literary Center of the Con-structivists
MAPP	Moskovskaya assotsiatsiya proletarskikh pisateley	Moscow Association of Proletarian Writers
OPOYAZ	Obshchestvo po izucheniyu poeticheskogo yazyka	Society for the Study of Poetic Language
Proletkult	Proletarskaya kultura	Proletarian Culture
RAPP	Rossiyskaya assotsiatsiya proletarskikh pisateley	Russian Association of Proletarian Writers
REF	Revolyutsionnyi front	Revolutionary Front
ROSTA	Rossiyskoye telegrafnoe agent-stvo	Russian Telegraphic Agency
SRs	Sotsialisty-revolutsionery	Socialist Revolutionaries
VAPP	Vsesoyuznaya assotsiatsiya proletarskikh pisateley	All-Union Association of Proletarian Writers
VOAPP	Vsesoyuznoe obedinenie assotsiatsiy proletarskikh pisateley	All-Union Organization of Associations of Proletarian Writers

VOKP	Vsesoyuznoe obedinenie krestyanskikh pisateley	All-Union Organization of Peasant Writers
Volfila	Volnaya filosofskaya assotsiatsiya	Free Philosophical Association
VUSPP	Vseukrainsky soyuz proletarskikh pisateley	All-Ukrainian Union of Proletarian Writers

5

The Jewishness of Babel[1]

Efraim Sicher

The typological problem of Jews who write in non-Jewish languages has long been a difficult, sometimes controversial one. Babel was, in fact, in his day considered a master of Russian style; the colorful images and unexpected metaphors of his concise prose reflect a concern for language which may be compared with the linguistic alienation attributed by George Steiner to Franz Kafka and by T.W. Adorno to Heinrich Heine. What concerns us in the present essay is that although Babel could have written only in Russian, he was nonetheless a Jewish writer. This is important not only for an understanding of Babel's writings but also for the wider discussion of Soviet Jewish culture.

Isaak Babel was born in 1894 in Odessa, a cosmopolitan Russian port in the Ukraine, whose population consisted of a large proportion of Jews—over 34 per cent according to the 1897 census. Babel's grandparents spoke Yiddish, and his parents also knew Yiddish, but they talked with their children in Russian. Nevertheless in this fairly assimilated middle class family Isaak Babel was tutored at home in Hebrew, Yiddish, the Bible and Talmud. From the age of six he was sent to *kheder*, and according to his sister was keen on his Jewish studies. Hence Babel, though brought up speaking Russian, had a command of Yiddish as well as some knowledge of Hebrew.[2]

While this linguistic background was a fairly common feature of those Russian Jews who were urbanized and socially upward moving, Odessa was unique in being a new city where traditional Judaism was less deep-rooted than in the *shtetl* and where the ideas of the *Haskalah* (Jewish Enlightenment) had found fertile ground in the second half of the nineteenth century.[3]

Odessa of the early twentieth century was an important cultural center of East European Jewry. This was the Odessa of Ahad Haam, Pinsker, Klausner, Jabotinsky, Bialik, Sholem Aleichem and Mendele Moykher-Sforim. Babel met Mendele on several occasions before the death in 1917 of the 'grandfather' of Yiddish literature[4] and in later years translated Sholem Aleichem into Russian. He wrote the sub-titles for Gricher's silent film adaptation of Sholem Aleichem's Menakhem Mendl stories 'Jewish Luck' (1925), starring Mikhoels whose great friend and fan he was. His filmscript based on Sholem Aleichem's novel 'Vagabond Stars' came out in 1926.[5] He spent many hours in his last years reading Yiddish and translating from Yiddish purely for pleasure. Babel, we know, often had to give up work on his own stories to undertake translating and editing work for financial reasons, but his devotion to Yiddish literature was genuine.

The break with tradition and the motif of escape from the stifling Jewish home into the outside world link the boy in Babel's 'Childhood Stories' and the intellectual in *Red Cavalry* with the romanticized heroes of *Haskalah* literature who were depicted as breaking out of the stifling restraints of the outdated Jewish home; however, after the pogroms and the failure to be accepted in Russian society the assimilated Jewish intellectual in Babel's 'Gedali' returns nostalgically to the Jewish *shtetl* only to find it ruined, doomed, just as the life has gone out of the unchanging old Jews in Bialik's 'Upon My Return'. In 'Alone' or 'At the Threshhold of the Study-House' there remains little but dark despair in traditional Judaism. There is no return and no way out. Feuerberg's question in the title of his novella 'Whither?' (1899) assumed new tragic proportions. At the same time Bialik's 'City of Slaughter' and other poems on the pogroms inspired Babel's generation with the flame of resistance. In 'First Love' Babel's ten-year-old narrator fantasizes that he is a member of a Jewish self-defense group during a pogrom.

Being a Jew in his house and a man in the street—this is what makes Benya Krik king of the gangsters of Jewish Odessa. Not only can he sleep with a Russian woman and satisfy her, says Arye-Leyb in 'How It Was Done in Odessa', but he also meets the Russian world on his own terms: the gangsters shoot back at the *pogromshchiki*. Babel's Odessa stories may seem a departure from traditional portrayals of the passive Jew but the burly Jews in Sholem Asch's 'Kola Street' could well count among the antecedents of Babel's rough Odessa Jewish carters. The Jewish underworld was dealt with by Sholem Asch (*Motke the Thief*), by Joseph Opatoshu (*Romance of a Horse Thief*) and later by Oyzer Varshavsky (*Smugglers*), not to mention Sholem Aleichem and Mendele. The positive Jewish hero who uses brawn as well as brain was an expression of national consciousness and the search for human dignity in Russia at the turn of the century.

Babel was probably active in Zionist groups[6] and worked for a Jewish welfare organization in Odessa.[7] His profound interest in the 'Jewish question' can be seen in most of his stories and is evident in the first story known to us, 'Old Shloyme', published in Kiev in 1913.[8] This contribution to a regular column on the 'Jewish question' concerns a senile Jew who chooses suicide rather than see his son convert and assimilate into Russian society. In Kiev, where from 1911 he was taking a course in business studies, Babel mixed with the assimilated Jewish intelligentsia and *nouveaux-riches*, whom he was to caricature in a later story, 'Guy de Maupassant'. At the home of Boris Gronfeyn, a business acquaintance of his father, Babel met his future wife Evgeniya, a painter, who shared his dedication to art and West European culture.[9]

On the outbreak of war Babel continued his studies in Saratov, where he wrote the first story in a series on Jewish childhood, 'Childhood. At Grandmother's' (November 1915). He moved to Petrograd and became a student at the Psycho-Neurological Institute whose doors were open to Jews. According to surviving records, Babel was not involved in the revolutionary activities which went on there.[10] In 'Ilya Isaakovich and Margarita Prokofevna', one of the sketches and stories he published in Petrograd periodicals, Babel introduces an Odessa Jew who dodges the police by spending the night with another victim of the Tsarist system, the Russian prostitute Margarita Prokofevna.

After having served on the Romanian front, Babel returned to revolutionary Petrograd in March 1918. Here he contributed to Gorky's anti-Bolshevik newspaper *Novaya zhizn*. He also published a Russian version of the Hershele Ostropoler story 'Shabos-nakhamu'[11] in which the eighteenth-century Jewish prankster tricks an innkeeper's wife into giving him a hearty meal. In a later *Red Cavalry* story the narrator tells the Zhitomir rebbe he is putting Hershele's adventures into verse; the rebbe replies: 'the jackal whines when it is hungry, every fool has sufficient foolishness for despondency and only the wise man can tear the veil of being with his laughter.'[12] For Russian readers, who were probably as cold and hungry as Hershele proverbially was, the Yiddish story not only contains a social message but also illuminates much of Babel's ironic humor. For Jewish readers, this is one of the most explicit examples of Yiddish influence in Babel's Russian prose.[13]

An unpublished pre-Revolutionary fragment, 'Three O'Clock in the Afternoon . . . ', depicts the Jew Yankel trying to save the imprisoned son of his landowner, the priest Father Ivan, while simultaneously putting up with abuse about Jewish 'exploitation'. The 'Story of My Dovecot' (1925) records the painful impression made by pogroms on the occasion of the

1905 Constitution,[14] while 'The Journey' and 'Beresteczko' reflect the atrocities of the Civil War period. Konstantin Paustovsky, attesting to Babel's sensitivity to antisemitism, quotes him as saying: 'I didn't choose to be a Jew . . . I am a Jew, a Yid. At times I think I can understand everything. But one thing I will never understand and that's the reason for that filthy treachery which goes by the humdrum name of antisemitism.'[15]

Like many secular Jews, Babel adhered to the humanitarian ideals and some traditional customs of Judaism, rather than to religious law. For him God had been officially dedeified in 1917, though he tried to buy *matsoth* for Passover and sent greetings for the Jewish New Year to his family abroad. In a letter of 1935 he speaks of re-discovering God and praying for his mother's recovery from illness,[16] but the diary he wrote on the Polish front in 1920 shows his unfamiliarity with a prayer-book during a Friday evening service.[17] His attitude is summed up in a letter he wrote in 1928. It was time, he remarked, to forget Jewish ailments, bitter memories and anxieties: 'We must decorate our houses with gaiety not with *tsores*. But how can one convince people of that?'[18]

As a war correspondent attached to Budenny's First Red Cavalry from May until September 1920, Babel came into close contact with the East European *shtetl* Jew, so different from the jovial Odessa Jew who 'bubbled like cheap wine' . . .

> The movements of the Galician and Volhynian Jew are impetuous, jerky and uncouth, but their sorrow is filled with a somber grandeur and their secret contempt for the Polish lord is limitless. Looking at them, I understood the poignant history of these parts, the tales of Talmud scholars who kept taverns, rabbis who lived off money-lending, and young women who were raped by Polish soldiers and fought over by Polish magnates.[19]

Babel adopted the ironic pseudonym Lyutov—'fierce'—and passed himself off as a Russian. Yet, although he was aware of the decay of this petty-bourgeois Jewry, they were his 'kin' and he opened his heart to them.[20] More than once he comforted credulous *shtetl* dwellers with fantastic stories of a Bolshevik utopia, but his true sympathies for the victims of looting and pogroms are revealed in his diary and in the articles he wrote for the front-line propaganda news-sheet, *Krasny kavalerist*.[21]

When Babel transformed his diary into the short stories which appeared from 1923 he introduced a fictional narrator who presents an ironic, at times cynical, portrayal of a post-Revolutionary Jewish intellectual. This intellectual cannot escape his Jewish identity—the spectacles, literacy and humaneness which alienate him from the Cossacks—and is nostalgic for his vanishing Jewish past. At the beginning of 'Gedali' the narrator sadly recalls his childhood when the sabbath candles were kindled and his grandfather would read the Bible commentator Ibn Ezra: 'On those evenings my child's heart rocked like a little ship on enchanted waves. Oh, the rotted Talmuds of my childhood! Oh, the heavy melancholy of memories!'[22] He wanders around the former market of Zhitomir—the thematic and biographical association with Bialik is striking—in search of a 'shy star' (the beginning of the sabbath), a 'Jewish glass of tea' and a bit of that 'pensioned-off God' in the glass of tea. The narrator's search brings him to the junk store of old Gedali who has witnessed the cruelty both of the Poles and the Bolsheviks. With Talmudic logic Gedali examines the warring camps, but neither offers him salvation. The Revolution cannot accommodate Jewish values: ' "To the Revolution we say 'yes', but are we to say 'no' to the Sabbath?" Thus Gedali begins and winds round me the silken straps of his smoky eyes. "Yes, I shout to the Revolution, yes, I shout, but the Revolution hides from Gedali and sends forth nought but shooting . . . . " '[23]

This was the dilemma facing many Jewish intellectuals who had forsaken Jewish life and pledged allegiance to the Revolution, but could not be totally indifferent to the destruction of the *shtetl* and its values. It is not by chance that Babel's stories, including 'Gedali', were the only translations to be included in the short-lived Soviet Hebrew journal *Be-reshit*.[24]

This lament for the past was accompanied by messianic yearnings, but it is presented by Babel with subtle irony. Gedali, who has studied the Talmud and loves Rashi and Maimonides, is blind to the rising sun of the Revolution and departs for the synagogue, a lone figure in the setting sun which symbolizes the end of the *shtetl*, but which also heralds the inauguration of the sabbath—day of rest and foretaste of the messianic age. As he departs in the setting sun, Gedali dreams of an 'International of Good People' who will distribute first-class rations to all.

The sunset metaphor appears frequently in Babel's writings. It is most explicit in the play *Sunset* (1926-28) which is based on the earlier unpublished short story of the same name. We recall that in Perets's dramatic poem *The Golden Chain* the hasidic Rabbi Shloyme wants to hold on to the Sabbath as long as he can, but his son restores the natural order; nevertheless, the hope for final redemption lives on. In Babel's play, Mendel Krik seeks to evade the sunset of his terrible reign and to cheat his sons Benya and Levka of their inheritance by selling his carter's business and running off to Bessarabia with the Gentile Marusya. However, in the words of the local oracle, Rabbi Ben-Zkharya, Mendel has repeated the 'mistake' of Joshua the Prophet, who 'stalled' the setting of the sun,[25] and Jesus of Nazareth, who 'stole' the sun.[26] All his life Mendel wanted to bask in the mid-day sun, to delay the coming of the sabbath: ' "But God has policemen on every street and Mendel had sons in his house. Policemen come and make order. A day is a day, and evening is evening. Everything is in order, Jews. Let's drink a glass of vodka . . . !" '[27]

The inevitability of social and historical change—the play is set in 1913—is emphasized by the allegory of King David, told by Arye-Leyb, the *shames* (synagogue sexton), after the downfall of Mendel under a blood-red sunset. Mendel and David both faced attempts by their sons to usurp power, both strayed from the strict path of morality. Arye-Leyb tells of King David's rise to power, his wealth and fame, and of how he took Batsheva, the beautiful wife of Uriah the Hittite...

Benya Krik is Ben Tsion, Son of Zion, and is modelled on the real-life gangster Misha Yaponchik, who helped to defend Odessa's Jews from the Whites but was afterwards killed by the Reds, as is Benya in Babel's film of the Odessa stories. Despite his mock-epic speech in 'How It Was Done in Odessa', in which he speaks of Joseph Muginshtein as a scapegoat for 'the whole working-class', Benya the King institutes no new social order. Indeed, the red dawn does not shine brightly in any of Babel's works, and the hope of a happy future for the new proletarian generation, voiced at the end of the play *Mariya* (published in 1935, but repressed while in rehearsal at the Moscow Vakhtangov and Jewish theaters), was elsewhere sceptical. The exotic adventures of the Odessa gangsters give way to melancholy for the old Odessa lost after the Revolution ('Froim Grach', 'End of the Old Folks' Home'). The final Odessa story, 'Karl-Yankel', is set against the background of the anti-religious campaigns of the 1920s. Naftula, red-haired *mohel* (circumciser) of old Odessa, finds himself in the dock at a show trial. The father, anxious about his application to join the Communist Party, cuts a ridiculous figure and the public prosecutor Orlov (né Zusman) was himself once circumcised by the defendant. For all the slogans of the Friendship of the Soviet Peoples (a Kirghiz suckles the Jewish child) and the promise that the unfortunate baby will be an airman—the spirit of the new age!—the fusion of the heritage of the Marxist and Jewish patriarchs in Karl-Yankel is not a happy one.

A synthesis of Judaic tradition and revolutionary zeal is also attempted by Ilya Bratslavsky in *Red Cavalry*. But Bratslavsky dies, a forgotten Elijah in an apocalyptic war, and the narrator receives 'the last breath of his brother', the conclusion of the first edition of the book (1926). Even the fulfilment of the narrator's dream in 'Argamak', added as a new ending to the *Red Cavalry* stories in 1933, to ride as one of the Cossacks, is not achieved without making more enemies. Similarly, acceptance by the Cossacks does not enable the narrator of 'My First Goose' to sleep with an easy conscience. Here the narrator has killed a goose, a sexual surrogate of the landlady—herself a bespectacled victim—whom he pushes around in order to earn the Cossacks' admiration. But he has sacrificed something within himself in descending to the Cossacks' bestial amorality. Lyutov's sole prayer at the end of 'After the Battle' is to be able to overcome his Jewish abhorrence of killing his fellow man.

Not all the stories in *Red Cavalry* are told by an alienated Jewish intellectual: some of them are narrated by Cossacks. But even in the folksy tales of the uneducated Cossacks Babel demonstrates with irony their misconception of the Revolution, their barbarity and their traditional hatred of Poles and Jews ('Konkin', 'Salt', 'Treason'). That the narrator appears indifferent towards the slaughter of his Jewish brethren serves to emphasize the horror of the deed which usually is passed off under a 'humdrum name'. In 'Beresteczko' the victorious Cossacks enter the town after staging an epic march past reminders of their glorious past as well as reminders of their defeat by the Poles in 1651, only to be greeted by barred shutters. The first act of these heroic descendants of Bogdan Khmelnitsky is to execute an old Jew; the narrator at this point has detached himself from their midst and watches from a window. 'Cemetery at Kozin', an elegy for centuries of unrevenged Jewish dead, is preceded and followed by stories of vicious Cossack vengeance, 'The Life of Matvey Rodionych Pavlichenko' and 'Prishchepa'. 'Cemetery at Kozin' ends with a question which echoes that posed by the pregnant Jewess in 'Crossing the Zbrucz' compelled to watch her father being butchered: why has the Angel of Death not once spared the Jews?

Themes of the Civil War and the post-Revolutionary intellectual were topical in Russian literature in the early 1920s, as were under-world heroes (among whom were also the Jewish gangsters in Kaverin's *End of the Gang*). But Babel's stories, with their distinctive Jewish point of view, also dealt with issues touched upon by contemporary Yiddish authors such as Dovid Bergelson, Der Nister, Perets Markish and Dovid Hofshteyn of the Kiev group. Like Babel, they were attacked by the proletarian critics for lamenting too much the passing of the *shtetl* and not drawing uncritical portraits of 'positive' socialist heroes. Their acceptance of the Revolution was not unambivalent—Markish, Kvitko, and Hofshteyn left the USSR for a while—and their tragic fates during Stalin's last years put paid to their desperate hopes after October, when East European Jewry lay devastated by war, revolution and pogroms.[28] Babel's stories were published by the Kiev *Kulturlige* in 1925[29] and Babel was a close friend of, among others, Mikhoels and (after his return in 1933 from emigration) Dovid Bergelson. Babel translated Bergelson's New York story 'Giro-Giro' and Bergelson translated Babel's play *Sunset* into Yiddish for the Moscow Jewish State Theater (though it was apparently not performed.)

Babel was too much of an individualist to toe the line, and in the 1930s, although it became increasingly dangerous to keep silent, fewer and fewer of his works were published. He was never a Party member and, apart from the obligatory references to Stalin, avoided voicing any definite political or literary views.[30] Certainly Babel was aware of the difficulty of publishing his own accounts of collectivization (only one part of *Velikaya staritsa* appeared), industrialization (in the story of a reformed gangster in Donbass mines, *Kolya Topuz*) and life in Kabardino-Balkariya (whose leader Betal Kalmykov was purged). The novella *The Jewess*, on which Babel worked in the late 1920s, dealt with the final demise of the *shtetl*. The Ehrlich family, once rich, are now destitute and denied work, and it is not clear whether this is a new beginning or a dreary, lonely end. The widowed Jewess agrees to go to Moscow with her son, the Red Army officer Boris, who has invested his fervent Jewish passion in the Revolution. Whether the move to Moscow was to be successful is unknown for there the surviving fragment of the manuscript breaks off.

Like the Yiddish 'fellow-travellers' Babel could not ignore the suffering and fate of the *shtetl* when depicting those who devoted their lives to socialist ideals. He did not give a full portrayal of a socialist hero, except for the steel-hard smithy Baulin in 'Argamak', and made clear the painful dilemma of the Jewish intellectual in post-Revolutionary Russia. In Dovid Hofshteyn's words,

> In Russian fields, at dusk, in wintry frost—
> where can one feel lonelier, more lonely, more lost?

Levka Krik, on leave from the Tsarist cavalry in the play *Sunset*, declares that a Jew who has mounted a horse has ceased to be a Jew and has become a Russian, but, for all their attraction to the open, Gentile world of physicality and nature, Babel's Jews remain alienated and intrinsically Jewish—unlike Levinson, the Jew on horseback in Fadeev's *The Rout* (1927), or Libedinsky's Mindlov in *Commissars* (1926). The Russian classics tended to treat the Jew as little more than a type of mythical enemy, not as a real phenomenon of Russian life.[31] The picture is not all black, of course, as evidenced by the contributors to Gorky's *The Shield* and others who championed the Jewish cause in Tsarist Russia. Jews who were smugglers and who made rowdy scenes in taverns were not unknown, but—to take an example—Kuprin's treatment of biblical motifs ('Shulamit') and of East European Jewry ('The Coward', 'A Wedding') lacked an inside view of Jewish life and Yiddish folklore: the *shtetl* is seen through the eyes of a Russian officer. The novelty of Babel's contribution to Russian literature was its very Jewishness. The stance of an outsider does not hide the attachment of Babel's Jewish narrators to the Jewish world they wish to abandon: they do not find it so easy to break free from their Jewishness.

Unfortunately, the fact of Babel's Jewishness has been almost totally ignored by both critics and scholars.[32] Nevertheless, F. Levin, a Soviet scholar and critic, writes: 'Portraying Gedali, the Bratslaver rebbe Motele and other Jews, Babel conveys in their speech a specific blend of the style of the Talmud and the actual colloquial speech of the inhabitants of the Jewish *shtetl*, with its aphorisms and humor.'[33]

The approach to the exposition of the plot (*syuzhet*) in many of Babel's stories is similar to a Talmudic discourse. The *syuzhet* is kept to a bare minimum of information while allusions and parallels direct the reader to that extra-textual conclusion which is the reader's own but planned by the author. This is how Arye-Leyb tells his story: 'Arye-Leyb began, as always, with allegories and parables that crept up from afar and towards an aim that not all could perceive'.[34] Such is the tortuous, insidious path of Talmudic logic. The object of analysis—and eventual comprehension—is isolated and the problems blocking the mind's way to full understanding are delineated and enumerated:

> . . . let's talk about Benya Krik. Let's talk about his lightning beginning and his terrible end. Three black shadows block up the paths of my imagination. There is the one-eyed Froym Grach. The russet steel of his deeds, can it really not bear comparison with the strength of the King? Here is Kolka Pakovsky. The simple-minded fury of that man contained everything necessary for him to wield power. And couldn't Khaim Drong make out the brilliance of a new rising star? Why then did Benya Krik alone climb to the top of the rope-ladder, while all the rest were left swaying precariously on the lower rungs?[35]

Babel's prose abounds in references and allusions to *tanakh* (Bible, Prophets and later holy scriptures). In texts that were worked on almost till perfection this can sometimes border on the dangerous ground of the subtext, that which lies below the non-literal, secondary meaning, as evidenced by the very style of Babel's Russian prose with its devices of repetition and refrain, a point made by A.B. Murphy who sees Biblical overtones dominating the story 'Salt'.[36] The use of rhythm, syntactic constructions—such as the conjunctions *i* ('and') with a temporal meaning and *togda* ('then') with a causal connotation (often beginning a sentence or paragraph)—parallelism and near tautologies, is characteristic of Biblical Hebrew, and for this reason also native to Yiddish.

All this has the effect of evoking the epic, being often a deliberate stylization, but it also on occasion draws attention to *parable*. By referring to *myth* and using it in a transferred or distorted sense the end result is actually a *demythicization* of the often stereotyped Jewish world.[37]

Jewish writers in Russian in the Soviet period generally appear in the official annals with little or no mention of their Jewish origin. The extent of their Jewish background varies greatly, but Isaak Babel's Jewishness is manifest when compared with, say, that of Boris Pasternak, Osip Mandelshtam, or Ilya Ehrenburg. For the baptized Pasternak, nations and ideologies had been rendered anachronistic by Christianity. Mandelshtam is a more complex example, his feeling for his blood brethren consisting largely of his conception of European civilization as rooted in Levantine Judeo-Christianity. Ehrenburg's *Stormy Life of Lazik Roitshvanets*, published in Paris in 1928 but never included in Soviet editions of Ehrenburg's works, was as critical of Judaism and Zionism as it was of Bolshevism and its enemies. Ehrenburg eventually returned to Russia and, until the Nazi invasion, any remaining Jewish tendencies were muted in his writings. Ever the chameleon, Ehrenburg declared he would remain a Jew as long as there was antisemitism.[38]

The above mentioned writers deserve, of course, fuller analysis than is possible here. Less complex is the position of the numerous Jewish writers, critics, artists, scholars and politicians who became prominent after the Revolution and who discarded any traces of their Jewish heritage. For the sincere Jewish revolutionary who had rejected Zionism or the Bund, the *shtetl* was an outdated survival of the Jewish bourgeoisie.

Babel's assimilated Jewish contemporaries did not generally express conflicts between Jewish roots and Revolutionary allegiance. No such conflict exists for Kogan, the heroic Jewish commissar of Bagritsky's *Ballad of Opanas*. Bagritsky (pseudonym of Eduard Dzyubin), a friend of Babel from Odessa, was hardly nostalgic for his Jewish childhood (see his 'Conversation with My Son' and 'Origins'). When Babel paid tribute to him after his death as embodying the communist pioneer combined with Rabbi Akiva he no doubt had Bagritsky's poetic genius in mind. For Bagritsky, as for Utkin and others, the Revolution had put an end to the 'Jewish question': in Bolshevik terminology, the pogrom was a class problem. Although Babel told Michael Gold in Paris in 1935 there was no longer a 'Jewish question' in Russia,[39] this is not borne out by his published writings. His 'Story of My Dovecot' leaves an unforgettable impression of what it meant for a Jewish boy in Tsarist Russia to grow up into the adult world of sex and pogroms. Rather than presenting a Marxist standpoint and portraying the pogrom as the work of reactionaries, as does Valentin Kataev in *Lone White Sail* or Nikolay Ostrovsky in *How the Steel Was Tempered*, Babel depicts the violence done to Jews before and after the Revolution as their natural lot. In 'Story of My Dovecot' the cripple Makarenko, seeing he is getting nothing but bonnets from the looting, strikes at the Jewish boy, squashing his newly purchased doves (a Biblical symbol of peace and sacrifice). His rage is matched by Katyusha's venom: ' "Their seed should be wiped out . . . I can't stand their seed and their stinking men." '[40]

In the story which followed, 'First Love', the boy, having joined his parents who are sheltering at the house of their Russian neighbors, cannot resolve the contradiction between reality—his father debasing himself in the mud, his own portrait thrown out of his father's store—and fantasy—his passion for the Russian Galina, the imaginary heroism of the Cossacks. He ends up with a nervous disorder and concludes that these events explain much in his later life.[41]

Babel was one of the few Jewish authors to portray pogroms in Russian after the Revolution, along with Mikhail Kozakov (*The Man Who Bowed to the Ground*, 1930), the children's author Lev Kassil (*Shvambraniya*, 1933) and Aleksey Svirsky (*Story of My Life*, 1935). The last two works were expurgated during the Zhdanov clamp-down after the Second World War.

Babel did not produce original work in Yiddish, unlike Ansky or other bilingual writers. There already existed a tradition of Jews writing in Russian dating back to the growth of the Russian Jewish press in the 1860s[42] and Simon Markish has, in fact, called Babel a fount of Russian Jewish literature in the Soviet period.[43] But Babel's prose style is easily distinguishable from the censorious, often publicistic tone of earlier Russian Jewish authors, such as Rabinovich or Semyon Yushkevich, who also portrays the Odessa Jewish under-world (as in *Leon Drei*, 1908).[44] The new generation's revolt against the patriarchal magnate's philistinism and imperviousness to the suffering of fellow Jews in Yushkevich's drama *The King* (1908) contrasts with the rebellion of Benya 'The King' against the vulgar, cruel regime of his father Mendel 'The Pogrom' in *Sunset*.

Like Bergelson and Der Nister on the one hand and Mandelshtam and Ehrenburg on the other, Babel began writing before the Revolution. However, he had little in common with many of the pre-Revolutionary Jewish *littérateurs* who wrote in Russian, either in social origin (his father dealt in agricultural machinery) or in outlook. For him Russian was not a conscious choice, but the natural culture in which he had grown up; no doubt because he had never had to make a choice he was not estranged from Yiddish.

The upheavals of war and revolution had, moreover, radically altered the fate of Russian Jewish writers. Several, including Mark Aldanov, Yuly Aikhenvald, Semyon Yushkevich, Nikolay Minsky and Sasha Cherny, went into emigration after the October Revolution. The nationalistic poet Semyon Frug had died in 1916; Andrey Sobol remained pessimistic about the attitude of Russian intellectuals towards Jews until his suicide in 1926; David Aizman died in 1922. The old social and geographical distribution of readers of Russian Jewish literature no longer existed, nor did the aim of amelioration of the Jewish position. Emancipation had unleashed a plethora of Jewish publications in Russian as well as in Yiddish; from the mid-1920s, however, a writer's allegiance to Soviet literature was expected to derive from class consciusness, not ethnic identity. In the view of the author of one typology of Soviet Jewish writers, the Revolution put the old God off-stage and the new generation followed very different gods, so that one could hardly speak of a Russian Jewish literature in the Soviet period.[45]

If Babel refers in any way to Russian Jewish literature it is ironically. In a 1916 sketch, 'The Nine', one of the characters awaiting the editor's beneficence is the Jew Korb who suffers from pains in the head as a result of wounds sustained during a pogrom. During the First World War he joined the Foreign Legion and was evacuated back to Russia after being wounded. Now he has written a drama which begins 'Ring the bells, Judea has perished!'[46] The only Russian Jewish author Babel mentions (in a conversation reported in Paustovsky's memoirs) is the emigré satirist Sasha Cherny.

It was pointed out in Babel's own day that what was of anecdotal or ethnographic significance in Russian Jewish literature Babel transformed into an expressive, convincing work of art of wide appeal.[47] Babel was acclaimed as the first Jewish writer to write from *within* Russian literature and to give the Jewish milieu color and depth.[48] Russian Jewish literature had no Heine and one could scarcely measure its writers on the same scale as the Yiddish masters Mendele, Sholem Aleichem or Perets, whereas, in the opinion of at least one contemporary critic, Babel and other Soviet Jews writing in Russian could aspire to the class of Turgenev and Tolstoy.[49]

Whatever ambivalence or disquiet Babel may have felt about the future of a Jewish writer in the Soviet Union, he could not possibly have resigned himself to becoming a taxi-driver in Paris, where he lived in 1927-28. Nor was he content to be an emigré writer: to begin with, the Western publishing system was no more adaptable to his laborious and uncompromising method of writing than was the Soviet system. He had hoped to bring his family back together again in Russia but October 1928 found him alone in Kiev, arranging the affairs of his deceased father-in-law: 'I feel fine on my native soil. There's poverty here, much that is sad, but it is my material, my language, something that is of direct interest to me.'[50]

Babel failed to re-unite his family and was able to visit them again only in 1932 and once more in 1935. Yet his destiny was too bound up with Russia and the struggle for socialist ideals for him to live and write abroad. His arrest and disappearance in May 1939 only confirmed the tragic paradox of history. As Simon Markish has written, Babel was symbolic for the 'Jews of Silence' of a modern Jewish writer[51] but there was to be no place for him in Soviet literature from the purges until Stalin's death, and again from the mid-1970s, during the reaction under Brezhnev and the curb on Jewish activism.

Notes

1 As only the issue of Babel's place in Soviet Jewish culture in the 1920s is tackled here, the reader interested in the image of the Jew and Jewish writers in Soviet literature is referred to Maurice Friedberg's 'Jewish themes in Soviet Russian literature' and 'Jewish contributions to Soviet literature', in L. Kochan (ed.), *The Jews in Soviet Russia since 1917* (3rd ed., Institute of Jewish Affairs, 1978), 197-216 and 217-25 respectively. The Jew in Russian literature is dealt with in J. Kunitz, *Russian Literature and the Jew* (New York 1929). On the theme and image of the Jew in Stalinist Russian and Yiddish literature, see Bernard Choseed, 'The Soviet Jew in literature', *Jewish Social Studies*, vol. 11, no. 3, July 1949, an article written before the execution of Yiddish writers in 1952 and before Khrushchev's exposure of Stalin's crimes; a revised version appeared as 'Jews in Soviet literature', in E.J. Simmonds (ed.), *Through the Glass of Soviet Literature: Views of Russian Society* (New York 1953), 110-58. A more detailed examination of Jewish themes in Babel's writings is available in the present author's unpublished doctoral dissertation 'The Works of I.E. Babel (1894-?1941) with Special Reference to Tradition and Innovation in the Style of his Narrative Prose in the 1920s' (University of Oxford 1979).

2 See Judith Stora-Sandor, *Isaac Babel: l'homme et l'oeuvre* (Paris 1968), 18-20 (based on a conversation with Babel's sister, Meri Shaposhnikov, in Brussels); cf. Isaak Babel, 'Avtobiografiya' (Autobiography), *Detstvo i drugie rasskazy* (Childhood and Other Stories), compiled with notes by Efraim Sicher (Jerusalem 1979), 7. Babel's stories will be cited from the complete and uncensored versions in this edition.

3 See S.J. Zipperstein, 'Jewish enlightenment in Odessa: Cultural characteristics, 1794-1871', *Jewish Social Studies*, vol. 44, no. 1, 1982, 19-36.

4 See Babel quoted in Ya. Eidelman, 'Mendele Mokher-Sforim: Na torzhestvennom zasedanii v Dome soyuzov' (Mendele Moykher-Sforim: At a festive meeting in the House of Unions), *Literaturnaya gazeta*, 5 March 1936, 6.

5 We may believe that Sholem Aleichem always remained close to Babel's heart despite the deprecatory preface to his 1926 film version of *Vagabond Stars*, which was a defence against ideological attacks on such 'unsuitable' material. In 1936 Babel was commissioned by the Soviet publishing house 'Akademia' to edit the works of Sholem Aleichem. He had previously edited a two-volume translation (Moscow-Leningrad, 1926-27).

6 O. Ronen, 'I.E. Babel', in *Kratkaya evreyskaya entsiklopediya* (Short Jewish Encyclopedia) (Jerusalem 1976), vol. 1, 272.

7 Judith Stora-Sandor, 19.

8 *Ogni* (Kiev), 9 February 1913, 3-4.

9 Nathalie Babel, 'Introduction', in Isaac Babel, *The Lonely Years, 1925-1939: Unpublished Stories and Private Correspondence* (New York 1964), xvi-xvii.

10 According to a file in the Leningrad Historical Archives, cited in L. Livshits, 'Protiv tendentsioznykh istolkovaniy tvorchestva i biografii I.E. Babelya' (Against tendentious interpretations of the works and biography of I.E. Babel),

Voprosy literaturovedeniya i yazykoznaniya (Kharkov), vol. 2, 1965, 22-5.
11 *Vechernyaya gazeta*, (Petrograd), 16 March 1918, subtitled 'Iz tsikla *Gershele*' (From the Hershele cycle). A version of the Yiddish source may be found in *Hershele Ostropoler, der Velt berihmter Vittsling* (Hershele Ostropoler, World Renowned Wit) (New York n.d.), 65-6.
12 I. Babel, 'Rabbi' (The Rebbe), *Detstvo i drugie rasskazy*, 134. It is not known whether Babel continued with the Hershele stories, but he did think of Hershele when watching the Hasidim pray in a Dubno synagogue (Diary entry for 23 July 1920, MS in the collection of A.N. Pirozhkova).
13 See the present author's article 'Yitskhak Babel, He-hakham Me-Odessa' (Isaak Babel, the wise man of Odessa), *Zehut* (Ramat-Gan), no. 2, 1982, 219-22.
14 There is no evidence that the Babel family were harmed by the violent outbreaks of 1904-5, and this is denied by Nathalie Babel, *The Lonely Years...*, xiv-xv.
15 Konstantin Paustovsky, *Vremya bolshikh ozhidaniy* (A Time of Great Expectations) (Moscow 1960), 151-2.
16 Letter of 9 October 1935, *The Lonely Years...*, 290.
17 Diary, 3 June 1920.
18 Letter of 15 December 1928, *The Lonely Years...*, 112.
19 'Uchenie o tachanke' (A discourse on the *Tachanka*), *Detstvo i drugie rasskazy*, 140-1.
20 Diary, 5 June 1920.
21 See 'Rytsari tsivilizatsii' (Knights of civilization), *Krasny kavalerist*, 14 August 1920; 'Nedobitye ubiitsy' (The unbeaten murderers), *Krasny kavalerist*, 17 September 1920.
22 'Gedali', *Detstvo i drugie rasskazy*, 125. The 'ship' and 'waves' presumably refer to the 'sea' of the Talmud.
23 Ibid., 126.
24 'Reshimot' (Notes), *Be-reshit*, (Moscow-Leningrad) no. 1, 1926, 15-38. Babel authorized these translations personally. See also Y.A. Gilboa, *Oktobraim Ivriim* (The Hebrew Supporters of October) (Tel Aviv 1974).
25 Joshua, 10: 12-15.
26 I. Babel, *Zakat* (Sunset) (Moscow 1928), 95. The reference to Jesus is missing in other editions.
27 Ibid., 96.
28 See Chone Shmeruk, 'Yiddish literature in the USSR' in *The Jews in Soviet Russia since 1917*, 242-80. Little attention has been paid to the thematic parallels with Perets Markish's *The Brothers*, Moshe Kulbak's *Zelmenyaner* or Bergelson's 'Civil War' in his *Stormy Days*. Indeed, these works attracted similar criticisms of a 'non-Marxist' standpoint levelled at Babel's *Red Cavalry*.
29 I. Babel, *Dertseylungen* (Stories) (Kiev 1925). There is no indication that this is a translation and Babel may have had a hand in this Yiddish publication of his stories. D. Feldman's translation appeared the same year in Kharkov, followed by Gitl Mayzl's in the Warsaw *Literarishe bleter*.
30 A rare example of Babel's signature of a public anti-Trotskyite denunciation is 'Lozh, predatelstvo, smerdyakovshchina' (Lies, treachery and 'smerdyakovshchina'), *Literaturnaya gazeta*, 26 January 1937, 4. Needless to say, Babel was under much pressure to join such mass declarations during the purges. He was subject to personal harassment and his fear is evident in the memoirs of Ervin Sinkó and Ilya Ehrenburg.
31 See, for example, David Goldstein, *Dostoevsky and the Jews* (Austin 1981). The

antisemitism of, say, Gogol or Lermontov, did not prevent Babel from valuing them as writers, just as it did not prevent many other Jews, particularly the nineteenth-century *maskilim* , who looked to the Russian classics for liberal humanitarian ideals.

32 For instance, Patricia Carden in *The Art of Isaac Babel* (Ithaca and London 1972) barely mentions Babel's Jewish background except to quote from Judith Stora-Sandor (*Babel: l'homme et l'oeuvre*, Paris 1968), who does not have a proper grounding in Judaism (and hence some strange conclusions). James E. Falen in *Isaac Babel: Russian Master of the Short Story* (Knoxville 1974) and in his thesis (University of Pennsylvania, 1970) quotes the *Hagada* as his only Jewish source, and claims Nietzsche and the Classics as literary sources and parallels. See on this problem Efraim Sicher, 'Babel's Jewish Roots', *Jewish Quarterly*, no. 3, 1977, 25-7.

33 F. Levin, *Babel: Ocherk tvorchestva* (Babel: A Sketch of His Work) (Moscow 1972), 139.

34 I. Babel, 'The End of the Old Folks' Home', *Detstvo i drugie rasskazy*, 301. For the high standards of euphemistic language set by the Babylonian Talmud, see the beginning of tractate *Psakhim*.

35 I. Babel, 'How It Was Done in Odessa', *Detstvo i drugie rasskazy*, 246.

36 A.B. Murphy, 'The Style of Isaac Babel', *Slavonic and East European Review*, 1966, vol. 44, 366-8.

37 For a discussion of Babel's use of myth, see Efraim Sicher, 'The road to a red calvary: myth and mythology in the works of Isaak Babel of the 1920s', *Slavonic and East European Review*, 1982, vol. 60, 528-46.

38 I. Ehrenburg, 'Lyudi, gody, zhizn' (People, years, life) in *Sobranie sochineniy* (Collected Works), vol. 9 (Moscow 1967), 571.

39 Michael Gold, 'A love letter from France', *New Masses*, (New York), 13 August 1935. This article was translated into Russian in *Literaturny Leningrad*, 14 September 1935, 1.

40 *Detstvo i drugie rasskazy*, 45. This story was, in fact, included in two Soviet anthologies of 1930 directed against antisemitism.

41 Like several such passages which reflect the narrator's nationalistic consciousness, the last lines of the story were omitted from the mid-1930s.

42 See Alexander Orbach, *New Voices of Russian Jewry: A Study of the Russian-Jewish Press of Odessa in the Era of the Great Reforms, 1860-1871* (Leiden 1980).

43 S. Markish, 'Russko-evreyskaya literatura i Isaak Babel' (Russian Jewish literature and Isaac Babel), in Isaak Babel, *Detstvo i drugie rasskazy*, 319-45: English translation, 'The example of Isaac Babel', *Commentary*, vol. 64, no. 5, 1977, 36-45. For a critique of the essay by Markish, see Dino Bernadino in *Ressegna sovietica*, (Rome), vol. 32, no. 5, 1981, 202-3.

44 For a comparison of Yushkevich and Babel, see Walenty Cukierman, 'Isaak Babel's Jewish heroes and their Yiddish background', *Yiddish* (New York), vol. 2, no. 4, 1977, 18-19. Others who had described Odessa's underworld and its racy slang—a mixture of Yiddish, Russian and Ukrainian—include L. Kornman ('Karmen') and the St Petersburg journalist E. Doroshevich.

45 M. Slonim, 'Pisateli-evrei v sovetskoy literature' (Jewish writers in Soviet literature), *Evreysky mir* (New York) no. 2, 1944, 163.

46 *Zhurnal zhurnalov*, (Petrograd), no. 49, 1916.

47 See V. Veshnev, 'Poeziya banditizma' (The poetry of gangsterism), *Molodaya*

gvardiya, (Moscow), no. 7-8, 1924, 276; A. Lezhnev, *Literaturnye budni* (Literary Workdays) (Moscow 1929), 266, 267, 269.

48 A. Lezhnev, *Sovremenniki: Literaturno-kriticheskie ocherki* (Contemporaries: Literary and Critical Sketches) (Moscow 1927), 124-7.

49 A. Kaun, 'Babel: Voice of new Russia', *Menorah Journal*, (New York), November 1928, 400-1. Such an identification of Jewish writers with the national culture of their country of residence was also applicable to contemporary Jewish writers in West European literatures such as Lion Feuchtwanger (whom Babel knew personally) (cf. C. Fadiman, 'The Jew on horseback', *Menorah Journal*, February 1927, 102—a review of Feuchtwanger's *Power*.)

50 Letter of 20 October 1928 in *The Lonely Years...*, 106. Babel's first wife had lived since 1925 in Paris, where a daughter, Nathalie, was born in July 1929. His sister had also left Russia in 1925 to live with her husband in Brussels and was followed by Babel's mother. Meanwhile, from 1925 until 1928, Babel continued a relationship with the future wife of Vsevolod Ivanov, Tamara Ivanovna Kashirna, who bore him a son, Mikhail. In 1934 Babel finally settled down with Antonia Nikolaevna Pirozhkova, an engineer on the Moscow Metro project, by whom he had a daughter, Lidiya.

51 'Russian Jewish literature...', in Isaak Babel, *Detstvo i drugie rasskazy*, 345.

6

Ilya Ehrenburg

Anatol Goldberg

'His name is always mud—somewhere or other. He is Ilya Ehrenburg, the renowned Soviet writer, who has shouldered the lifelong burden of always being blamed by somebody, somewhere, for something.'

The London *Daily Mirror* said this on his seventy-fifth birthday in January 1966 and it was true. Ehrenburg was too complex a character for those who prefer to see the world in black and white. He had been a Bolshevik who left the Party before he was twenty-one and never rejoined it. He was a cosmopolitan and a Russian patriot. A hater of the capitalist system who had been afraid of communism. An agnostic in search of faith who once nearly entered a Catholic monastic order. A Paris Bohemian who was absorbed by the Soviet literary establishment. A rebel who was protected by Stalin and rebelled against Stalinism as soon as Stalin died. A basically anti-Zionist, non-religious Jew who proudly proclaimed that he would call himself a Jew as long as there was a single antisemite left in the world.

To Russian literature, which had no *Candide*, no *Gulliver's Travels* and no *Gargantua and Pantagruel*, Ehrenburg gave its first *roman philosophique*, *The Extraordinary Adventures of Julio Jurenito*, thus filling a gap—even though a famous Russian critic said about it at the time: 'We are still waiting for a Russian Rabelais.' To the Soviet Union Ehrenburg gave *The Thaw*—a book whose content was soon forgotten but whose title acquired world fame: it became the symbol of an era in Soviet politics and an inspiration to statesmen at home and abroad who, thanks to Ehrenburg, though they often did not know it, developed a taste for meteorological metaphors and talked about melting or breaking the ice of the Cold War. To the men and women who grew up in the Soviet Union after Stalin's death Ehrenburg gave his memoirs—a unique, though incomplete, collection of facts which his public could learn from no other source.

He also helped the Soviet Union to win the war against Nazi Germany—by telling Soviet soldiers day after day why they must go on fighting. He talked to them through the Armed Forces paper *Krasnaya zvezda* (Red Star) and they adored everything he said. It is remarkable that a man like Ehrenburg, who until 1941 had spent most of his adult life in Paris, should have found words that went straight to their hearts. Some people regard this as his greatest achievement, and indeed while war-time articles—the kind of writing that is avidly read today and goes out of one's head tomorrow—may not rank as a contribution to a nation's culture, they did in this case contribute to Russia's survival.

Julio Jurenito

Ehrenburg wrote *Julio Jurenito* after he had seen the world war in France and then the Communist Revolution, followed by civil strife and chaos in Russia. In 1921, when he returned to the West, he found refuge in a Belgian seaside village where he worked on his book. He finished it in a month, which means that it must have been ready in his mind before he put pen to paper. It is written in the first person singular. Ehrenburg casts himself in the modest role of a disciple who expounds the philosophy of his Master, a Mexican adventurer called Julio Jurenito. Jurenito is supposed to be what Ehrenburg would dearly have liked to be himself: a cynic. They meet in Paris at a popular Bohemian café shortly before the outbreak of the First World War. Ehrenburg, the romantic, is in the depths of despair because of the wickedness of the world round him and Jurenito puts to him the simple proposition that since everything is so manifestly evil, everything should be destroyed. But to rely on an anarchist's bomb would be childish. Jurenito has devised a more effective method: to cultivate the sores and to foment decay, thus accelerating the process by which society will destroy itself.

Having recruited Ehrenburg as his first disciple—the only one who knows what the Master is planning to do—Jurenito chooses six other companions of different nationalities, who are supposed to assist him in his undertaking without being aware of it. His selection is not entirely logical. Three are evil men and as such eminently qualified to act as his unwitting accomplices since everything they do automatically helps the process of decomposition. But the others are harmless and even endearing people, which means that they can hardly be of much use.

One of the evil men is Mr Cool, the American. A businessman by profession and a missionary by inclination, he is confident that he can solve every problem with the help of two books: the cheque book and the Bible. His belief in the power of the former is absolute. Whether it is a matter of going to bed with someone else's fiancée, or of breaking a strike—not in his own factory, but purely for the sake of maintaining the established order—or of ruining the life of an artist whose style he happens to dislike, it can all be arranged by signing a cheque and handing it to the right people. The Bible, or rather the use he makes of it, enables him to find a moral justification for everything he does. At one point Ehrenburg asks Jurenito: 'Master, why didn't you kill Mr Cool?' Yet for all his iniquity, Mr Cool is a human being. By contrast, there is nothing human about Jurenito's German disciple, Karl Schmidt, who is the nearest approach to an automaton equipped with what would now be called an electronic brain. Schmidt stands for dictatorship and regimentation. He is not interested in gain or pleasure—his only ambition is to organize the world and he is prepared to accept any doctrine whose declared purpose is to set up an orderly system. He admires both the Kaiser and Karl Marx: during the war he becomes a general in the German army; after Germany's collapse, he turns communist and goes to Russia where he hopes to put his ideas into practice. Schmidt fills Ehrenburg with dismay. Ehrenburg is much kinder to the Frenchman, Monsieur Delhaie, who personifies bourgeois selfishness. He, too, is a loathsome creature, but he appreciates good food, a quiet life and the pleasures of love, and one can see that Ehrenburg has a sneaking admiration for his *savoir vivre*.

While the 'wicked' disciples all belong to privileged nations, Aleksey Spiridonovich Tishin, the idealistic, tearful and hopelessly muddled Russian intellectual, Ehrenburg, the Jew, and Aysha, the negro, represent the underdogs. At one point Jurenito and his friends—all except Schmidt—are interned in a German prisoner-of-war camp. 'Whenever our guards were angry with the Master, Mr Cook or Monsieur Delhaie,' says Ehrenburg, 'they would invariably punish Aleksey Spiridonovich, Aysha or myself.' The status of Ercole Bambucci, the Italian member of Jurenito's team, is somewhat indeterminate: the guards do not treat him as a whipping-boy but do not hesitate to punish him for his own misdemeanors. As an Italian, Ercole represents, in Ehrenburg's eyes, true Western culture, even though he has never learned to read or write. He is a joyous anarchist, has never done a stroke of work in his life and despises wealth, but has mastered the art of living to no lesser extent than the prosperous and respectable hedonist Monsieur Delhaie. As for Aysha, the negro, he is the best of the lot. Civilization has passed him by—he is kind, affectionate and pure of heart.

Ehrenburg differs from the other six in that he is a Jew and, unlike them, he claims that if he had to choose between the two most important words in the human vocabulary, he would choose 'No' rather than 'Yes'. This in fact is supposed to be the basis of Ehrenburg's and Jurenito's philosophy—'No' to society—and wherever they go, the Master holds forth about the *impasse* civilization has reached. Religion has been destroyed by dogma. The Almighty of the Old Testament had once placed a bet on Job's endurance and has been playing with men's lives like a reckless gambler ever since. The Church has devalued the currency of the Kingdom of Heaven, which has fallen as low as it can possibly fall. Protestantism stripped the beautiful doll of Rome of its vestments, without realizing how precious they were, and found only a handful of stuffing inside. Atheists, with nothing to cling to, rant and roar in public but seek refuge in cowardly superstition when they are unobserved. Faith exists only among such primitive and tender-hearted persons as Aysha: nothing can shake his trust in the power and the kindness of the idols he carves out of coconut shells, whereas among Europeans a believer is as rare as a good-looking virgin or an upright statesman. Love, as a natural relationship between the sexes, was killed by St Paul whose teachings Jurenito calls 'scabrous'. Unable to castrate the whole of mankind, the Apostle's followers had no choice but to tolerate sex 'sanctified' by marriage, with the result that the world has become a gigantic brothel, since marriage in a bourgeois society is more corrupt than prostitution; prostitutes are at least good at their job.

However, in spite of all this big talk, the attempt to present Jurenito as a true cynic does not come off. Yes, he does regard marriage as worse than prostitution and organized religion as a fraud. But why is he so indignant about it? Strictly speaking, he should not give a damn. The reason is of course that while Jurenito is not supposed to care, Ehrenburg does—because whatever he may say in the book about the Jews' negative approach to life, Ehrenburg does not in the least prefer 'No' to 'Yes'. A 'No'-lover would have relished the world war as the ultimate negation of everything the so-called civilized world had ever stood for, whereas, while the war goes on, Ehrenburg, the narrator, laments: 'They brought a little girl in a light-blue dress, her legs had been torn off by a German bomb . . . The newsboys screamed: "killed, lost, blown up!" I was suffocating—I could not bear the stench of blood, anaesthetic and printer's ink . . . ' Some 'No'-lover!

In 1917, after the February Revolution in Russia, Jurenito and his disciples go there (as Ehrenburg did in real life). As they watch the orgy of freedom which sweeps the country and the chaos this creates in people's minds, Jurenito quickly comes to the conclusion that freedom is too heavy a yoke to bear and that its twilight is at hand. Later, after the establishment of the Soviet regime, he discusses the issues of freedom and power with the 'man on the captain's bridge', whom he does not name but who is easily recognizable as Lenin. In Dostoevsky's 'Legend of the Grand Inquisitor' the man whose voice is the voice of power talks about freedom to Christ. Ehrenburg called his account of Jurenito's imaginary conversation with Lenin 'The Grand Inquisitor outside the Legend'.

Jurenito, as he speaks to the 'captain', mingles irony with respect. He compliments Lenin on his healthy single-mindedness; he quite understands that people like Lenin must wear 'merciless blinkers'. 'Reflection', says Jurenito, 'is a dessert served at the last supper before death. Can anyone do anything unless he is blind? The bandage round your eyes is a splendid suit of armor against the devil of wisdom.' Lenin listens to this placidly. But then Jurenito mentions the inevitable by-product of this type of healthy approach: the list he saw in *Izvestiya* of people who had been shot the previous day. This would have made no impression on the Inquisitor, but Lenin becomes emotional and excited. He jumps to his feet, paces up and down the room, launches into a tirade trying to prove—not so much to his visitor as to himself—that there is no other way, even if he finds it terrifying and hard to bear: 'I am not going to pray away my sins or wash my hands clean. I am simply telling you it is hard. But it has to be, do you hear?'

Thus, while Lenin is not as impassive as Dostoevsky's Inquisitor would have been in a similar situation, he does feel that people 'must be driven to Paradise with iron whips', which tallies with what the Inquisitor tells Christ: 'Only now that we have at last suppressed freedom, has it become possible for the first time to think about people's happiness. Man is rebel by nature. Can a rebel ever be happy?' Dostoevsky's 'Legend' ends with Christ imprinting a gentle kiss on the Inquisitor's lips. Outside the Legend, Jurenito ends the conversation by kissing Lenin on his 'high vaulted forehead'. 'Out of reverence or out of pity?' asks Ehrenburg. 'No,' says Jurenito, 'it was a ritual kiss in deference to Russian tradition'—a clever answer, considering that Jurenito is supposed to be a cynic and cannot afford to be emotional. Ehrenburg, however, does not conceal that he feels pity for the man who, having acquired power and become its slave, is following in the footsteps of the Inquisitor, while Schmidt, Jurenito's unwitting accomplice in ruining the world, and thousands like him, are swinging their iron whips, eager to suppress freedom without even beginning to comprehend the meaning of the word 'happiness'. True, not all Bolsheviks are like Schmidt. Some understand what happiness means and passionately desire it for others. There exist selfless people who are doing dull jobs and are intoxicating themselves with work in the belief that what they are doing will in the end mitigate the hardships the country has to endure. Ehrenburg describes one such man who bursts into tears when in a moment of truth he sees the futility of his efforts. Such men do not think or speak of freedom; they are much too pre-occupied with other things. Ehrenburg admires their integrity but for him freedom remains the key issue.

Ehrenburg had a gift for prophecy, of which he was aware and proud. He used to say that a writer's mission was not only to see but to foresee. At a time when art and poetry are flourishing in Russia (as they did in the first years after the Revolution), Jurenito is firmly convinced that under the Soviet regime there will be no room for artistic freedom or for art itself. He predicts that art will disappear and will be replaced by what is now known as industrial design. Here Ehrenburg turned out to be both right and wrong: right because an attempt to do away with art was indeed made by Stalin who instructed his deputy, Andrey Zhdanov, to supervize this unprecedented experiment; wrong, because Stalin tried to replace art by old-fashioned vulgarity and was not interested in the aesthetic side of industrial design or in any other form of aesthetics.

The most remarkable prophecy in the book is of a different kind. During the war Jurenito invents a terrifying weapon of mass destruction (that in itself was not an original idea—science-fiction writers had often predicted the advent of a weapon equivalent to the atomic bomb). But when Jurenito hands over the blueprints to his friend Mr Cool, who owns huge armament factories working non-stop, the American is in no hurry to start producing that devilish instrument; not because he has a vested interest in prolonging the war but because he feels—as Ehrenburg puts it—that Germany can be finished off with French bayonets and that it would be more practical, from the American point of view, to keep Jurenito's deadly gadget in reserve—for future use against Japan.

Candide, which Ehrenburg claims not to have read before he finished *Julio Jurenito*, ends on a note of resignation: the hero, cured of his optimism, contents himself with working in his garden and no longer believes in the best of all possible worlds. Gulliver's conclusion is deeply pessimistic: he no longer wants contact with human beings. By contrast, Ehrenburg, the incurable romantic, ends his kaleidoscopic account of the horrors he has witnessed by sounding the trumpet of hope. He knows he will never see a world where men have been set free. 'But the inevitable will come. I believe it, and to all who await it, to all my brothers without a god, a program or an ideal, to those who are naked and despised and love only the wind and the outrage, I send my last kiss.'

Julio Jurenito was first published in Berlin and shortly afterwards in the Soviet Union. There it appeared with a preface by Nikolay Bukharin, who had known Ehrenburg as an adolescent—it was he who had induced Ehrenburg to join a Bolshevik organization. Things had changed since that time. Ehrenburg had long ceased to be a Bolshevik, while Bukharin was by now a member of the Politbureau, one of the leaders of the Comintern and editor of *Pravda*. This, however, did not stop him from treating *Julio Jurenito* as a piece of literature. He pointed out that he could have written all sorts of 'meaningful phrases' about the author's 'individualistic anarchism', nihilist 'rowdyism', latent scepticism and what not. It was easy to see, said Bukharin, that Ehrenburg was no communist, that he had no great faith in the coming order of things and was not particularly keen on it either. But this did not alter the fact that the book was a fascinating satire. Ehrenburg's own particular brand of nihilism had enabled him to describe some of the laughable and loathsome aspects of life under all regimes – predictably, Bukharin singled out for special praise Ehrenburg's denunciation of capitalism and war. 'The author', he went on, 'is a former Bolshevik, a man of broad vision, who has an excellent knowledge of the West European way of life, a sharp eye and an acid tongue. He has written a humorous, thrilling and intelligent book.' One must not argue about tastes, said Bukharin. 'But we hope that the public will show good taste and will enjoy the amusing *Julio Jurenito*.

Those were the days. But as time went on, Soviet critics began to condemn *Julio Jurenito* on political grounds. One of them objected particularly to Ehrenburg's fanciful description of Lenin. Ehrenburg, he claimed, had made the 'captain' a hysterical Bohemian and a pathetic figure; no wonder he opened his heart so readily to a petty bourgeois interviewer who plied him with loaded questions. 'Fortunately,' said the critic, 'Russia had a different type of man on the captain's bridge in those fateful days.' The critic wrote this after Lenin's death, which was just as well, since the 'captain' himself was less touchy. Lenin remembered Ehrenburg as an untidy youth he had met in Paris, and when he read *Julio Jurenito*, he said to his wife, Nadezhda Krupskaya: 'This is by shaggy Ilya. It's good stuff.'

The Thaw

During the decades that followed Ehrenburg went through many different phases*, including one of almost total submission to Stalin's tyran-

---

* *In the 1920s, Ehrenburg published a number of works which, although translated into many European languages, remained unknown to the Soviet reader; some of them were not included in his nine-volume 'Collected Works' published in 1961. Among these is his most Jewish novel,* The Stormy Life of Lazik Roitschwantz, *which first appeared in 1927. It describes the trials and tribulations of the titular hero, a Jewish tailor from Homel, who faces the cruel contemporary world in revolutionary Russia, Western Europe and Palestine. (Ed.)*

ny. But in 1954, when *The Thaw* appeared in a literary magazine, Stalin was dead and one of the most daring passages in that novel contained a reference to the terrifying episode which had occurred shortly before his death.

Ehrenburg did it very discreetly. A woman doctor, called Vera Sherer, examines a sick child and finds that there is nothing wrong with it. The child's over-anxious mother, still too frightened to rejoice, says, 'Are you quite sure?' To which the doctor indignantly replies: 'If you have no confidence in me, why did you call me?' Then, realizing that this is not the way for a member of the medical profession to behave, the doctor explains that her nerves are in a bad state because of 'the things one has to listen to nowadays . . . after that announcement . . . '

Ehrenburg must have known that future generations would not be able to make head or tail of this and that future editors, should they decide to republish the book, would have to supply a lengthy footnote. The 'announcement' is the one that was issued by TASS, the official Soviet news agency, on 13 January 1953 concerning the arrest of a group of doctors—mostly Jews—accused of having poisoned some of the Soviet leaders and of planning to poison others; Vera Sherer is Jewish, as can be gathered from her surname, and is hinting at the effect the announcement has had on hospital patients who have become suspicious of all Jewish doctors and do not hesitate to voice their distrust. All this would have to be explained. Ehrenburg however, was thinking of the present and there was no need to explain it in 1954. By referring to the 'Doctors' Plot' he was destroying a taboo. True, after Stalin's death the doctors had been rehabilitated and released from prison (except those who seem to have died there), but having made this public and condemned officials for what had happened, the Soviet authorities clearly did not want anyone to mention that monstrous business again. Ehrenburg was bold enough to do so and many marvelled at his boldness.

The Thaw was even more daring in another respect, and here Ehrenburg had to phrase what he was trying to say with even greater care, considering that in 1954 Khrushchev had not yet denounced Stalin. One of the most important features of the book is the symbolic role played by one of its characters—a powerful bureaucrat called Zhuravlev, who is the head of a large industrial enterprise in a provincial town. He has a good war record, works hard and is generally regarded as efficient. When he was young he used to be cheerful and optimistic; now he has acquired an imperious voice and when he laughs people no longer feel cheered by his laughter. During the war he was not afraid of death; now he is frightened of his superiors in Moscow. He has grown fond of lickspittles. A local artist has painted his portrait, showing him, with all his decorations pinned to his lapel, as he sits behind an enormous desk and stares at a model of a new machine tool. He is in love with the enterprise he is directing and is fond of saying, 'The factory and I are one'—in fact he is so much in love with it that he has spent the funds allocated to housing on a new shop at the steel foundry in order to raise production. Whenever he sees the miserable communal huts in which the workers have to live as a result, he feels momentarily depressed but manages to persuade himself that these frail structures are not all that bad and that, in any case, the men are better off now than their fathers had been in the old days.

Gradually Zhuravlev ceases to be human. His wife leaves him and, although he is not particularly upset about this, he becomes morbidly suspicious of everybody. People who used to respect his efficiency—and especially his ability to keep a cool head in a crisis—now call him a scoundrel and one of them says that after talking to Zhuravlev one feels as if one had wallowed in mud. Finally, his disregard for human beings and their needs causes his downfall. A storm destroys the workers' huts, Zhuravlev is summoned to Moscow and while he keeps telling himself that he is not responsible for the weather and has always worked hard for the good of the cause, he knows he is doomed. Soon rumors reach the town that he has lost his job, and his favorite sycophant, getting ready to lick the boots of Zhuravlev's successor, starts saying nasty things about his former chief. People quickly forget Zhuravlev. 'Where was he? What had become of him?' asks Ehrenburg . 'No one cared. There had been a storm which caused much trouble and then moved away. Who thinks of a storm after it has stopped raging?'

There remains the question: who was Zhuravlev? Did Ehrenburg try to portray a basically decent man gone wrong, utterly corrupted by the Stalin era? Or was Zhuravlev meant to be not just a miniature Stalin (of whom there were a great many in Russia) but, symbolically, Stalin himself? There are certain parallels in the lives of the two men that go beyond the urge felt by the slave to imitate his master. Zhuravlev's wife leaves him; Stalin's wife committed suicide—neither could bear the inhumanity of her husband. Zhuravlev is fond of saying, 'The factory and I are one'; Stalin, the absolute ruler, personified the very essence of the maxim '*L'état c'est moi*'. People pay tribute to Zhuravlev's ability to keep a cool head in a crisis; in 1954 Stalin, the late war lord, still ranked officially as the unquestioned architect of the Soviet Union's victory over Nazi Germany, and Ehrenburg could not afford to question this even though he remembered how Stalin had lost his head in the first few weeks after the Nazi attack.

However, in 1954 Soviet readers were still too frightened to speculate openly about the symbolism of Zhuravlev's life and downfall, and most of the public discussion centered therefore on the second theme of *The*

Thaw: the pitiful state to which art and literature had been reduced under Stalin. This was a subject which was no longer taboo; in fact, since Stalin's death there had been several signs of what amounted to a rebellion against the virtual ban which Stalin, through his deputy Zhdanov, had imposed after the war on all true art and all creative writing. A stir had been caused by the publication of an article in the *Novy mir* magazine in which a Soviet writer called Vladimir Pomerantsev dealt with the question of 'sincerity' in Soviet literature. Earlier, I had heard an eminent Soviet theatrical producer declare very emphatically at a meeting in London that no work of art could be created to order, no matter whether the order came from a private person or the state. Earlier still, in October 1953—only seven months after Stalin's death and, as it happened, seven months before the publication of *The Thaw*—Ehrenburg himself had done some probing. In an article which appeared in a monthly journal called *Znamya* he analysed at great length and with utmost caution a question which, he said, had been put to him by one of his readers: why did so many Soviet books no longer grip one's heart and why were the characters in these books so unlike real people? Ehrenburg used a great deal of verbiage to soften the impact of his conclusion, but there was no mistaking the conclusion itself: writing was the business of the writer and not of the rulers or of those who were acting on the rulers' behalf. No one had ever dared to tell Chekhov what he should write about; nor could one imagine anyone 'ordering' Tolstoy to produce *Anna Karenina*. The time had come, said Ehrenburg, to resurrect certain words which had fallen into disuse—words like 'vocation' and 'inspiration'—and also to stop being afraid of literary critics. Without using the word 'censor', Ehrenburg attacked the type of critic who in effect was merely a censor's stooge; such people were so frightened of praising a book which had not been awarded a prize—i.e. had not been lauded officially—that they sought refuge in listing all the things it did not contain and blamed the author for omitting them. It was sad to see, said Ehrenburg, pages of indifferent stuff being inserted in a narrative purely in order to prevent the critics from saying, 'Why did the author not deal with this or that . . . ?'

Ehrenburg got away with this (unlike Pomerantsev, who used some unfortunate similes as he was trying to prove his point and thus made it easier for the establishment to voice its displeasure) and, having got away with it, Ehrenburg ventured to go much further in *The Thaw*. No more verbiage to blunt the effect of what he was trying to say. Instead, a straightforward account of what happens to two friends who are both talented painters. One of them, a man called Pukhov, lured by the prospect of money and success, has done what Stalin wanted him to do—he has abandoned art and concentrated on producing vulgar and worthless stuff. The other painter, Saburov, has chosen poverty and starvation with no hope of acknowledgement or even of showing his work to the public, but has remained a true artist. In this moral anti-Stalinist tale there is, however, one complication: Pukhov tries to be cynical but, like most would-be cynics in Ehrenburg's books, does not really succeed. While he appreciates the money, official praise makes him sick, and when he sees the other man's work, he is overwhelmed. 'Envy is an ugly emotion,' he says to Saburov. 'But I envy you,' and he meditates gloomily on his way home: 'I shall never be able to paint like him—not even if I go mad. I have no longer any feeling for art. Even in a loony bin,' he says to himself, having just finished a mural for an agricultural exhibition, 'even in a loony bin I would still be painting chickens to order . . . ' At home he is gripped by icy cold although the room is well heated.

Frost and ice—outside and in the hearts of men—is the leitmotiv of the novel, but in the end Ehrenburg leaves it to Pukhov, the repentant sinner against art, to make the first gesture welcoming the thaw. As Pukhov goes for a walk in the park with his mistress and sees the first snowdrop, he recalls how much he used to enjoy breaking the thin film of ice which covers the puddles when the end of the winter is near. He sees such a frozen puddle now, runs towards it and tramples upon it with unspeakable pleasure, breaking the ice—the ice of the Stalin era. This joyful gesture coincides with the news (since this is supposed to be 1954) that two of Saburov's paintings are going to be exhibited. Characteristically, the management of the exhibition has chosen the weakest (at least that is what the artist thinks), which suggests that the thaw will be a slow and difficult process. But it has begun.

Like the article Ehrenburg had published seven months earlier, *The Thaw* was an experiment in controversial writing, but on a grander scale—its purpose was to establish what the authorities were prepared to put up with one year after Stalin's death. For every true artist or writer in Russia this had become the crucial question. By now the situation was fluid. The state no longer prohibited literature and art, as it had done in Stalin's time, and thus implicitly granted a certain degree of creative freedom. Its limits, however, were not defined—besides, it was obvious that different factions at the top and among literary bureaucrats had different ideas of what the limits should be. In these circumstances, every true writer or artist was bound to ask himself whenever he started work, 'How far can I go?' Leonid Leonov, a well-known Soviet author, later described this rather colorfully in a lecture he gave to a British audience in London. 'Wily serpents are hissing into one's ear, "Take the plunge and the angels of the Lord will take charge of thee . . . ," ' said Leonov paraphrazing one of the Gospels. 'It's dangerous to tempt the little ones . . . ' Many Soviet writers must have wondered at the time whether the angels of the Writers' Union would protect them if they dared to take the plunge.

Ehrenburg took the plunge for them to find out how things stood. *The Thaw* seemed to be based on the following calculation: if it was praised, which was improbable, this would be an historic landmark; but even if it merely managed to escape complete annihilation by the official critics, it would still be legitimate to regard the experiment as a success—it would mean that some movement towards freedom in art and literature was possible. What gave added weight to this experiment was the fact that the man who undertook it was himself a member of the literary establishment. This was particularly important because by the middle of the year—by which time the authorities and the critics had digested *The Thaw*—the reactionaries became extremely active. The liberal editor of *Novy mir*, Aleksandr Tvardovsky, was sacked for publishing Pomerantsev's article on sincerity in literature, and Pomerantsev as well as a few other 'rebels' were dealt with rather unceremoniously in one of the literary monthlies by the head of the Writers' Union, Aleksey Surkov. *The Thaw* had to be handled more carefully, and the task of combating its effects was entrusted to a subtler person, the poet and novelist Konstantin Simonov, who, like Surkov, had acquired a bad reputation under Stalin but, unlike Surkov, seemed ready to admit that times were changing, though he chose to tread warily. By 1954 one could describe him as an enlightened reactionary, not averse to gradual, very gradual reform.

Simonov's lengthy review of *The Thaw* appeared in the Moscow *Literaturnaya gazeta* (Literary Gazette) and was published in two instalments. In many ways it was a remarkable document, as typical of the period as Ehrenburg's novel. It showed how one could make a piece of writing look like a serious book review, containing much that was true, and yet ignore most of the points that mattered. Simonov could not help mentioning the title of the book but completely ignored its significance. He also ignored the symbolism of Zhuravlev, but that was something he could not afford to analyse. Readers were free to think what they liked; if it occurred to them that Zhuravlev was meant to be Stalin, that was their business—an official critic was not supposed to encourage this kind of speculation. Simonov dealt with Zhuravlev as if he were just a bad factory director, and Simonov emphatically agreed with the author that a man who was not interested in the welfare of the workers should not have been given a responsible job in industry. But while he agreed with Ehrenburg on the worthlessness of Zhuravlev, he objected to Ehrenburg's overall picture of Soviet life. In Ehrenburg's book, said Simonov, decent people were exceptions (perfectly true). Zhuravlev's wife met a decent and intelligent man and was surprised; why was she surprised? She herself was supposed to be a highly intelligent woman – such as one rarely met in Moscow; why 'rarely'? Ehrenburg appeared to suggest, said Simonov, that evil (in the Soviet Union) was common and good was something unusual (perfectly true – this was exactly what Ehrenburg did in *The Thaw*).

Moreover, said Simonov, the book must have been written in a hurry and its literary quality was uneven. This, too, was true. *The Thaw* has no special literary value and Ehrenburg must indeed have written it in a hurry – because he felt that the experiment could not wait. 'In my opinion,' said Simonov, 'this novel is much weaker than anything Ehrenburg has written in the past fifteen years.' This was not true: *The Thaw* is not a work of art but from the purely literary point of view it is still better than, for example, 'The Ninth Wave', a book which was written to order shortly before Stalin's death and which Ehrenburg did not allow to be republished.

Simonov then dealt with the second theme of *The Thaw*: the arts and the plight of the Soviet artist. Here, at least, because it was no longer a prohibited subject, Simonov did not have to ignore the points that mattered. He attacked Ehrenburg's basic assumptions. He said that, according to Ehrenburg, one could be either like Saburov or like Pukhov, one either starved or one betrayed one's art (perfectly true). Worse still, Ehrenburg did not seem to regard Pukhov as an enemy – or a 'petty executioner' – of socialist art, but as a victim of the circumstances – as someone who in the depth of his heart loved art but had been compelled to betray it, not being able to withstand the force which inexorably dragged him towards hack-work (perfectly true). Simonov described this as a travesty of the real situation and the book as a 'regrettable failure'.

However, in his final conclusion Simonov did take into account that this was 1954 and that Stalin had been dead for over a year. Simonov admitted that the standard of Soviet art was not invariably high and the example he chose showed that times were indeed changing: he criticized the President of the Academy of Fine Arts, Aleksandr Gerasimov, a master-vulgarian who used to be Stalin's favourite painter and who typified the worst of what Ehrenburg later described as 'that cursed photography in visual art'. Simonov, too, attacked such 'photographers' together with the 'naturalists' who refused to accept that socialist realism could express itself in different styles and who tried to strangle everything that was new. Had Ehrenburg written about that, said Simonov, and had he paid tribute to what was good in Soviet art, he would have received wide support. Yet all he had to offer was Saburov, a formalist divorced from life – Ehrenburg was thus playing into the hands of the 'naturalists' who would use his book to prove their point. Simonov, the enlightened reactionary, evidently felt that Ehrenburg was moving too quickly and had gone too far.

Years later, a reactionary Soviet lady critic, attacking as 'ideologically harmful' an exhibition arranged by young Soviet artists, who, by Soviet standards, must have ranked as *avant-garde*, pointed out gloomily that it had all started with Ehrenburg's 'Thaw'. She was right. In spite of Pomerantsev and other early signs of rebellion, in spite of the probing done a few months after Stalin's death by Ehrenburg himself, it was *The Thaw* that marked the beginning of the real battle between Stalinists and liberals, which was also a battle between those who had talent and the literary and artistic mediocrities who were defending their own vested interests—with authors like Simonov (talented but too cautious to use their gifts) hovering somewhere in between. The struggle that followed was a succession of victories and defeats—on balance, there was for quite a time a steady but slow movement in the right direction. Politically, the Thaw was triumphant in the first part of 1956, after Khrushchev had denounced Stalin at the 20th Party Congress, and there was a leap forward in literature and art. By contrast, after the Soviet intervention in Hungary, one could expect a setback, and some of the official critics were only too eager to stress that it was essential for the Party to reassert its role in literature, especially in view of the deterioration of the international situation. Ehrenburg, however, seemed undismayed. In February 1957, in an article which appeared in *Literaturnaya gazeta*, he claimed that there was still not nearly enough freedom for true art and creative writing and, invoking the authority of the 20th Congress, he asked for more—in spite of the current anti-Soviet propaganda campaign abroad (i.e. the storm caused by the Soviet action in Hungary). He emphasized that he was addressing both the Soviet public and his friends in the West. For the benefit of the former he once again wiped the floor with those official critics who analysed each new book 'for the amount of sugar and acid' it contained to see if 'the right proportion' had been observed; after the 20th Congress, said Ehrenburg, this kind of approach had become anachronistic. To his friends in the West, especially to those who had been deeply perturbed by the events in Hungary and were beginning to wonder whether Soviet literature and art would 'follow the road mapped out by the 20th Congress', he said with surprising confidence: 'We are advancing steadily; there will be no retreat.' The publication of this article, said Ehrenburg, was the best proof of that.

He sounded as if he had official backing, and he had indeed consulted some people near the top. Two weeks later, however, the Soviet Party journal *Kommunist* came out with an editorial which made some people think that Ehrenburg had been over-confident. The editorial looked at first sight alarming. It recalled the Zhdanov decrees, which in the late 1940s and early 1950s had paralysed all creative writing and art. It claimed that these decrees were 'basically' still valid. It rebuked editors for having published harmful books. Yet *The Thaw* was not included in that list, and *Kommunist* admitted that things had at one time been carried too far, that the cult of Stalin had adversely affected the situation, and that it had been wrong to ban works by certain authors. On closer examination, the article appeared to suggest that, while the authorities were determined not to let things get out of hand, they had no intention of going back to the Zhdanov-Stalin era. In May Khrushchev had meetings with Soviet authors and artists and told them that Party control over literature and art was essential and would continue; what he had said about Stalin did not mean that they could now do as they pleased. He criticized in particular a new literary almanac which had been started by a group of progressive writers in the mistaken belief that the Thaw would soon be followed by spring. Khrushchev was angry with a member of that group who tried to defend it. At the same time he expressed the hope that those who had gone wrong would soon see the error of their ways. It was a warning and an admonition, not a pogrom.

Yet, while the general situation could have been worse, Ehrenburg did not have an easy time. Those who hated the Thaw assumed that they could now attack him with impunity and some of the attacks were so scurrilous that at one point he complained to the Secretariat of the Party Central Committee. The most vicious onslaught was launched upon Ehrenburg in the summer of 1958, by someone who, judging by his behavior, would have relished a literary pogrom, had he been permitted to organize one: the Stalinist die-hard, Vsevolod Kochetov, whose novel 'The Brothers Ershov' was serialized by a Leningrad magazine. As he was writing it, Kochetov must have imagined that after Hungary he would be able to settle accounts with Ehrenburg once and for all. He attacked the Thaw, *The Thaw* and even the thaw, i.e. he denounced it in all its manifestations—political, literary (as a piece of Ehrenburg propaganda) and climatic: the thaw, said Kochetov, was a 'rotten slushy season', the season of 'flu germs' and he drew a parallel between it and the Hungarian rising. He had to be more careful in his attack upon the Thaw since this was generally identified with Khrushchev's anti-Stalin speech, but he must have been cheered by the fact that Khrushchev in his address to writers had mentioned Stalin's achievements as well as Stalin's mistakes, and Kochetov reinsured himself by mentioning briefly the Party's efforts to liquidate the consequences of the personality cult. At the same time he sneered at those who had kept silent for decades and then became extremely vocal when they saw that they could jump on the band-wagon; he compared them to vermin which had been hiding in the cracks of walls during the long winter and crept out into the open 'at the first signs of the thaw' (another politico-climatic metaphor). Finally, Kochetov poured venom on Ehrenburg's *Thaw*, without naming him or it but making his meaning absolutely clear; in this context he also spoke out in defense of Stalin, without naming him either. Kochetov had no hesitation in accepting that Stalin and Zhuravlev were one and the same person. He recalled how 'a couple of years ago' an author had written a story about the director of an industrial enterprise (i.e. Zhuravlev) whom—said Kochetov sardonically—God had punished for producing steel instead of building homes for workers. Yet the director (this time it is evidently Zhuravlev-Stalin) had been right and the author, instead of throwing mud at him, should have bowed before him in gratitude—because if the director (i.e. Stalin) had been less keen on constructing steel foundries, the author would probably have landed in some ravine feeding worms with his body (i.e. in Baby Yar, where the Nazis massacred the Kiev Jews).

However, by the time Kochetov's novel appeared, the panic over Hungary had subsided, though the star of the reactionaries was still in the ascendant. When the novel was subsequently published in book form, a special effort was made to publicize it. Nevertheless, the *Pravda* reviewer tempered his praise with an expression of regret: Kochetov, he said, had attributed 'formalistic' tendencies to too many people and had failed to take into account that a number of authors, who had been guilty of 'formalism' in the past, had since mended their ways. 'The Brothers Ershov' did not destroy Ehrenburg, but the atmosphere was still such that some people felt it was safer to treat him as if he were under a cloud. A Moscow publishing house, having accepted a collection of his essays on French culture, including one in which he defended the art of Picasso (' "a corrupting influence" to some, "formalism" to others, and to yet others "Bolshevism in art" '—i.e. to a certain type of people in the anti-Soviet camp), did not dare to bring the book out and, finally, when the persecution of Pasternak began, demanded of Ehrenburg that he should delete a passing reference to one of Pasternak's poems. Ehrenburg was furious. He appealed for help to a senior Party official, who had helped him in the past, and the text remained unaltered.

Pasternak's *Dr Zhivago* was beyond the range of the Thaw, and the Thaw continued in spite of that sordid affair. In 1959, the year in which Harold Macmillan, the British Prime Minister, visited Moscow and Khrushchev went to the United States, the Thaw became a fashionable term in international politics—statesmen and observers made ample use of it in their comments on East-West relations, contrasting it with the glaciers of the Cold War. Meanwhile in Russia the battle for the cultural Thaw went on.

There were, of course, many people engaged in it on the side of the liberals—the poet Aleksandr Tvardovsky, long reinstated as editor of *Novy mir*, was fighting with particular vigor and with good results. Ehrenburg, apart from writing his memoirs, which were to play a major part in the struggle, always kept a sharp eye on the enemy. When the lady critic who suggested that *The Thaw* had been the cause of all the trouble charged Ehrenburg with being at least partly responsible for such harmful ideological phenomena as the exhibition that had aroused her displeasure, he replied that he did not consider *The Thaw* an ideological error and recalled proudly that he had written that book two years before the 20th Congress (i.e. before Khrushchev's speech). He added that he was only too glad to take full moral responsibility for the works of those artists who preferred to use their own eyes instead of relying on the lens of a camera, and he deplored the way some of the most talented Soviet artists had been treated: in one case the artist's first exhibition had been arranged posthumously, in the case of Ehrenburg's friend Falk a few months before his death, and the works of the great Armenian painter, Martiros Saryan, had been shown to the public after a lengthy hiatus by which time Saryan had reached the age of seventy-five. In numerous articles and interviews Ehrenburg kept stressing that the purpose of literature was not to describe industrial or agricultural production but to portray human beings and to uphold human values. He was saying in effect that literature must be literature and not crude advertising copy—such as Stalin and Zhdanov had been telling authors to supply. From time to time he pounced on his old enemies, the official critics. In the past, said Ehrenburg, they used to wait for a book to be awarded a prize before they dared to praise it; nowadays they eyed one another with suspicion, each wondering what the other was going to say.

In 1960 *Novy mir* began to print Ehrenburg's memoirs—a book that was unique by Soviet post-war standards—and in 1962 the November issue of *Novy mir* contained Solzhenitsyn's classic *One Day in the Life of Ivan Denisovich*. It looked as if the Thaw was over and spring had come. Who would have thought that in a few months' time the Soviet Premier and Communist Party leader Nikita Khrushchev, deploring the publication of books which, 'in his opinion', gave a 'wrong and one-sided picture of the phenomena connected with the cult of personality and of the essence of the fundamental changes' which had occurred after the 20th Congress (i.e. after he had denounced Stalin)—who would have thought that Khrushchev would say, 'I rank Comrade Ehrenburg's story *The Thaw* among such books'?

Part of Khrushchev's statement was plainly nonsensical. *The Thaw* did not and could not give any picture, true or false, of the changes that followed the 20th Congress because the book had appeared two years before the Congress was held. By now the political content of *The Thaw* had long been overtaken by events and was largely forgotten. All that was remembered was the title, the image of the Thaw. Khrushchev knew it and went on to explain that this was an image which he did not accept. He said: 'The notion of the thaw is generally associated with a period of instability, with unfinished business and with fluctuations of temperature when it is difficult to forecast what the weather will be like.' A literary image of this kind, declared Khrushchev, did not reflect the real significance of the changes which had taken place in Soviet society since Stalin's death. This made more sense. Khrushchev evidently did not want his rule to become known permanently as the era of the Thaw—because the Thaw, though it is preferable to the Ice Age, does imply instability and fluctuation, whereas he, like all statesmen, was anxious to be known as the creator of something enduring and complete. In theory this could have meant enduring progress, it could even have meant spring. Unfortunately, it was clear from the context that it did not.

Khrushchev made this speech in March 1963. It marked the climax of an offensive launched three months earlier, and Ehrenburg was one of the main targets of that reactionary campaign. Since 1956 he had experienced a great deal of unpleasantness from people whom the authorities regarded as useful dinosaurs but who did not matter all that much. Now shots were being aimed at him from high places and in the end a shell was fired from the summit.

It all began on 1 December 1962, at the time when hopes had been roused by the publication of Solzhenitsyn's story and by other signs of what looked like the approaching spring. On that day Khrushchev visited an exhibition where he saw some experimental Soviet paintings—he called them 'shit' and bullied the artists. On 17 December he and Leonid Ilichev, the Party Secretary in charge of cultural affairs, had a meeting with writers and artists at the Kremlin. Ehrenburg's contribution to the debate was not published, but from a later statement by Ilichev one could gather what he had said. His main point had been that there was no arguing about tastes (something which Bukharin had said in his preface to *Julio Jurenito*), that innovations were always opposed by somebody and that Lenin, who disliked modern poetry, had never tried to impose his taste upon the public. Such references to Lenin always infuriated the diehards. Ilichev, on this occasion, cursed modern art but, as far as one knew (his speech seems to have been published in abridged form), did not mention Ehrenburg. Ehrenburg, however, was slandered by the writer Galina Serebryakova, a reactionary whose views had not changed in spite of the fact that her two husbands had been destroyed by Stalin and she herself had spent many years in prison and exile; she charged Ehrenburg was an accomplice of

Stalin and repeated a rumor which alleged that he had betrayed his colleagues on the Jewish Anti-Fascist Committee. The campaign went on. Shortly afterwards, in January 1963, the painter Aleksandr Gerasimov, who by now was over eighty, published an article in which he attacked Ehrenburg and certain other writers for defending modern art. Gerasimov complained that the Soviet media were being placed much too readily at the disposal of the patrons of 'formalism', which he called 'a worm-eaten pear', of abtract art, which he described as 'pathological', and of the monstrosities produced by Falk (Ehrenburg's friend).

However, the controversy over art proved to be merely a preparatory exercise—insofar as it affected Ehrenburg. The real storm broke over a passage which occurs in his memoirs and has nothing to do with art. The memoirs had been appearing for some time in *Novy mir* and in one of the instalments Ehrenburg said that he had lived through the years of the Great Terror (1937-38) with clenched teeth and had learned to remain silent without losing faith—in spite of the agonizing doubts about the intelligence of the people in command. This implied that he had never doubted the innocence of the victims and an official critic, called Ermilov, took him to task for this. Writing in *Izvestiya*, Ermilov observed sardonically that Ehrenburg must have had a great advantage over the overwhelming majority of ordinary Soviet men and women who had had no such doubts but had felt shocked and grieved that there should be so many enemies of the people; since Ehrenburg appeared to have known so much, why had he kept silent? Ermilov claimed that others who had doubted 'the propriety of some action' (by the authorities) had fought to put things right and their weapon had not been silence. Ehrenburg replied that he had not been present at a single meeting at which a voice had been raised in protest against the persecution of innocent people once they had been arrested. But *Izvestiya*, in an editorial postscript, took Ermilov's side.

It was a belated storm and an artificial one. The instalment of Ehrenburg's memoirs, which contained that particular passage, had appeared in May 1962. By now it was the end of January 1963—a long time to nurture one's indignation. It looks as if towards the end of 1962 when Khrushchev was in an 'illiberal' mood, someone persuaded him that the time had come to rap Ehrenburg over the knuckles or, preferably, to hit him on the head. This was now being done and one could see that some people were enjoying it enormously. At the beginning of March there was another meeting between the Party leaders and the intellectuals, and this time Ilichev did not spare Ehrenburg. He made the poisonous remark that Ehrenburg's 'theory of silence' had not really been practised by Ehrenburg himself. 'After all,' sneered Ilichev, 'you were not silent in those days, Ilya Grigorevich—you eulogized!' and Ilichev quoted a sentence from the speech Ehrenburg had made at his sixtieth birthday celebration in 1951; it had been a pretty servile speech in which Ehrenburg thanked Stalin for helping him to write what he had always dreamed about, and Ilichev related this with gusto. Oh, what a pleasure it was for some of those present to hear the Great Liberal, the author of *The Thaw*, the Prophet who had foreseen the Thaw, the Patron of modern art, the cultured Westerner—what a pleasure it was to hear him being told in effect that not very long ago he had been as everyone else! Ilichev went even further: he suggested that they had been better than Ehrenburg. Ilichev conceded magnanimously that he was not blaming Ehrenburg for having eulogized Stalin in 1951 because 'we all spoke and wrote thus at that time.' 'But *we* believed . . . ,' said Ilichev, 'whereas *you*, as it turns out now, did not believe but wrote those things all the same . . .' At this point, according to *Pravda*, there was applause—the Stalinists were having a grand time. It was a fantastic situation. People to whom lying had become second nature had the nerve to pretend that they had always been truthful and sincere, and to charge with hypocrisy someone, who—like them—had submitted to the dictator but at least had the courage to state now that he had done so knowingly.

Finally, the next day, there spoke Khrushchev, contributing his share to the Ehrenburg-hunt: ranking *The Thaw* among harmful books; contrasting Ehrenburg's attitude with that of Sholokhov—Sholokhov, raved Khrushchev, was such an outstanding, such a patriotic writer (Khrushchev must have known that the two were at daggers drawn); contrasting Ehrenburg's approach with that of Galina Serebryakova who had slandered him three months earlier by repeating a vile rumor—unlike Ehrenburg, said Khrushchev, she had been imprisoned for many years; yet she had not lost heart and was now writing books that were needed by the people and the Party.

Ehrenburg was crushed. True, there must have been worse moments in his life—during the Great Terror when he had returned to the Soviet Union from Spain and was expecting arrest, or just before Stalin's death, at the time of the 'Doctors' Plot' when he refused to sign a document 'asking' the Government to deport nearly all Soviet Jews to Birobidzhan. But, as a writer and journalist, he had not felt so depressed since the spring of 1945 when he, the greatest Soviet war-time propagandist, was attacked in *Pravda* and prevented from following the troops to Berlin to report its capture. Now he was over seventy—at that age one begins to feel tired after an exhausting struggle. He did not know whether the next volume of his memoirs would be published or whether he would ever again be allowed to go abroad, which had become part of his life (in that respect he had been in a very privileged position). One wondered whether his career as a writer and journalist had come to an end.

Yet, as had so often happened to him in the past, things took a turn for the better. The regime needed him and, having hit him on the head, was prepared to disregard his further eccentricities. Within a few months Ehrenburg spoke at a European writers' forum in Leningrad, his speech was printed in *Literaturnaya gazeta*, and while at this meeting with their Western colleagues other Soviet writers obediently toed the official line, Ehrenburg seemed determined to show that his attitude towards art and literature had remained unchanged. Soon there was an article by him in *Pravda* on an international topic, and although the next volume of his memoirs did not appear in *Novy mir* until the beginning of 1965 (by which time Khrushchev was no longer in power), what mattered was that it did appear and the memoirs were in due course published in book form.

On balance, he won. He had not written *The Thaw* in vain. He had acted as a pathfinder—as the disgruntled lady critic said, it had all started with *The Thaw*. Later, officially approved Soviet writing was overshadowed by the emergence of Solzhenitsyn and other dissident literature but, as Nadezhda Mandelshtam says in her book, Ehrenburg was one of those who had taught people to read *samizdat*. He sat on many rehabilitation committees and played a major part in securing the posthumous publication or republication of masterpieces written by victims of the Stalin era. His greatest achievement, however, during that period was probably in the field of visual art. It was largely owing to him that the Soviet attitude to art underwent a gradual change, and this happened in spite of the fact that to Khrushchev modern art meant 'painting fir-trees upside down' (as he once put it) or worse things (when he was in a bad mood). Kochetov had warned the establishment in his book 'The Brothers Ershov' that if one allowed socialist realism (the official style) to co-exist with what he ironically called 'socialist' impressionism, this would spread to 'socialist' formalism, then to 'socialist' abstractionism, and would eventually lead to 'socialist' capitalism. Yet during the Thaw the impressionists were taken out of the museums' store rooms and put where the public could see them. Things did not stop there. It was a great day for Ehrenburg when he opened the Picasso exhibition in Moscow and saw the crowds queuing in the streets. Other exhibitions were arranged and, if so many Picassos and Matisses can now be viewed at the Hermitage in Leningrad and at the Pushkin Museum in Moscow, much of the credit for this goes to Ehrenburg.

The Thaw was an era of hope, of prisoners returning from camps and exile, of East-West contacts and East-West détente. Ehrenburg foresaw it a year after Stalin's death. But as he gave that title to his historic novel, he unwittingly chose the right image in yet another respect: the thaw, as Khrushchev correctly remarked, is a season of instability and fluctuations, and so it was. During those exciting, hopeful and maddening years one never knew which way the wind would blow next, and the Thaw was not followed by spring.

The Memoirs

Ehrenburg's memoirs, which appeared in the 1960s and which he called 'People, Years, Life', were his last major work and his best since *Julio Jurenito*.

He said they were a confession rather than a chronicle. By that he did not mean anything resembling Jean-Jacques Rousseau's exercise in self-castigation—in fact, he makes it clear that he had no intention to deal with 'affairs of the heart'. All he meant was that he would try to tell the truth—about the people he had known, the epoch through which he had lived and the things life had done to him and to others while history was being made. To tell the truth, as he himself admits, proved impossible. Time and again he apologizes for having to fall silent on vital topics. But even so, he does manage to say a great deal.

Where else, in a country where poetry is part of people's lives, could readers find in the early 1960s the first proper tributes to the poets they worshipped—Osip Mandelshtam and Marina Tsvetaeva? Both were victims of Stalin's terror; Mandelshtam had died in a camp and Tsvetaeva had committed suicide. Later a Soviet literary magazine published Tsvetaeva's childhood memories and Nadezhda Mandelshtam wrote her wonderful books which were available in Russia only as *samizdat* publications. But in 1961, when Ehrenburg's memoirs were appearing in *Novy mir*, the chapters on Mandelshtam and Tsvetaeva earned him much love and admiration.

Where else in Soviet literature could one find anything approaching Ehrenburg's appreciation of Yuly Martov, the well-known Russian Menshevik leader, who at one time worked together with Lenin, then—in the first years after the Revolution when Mensheviks could formally still take part in public life—tried to speak on behalf of a peaceful opposition in Russia, and finally left the country in 1920? The 'Great Soviet Encyclopedia', in a volume passed for publication one year *after* Stalin's death, calls Martov a renegade and a traitor who in 1905 betrayed the interests of the Russian workers and during the First World War helped the bourgeoisie to deceive the people. Later, a Soviet play, called 'Lenin in Geneva', turned Martov into a figure of fun, trying in vain to make peace with Lenin. The new 'Great Soviet Encyclopedia', an infinitely more civilized publication than the one started under Stalin, contains a much more sober and objective account of Martov's activities, but this appeared only in 1974. Ehrenburg says in his memoirs that Martov, whom he met at the beginning of the First World War in Paris, was an attractive and gentle person, a man of utmost integrity, even though he struck him as bookish and remote from life. Ehrenburg describes him with so much warmth that one can vividly picture the incurable Russian Jewish idealist, freezing and in poor health because he had no winter coat, and deeply depressed by the failure of the Second International to prevent the War. Ehrenburg himself loathed but supported the war against Germany.

Where else in the early 1960s could Soviet readers find a record of the kind of conversation Ehrenburg had in 1924 with a Jewish watchmaker in Odessa, who summed up in a few words what many people felt during that early period in Soviet history after private enterprise had been restored on a limited scale? 'I see from the papers,' said Ehrenburg's interlocutor, 'that they are once again pouncing on Curzon' (who at that time ranked as Soviet Russia's Enemy Number One). 'But I don't think Curzon is afraid of them. I am the one who is afraid. I am afraid of the tax inspector, I am afraid of the GPU, and I am afraid of you. How do I know what sort of person you are and why you want me to tell you so many things? . . . '

Who else could inform Soviet readers, or at least remind them of the fact that in 1943-44 Ehrenburg, together with the writer Vassily Grossman, who fell into disfavor after the Second World War and never recovered from it, had compiled what looked like a unique collection of documents relating to the persecution and extermination of Jews in Nazi-occupied areas of the Soviet Union, that a few excerpts from that 'Black Book' (as they called it), appeared in a Soviet magazine (Ehrenburg later showed it to Albert Einstein), and after a lengthy delay a number of copies of the book were actually printed—only to be destroyed in the late 1940s when the Soviet Jewish Anti-Fascist Committee was disbanded and the anti-cosmopolitan, i.e. antisemitic, campaign began? Ehrenburg reveals that the 'Black Book' figured in a number of 'judgments' passed during that period by Soviet tribunals on Jews who were sentenced for crimes they had never committed. He was told this in 1956 by a state prosecutor who had been instructed to rehabilitate these people and who asked Ehrenburg what the 'Black Book' was, since his name had been mentioned in that connection.

It had not been customary to refer to declared opponents of the Soviet regime as men of integrity. Now, in the 1960s, Ehrenburg the Pathfinder proved that this could be done provided the people concerned had been dead long enough. I think one might have got away with it in the 1970s as well—except that in the 1970s Ehrenburg's memoirs could not have appeared for another reason: because of the way he had described the Stalin era. In 1971, having stopped short of rehabilitating Stalin, Leonid Brezhnev announced that the 'cult of personality' had been sufficiently exposed and that the time had come to stop denouncing it. Naturally, Ehrenburg had not been the only one to deal with this subject as long as it was permitted. One outstanding piece of writing—apart from Solzhenitsyn's *One Day in the Life of Ivan Denisovich* which was in a class by itself—concerned the fate of Mikhail Koltsov, who had been *Pravda* correspondent and Stalin's personal envoy in Spain during the Civil War. This remarkable account of how Koltsov, on his return to Russia, was gripped by an invisible hand which led him step by step to his doom, was contributed by his brother to a volume of essays on Koltsov's life and work. Ehrenburg, when he reached the point in his memoirs at which he had to deal with the Great Terror, as usual, did some probing and went further than others, supplying as many hitherto unpublished details as he could. He revealed, for example, that the famous theatrical director, Vsevolod Meyerhold, who was generally believed to have died in a labor camp, had managed to insert two lines containing an official admission that Meyerhold had 'died' the day after he had been sentenced to imprisonment 'without the right to send or receive letters', which meant that he was shot within twenty-four hours after the passing of the sentence.

During their anti-Ehrenburg campaign of 1963 Khrushchev and Ilichev had concentrated on what they felt concerned them most closely: Ehrenburg's 'theory of silence', i.e. his claim that during the Great Terror many people, including himself, had not believed in the guilt of the accused but, like himself, had kept silent because that was all they could do. Official literary critics, however, made two other points. Ermilov, who fired the first broadside in the campaign, drew attention to Ehrenburg's heretical views on freedom. Others remarked that he seemed to ignore the division of the world into two 'contrasting antagonistic systems'. Factually, both observations were correct.

Ermilov quoted a passage from the memoirs, which said that in 1918 Ehrenburg had been unable to support the Bolshevik Revolution because he had been brought up on the nineteenth-century concept of freedom. Here it is worth noting that in the 1960s, nearly half a century after the event, it was quite all right for a convert to admit that he had opposed the Revolution initially. But to suggest that he had done so because he felt that the Revolution was incompatible with freedom and to present this as a legitimate excuse, as Ehrenburg appeared to be doing, did point to a dangerous heresy. When in the early 1930s Ehrenburg made peace with the Soviet Government (until then relations had been tense), he in effect chose unfreedom. But he started worming his way towards freedom as soon as Stalin died, and now he used every opportunity to press for it. In his memoirs he pointedly recalls how in 1909, when he first arrived in Paris, the *concierge* at his hotel refused to look at his passport and told him that she was not interested in that sort of thing. In another part of the book he quotes a passage from Miguel Cervantes: 'Freedom, Sancho,' says Don Quixote, 'is one of the most precious blessings bestowed on us by Heaven. No treasures can compare with it; neither those that are hidden in the bowels of the earth nor those concealed at the bottom of the sea . . . whereas unfreedom is the worst of all misfortunes that can befall man'. Ehrenburg reproduces this passage as he tells how he was driven through La Mancha, Don Quixote's homeland, during the Civil War in Spain. No Soviet censor could legitimately object to Cervantes being quoted in this context, and yet every intelligent reader knew that this was a *cri de coeur* on behalf of countless Soviet intellectuals, and not only intellectuals. As for the disastrous effects of unfreedom — 'the worst of all misfortunes that can befall man' — these are described everywhere in the book. Ehrenburg warns his readers, and particularly the young Soviet writers, that the questions he had raised at the Writers' Congress in 1934 (where he clamored for creative freedom) are likely to remain 'topical' for a very long time, and he adds that an author is always hounded if he dares to express a thought before it has become a truism. 'Yet,' says Ehrenburg to those Soviet critics who condemn every original idea simply because it is safer to do so, 'it is not an author's business to reproduce axioms.'

To justify the absence of cultural freedom, the Soviet establishment claimed that 'the division of the world into two contrasting antagonistic camps' applied not only to politics and economics but to culture as well. This went against everything Ehrenburg the Cosmopolitan (and he was a true cosmopolitan, not just a Jew) had always stood for. For him the opposite of literature was trash, the opposite of good taste was vulgarity, and culture was culture — regardless of the political system, though he naturally realized that in certain situations the latter could kill the former. Since, in addition to being a Russian and a Jew, he was a European, he thought of the arts first and foremost in terms of one all-embracing European culture.

He was acutely aware of the fact that a large number of people both in Russia and in the West could not bring themselves to accept this. In his memoirs he gives some amusing examples of prejudice, mutual ignorance and misunderstanding between the nations of East and West Europe, ranging from the writer Aleksandr Tolstoy, who was Ehrenburg's contemporary, being mistaken in Paris for Leo Tolstoy ('The news of your death must have been a *canard*!') to a Russian emigré who, after spending a few days in Paris, was repelled by French 'lechery' merely because he saw couples kissing in public places. What particularly annoyed Ehrenburg was the habit, prevalent among French highbrows, of looking on every Russian as a spiritual masochist tormented by his *âme slave*. All this, however, paled into insignificance compared with Stalin's post-war policy of isolating Russia from the outside world—a policy reinforced by a campaign against those who 'toadied to the West'. Yet even in those days Ehrenburg found opportunities to make his point. When Western propagandists, who were often too lazy or too ignorant to distinguish between Russian culture and the mess Stalin had made of Soviet cultural life, attacked Russia as barbaric, Ehrenburg retorted haughtily that world literature was unthinkable without *War and Peace* as it was unthinkable without *Madame Bovary*. Ostensibly, he was defending Russia's honor and the censor did not object. But it was his way of restating, in the midst of a chauvinist orgy in Russia, that culture was one and indivisible.

Now that Stalin was dead, Ehrenburg set himself the task of making the new generation understand that theirs was part of a much larger European cultural heritage. The young people had a right to know both about the Rotonde of Paris—the Bohemian café where Ehrenburg spent his formative years in the company of Modigliani, Soutine, Guillaume Apollinaire and other future celebrities—and the Poets' Café in Moscow, the haunt of Mayakovsky and his friends in the early years after the Revolution in Russia. These were the years of free experiment in art and literature under the patronage of the enlightened People's Commissar for Public Enlightenment, Anatoly Lunacharsky—when there was little to eat but an abundance of creative enthusiasm, when it was cold and dreary outside but as soon as one entered a theater, one was transported into the fairy-tale world of E.T.A. Hoffmann ('Princess Brambilla') or Carlo Gozzi ('Princess Turandot'), when a great deal of exhibitionist nonsense was talked and much lovely verse was written. (When the memoirs appeared, an official critic took Ehrenburg to task for his nostalgic description of that period.) The young people were now hearing about the Poets' Café from Ehrenburg as well as from others. But only Ehrenburg could tell them about the Rotonde.

To tell them about it was relatively easy, even if later some of the critics grumbled about Ehrenburg's unorthodox views on art. But in order to include some of the other things which he felt were vital, he had to fight a battle which went on for years—while the memoirs were being published in instalments in *Novy mir*, as a separate edition in book form, and, finally, as part of his 'Collected Works'. It was a battle with editors and publishers. At times it was a war of attrition, at other times it flared up with tremendous force. Ehrenburg was a stubborn fighter and, on balance, he won. His memoirs do not contain everything he would have liked them to contain, but all the six parts—ending with Stalin's death, as he had originally planned—did eventually appear in print.

In the first months of 1963, during the anti-Ehrenburg campaign, it looked as if the last two parts might not appear at all. Until then Ehrenburg had merely encountered difficulties, in spite of the fact that the editor he had to deal with was the poet and writer Aleksandr Tvardovsky. Tvardovsky had made *Novy mir* a world-famous publication which stood for everything that was progressive in Soviet literature. But Tvardovsky was doing not only a magnificent but also an extremely difficult and delicate job, and did not want to make his journal more vulnerable than it already was. Besides, his views on a number of questions did not tally with Ehrenburg's. As a result, when Ehrenburg dealt with certain explosive issues, Tvardovsky insisted on cuts and alterations. One such demand concerned, for example, a passage on the Nazi-Soviet pact. I do not know what Ehrenburg had written about it originally, but it could hardly have been stronger than the brief agreed version which finally appeared: 'On 1 September (1939) Molotov declared that this treaty served the interests of universal peace. Yet two days later Hitler started the Second World War.'

Such difficulties could be considered routine. But in 1963, when the Ermilov article appeared, Ehrenburg's position became precarious, especially after Ehrenburg's protest and Ermilov's arrogant reply which showed that he was acting on instructions from above. The effect on the readers and the publishers was immediate. Admirers sent messages to Ehrenburg telling him to stand firm; a sixteen-year-old girl even assured him that if the publishers refused to have his writings printed, she and her friends would copy them by hand. For a while it seemed that Ehrenburg would have to avail himself of this touching offer. The first instalment of part five of his memoirs had just appeared in *Novy mir* but it was now being suggested that no more should be published. Ehrenburg protested and complained, pointing out that this would make a disastrous impression both at home and abroad. The two remaining instalments of part five duly appeared, yet the situation kept deteriorating: Ermilov no longer mattered, Ehrenburg had now been attacked by Ilichev and Khrushchev. In the circumstances it seemed doubtful that part six, which was to deal with the most controversial events of the post-war period, would ever see the light of day, or that the publishing house which had already brought out one volume of his memoirs in book form would wish to go on with it. The director of that enterprise was a left-over from the Stalin era and acted predictably—on the principle that when a man was down it was both prudent and pleasurable to give him an additional kick or two. Consequently, before publishing the next volume, he demanded that Ehrenburg should completely alter certain chapters in spite of the fact that these were already known to the public from the *Novy mir* version. Fortunately, while the behavior of bureaucrats was predictable, Khrushchev's was not.

Soon after Khrushchev had made his final speech in the anti-Ehrenburg campaign, Ehrenburg wrote to him to say that though he was seventy-two, he had no wish to retire and felt that he could still be of value; what should he do? For about three months Khrushchev did not reply. Then, suddenly, he asked Ehrenburg to come and see him. They had a long conversation during which Ehrenburg is said to have spoken with great frankness and to have told Khrushchev that the kind of control over the arts, which was now being envisaged, would not work unless the authorities were again allowed to put people in jail—a practice which, surely, Khrushchev would not wish to restore. Khrushchev appeared to be in a conciliatory mood. He said to Ehrenburg that he did not want him to stop writing and that Ehrenburg should complete part six of his memoirs. Shortly afterwards Ehrenburg was invited to address the meeting with foreign writers in Leningrad and it looked as if his troubles were over.

In actual fact, they were not. The director of the publishing house naturally had to cave in and to accept the text as it stood. But part six of the memoirs did not appear in *Novy mir* until nearly eighteen months later, after endless bargaining over cuts and changes with Tvardovsky, threats by editors to stop publication, threats by Ehrenburg to withdraw the script, more complaints to Khrushchev, acrimonious bickering in the course of which Ehrenburg accused his publishers of letting down the readers, who had ordered the book in advance, and himself was accused of trying to please a narrow circle of young *frondeurs* (the equivalent of the 'bright young set'). At the last minute *Novy mir* tried to suppress a whole chapter which was no more controversial than many of those already published but which must have frightened someone on the editorial board—perhaps because of the politically uncertain situation after Khrushchev's dismissal (by now it was 1965). Finally, the last instalment of the memoirs appeared in *Novy mir*. But it took another year until the last volume was published in book form and six more months until it was republished as part of the 'Collected Works'. All that time he had had no peace.

The struggle had been long and exhausting but it had been worthwhile. In book form the memoirs contained more material than had been included in the *Novy mir* serialization. This was quite an achievement. But there was something Ehrenburg had not been able to achieve.

In one of the very first chapters, as he recalls his revolutionary past (he joined a militant Bolshevik organization while he was still at school but this was a short episode in his life before the Revolution and he never became a member of the Party during his long career as a Soviet writer). Ehrenburg mentions someone called Nikolay Ivanovich: he tells how he and Nikolay Ivanovich used to visit friends and how cheerful Nikolay Ivanovich had been. There is no other clue to the man's identity. Yet Ehrenburg must have assumed that at least some readers would guess who this was.

After the whole of the memoirs had been published, there was a 'readers' conference' — at which authors meet their public — and someone asked Ehrenburg whether he did not feel that the time had come to name 'the friend' who had helped him to join the clandestine Bolshevik organization in Moscow. Ehrenburg replied with mock indignation: 'You are insulting me. I always felt that the time had come to name one of my best friends, Nikolay Ivanovich Bukharin. But I do not decide what may or maynot be printed. All I do is write.'

In the *Novy mir* version Nikolay Ivanovich appears only in that early chapter, probably because Tvardovsky had overlooked it; subsequently, he saw to it that there was no further mention of Bukharin in any shape or form. But in the separate edition Bukharin is named a few times in a neutral context — as editor of *Izvestiya* — and towards the end Ehrenburg points out that he had become a revolutionary thanks to a number of slightly older friends and, especially, his 'friend Nikolay'. Ehrenburg had intended to pay a glowing tribute to the man who had played a decisive part in his youth, who had so warmly recommended *Julio Jurenito* to the Soviet readers even though he disagreed with Ehrenburg's views, and whom Ehrenburg had last seen in the court room where he was tried and sentenced to death. But all Ehrenburg had managed to wrench from the censors was a few token concessions. However, token concessions matter to a public used to reading between the lines. The question asked at the readers' conference proved that some people understood perfectly what it was all about. One may say that Ehrenburg rehabilitated Bukharin which was something Khrushchev had failed to do.

The published editions of the memoirs end with Stalin's death. But Ehrenburg had a great deal more to say and before long he was writing again. Tvardovsky, who must have breathed a sigh of relief when part six was finished and done with, was too good an editor not to express interest in part seven, but Ehrenburg advised him to wait until it was completed. He did, however, as he had often done before, send a few excerpts to another magazine. This time it was *Nauka i zhizn* (Science and Life) which published the material with cuts. Ehrenburg, who had not been consulted about these, resented it bitterly. This happened less than two months before his death.

'I wish I could be certain,' said a young reader to Ehrenburg, 'that by the time I reach your age I shall have seen a quarter of what you have seen and have acquired one-tenth of your knowledge.' To young people, thirsting for knowledge and starved of contacts with the outside world, Ehrenburg's memoirs were a revelation.

'A spoonful of tar'

He was born of Jewish parents and remembered how his mother used to write long letters in Yiddish—from right to left, which puzzled him as a child. But he did not practise Judaism, and Israel, when it came into being, was for him not the fulfillment of a dream but merely an accomplished political fact. He understood religion and was fascinated by Hasidic legends, but he knew at least as much and probably more about Roman Catholicism and in his youth had nearly become a Benedictine monk: he admired the fourteenth-century Spanish and Hebrew poet Santob de Carrión (Shem Tov ben Isaac Ardutiel) but was no less fond of the poems of Santob's contemporary, Juan Ruiz, archpriest of Hita. Is it right to look upon Ehrenburg as a Jew?

People often argue about such things when a man is dead. Fortunately, Ehrenburg himself gave the answer while he was still alive. After Hitler had invaded Russia, he said at a public gathering: 'I am a Russian writer. But my mother's name was Hanah—I am a Jew!' Later he declared: 'As long as there is a single antisemite left in the world, I shall always proclaim myself a Jew.' He said this loudly, on his seventieth birthday, in a broadcast to the Soviet people over Moscow radio.

Was there anything specifically Jewish in the influence he exerted? Did he feel that there was such a thing as Jewish influence? He did. He called it 'a spoonful of tar' and wrote an essay about it in the 1920s. In that essay he says: 'I am going to speak about tar, i.e. the infusion of Jewish blood into world literature. It is a subject that is usually discussed by naive Jew-baiters, who are laboriously compiling black-lists for the future' (Ehrenburg, as he wrote this, probably did not realize how right he was) 'or by equally naive Jewish patriots—it is therefore normally associated either with abuse or with self-praise.' Ehrenburg believed he was looking at it dispassionately. There is a Russian proverb which says that a spoonful of tar will spoil a barrel of mead. He claimed the opposite was true. Pure mead for him meant conformity; tar stood for scepticism and dissent. Ehrenburg preferred mead with tar. In the same essay he quoted one of Santob's 'Counsels to King Pedro': 'Which is the better of the two—Andalusian wine or a thirsting mouth? The taste of the most wonderful wine is soon forgotten. Unquenched thirst stays.' The Jews, said Ehrenburg, had been making good wine—they had discovered many religious, philosophical and social remedies. But they had not bothered to use them—they had left that to others. They had chosen thirst.

Ehrenburg's writings were a spoonful of tar. Some more than others, but even when he had to go through a period of almost total submission, the taste or the smell of tar was never totally lost—it was always noticeable against the background of Soviet conformity. He had no imitators. He influenced readers, not writers. Whole generations of young readers came under his spell in the 1920s, during the war and, especially, after Stalin's death. Like Shem Tov, he taught them the blessings of thirst.

7

Jews in Soviet Philosophy

Yehoshua Yakhot

It has long been thought that there is a high proportion of Jews amongst Soviet philosophers. There are good grounds for this view. A whole generation, for example, was nurtured on the works of A. Deborin, who was officially considered the head of a whole school of philosophy. L. Akselrod (pseudonym — Ortodoks) was regarded as perhaps the most gifted of Soviet philosophers; she was the closest collaborator of Plekhanov, who had a high opinion of her literary and philosophical talents. I. Razumovsky published a textbook on philosophy as early as 1924, and his was a household name to countless numbers of students. M. Leonov's 'Outline of Dialectical Materialism' (Moscow 1948) was for many years the most famous textbook at a time when there was virtually nothing on this topic in the bookshops apart from the notorious 'Chapter Four' of Stalin's *History of the CPSU (B), Short Course*. The same may be said of M. Rosental's 'The Marxist Dialectical Method' (Moscow 1951), the only textbook on its subject. V. Pozner's 'On Lenin's *Materialism and Empirio-Criticism* (Moscow 1948) gave a rather ponderous but fairly detailed exposition of Lenin's main philosophical work. The textbook by M. Kovalson and V. Kelle (a Latvian) 'Historical Materialism' (Moscow 1963) is one of the best on its topic. In addition there are dozens of books by T. Oyzerman, B.E. Bykhovsky, O. Trakhtenberg and others. All this is enough to show why Soviet philosophy is so often associated with Jewish authors: they were the best-known and the most widely read.

Nevertheless, let us cite some statistical data in corroboration of what public opinion has long regarded as an incontestable fact. In the 'Philosophical Encyclopaedia', published in Moscow in the mid-1960s, there are short biographies of Soviet philosophers: of these, sixty-four are Russians (excluding the national republics) and thirty-nine are Jews. Even if we did not know that a large proportion of Soviet philosophers were Jews, these figures are very striking when we bear in mind that Russians form over half the population of the Soviet Union, but Jews only one or two percent. This is in spite of the fact that, firstly, these data largely exclude people from the 1920s and early 1930s, and, secondly, that since the late 1940s the admission of Jews to philosophical departments in universities and to post-graduate work in philosophy has been severely restricted.

The proportion of Jews in Soviet philosophy was especially high in the 1920s and early 1930s. But the fact is that at that time there was a high proportion of Jews amongst the intelligentsia as a whole—in engineering, in the fine arts and in the academic world: they filled a vacuum. In philosophy, for instance, Russian philosophers such as Radlov, Berdyaev and many others had been prevented from working at their profession and in 1922 were finally expelled from the country. By the end of the Civil War there were practically no philosophers of the kind required by the new regime. The vacuum thus formed was perhaps greater in philosophy than in other fields of scholarship and in technology. Whereas in technology, for example, 'bourgeois specialists' could be used, in philosophy the Bolsheviks had to start virtually from scratch. For this educated young people were needed, and these were to be found, of course, largely amongst the Jews. So it is not surprising that, when the Institute of Red Professors was founded in 1921, it included many Jews. Age-old messianic longings, given new life by devotion to world revolution, in this case took the form of working for a revolutionary theory which showed the way to social justice.

Let us consider some examples which indicate how great a part Jews played in the philosophical life of that time. In 1930 the theoretical journal of the Central Committee, *Bolshevik* (no. 3-4, p.12), announced that the first All-Union Philosophical Conference would be held that summer, noting that this was the first such conference both in the history of Marxism and in the history of Russian philosophy. Characteristically, in all three sections (dialectical and historical materialism and the history of philosophy) the main papers were given by Jews: A. Deborin, B. Gessen, E. Yaroslavsky (Gubelman), M. Mitin, S. Levit, Yu.S. Semkovsky, Sapir, Yu. Frankfurt, G. Tymyansky, I. Razumovsky, D. Kvitko (who had participated in the revolutionary movement in the USA) and G. Bammel. In fact, this conference was never held. The summer saw the start of the controversy directed against A. Deborin and his school. When, by the end of 1930, the Deborinites had been debarred from active work, the projected conference was cancelled by the new philosophical leadership.

In 1929 the Society of Militant Materialist-Dialecticians (OVMD) was founded. In *Vestnik Kommunisticheskoy akademii* (Bulletin of the Communist Academy) (no. 31 (1), 1929) there appeared a list of the first full members, thirteen in all, of whom seven were Jews: Boris Mikhaylovich Gessen, Abram Moiseevich Deborin, Solomon Grigorevich Levit, Lev Aleksandrovich Mankovsky, Mark Borisovich Mitin, Isaak Petrovich Razumovsky, Grigory Samoylovich Fridland. This list reflects quite accurately the proportion of Jews in philosophical scholarship.

On 18 June 1930 a plenary session of the Communist Academy was held at which new full and corresponding members were elected. Half of them were Jews: I.I. Agol, Ya. L. Berman, R.E. Vaysberg, N.N. Vinich, B.M. Gessen, S.I. Gopner, P.O. Gorin, S.M. Dimanshteyn, G.I. Krumin, L.K. Martens, A.S. Mendelson, B.P. Pozern, M.I. Rubinshteyn, G.S. Fridland, A.G. Shlikhter, A.S. Gonikman, G.S. Zeydel, E.V. Zelkina, D. Kin, A.F. Kon, I. Matsa, G.S. Tymyansky, E.L. Khmelnitskaya.[1]

When Mitin, Yudin and Raltsevich published in *Pravda* on 7 June 1930 the first article against the leading philosophers of that time, thus marking the beginning of the 'Stalinist offensive on the philosophical front' a group of philosophers was bold enough to criticize it in the philosophical journal *Pod znamenem marksizma* (Under the Banner of Marxism) (1930, no. 5). Apart from E. Luppol, N. Karev and Ya. Sten, these included A. Deborin, I. Podvolotsky, B. Gessen, M. Levin, I. Agol and S. Levit, who defended their convictions with dignity and honor against the spokesmen for the Central Committee, who were supported by Stalin. M. Levin, I. Agol and S. Levit were distinguished biologists, who comprised the main leaders of the Society of Materialist Biologists, while A. Deborin and I. Podvolotsky were the leading lights in philosophy; together they symbolized a union of philosophers and natural scientists which at that time was a matter of pride. Most of this group were Jews.

Unfortunately, the percentage of Jews was also high amongst the philosophers subjected to reprisals in the terrible years 1936-37. Many of the Jewish philosophers we have mentioned were declared 'enemies of the people' (e.g. Vaysberg, Samoylovich, Semkovsky, Gessen, Levin, Bammel); others were accused of Trotskyism. Not only did the overwhelming majority of Jewish philosophers meet their end in these years, but their names were consigned to oblivion, being expunged, with rare exceptions, from the history of Soviet Russian thought. Many of them have not been mentioned once since that time. For example, it is hard to find a good word in Soviet sources about Akselrod (Ortodoks), who merely enters the history-books under the label 'head of the Mechanist school'. Hence we regard this study partly as an attempt to restore the good name of those who innocently suffered and have been frequently forgotten in the Soviet Union.

About 1921 the first steps were taken by A. Deborin, L. Akselrod and

L.D. Trotsky to form what came to be known as 'the philosophical front'. At that time the shortage of trained personnel, both for teaching and research, was an especially acute problem in philosophy. In those circumstances it would have been incredible not to have thought of the two outstanding philosophers Akselrod and Deborin. Lyubov Isaakovna Akselrod, whose pen-name was 'Ortodoks', was active in the revolutionary movement as early as 1884. An energetic member of the 'Liberation of Labor' group started by Plekhanov, she soon became his trusted assistant, especially in theoretical and philosophical matters. By 1906 she had published her own collection of essays called 'Philosophical Studies', in which she attacked neo-Kantianism at a time when E. Bernstein's slogan 'Back to Kant' was still new and fashionable. Lenin asked her to deliver a similar attack on A. Bogdanov's 'empiriocriticism' which she duly did in a series of articles published in 1907-10, later incorporated into her collected essays 'Against Idealism' of 1922.

Abram Moiseevich Deborin (Ioffe) graduated in philosophy from the University of Bern in 1908. After joining the Bolshevik Party in 1903 he became one of its chief protagonists in the struggle against Machism. His 'Introduction to the Philosophy of Dialectical Materialism', published at the beginning of the century, had gone through six editions by 1930, which shows that he must have seemed irreplaceable early in 1921 when trained scholars were so hard to come by.

But at this point other factors intervened. Akselrod had been not only a Menshevik, but a member of the Menshevik Central Committee, and still worse, she had been an opponent of Lenin on many philosophical and political questions. For example, in 1909 she had come out with a strongly critical review of Lenin's chief philosophical work *Materialism and Empirio-Criticism*; she especially objected to the rude, 'uncomradely' tone of Lenin's polemic, which she called 'intolerable' and 'offensive to the aesthetic feelings of the reader'.[2]

Deborin too had at one time gone over to the Mensheviks (from 1907-17) and had publicly criticized Lenin and the Bolsheviks. He wrote in an article published in the journal *Golos sotsial-demokrata* (Voice of the Social-Democrat):

> The stamp of subjectivism and 'voluntarism' is manifest in all the *tactics* of so-called 'Bolshevism', the philosophical expression of which is Machism. Machism, that world-view without a world, is an individualist and subjectivist philosophy which, when combined with Nietzschean immoralism (which justifies 'evil', exploitation, etc.), creates an ideological fog which obscures the practical aims of the bourgeoisie. In their 'ideology' the Bolshevik philosophers do not transcend the mental outlook of the petty bourgeoisie. As for the Bolshevik strategists and tacticians, with their

> Romantic revolutionism and petty bourgeois radicalism, they apply in practice the theoretical principles of philosophical nihilism, which is based on the denial of objective truth and the recognition of the right of each individual to determine the nature of what is and what is not permitted, of truth and falsehood, of good and evil, of justice and injustice.[3]

It is therefore not surprising that when in 1921 the Ya. M. Sverdlov Communist University requested permission to invite Akselrod and Deborin to give courses of lectures, the Central Committee Organization Bureau rejected the application. Thereupon E.M. Yaroslavsky, at that time a Secretary of the Central Committee of the Bolshevik Party, wrote to Lenin on 20 April 1921 as follows:

> Do you consider it possible to invite Deborin and Akselrod to give lectures on philosophy (the history of philosophy and historical materialism)? The educational council of Sverdlov University has made an enquiry about this. We on the Organizational Bureau decided against Akselrod, but now the question has been raised again by a group of lecturers.[4]

Lenin replied that same day:

> I think both should be invited *without fail*. This would be useful, because they would defend the Marxist point of view (if they start agitating in favor of Menshevism, we'll catch them: they'll have to be watched). They should be invited to work out a *detailed program* (and a *synopsis* of their lectures) on philosophy and a scheme of *publications* on philosophy.[5]

Lenin knew perfectly well that there could not be found any better scholars than these for helping to draw up a detailed program of lectures and to write the necessary textbooks, and thus gave his agreement for them to be 'used', just like many other 'specialists' in other fields of scholarship and technology. As regards his advice 'they'll have to be watched', future developments showed that this did not go unheeded. But at that time, in 1921, Akselrod and Deborin were allowed to get on with their work, which they did with great enthusiasm, both in the development of philosophical education and in the organization of academic study, and were duly appreciated as specialists who were capable of carrying out both tasks. Contemporary evidence suggests that their philosophical gifts were judged more or less on their merits. V. Rozhitsyn, an authoritative writer of that period, wrote in the Central Committee's official journal *Agit-propaganda* (no. 7, 1922) that the way now lay open for the restoration of the 'authority of the four Russian founders of a consistent, genuine dialectical materialism, unadulterated by any admixture of idealism, namely Plekhanov, L. Akselrod (Ortodoks), Deborin and Lenin'.

A. Deborin was particularly successful. When the first Soviet philosophical journal—*Pod znamenem marksizma*—was founded in 1922 he became its first editor-in-chief (though V. Ter was responsible for routine editorial work). This journal played a notable part in the philosophical life of those years, forming a point of coalescence for new philosophical cadres, headed by Deborin. For ten years he was not merely in charge of the journal, but became the recognized leader and main authority in the field of philosophy. He wrote energetically on the most controversial and pressing historical and philosophical problems. For example, it was he who first came out against Oswald Spengler's philosophy, in a very critical article in the first issue of *Pod znamenem marksizma*, at a time when Spengler's ideas were very fashionable even amongst Marxists.

L. Akselrod fared somewhat differently. Right from the start her work displayed not only enormous literary talent but also independence. For example, on one occasion the Executive Committee of the Comintern published an Appeal, some of the formulations of which could be taken as implying that, in the Comintern's view Plekhanov was not a Marxist in the last years of his life. Together with L. Deych, another close associate of Plekhanov, Akselrod wrote an angry and impassioned letter, the point of which was abundantly clear from the heading: 'Plekhanov never ceased to be a Marxist.'[6]

This letter reflected a widespread feeling in the early 1920s, when there was great interest in Plekhanov's work. A large number of works were published about him which tended to idolize the first Russian Marxist. S. Ya. Volfson brought out two books: 'A Great Socialist: A Short Account of the Life of G.V. Plekhanov' (Minsk 1922) and 'Works on Plekhanov' (Minsk 1923). The first book contains a short biographical outline and a cursory treatment of the significance of Plekhanov as a philosopher and as a publicist. Volfson's second book is a guide to the literature on Plekhanov up to 1922, including a fairly detailed summary of the content of the various articles on Plekhanov. One such article by A. Frenkel in the first issue of *Pod znamenem marksizma* says of Plekhanov: 'He produced on Russian soil the best literature on the philosophy of Marxism' (p. 68).

Another Soviet philosopher of that period, Sh. Dayan-Ginzburg, examined in 1924 the relationship between free will and determinism on the basis of Plekhanov's works.[7] He devoted most of his attention to the problem of determinism and the role of the individual in history. He was one of the first to raise a question which for many years was continually discussed in philosophical works: if social development occurs exclusively as a result of causal necessity, what is the point of our furthering social development? Who would try to further an impending lunar eclipse? Using factual material from the history of philosophy, Dayan comes to the conclusion that Plekhanov gave the best solution to this problem and gives a detailed account of his ideas, which tried to show that determinism not only does not deny the individual an active role in history but is in fact the basis of the individual's activity.

As we have seen, L. Akselrod also came to Plekhanov's defense. The tone of her letter about Plekhanov sheds light on all her subsequent work. Her unwillingness to compromise and her adherence to principles put her at variance with the official leadership in philosophy; she fell continuously into disfavor with the 'authorities' and was attacked by all manner of critics, whose blows she parried time and again tirelessly and brilliantly. We may note in passing that ten years later, in 1932, when M. Mitin headed the 'philosophical front', he said of Akselrod's letter on Plekhanov: 'Here we have a direct Menshevist attack, a direct Menshevist appeal against the view of the Comintern, which Akselrod accuses of making insinuations' etc.,[8]

It was only in the first few years that Akselrod was able to work comparatively comfortably. She published a number of works: 'Karl Marx as a Philosopher' (Kharkov 1924), 'The Materialist Conception of History and a Critique of the Fundamentals of Bourgeois Social Science', vol. 1 (Ivanovo-Voznesensk 1924), 'Sketches and Reminiscences' (Leningrad 1925) etc. But from about 1925, when she wrote several works on Spinoza, she began to disagree seriously with the official philosophical line on many questions, and for many years, right up to her death in February 1946, she was in disfavor. From the first she had done fruitful scholarly and teaching work, but not in a 'leading' capacity. She was not even on the editorial board of *Pod znamenem marksizma*.

The official representatives of the regime attached a great deal of importance to this journal at that time, regarding it as the keystone of their attempt to form new cadres for the 'philosophical front'. Of the Bolshevik leaders Trotsky played the chief role here. Lenin was unquestionably dominant in Soviet political writing, and his article 'On the significance of militant materialism', which was published in the journal *Pod znamenem marksizma*, was considered his philosophical testament. But it should not be forgotten that by that time Lenin was very ill, and hence was not included in the list of participants in the work of the newly founded journal (no. 1, 1922, p.1). The only members of the Politbureau appearing there are Trotsky, Bukharin and Kamenev. Nor is it surprising that the first issue of the new journal should open with a letter by Trotsky, which, together with Lenin's article (which appeared only in the third issue), may be regarded as setting out the journal's program. Trotsky saw the journal's main aim as 'the materialist upbringing of working-class youth'.

But Trotsky's key role in the organization of Soviet philosophy was not confined to his letter of advice and greetings to the new journal. He also published some important articles, notable for their firm adherence to principles. For example in his article 'Some cursory thoughts on Plekhanov', published in *Pod znamenem marksizma*, no. 4-5, 1922, he gave an authoritative assessment of Plekhanov, not only as a philosopher (in which field we have seen that his worth was generally recognized at this time), but as a theoretician and politician, in which fields Plekhanov was a controversial figure, considered to be far removed from Bolshevism. Trotsky, in a work of great literary style, strongly praised the latter side of Plekhanov's activity, calling him 'the first Russian crusader of Marxism', while also admitting his weak sides. Trotsky similarly made an authoritative defense of Einstein's theory of relativity and Freud's theory of psycho-analysis, both of which had been strongly criticized in the early years of the Revolution; he appealed for a less dogmatic approach in deciding whether these theories were 'reconcilable with Marxism' or not.[9] Trotsky was one of the organizers of a general meeting in June 1924 of the founder-members of the Society of Militant Materialists. Unable to be present himself, he sent a message of greeting, published in *Pod znamenem marksizma*, no. 6-7, 1924, in which he urged that materialist dialectics should be linked with ever-expanding scientific knowledge: a far cry from the later empty quotation-mongering and 'theoretical dictatorship' under Stalin. Trotsky had earlier argued that Marx's method 'is today useful primarily, almost exclusively, for *political* purposes. The extensive cognitive application and the methodological development of dialectical materialism lies wholly in the future'.[10] These plans, in spite of positive developments in Soviet philosophy in recent years, are still far from being realized.

But Trotsky's active work in the philosophical field did not last long. When his serious disagreements with Stalin began, Trotsky several times informed the editor of *Pod znamenem marksizma* that he could not complete promised articles, pleading pressure of work. By the end of 1924 his collaboration with philosophers was at an end. Soon his name would again figure frequently in the journal, but in a quite different guise.

In the early years the main focus of philosophical work, along with the creation of the 'philosophical front', was the writing of textbooks on philosophy. This was because Marx and Engels left no coherent philosophical textbook: their thoughts were scattered through many different works, often polemical in tone, which made them not always suitable for teaching texts. Still more was this true of Lenin's *Materialism and Empirio-Criticism*. Since the study of theory has always been accorded paramount importance in the Soviet Union, this has entailed a similar urgency in the composition of textbooks for teaching purposes. Of these the most famous was Bukharin's *Historical Materialism*, the bed-side book of all students at that time. But Deborin's 'Introduction to the Philosophy of Dialectical Materialism' was also very important. The fact that Plekhanov, the dominant influence of those years, had written a preface for the book made it still more popular with students.

No less important were the textbooks 'A Course of Lectures on Historical Materialism' and 'A Reader in Marxism'[11] by Yu. S. Semkovsky (Bronshteyn), a professor at Kharkov University. His 'Course of Lectures' was highly original in structure: though formally concerned only with historical materialism, it actually expounds a whole philosophical system. The first part is called 'Dialectical materialism (the philosophy of Marxism)' and the second 'Historical materialism (Marxist sociology)'. The book defines the nature of philosophy, matter, dialectics, free will and causal necessity, and determinism and indeterminism. The 'Reader', a weighty 570-page volume, was highly praised at the time. In fact, in one issue of *Pod znamenem marksizma* (no. 3, 1931, p.2) it is said that Semkovsky's work is 'extremely varied and rich' and 'has strongly influenced the philosophical movement in the Ukraine'.

I. Razumovsky's 'A Course in the Theory of Historical Materialism' (Moscow 1924) is an exposition of a rather different type, one of the first books setting out the basic categories of Marxist philosophy. It is a transcript of lectures given to students at Saratov State University, but is more of a scholarly study than a popular lecture-course. The author expresses several views which were to become 'seditious' within a few years. For example, he criticizes the very concept of causality, which, he argues, is an anthropocentric idea, since it is man who introduces causal relationships, which do not exist in nature itself. Furthermore, he divides Marxist philosophy into ontology and epistemology, a division rejected as heretical by subsequent dogma. This is not a simple book and its permanent value lies in the constant evidence of independent thinking by the author and in his attempt to investigate many difficult philosophical problems. This explains its success: the book ran to a third edition in 1929.

Of similar quality was G. Tymyansky's book 'An Introduction to Dialectical Materialism', which ran to two editions. Tymyansky possessed exceptional ability as a teacher, and also as an investigator of very complex philosophical problems—in sharp contrast with the practice of many authors who reduced philosophy to a mass of quotations without investigating its concepts. In his emphasis on the primacy of logic for the study of the empirical and social sciences (see his 'Introduction to Dialectical Materialism', *Priboy*, 1930, p.147) we see the influence of Hegel, whose philosophy played an important part in the concepts of the Deborin school, of which Tymyansky was an eminent representative. In contrast to the later reduction of philosophy to being simply an attitude to life, Tymyansky viewed it as 'a process of developing concepts and of applying them to facts' (ibid., p.197).

S. Gonikman's book 'Historical Materialism' (Moscow 1928) is of undoubted interest. This was one of the most fruitful attempts to expound this branch of philosophy on the basis of the appropriate logical categories (general and individual, quality and quantity, etc.). Historical materialism is, of course, the most 'politicized' branch of Soviet philosophy. The philosophy of history is often reduced to an exposition of the part played by classes and the struggle between them and to a mass of examples of the decisive role of the 'economic factor' etc. Gonikman's attempt at a philosophical approach to the philosophy of history was promising. For example, he tried to give an interpretation of the problem of the unity of subject and object in the process of historical development and of the role of empirical practice as the basis of understanding historical processes. This approach did not endear him to his later critics.[12]

One of the first to publish a course on Marxist philosophy was S. Ya. Volfson, a full member of the Byelorussian Academy of Sciences and Director of its Institute of Philosophy and Law. His 'Dialectical Materialism', in two parts (1922), was an accepted textbook and successfully used far beyond the bounds of Byelorussia, as is clear from the fact that it had run to six editions by 1926.

The book by B. Fingert and M. Shirvindt, 'A Short Textbook on Historical Materialism' (Moscow 1928), was also quite important. Recommended, with qualifications, by the journal *Pod znamenem marksizma* in 1928, with the change of direction in 1931 it was sharply criticized for its mistaken 'Menshevizing idealism' (no. 3, 1931, p.171). Very popular with students were the two textbooks by O.V. Trakhtenberg: 'Historical Materialism', parts 1-6 (Moscow 1929) and 'Conversations with a Teacher on the Subject of Historical Materialism' (Moscow 1924); Trakhtenberg was a professor at Moscow University and senior research fellow at the USSR Academy of Sciences Institute of Philosophy.

When Bukharin's textbook *Historical Materialism* came out in 1922 it had a rapturous reception. But V. Sarabyanov and S. Gonikman published a critique of Bukharin. A. Kon came to Bukharin's defense with a severe 'Critique of the "critics" ' in *Pod znamenem marksizma* (no. 5-6, 1922). He argued that there had not previously been a work which gave a systematic and full exposition of the Marxist teaching on the nature of society in a positive rather than a polemical form, and that Bukharin tried to give an original treatment of a large number of questions. Kon also pointed out that the aim of the book was to provide a *textbook* in Marxist sociology for Party schools, and criticized the 'unacceptable style of criticism and willful and contemptuous tone' of the reviews by Sarabyanov and Gonikman published in *Pod znamenem marksizma* (no. 3, 1922).

The official textbook on philosophy edited by M. Mitin, 'Dialectical and Historical Materialism' (Moscow 1933), is worth special attention. It was intended to replace previous textbooks on philosophy, some of which have been mentioned above, after many Deborinite authors had been 'censured' and excluded from active academic work. M. Mitin became the 'head of the philosophical front' and hence naturally headed the group of authors chosen to write a textbook expounding philosophical problems 'in the spirit of the times', i.e. in accordance with Stalin's developing personality-cult. The textbook is a clear and typical example of all the work done by Mitin in his struggle with 'Menshevizing idealism'. In a review of the work G. Glezerman, a well-known Soviet philosopher, first does justice to the merits of the book in 'bringing out and illuminating the new, distinctive contribution made by the Marxism-Leninism of Lenin and Stalin to the general treasure-house of Marxism'. But then he goes on:

> But at the same time the first part of the book is still more difficult to read; its language is dry and abstract, completely neglecting teaching methodology. Experience in using this part of the book in the current academic year indicates that it is very difficult for the average student at a communist university . . . [The textbook] suffers, in our view, from the same schematic and abstract approach that characterizes the textbooks on general history. Philosophical trends (e.g. that of French materialism) are expounded simply by listing names, without any attempt to give details about individuals who played an important part in the struggle between materialism and idealism, and even without any chronological references.[13]

One can imagine the 'quality' of this work if a review like this could appear when Mitin was at the height of his power in philosophy. It was quite clear from the 'experience in using . . . the book in the current academic year' that the students hardly understood anything in the textbook. Hence pragmatic needs took precedence even over consideration for Mitin's authority: the position had to be rectified. Such was Mitin's first scholarly achievement when he took charge of the philosophical front.

Great attention was paid during this period to problems in the history of philosophy. French materialism as a whole, for example, was accorded great importance throughout the 1920s and 1930s. Here we should note the contribution made by E. Sitkovsky, especially with his monograph 'The Philosophy of J.B. Robinet' (Moscow 1936). Also noteworthy is Sitkovsky's study of the philosophy of Kant, Hegel and Feuerbach.[14] Sitkovsky worked successfully in the field of the history of philosophy until his arrest in 1943.

He was released only in 1956, but managed to return to academic and teaching work.

Research was also done on ancient Greek philosophy, especially on the materialists. A number of works on this topic were written by G. Bammel, well-known in the 1920s and 1930s for his studies in the history of philosophy (including Soviet philosophy), such as 'Democritus: Fragments and Ancient Source Material' (Moscow 1935) and 'The Materialist System of Democritus'.[15]

Special mention should be made of the work of translating into Russian and editing world classics of philosophical thought, which was begun in the 1920s and 1930s. On this task a really enormous amount of labor was expended by A. Rubin, B. Slivker, B. Stolpner, G. Tymyansky, M. Dynnik and B. Fokht. Thus A. Rubin translated some chapters of the work by Maimonides, *A Guide to the Perplexed*,[16] which is one of the few sources on the history of Jewish philosophy accessible to the Soviet reader. He also translated Ibn Rushd's (Averroes) work *Tahafut al-Tahafut* (The Incoherence of the Incoherence).[17] Another translator-philosopher, B. Stolpner, made the first translation into Russian of most of Hegel's works, which made them accessible to a wide Soviet public. Stolpner is also well-known for his translations (made before the Revolution) of H. Höffding's *A History of Modern Philosophy*, H. Gomperz's 'The Doctrine of the World-View', and E. Cassirer's 'Cognition and Reality'.

G. Tymyansky translated into Russian Spinoza's *Treatise on the Improvement of the Intellect*, with a very full commentary. He also translated a number of works by Bacon and Toland. M. Dynnik translated the fragments of Heraclitus and Parmenides's 'On Nature',[18] Giorddano Bruno's *On Cause, Beginning and the One* (Moscow 1934) and Helvetius's *Happiness* (Moscow 1936). B. Fokht, who had studied at Marburg University, was considered an 'idealist' and was allowed to lecture on the history of philosophy at Moscow University only for a few months during World War II. Hence his main job was teaching Latin at the Lenin Pedagogical Institute in Moscow. He translated Aristotle's *Analytica Priora* and *Analytica Posteriora* and several works of Kant, with commentary.

In this period great importance was attached to the philosophical systems of Hegel, Feuerbach, and Spinoza, who were considered to be the theoretical precursors of Marxism. Deborin was one of the first to do work on them, and wrote a number of articles and books which still retain their importance today (e.g. 'Ludwig Feuerbach. His Personality and Outlook', (Moscow 1923)) because of their erudition, use of original sources and wide historical and philosophical range. He paid special attention to Hegel, in the firm conviction that Marxism could not be understood without a thorough knowledge of Hegel's dialectics. He consistently defended this opinion against the so-called 'Mechanists' (especially Akselrod and A.I. Varias), who several times accused him of a 'passion for Hegel' and of blurring the distinction between the dialectics of Marx and Hegel. Akselrod strongly criticized the exaggeration of Hegel's importance in the origins of Marxism, especially in her book of 1928 'In Defense of Dialectical Materialism', in which she argued that Hegel's dialectic was closely bound up with mystical and abstract-idealist notions and this chaff must be winnowed out from the valuable grain. Curiously enough, a few years later the new 'philosophical leadership' headed by Mitin was to repeat this argument, especially in the philosophical discussion in 1947 on G. Aleksandrov's book 'A History of West European Philosophy' (Moscow 1946), but with the qualification that while Deborin had 'overrated' Hegel, Akselrod had 'underrated' him, so the struggle had to be waged on two fronts. But in fact a negative attitude towards Hegel clearly predominated in the philosophical discussion of 1947 and especially in the Central Committee's decree on German philosophy (1943).

The research undertaken by two well-known Soviet philosophers, E. Kolman and S. Yanovskaya, into the place of mathematics in Hegel's system is of undoubted interest. Kolman's case is a complex and interesting one. Born in Czechoslovakia, he was captured by the Russians during the First World War. He was a mathematician and philosopher, and after the Revolution he decided to help the Soviet regime, which badly needed academic personnel. Kolman played an active part in the philosophical life of the Soviet Union; then after the Second World War he returned to Prague to head an Institute of Philosophy. He was arrested after 1948 and held in solitary confinement in Moscow. In the Soviet Union he was associated with work on philosophy and natural science, especially for his books: 'The Subject and Method of Modern Mathematics' (Moscow 1936); 'Engels and Natural Science' (Moscow 1941); 'Cybernetics' (Moscow 1956); 'Lenin and Recent Physics' (Moscow 1959), etc. S. Yanovskaya was one of the few women to make a notable mark in Soviet philosophy, especially in the field of mathematical logic. An interesting essay by her on this topic appeared in the collection 'Hegel and Dialectical Materialism' (1931) and a more detailed treatment of this question, 'Hegel and mathematics' (written jointly with E. Kolman) appeared in *Pod znamenem marksizma* in 1931 (no. 11-12), which supported Hegel against Kant on the problem of the nature of mathematics and its relation to material reality.

We will now deal in greater detail with 'the problem of Spinoza', which to a certain extent was the central point of debate in Soviet intellectual life for most of the 1920s. To begin with, let us take Akselrod's appraisal of Spinoza's philosophy. What sharply distinguishes her treatment of the question from other Soviet philosophical writings on Spinoza is that she is one of the few Soviet authors to link his philosophy with his Jewish origins. Akselrod turned to Spinoza's 'Jewish upbringing' in order to help elucidate the meaning of one of the most important concepts in the philosopher's system—'God'. The problem of whether Spinoza was a 'consistent materialist' was a central one both for Marxist writings as a whole and for Soviet philosophy in particular. Saddled with Plekhanov's authoritative definition: 'Marxism is a type of Spinozism', Soviet philosophers could not avoid the question of what place God occupied in Spinoza's thought. Was it just a terminological 'inconsistency' or did the concept have a more important function in Spinoza's system? And if it did, how could Marxism be considered a type of Spinozism? Hence the central importance of these problems.

Some authors, in view of Plekhanov's definition, did not bother themselves with a deep analysis. They developed a view of Spinoza's system as one of strictly consistent materialism, maintained from beginning to end. Akselrod criticized this view in her article 'Spinoza and materialism',[19] which is an expanded version of the preface written for the new edition of Plekhanov's *Fundamental Problems of Marxism*. Her subject was the relationship between Spinozism and materialism, but she devoted most of her attention to elucidating the so-called 'theological element' in Spinoza's system.[20]

The problem of the relationship between Spinozism and materialism has a history behind it. When Plekhanov gave his enthusiastic and clearly exaggerated estimate of the proximity of the systems of Marx and Spinoza he nevertheless added an important qualification: he noted the presence of a 'theological appendage' in Spinoza's system. It could not be said that Soviet authors of the 1920s disavowed this assessment and hushed it up—they simply did not pay attention to it, and spoke of the 'theological appendage' only hastily and in passing—after all, an 'appendage' is something inessential. As a result Spinoza's philosophy was interpreted without any reference to Plekhanov's qualification but only from the viewpoint that the philosopher 'had come very close to dialectical materialism'.[21] Not only did Plekhanov's enthusiastic and exaggerated assessment of the proximity of Spinozism and Marxism retain its validity, but it was made even stronger than Plekhanov had intended. That is why Akselrod's article was crucially important: because in it she makes a special study of the essential meaning of the 'theological appendage' in Spinoza's system and of the problem of 'God' which is bound up with it. She was one of very few Soviet philosophers to realize that it was not a question of 'God in general' but specifically of the God of the Jews; in brief, she realized that the problem had to be studied in close connection with the thinker's Jewish origins. She refers to the seventh chapter of the *Tractatus theologico-*

politicus, in which the philosopher, when defining a historico-philological method for studying the Bible, says that the more we know about an author's life, the more easily we will be able to interpret his words. Akselrod applies this methodological rule to Spinoza himself in order to explain the meaning of the word 'God' in his system. And Spinoza's life was, of course, very closely bound up with his 'Jewish upbringing' or 'Jewish origin'.

For a Soviet author it was very unusual to investigate the national characteristics of a philosopher's work and not the 'front of class struggle' of the age in which he lived. This is what makes Akselrod's study very original and unlike anything else written on Spinoza in the Soviet Union. She quite justifiably comes to the conclusion that Spinoza's life and spiritual development differed sharply from those of thinkers with a Christian background. The latter did not experience the tremendous inner dramas endured by thinking people emerging from Orthodox Judaism.[22] Christian peoples possessed their own territory, their own statehood, their own national culture. For this reason, the Christian religion, in spite of everything, had to make and did make concessions to scientific aspirations contrary to the basic essentials of its doctrine, without any fear that it might thereby 'destroy' its peoples or 'disperse' them among all the other peoples by whom they were surrounded. The surety against this was the possession of firm roots in one's own land. This gave rise to an interesting phenomenon: however strong the religious traditions, religious upbringing and the religious feeling which developed out of these may have been in the Christian world, these elements were dissolved in the general stream of historical culture: in science, art, politics, etc. This is the reason why in the case of Christian thinkers religious traditions co-existed more or less peaceably with the scientific aspirations and cultural needs of a given age which contradicted these traditions. There was a more or less practicable possibility of, on the one hand, preserving one's religious beliefs and, on the other, contributing to the advance of scientific thought. This does not, of course, mean that there was no persecution of thinkers whose teachings, in the opinion, say, of the Inquisition, ran contrary to the basic dogmas of the Church. But these outward persecutions, however cruel they may have been, could not, in the opinion of Akselrod, cause in people of strong character tragic inner conflicts, i.e. conflicts over one's outlook on the world.[23]

This analysis forms a background against which Akselrod develops her main idea, namely that the situation is quite different with innovators who come from a Jewish environment. For thousands of years the Jewish people has been deprived of its own territory, its own statehood and, consequently, of its own national culture in the broadest sense. Therefore, the Jewish people, being highly cultured as regards its spiritual needs, cultivated and piously guarded the remains of its intellectual and moral development of its historical past. Religion is one of those remains. The Jewish religion in itself, as regards its dogmas, is the most realistic of all religious doctrines, capable of all manner of compromises to meet the demands of reality, but as a result of the isolation of the Jewish people it increasingly hardened and ossified. The Jews' religious outlook on the world remained virtually the only national element which unified national spiritual consciousness, i.e. the only form of national ideology. And since scholarship, art, politics and literature are the cultural blessings of the Christian world, i.e. of a world hostile to Judaism, Orthodox Jews cultivated a religious hatred of all these cultural values. Cultural values of a secular nature were pronounced to be forbidden fruit, which could only entice Jews away from the faith of their ancestors and impede true devotion to God. Devoted service to God was the sole, chief and highest aim of earthly existence. Thus, Akselrod concludes, it was in the heart of this ideology that Spinoza received his first spiritual upbringing. This upbringing became firmly embedded in the thinker's impressionable, sensitive and poetic soul. All Spinoza's works are imbued with the same religious feeling, in spite of his strict rationalistic and geometric method of argumentation. It is evident and perceptible that the cult of Jehovah, in which Spinoza had been brought up, had taken firm possession of the touchingly poetic soul of the great philosopher. The atheistic thinker never abandoned the central idea of Judaism, that the aim of life and its highest, supreme good is the service and love of God. The very same idea, in another form and essentially different content, became the crowning apex of his rationalistic scheme, in the guise of the '*amor dei intellectualis*'.

But how does this love of God, instilled in Spinoza by all his Jewish upbringing, manifest itself? This question is connected with an understanding of the notion of substance, also a central problem in the discussions of that period.

The focus of the Marxist philosophical writings on Spinoza at that time was the identification of substance (God) with matter. It was on the basis of this that the inference about Spinoza's materialism was made. Akselrod decisively rejects this inference. This is not the basis of Spinoza's materialism for, in her view, substance cannot be identified with matter. This conclusion was at variance with everything written on Spinoza in Soviet works at that time. In an article published in the same journal two years later she develops this idea in the following decisive manner:

> What an absurdity it is to maintain that Spinoza's substance is matter. Recognizing substance as matter involves constructing the following strange entity: substance is matter, one of its attributes is matter, its second attribute

> is thought; and besides this the same substance is supposed, according to Spinoza, to have an infinite number of other infinite attributes.[24]

The essential feature of substance is not that it is matter, for matter is only one of its attributes, but that it is *causa sui*, its own cause. Akselrod sees the key to discovering the essential meaning of substance in an investigation of the meaning of causality and the natural order in Spinoza's system. And this is connected with the problem of the consideration of ends.

Spinoza discards transcendental teleology and simultaneously rejects God as the goal-setter. This is the essence of Spinoza's atheism. Everything in the universe, including the weighing of goals, must be considered from the view-point of necessary laws of nature, in so far as we aspire to true, identical cognition. Once the idea of a transcendental teleology has been critically discarded and with it the notion of a setter of ends, the universe seems to be a *causa sui*, an absolutely self-sufficient necessity, an entity both independent and unique, caused by nothing and (which amounts to the same thing) created by no one. From the viewpoint of the universe as a whole, each phenomenon and each sequence of phenomena is caused by the general network of causal connections in the world, forming an immutable, necessary and ordered whole. All aims, whatever their nature and content, are occasioned and in the strictest possible manner caused by the law of mechanical causality. The law of absolute necessity, the most stringent natural order, which permeates all phenomena, is in Spinoza's system the supreme law, which governs all the universe. Akselrod's main conclusion is that this supreme, absolute law, is in fact, substance or (which is one and the same thing) Spinoza's 'God'. 'Imbued to the core with a deeply embedded religious feeling, Spinoza colors with this religious feeling the highest, supreme law of the world order'.[25]

The infinite power of God is transformed into the infinite power of nature herself and, consequently, Spinoza contrasts the religious anthropomorphic world-view with his own outlook, which is permeated through and through by a reverential worship of the limitless power and infinite might of the world order. With Spinoza, true religious feeling and genuine reverential worship are aroused by the necessary, immutable connection between phenomena in the universe, by their stringent, as it were, divine, order, which holds sway over everyone and everything, penetrating the whole universe, all phenomena in the world without exception. Here is the power, here is the grandeur, here is infinite might. This is Spinoza's true God, and not substance in the sense of 'matter'. This, of course, is not the God of theology, and in that sense Spinoza's system is atheistic. But this in no way rules out the conclusion, which Akselrod in fact made, namely that God existed in Spinoza's soul and found expression in the system. Because of the psychologically deeply embedded religious mood which remained from his previous reverential worship of God the Creator, the philosopher transferred this religious feeling of worship to the world order. The consequences of this religious worship was the isolation and alienation of the world order, i.e. of the natural laws of the universe, from the universe itself. Thus, religious feeling created out of an anti-religious principle an abstract entity, imbued with a religious spirit, and in particular with the spirit of the Jewish religion. As Feuerbach put it: a denial of theology, but on the basis of that very theology. This was certainly very far from the interpretation then current in Soviet philosophy according to which Spinoza's God was just an inessential 'appendage'.

One may easily imagine what a storm Akselrod's analysis aroused. All the orthodox Plekhanovites fell upon her. Writing of the sensation and wrath caused by her article 'Spinoza and materialism', she said: 'I'm tired of it all. Quantity has turned into quality. All of a sudden, absolutely without any cause, attacks on me have begun to appear in *Pod znamenem marksizma*. At first timidly, then becoming bolder and bolder both in quantity and quality.'[26]

But what arguments did the opponents of Akselrod's reasoning advance against it? Nothing, no arguments at all. Just abuse and accusations of revisionism. Akselrod believes Spinoza's system bears the imprint of the Judaic religion. Consequently, she is a Zionist. She does not consider Spinoza's substance identical with matter. Consequently, she is a revisionist, since she is at variance with Plekhanov. Deborin tried to show that Akselrod had completely fallen under the influence of idealist historians of philosophy and, together with them, distorted Spinoza's philosophy. In his view, this was evident first and foremost in the fact that her explanation of Spinoza's philosophy took the form of 'a Zionist conception of Jewish history'.[27]

Deborin remarks that anyone familiar with Zionist writings would immediately detect in Akselrod's conception the borrowing of a philosophical-historical idea from Zionist writers. In Deborin's opinion, the essence of Spinoza's system, its unique character, could not be derived either from national psychology or from the fact that the Jewish people had no land of its own, or even from the particular upbringing which the thinker received in his childhood, but only from the social relationships of the age in which he lived. Once again, in place of arguments we have abuse and labeling, in this case pinning on the label of 'Zionism'.

The question of the link between Spinoza's philosophy and Judaism has surfaced from time to time in Soviet philosophical writing, in particular in connection with the publication in 1935 of a translation of Spinoza's *Theological-Political Treatise* by Grigory Samuilovich Tymyansky, for which the latter had written an introductory article and a commentary. He emphasized the political nature of the 'Treatise', pointing to the fact that in the seventeenth century political struggle was expressed in religious forms. Thus, religious questions had primarily a political significance. Tymyansky explains the fact that Spinoza abandoned for several years work on his 'Ethics' and wholly switched over to writing the *Theological-Political Treatise* by his wish to take part in this political struggle: Spinoza wanted to intervene directly in the struggle at that time between the free-thinking party of De Witt and the Calvinist conformists. Spinoza came out in defense of free thought with no restrictions at all.[28] Tymyansky takes this as grounds for concluding that Spinoza was a philosopher on a European rather than a merely national scale and points out, in particular, that 'any attempts to derive Spinoza's philosophy from Judaism are erroneous' (ibid).

This last point was made again by Tymyansky in a paper read before the Institute of Philosophy on 22 December 1934 and published in no. 1-2 of *Vestnik Kommunisticheskoy akademii* for 1935. In the discussion on the paper A.I. Rubin disagreed with this interpretation of the origins of Spinoza's philosophy and virtually supported Akselrod's position, without, it is true, referring to her. A.I. Rubin insisted that it was impossible to understand the essential features of Spinoza's philosophy in isolation from Judaism (see ibid.).

The debate on the questions of the relationship between substance and matter and of whether Spinoza was a materialist followed similar lines to the debate on the relevance of his Jewish origins. Deborin attacked Akselrod not by appealing to what Spinoza actually said, but by quoting pieces from the Marxist classics to show that her interpretation was ideologically unsound. He tried to blacken her name by identifying her interpretation of matter as basically deriving from determinism and rejection of teleology with statements by the Machist heretic A. Bogdanov. He also maintained that Akselrod had changed her position on the question of Spinoza's materialism since her 'Philosophical studies' of 1925, which was quite untrue, as she showed. But the basic issue raised by Akselrod's interpretation of matter and materialism in Spinoza, which Deborin either did not see or made no attempt to answer, was that Engels's categorical assertion of the 'great divide' in philosophy between materialism and idealism was impossible to apply in practice, since it ignored the possibility of subtler intermediate positions. If Akselrod was right in seeing Spinoza's 'materialism' in his denial of teleology and his determinism, this would let in many 'idealists' who also rejected teleology—and where would this leave the classic Marxist distinction between 'idealism' and 'materialism'? However this was no argument against Akselrod's position, but a demonstration of the inadequacy of a dogmatic and outdated criterion.

The complex issues involved were partially recognized by scholars other than Akselrod in the 1920s. S. Volfson, one of the most serious investigators of Spinoza's philosophy, called the Dutch thinker's world-view 'naturalistic monism', emphasizing the materialistic nature of his doctrines.[29] But he paid special attention to the thinker's ethical doctrines. In the same article he argued that Spinoza 'developed a naturalistic conception of the world which was permeated by the principle of the most stringent mechanical necessity and the causal inter-dependence of phenomena.' He defended the position that Spinoza's system, freed from its theological shell, was materialist (see ibid.). On the other hand, a no less major researcher, the well-known Soviet philosopher B.E. Bykhovsky, put forward, in the late 1920s the formula of 'parallelistic monism' as a definition of the nature of Spinoza's philosophy. In Bykhovsky's view, this formula stressed the single source of mutually impermeable elements, which qualitatively distinguished Spinoza's monism from Descartes's dualism.[30] At the same time, Bykhovsky objected to the assertion made by several authors (in particular, by Plekhanov) that Spinoza had completely overcome the dualism of Descartes, arguing that this was true only on a very general level: Spinoza elaborated a doctrine whereby a unified 'substance' was the bearer of the attributes of both space and thought. In Bykhovsky's view, the fact that Spinoza continually insisted that the attributes of space and thought were mutually impenetrable does not suggest that he had completely overcome Descartes's dualism in the solution of the psycho-physical problem.

In a later pamphlet, 'Was Spinoza a Materialist?' (Minsk 1928) Bykhovsky rejected the accepted view that Spinoza was a materialist precursor of Marxism, arguing that his position was 'monism unresolved either into materialism or into objective idealism' and, in fact, a form of pantheism. This interpretation was attacked by K. Skurer and I. Vaynshteyn, who maintained that Spinoza regarded the attribute of space as primary and that of thought as secondary, derivative, which made him a 'materialist' and proved the correctness of Plekhanov's maxim that Marxism is a type of Spinozism.[31]

In the early 1930s there began a general 'reconsideration' of what was said and written both by the 'dialecticians' (Deborinites) and the 'Mechanists' (supporters of Akselrod). This reconsideration also touched on Spinoza's philosophy. On all the main problems Mitin now became the chief theoretician. We have already seen how this reconsideration went with regard to his assessment of Hegel's philosophy: he dealt with Spinoza in exactly the same way, arguing that he was fighting on 'two fronts'. At a session of the Communist Academy and the Institute of Philosophy to mark the 300th anniversary of Spinoza's birth he delivered a paper 'Spinoza and dialectical materialism'.[32] He criticized Deborin for hushing up the 'metaphysical character of Spinoza's system' and for not seeing his 'shortcomings', which, in Mitin's view, lay in his conception of an 'abstract, contemplative materialism and in his understanding of the attribute of thought and the category of motion' (p. 173). He literally repeated Akselrod (without, of course, referring to her) saying that the 'theological costume' or 'theological shell' of Spinoza's system was 'not something foreign to his basic ideas but rather shows the very serious inconsistencies in his philosophy, indicating that he had not yet reached a consistently materialist position' (ibid.). He stressed that Marxism could not be considered 'a type of Spinozism' (another echo of Akselrod). One curious feature was that Mitin attacked Deborin for stressing, in his description of Spinoza's social ideals, his doctrine that man could attain the highest happiness by organizing the sort of links and relations which might harmoniously coordinate mankind's collective powers to produce a happy life on earth. Against this Mitin says:

> Here Deborin makes not only theoretical errors in his assessment of Spinoza's philosophy but also an exclusively political error. Spinoza's vague assertions, typical of his position as the ideologist of the revolutionary bourgeoisie of his age, his statements about 'the general and highest happiness', about the necessity of coordinating mind and body as Spinoza put it, the necessity of mutual help for the satisfaction of needs and escape from dangers, the necessity of harmoniously coordinating the collective forces of mankind—all these are typically bourgeois ideals, occasioned by the particular historical and class conditions of his age. These were the ideals which were later written on the banners of the bourgeois French revolution in the form of 'liberty, equality and fraternity', etc. All these ideas Deborin passes off as purely socialist (ibid., p. 176).

The necessities of 'coordinating mind and body', of 'mutual help for the satisfaction of needs and escape from dangers', of 'harmoniously coordinating the collective forces of mankind' were, in Mitin's view, so contrary to the principles of socialism that he fiercely attacked those who mentioned these ideals of Spinoza. He did not even realize what a testimonial he had given to socialism.

When criticizing Deborin Mitin had repeated Akselrod's main arguments: when proceeding in the course of his paper to a critique of Akselrod, he literally repeated Deborin's arguments, as can be seen in this extract:

> In her assessment of Spinoza's philosophy Akselrod withdrew completely from the most important problems of the materialist world-view. She wrote: 'I absolutely deny that Spinoza's substance is matter, yet nevertheless I consider him a materialist.' The question then immediately arises: what does Spinoza's materialism amount to, what is the real meaning of his 'substance'? She replies as follows: 'Spinoza belongs with the materialists because of his doctrine of the unity of the world, his exhaustive criticism of transcendental teleology and his denial of the act of creation, which all show his materialist conception of the world'. It must be said that in Akselrod's really completely monstrous thesis there is not a grain of Marxism or of materialism. Firstly, Akselrod, as we have seen, is prepared to call Spinoza a materialist without his commitment to a material substance, in other words she admits the possibility of materialism without matter (ibid., p.177).

Mitin was manifestly not squeamish about making use of Deborin's arguments. Even his accusation that Akselrod 'was repeating Höffding' was taken from Deborin. This was Mitin's idea of 'fighting on two fronts'. But he had someone to learn from: Stalin was a recognized master at fighting on two fronts.

One other aspect needs to be stressed. In spite of the bitterness of the discussions in the 1920s they were conducted on the whole in good faith. One may agree or disagree with this or that thesis of Akselrod or Deborin, with the forms of polemic they adopted, but these were scholars who were defending their positions. Everything radically changed at the very beginning of 1931. We have already seen this in Mitin's case: he usually did not bother with a conscientious analysis of the facts but used any means to substantiate a particular 'line'. We will cite one example which illustrates the new ways, which spread as quick as lightning with the 'Stalinist offensive on the ideological front'.

For several years after 1931 the mass media were engaged in 'exposing Menshevizing idealism'. Moreover, the idea of scholarly good faith faded into the background. Any means were considered suitable. The following fact is typical. We have already seen what was the attitude of Deborin, the head of the 'Menshevizing idealists' towards the 'Zionist interpretation of Spinoza': highly unfavorable. In spite of this, the journal *Voinstvuyushchy ateizm* (Militant Atheism), no. 11, 1931 published an article by M. Leningradsky entitled 'Menshevizing idealism as an apologist for Judaism', in which the 'Menshevizing idealists' were condemned for maintaining what they so vigorously attacked. An article by B. Rakhman, 'Spinoza and Judaism', published in *Trudy Instituta krasnoy professury* (Transactions of the Institute of Red Professors) (no. 1, 1923), served as grounds for this. The article did indeed analyse in detail the influence of Judaism on Spinoza. Rakhman described, in particular, Spinoza's 'Ethics' as 'polished Judaism expounded by the Cartesian method' (p. 93). But the editors of the journal clearly felt that criticizing one author was insufficient so the accusation is made against the whole of 'Menshevizing idealism', although there was not a grain of truth in the accusation. Such was the established style of that period.

As soon as the 'philosophical front' was organized there began to appear in the press discussions of problems which riveted the attention of all. Let us now examine some of these.

No. 5-6 of *Pod znamenem marksizma* for 1922 published an article by S. Minin 'Over the side with philosophy!', the intention of which was clear from the title. Minin's formulation of his thesis was so strong that it could have been taken as an attempt to abolish Marxist philosophy and the very idea of a Marxist ideology. But the problem has a deeper significance: this was the first attempt to liberate natural science from the stifling influence of *a priori* philosophical schemas, the first claim that positive knowledge had priority. This was vividly expressed by V. Miller, a professor at Smolensk State University. He gave a thorough justification for his argument that it was Plekhanov who first gave an excuse for speaking about a philosophy of Marxism, 'when he used the incautious expression "the philosophical foundations of Marxism" '; his critique 'The main problems of Marxism', in Miller's view, 'was quite capable of enticing the reader along the completely false path of apriorism'.[33] This was not simply an 'abolitionist' position with regard to philosophy, but a carefully thought-out conception which demanded 'the determined and whole-hearted advocacy of the slogan of the sovereignty of the specialized sciences, or rather of a single positive science with all its natural or historically-conditioned sub-divisions' (ibid., p.71). Thus, he posited the necessity of freeing science from the guardianship of philosophy. The perspicacity of this scholar is surprising, in that as early as 1924 he foresaw the danger of reducing philosophy to abstract deductions and dogmatic ideas, to *a priori* schemas which were then called 'science' and 'scientific'. The later development of events showed how justified these fears were.

A.Z. Tseytlin, a physicist and philosopher, also warned against an over-simplified conception of dialectical materialism as a 'master-key' for solving specific scientific tasks. In a speech at the Second All-Union Conference of Marxist-Leninist Scientific Institutions in 1929 he remarked that dialectics, which even by that time was predominant as the official scientific and philosophical method, 'could in no way be applied to natural science, especially not to the exact sciences such as physics'.[34]

This positivist tendency, which demanded the freeing of scientific knowledge from the domination of abstract philosophical models, was especially evident in the work of Emmanuel Semenovich Enchmen. An entire school of Soviet philosophy—'Enchmenism'—which gave rise to stormy debates, is named after him.

Unfortunately the author has not managed to consult Enchmen's works, which have been withdrawn from circulation in the Soviet Union. But it is possible to understand the essentials of his position from the long passages from his books cited by his opponents. He produced the 'theory of the new biology' as a 'direct and inevitable development of genuine, orthodox Marxism'. The basis of the theory was 'the complete abolition of psychology in connection with the incipient degeneration of critical positivism'. In spite of its rather exaggerated and extreme form ('the abolition of psychology'), Enchmen's approach contained a highly rational element: it set as its aim 'the natural-science study of social phenomena in contrast to the traditional psychological approach', and also 'the full scientific generalization of biological phenomena together with social phenomena in a new revolutionary theory of historical physiology'. He wanted to take his stand on the foundation of pure biology, in order to give a 'purely causal explanation' of social phenomena, or, as he put it, a reciprocally-physical, natural-science explanation of the physiological reactions which correspond to the appropriate social phenomena.[35]

All this, of course, meant the ascription of excessive importance to physiology in the study of psychology. However, Enchmen's design can only be understood if we bear in mind that his conception was a reaction against the same sort of exaggeration of the role of ideology in the analysis of social events. This is the viewpoint of a positivist searching for scientific, positive methods of studying society.

Enchmen's theory caused a veritable storm because he came out in a positivist spirit against any world-view, including a proletarian one, against any sort of philosophy, including dialectical materialism. 'A world-view', said Enchmen, 'is an exploiter's invention . . . And with the coming of the dictatorship of the proletariat we are against a "world-view" '. He continues:

> Psychology, idealism and materialism are words to which one can apply the brilliantly daring passage in Descartes: 'People often use incomprehensible words in their assertions, for they assume that at one time they were understood or had been handed down by people who did understand them.' (ibid.). A certain philosophical world-view, called dialectical materialism, will be reduced to ashes, for thanks to a training in biology the need for logic will disappear, the knowledge of it and the use of it in thought will die out, and only the physiological reaction of the guffaw will call to mind exploitist dialectical materialism, which fooled the innocent minds of advanced revolutionary workers.[36]

It was natural that Enchmen, starting from these premises, should see as his task the elimination of a special science of sociology, for he considered there was nothing in social phenomena which could not be subjected to biological analysis. He criticized sociology on the grounds that this science aimed at studying, as the sociologists put it, the so-called 'abstract laws' of social life, i.e. those laws which are to 'fix' the specific events of social life, events which must unconditionally distinguish the science of sociology from the other sciences and turn it into a purveyor of ready-made schemas to which the positive sciences must be subordinated. And since Marxist philosophy in this respect is not only no exception but is the most determined purveyor of ready-made truths of the highest instance, then, in Enchmen's view, it deserves no mercy.

Enchmen's theory caused considerable anxiety in official Soviet circles, since it attracted enthusiastic supporters amongst young workers and students and in a short time had firmly won their sympathies. This is primarily because Enchmen adopted a position of extreme radicalism, giving a left-wing critique of all the old culture. Students looked upon his theory as the broadside of a revolutionary who had taken up the fight against the conservatism of the old way of thinking. This made 'Enchmenism' a social and psychological phenomenon which seriously worried those people on whom the 'young succession' began to turn its back. This is why heavy guns were brought in to deal with Enchmen. Bukharin criticized Enchmen in his book 'The Attack' (which had two editions). A. Bubnov, a major Party figure and subsequently People's Commissar for Education addressed an appeal to young people in *Pravda* (on 15 January 1924). A special collection of essays was published called 'Yet Another Distortion of Marxism (on Enchmen's Theory)', edited by S. Girinis (Moscow 1924). G. Bammel strongly criticized Enchmen in his book 'On the Philosophical Front after October' (Moscow-Leningrad 1929). *Pravda*, in a leader on 14 December 1923 posited a link between Trotsky's idea of the bureaucratic ossification of the old guard and pressure upon young people by means of Enchmen's theory, commenting ironically that certain 'ideological tendencies amongst young people have proclaimed "the old guard" not merely old but antiquated and have refused to issue it Enchmenist "physiological documents" '.

For several years 'Enchmenism' was stigmatized in many university departments at seminars, in articles and in books, and it gradually acquired a pejorative and even odious connotation. But in actual fact, in spite of the exaggeration of the role and importance of biology as a means of studying psychology, this was a positive phenomenon in Soviet sociopolitical thought, since Enchmen was one of the first to demand publicly a 'positive' and not abstractly dogmatic study of social phenomena.

In connection with the demand for a more thorough study of the theoretical problems of Marxist sociology, something must be said about Boris Isaakovich Gorev (Goldman). He began his work as a Soviet historian and philosopher in very inauspicious circumstances: he had been a Menshevik, and after the February Revolution even a member of the Menshevik Central Committee. But after he had officially left the Menshevik Party in 1920, he began his work as a university teacher and researcher. Thus, in 1923 the journal *Pod znamenem marksizma* (no. 10) published his article 'Some problems of the Marxist theory of classes'. He remarks that there is 'a considerable amount of truth' in the statements by Yu. Danilevsky, M.I. Tugan-Baranovsky and P. Sorokin to the effect that neither Marx nor his successors had provided an integral and systematic theory of classes, and that in particular Marx himself gives several varying definitions of the concept of a 'class'. Against this background he gives a critical analysis of Bukharin's book *Historical Materialism*, which was then considered an official textbook and, to use his words, 'had been distributed on a grandiose scale'. To this day Gorev's work has not lost its topicality: in the Marxist theory of classes there are indeed many 'blank spaces', obscurities and inaccuracies. If there are two main classes in every social formation, how, writes Gorev, is this thesis to be applied 'to society, where most of the population are small commodity-producers, and industrial capital and the proletariat exist only in embryonic form, i.e. to the population of the colonial countries and to the USA (where there was no [historical stage of] slavery) in the first decades of the nineteenth century?' Gorev's main objection was that if a society is to be divided on the criterion of the relationship to the means of production, the result will be, on the one hand, all the proprietors, from the big landowners down to the petty bourgeoisie, and, on the other, the industrial proletariat and the lumpen-proletariat. The numerous discussions about classes which have taken place at various times in the communist press show how right Gorev was in drawing attention as early as 1923 to contradictions in the application of the Marxist theory of classes to the analysis of the actual phenomena of social life.

B. Gorev published a number of monographs: 'Studies in Historical Materialism' (Kharkov 1925), 'A History of Socialism in Connection with the Development of the Working-Class Movement' (Moscow 1925), 'From Thomas More to Lenin' (Leningrad 1924), 'Bakunin, His Life, Work and Teachings' (Ivanovo-Voznesensk 1922), and 'Marxism and the Place of War in History' (Moscow 1930).

Great importance was attached to questions of the links between philosophy and natural science, especially after the publication of Lenin's 'On the Significance of Militant Materialism', in which the demand for the formation of an 'alliance between philosophers and natural scientists' is of central importance. For instance, in 1924 a Society of Materialist Doctors was founded, headed by Solomon Grigorevich Levit. Soon this organization reached All-Union proportions and was praised for its work by the then People's Commissar for Health N.A. Semashko.[37] Such well-known scientists as L.A. Zilber, I.G. Lukomsky, S.Ya. Kaplansky, S.S. Vayl, G.A. Batkis, etc. took an active part in the work of the Society. Biologists, particularly from the K.A. Timiryazev Institute, were closely involved in the work of the Society, which was headed by Izrail Iosifovich Agol.

As regards theoretical questions, we will discuss in detail reactions to Einstein's theory of relativity, which attracted universal attention at this time.

In many studies dealing with the influence philosophy has had on the development of science in the USSR it is stated that the theory of relativity was for a certain time rejected in the USSR since it, in the words of the German scholar H. Falk, 'contradicted dialectical materialism'.[38] F. Frank in his book 'The Philosophy of Science' shares this opinion, when he writes that 'Soviet authors have a strong tendency to consider that the theory of relativity contradicts materialism. This presupposes, of course, the condemnation of the theory of relativity as a "reactionary theory" which leads to undesirable political behavior.[39] D. Joravsky also maintains that Soviet Marxism proceeds from the assumption that 'anti-materialism' is inherent in Einstein's theory'.[40]

This view is disputed in recent Soviet philosophical writings. The journal *Filosofskie nauki* (The Philosophical Sciences), when reviewing the history of the 1920s and 1930s, pointed out that these authors were not being objective: they had taken into consideration only one type of assessment of this theory which was far from being shared by all Soviet physicists and philosophers. It gives the names of a large number of philosophers and physicists who gave a completely contrary assessment of Einstein's theory of relativity, such as A. Fridman, A. Ioffe, S. Semkovsky, E. Kolman, B. Gessen and others.[41]

All this is true: there were indeed fierce arguments on the nature of the theory of relativity. However, the fact is that the official new leadership in philosophy which dominated intellectual life in the country from the end of 1930 was highly unfavorable towards the theory of relativity. This is especially clear in the work of Mitin's closest assistant and 'authority' on the philosophical problems of natural science—A.A. Maksimov, of whom the 'Philosophical Encyclopaedia' was later to write that he 'made a nihilistic and both philosophically and scientifically mistaken assessment of quantum physics and the theory of relativity'.[42]

A. Maksimov nurtured this 'nihilistic position' for a long time. Here is a typical example. In 1923 a circle for the study of dialectical materialism, headed by Maksimov, was formed under the aegis of the Party cell of the physics and mathematics faculty of the first Moscow State University. In 1923 A. Goldshteyn, who took part in the circle, wrote: 'We are sharpening our materialist and dialectical teeth not only on the forgotten Dühring, but also on fresh young professors like Berg, Vernadsky, Novikov, Einstein etc.'[43]

It is not without interest that Maksimov's obscurantism was so obvious that after numerous protests from leading physicists he was forced to withdraw from active work and to go into retirement. But that was in the 1950s after Stalin's death. In the 1930s his opinion was considered the official view of the philosophical leadership. Therefore, it is not surprising that in both scholarly works and textbooks the dominant view was that the theory of relativity should be identified with Machism. In an article with the typical title 'On the reflection of the class struggle in modern science' Maksimov wrote: 'Einstein himself shows where the roots of his idealistic vacillations lie. In an article in the journal *Physikalische Zeitschrift*, no. 7, 1916, Einstein wrote concerning the death of Mach: ". . . at least for my own part I know that it was especially Hume and Mach who influenced me directly and indirectly." '[44] Those who were active in the philosophical field in the 1930s, 1940s and early 1950s know that that 'count of the indictment' against Einstein was repeated many times in university departments, at theoretical conferences and in the press. This is why the interpretation by Frank, Joravsky and Falk of the essence of the affair does correspond to the facts. All the more important is the work of those Soviet physicists and philosophers who actively resisted this position.

In the 1920s the 'campaign' against Einstein's theory of relativity was led by the physicist A.K. Timiryazev, son of the famous Russian biologist K.A. Timiryazev. This was a time when, in the words of the Soviet philosopher B. Gessen, speaking at the Second All-Union Conference of Marxist-Leninist Academic Institutions, 'in the field of theoretical natural science the position as regards Marxist cadres is catastrophic'.[45] In these conditions the bold and unambiguous defense of Einstein and his theory by S. Semkovsky, B. Gessen, E. Kolman, and A. Goltsman is of paramount importance. It can be said without exaggeration that the public statements by these scientist-philosophers have great historical value, since they parried the attacks on Einstein's work. Thus S. Semkovsky in an article 'On the argument in Marxism over the theory of relativity' expressed his disagreement with the main ideas in Timiryazev's paper at the Communist Academy on 7 November 1924. He showed convincingly that from the viewpoint of dialectics of nature, which rejects the idea of absolute rest, there is no logical possibility of talking about 'absolute movement'.[46]

The opponents of the theory of relativity advanced, along with several other arguments, one which was very typical of them: namely that since Einstein sympathized with the views of Mach, whom Lenin had energetically attacked, his theory could not be acceptable. Semkovsky advanced a number of counter-arguments, the irrefutability of which is self-evident. He pointed out that three questions must be distinguished: (1) Einstein's personal philosophical sympathies; (2) the historical influence of Mach's 'mechanics' on the elaboration of Einstein's theory of relativity; and (3) the essential inter-relationships between the theory of relativity and the philosophy of Machism (empiriocriticism) (ibid, p. 155). Elsewhere he wrote: 'The confusion introduced by A. Timiryazev into the theory of relativity starts with the basic distinction between absolute and relative movement', for 'there is no absolutely immobile ether, and there are no bodies which are in a state of absolute rest'.[47] In his 'Introduction' to this book Semkovsky stated still more definitely:

> The complicated and new problems brought out by the theory of relativity have caused fierce arguments in Marxist circles. But the polemic on this subject, as it is conducted in the journal *Pod znamenem marksizma*, is, it must be said bluntly, rather superficial and confused; it shows the lack sometimes even of a relative understanding of the theory of relativity, and this fact, as usually happens, is compensated for by the lowest tricks of polemic.

Semkovsky was actively supported by A. Goltsman, who wrote, in one of the first articles published on this topic in the Soviet press: 'Einstein's doctrine is the doctrine of dialectics of nature.'[48] And when A. Timiryazev criticized him for this he published a closely-reasoned article in defense of the theory of relativity and of his own position.[49]

E. Kolman also consistently defended the theory of relativity against attacks. In his paper at the academic session of the Institute of Philosophy of the Communist Academy to mark the twenty-fifth anniversary of the publication of Lenin's *Materialism and Empirio-Criticism* Kolman expressed his solidarity with the physicist Academician A. Ioffe, who declared at the same session: 'There is no doubt that even now attacks still occur, when philosophers stand in the way of the historical progress of physics and say: "Back, back, I won't allow any of it, it's all idealism." '[50] Continuing in this vein Kolman remarked that 'voices have been heard trying to drag physics back fifty years, standing in the way of all progress, denouncing as idealism the theory of relativity, the quantum theory and anything that does not accord with Maxwell and Faraday'.[51]

The problem of the participation of Jews in the development of Soviet philosophy is complicated and multi-faceted. Within the limits of this article we have been able to shed light only on certain aspects of the problem.

But even from what has been said it is obvious that from the very first moves to revive academic and scholarly work in the philosophical field, the part played by Jews was considerable and, in a certain sense, predominant.

Notes

1 See *Vestnik Kommunisticheskoy akademii* (Bulletin of the Communist Academy), no. 39, 1930, 88.
2 See V.I. Lenin, *Sochineniya* (Works), 3rd edn. (Moscow), vol. 13, *Materialy i dokumenty* (Materials and documents section: L. Akselrod, 'A review of a book by V.I. Lenin').
3 A. Deborin, 'The philosophy of Mach and the Russian Revolution', in *Golos sotsial-demokrata* (The voice of the Social-Democrat), no. 4-5, 1908, 3-12.
4 Lenin, vol. 52, 393.
5 Ibid., vol. 52, 159.
6 See *Pod znamenem marksizma* (Under the Banner of Marxism), no. 5-6, 1922, 155.
7 See the journal *Sputnik kommunista*, no. 29, 1924.
8 See M. Mitin, 'On the philosophical heritage of V.I. Lenin', in *Pod znamenem marksizma*, no. 3-4, 1932, 23.
9 L. Trotsky, 'Proletarian culture and proletarian art', in the collection of his works *Literatura i revolyutsiya* (Literature and the Revolution), 2nd edn. (Moscow 1924), 162.
10 Ibid., 150.
11 Both published by State Publishers of the Ukraine in 1923.
12 See the editorial 'On certain problems in the philosophy of Marxism as expounded by Menshevizing idealism', in *Pod znamenen marksizma*, no. 11-12, 1931, 205, 206, 209.
13 G. Glezerman, in the journal *Za bolshevistskuyu knigu* (For the Bolshevik Book), no. 4, 1935.
14 See the article 'Neokantianism' in the collection of essays, *Iz istorii filosofii XIX veka* (Essays on the History of Philosophy in the Nineteenth Century) (Moscow 1933); and the book *Filosofskie predshestvenniki dialekticheskogo materializma: Gegel i Feyerbakh* (The Philosophical Precursors of Dialectical Materialism: Hegel and Feuerbach) (Moscow 1941).
15 *Vestnik Kommunisticheskoy akademii*, no. 14, 1926.
16 See the appendix to the book by S.N. Grigoryan, *Iz istorii filosofii Sredney Azii i Irana VII-XII vekov* (On the History of Philosophy in Central Asia and Iran in the 7th-12th Centuries) (Moscow 1960).
17 See the book *Izbrannye proizvedniya myslitelei stran Blizhnego i Srednego Vostoka IX-XIV vekov* (Selected Works of Thinkers of Near and Middle Eastern Countries in the 9th-14th Centuries) (Moscow 1961).
18 See the collection *Antichnye filosofy* (Philosophers of the Ancient World) (Moscow 1935).
19 In the journal *Krasnaya nov* (Red Virgin Soil), no. 7, 1926.
20 Akselrod's article and Deborin's reply are translated into English by G. Klein in his book *Spinoza in Soviet Philosophy* (London 1952).
21 See *Vestnik Kommunisticheskoy akademii*, no. 20, 1927, 68.

22 See Akselrod, 'Spinoza and materialism', in *Krasnaya nov*, no. 7, 1925, 146.
23 Ibid. See also Akselrod's preface to Plekhanov's *Osnovnye voprosy marksizma* (The Main Problems of Marxism) (Soviet Village Publishers, 1925), 6-7.
24 Akselrod, 'I'm tired of it!', *Krasnaya nov*, no. 3, 1927, 172-3.
25 Akselrod, 'Spinoza and materialism', 154.
26 Akselrod, 'I'm tired of it!', 171.
27 A. Deborin, 'Revisionism under the mask of Orthodoxy', in *Pod znamenem marksizma*, no. 9, 1927, 13.
28 G. Tymyansky, 'Spinoza's "Theological-political treatise" ', in *Vestnik Kommunisticheskoy akademii*, no. 1-2, 1935, 59.
29 See S. Ya. Volfson, 'The ethical world-view of Spinoza', in *Trudy BGU* (Transactions of the Byelorussian State University), no. 14-15, 1927, 1.
30 See B.E. Bykhovsky, 'The psycho-physical problem in Spinoza's doctrine', ibid., no. 14-15, 1927, 2.
31 See K. Skurer, 'Spinoza and dialectical materialism', in *Vestnik Kommunisticheskoy akademii*, no. 20, 1927, 68; I. Vaynshteyn, 'Spinoza and materialism', in *Pod znamenem marksizma*, no. 3 1926, and 'Spinoza's system as interpreted by bourgeois philosophy', in *Vestnik Kommunisticheskoy akademii*, no. 11-12, 1932.
32 See *Pod znamenem marksizma*, no. 11-12, 1932.
33 V. Miller, 'On the problem of the philosophical heritage', in *Nauchnye izvestiya Smolenskogo gosudarstvennogo universiteta* (Academic Transactions of Smolensk State University), 17-20, 1924.
34 See *Sovremennye problemy filosofii marksizma-leninizma* (Contemporary Problems in the Philosophy of Marxism-Leninism) (Moscow 1929), 157.
35 Cited in G. Bammel's article 'On our philosophical development in the course of ten years', in *Pod znamenem marksizma*, no. 10-11, 1927, 81.
36 Cited by A. Deborin in his *Filosofiya i politika* (Philosophy and Politics) (Moscow 1961), 11.
37 See *Izvestiya*, 24 July 1927.
38 H. Falk, *Die Weltanschauung des Bolschewismus* (Würzburg 1956) 24.
39 F. Frank, *Filosofiya nauki* (The Philosophy of Science) (Moscow 1960), 287.
40 D. Joravsky, *Soviet Marxism and Natural Science (1917-1932)* (New York 1961), 71.
41 See the journal *Filosofskie nauki* (The Philosophical Sciences), no. 4, 1967, 125.
42 See *Filosofskaya entsiklopediya* (The Philosophical Encyclopaedia) (Moscow 1964), vol. 3, 284.
43 See *Pod znamenen marksizma*, no. 4-5, 1923, 247.
44 Ibid., no. 5-6, 1932, 33.
45 See 'The tasks of Marxists in the field of natural science', *Trudy II Vsesoyuznoy konferentsii marksistsko-leninskikh nauchnykh uchrezhdeniy* (Transactions of the Second All-Union Conference of Marxist-Leninist Academic Institutions) (Moscow 1930), 32.
46 S. Semkovsky, 'On the argument in Marxism over the theory of relativity', in *Pod znamenem marksizma*, no. 8-9, 1925, 129.
47 Id., *Teoriya otnositelnosti i materializm* (The Theory of Relativity and Materialism) (Kharkov 1924), 19.
48 See *Pod znamenem marksizma*, no. 1, 1923, 10.
49 Ibid., no. 1, 1924.
50 A. Ioffe, paper at the academic session of the Communist Academy Institute of

Philosophy held to mark the twenty-fifth anniversary of the publication of Lenin's *Materializm i empirio-krititsizm* (Materialism and Empirio-Criticism); see *Pod znamenem marksizma*, no. 4, 1934, 65.
51 Ibid., no. 4, 1934, 108.

8

The Jewish Contribution to the Development of Oriental Studies in the USSR

Inessa Axelrod-Rubin

Introduction

The purpose of this study is to give a factual account of the part Jews have played in the development of Oriental studies in the USSR. The main source used for our analysis is the 'Bibliographical Dictionary of Soviet Orientalists', which was published in Moscow at the end of 1975.[1] To quote the preface:

> This dictionary contains information about scholars with higher degrees and academic titles,[2] who gained their Candidate of Sciences degrees in the main before 1968 and who have published not less than 240 printed pages of scholarly work on the history, ethnography, archaeology, history of architecture and mathematics, economics, geography, law, art, literature and linguistics of the countries of Asia outside the USSR and of Africa. It also contains information about scholars without a higher degree who have nevertheless made a big contribution to the development of Oriental studies (p.5).

This is the first work of its kind which claims to be fairly exhaustive. The dictionary includes details of 1,488 scholars who worked in all fields of Oriental studies in the period 1917-72, thus giving us a relatively complete selection of material on which to base our analysis. While there are gaps in the 'Dictionary' and also, as we shall show below, instances of distortion and sometimes even definite falsification in the biographical details of certain scholars occasioned by political motives, nevertheless in general this material enables us to make a large number of interesting observations. In particular we intend to present some comparative statistical material and try to trace the changes in the Soviet leadership's policy towards Jews in the Soviet Union as seen in the situation of Jewish Orientalists in the USSR.

Since the nationality of scholars is not indicated in the biographical information given in the 'Dictionary', we have made our selection largely on the basis of their first names and surnames and of our personal acquaintance with the scholars concerned and, in doubtful cases, after consulting emigré Soviet Orientalists now working in Israel (for this the author would like to express her thanks to Yu. Bregel, M. Zand, M. Heltzer and V. Rubin for their help).

Here it seems necessary to say a few words about who exactly is to be considered a Jew. Unlike most countries in the world, the Soviet Union officially requires the heading 'nationality' in the internal passports which are compulsory for all citizens over the age of sixteen. It is usual for this 'nationality' to be determined from that of the parents. Thus if according to their passports both parents are Jewish, their son's or daughter's passport will automatically state 'Jew' or 'Jewess' under this heading. In the case of mixed marriages the young person receiving the passport has the right to choose his father's or mother's nationality but once the appropriate nationality has been entered in the passport it cannot be changed.[3]

After the February Revolution, when all the laws which had restricted the rights of Jews in Tsarist Russia were repealed, Jews gained access to all spheres of political, administrative and cultural life. At first the decrees passed after the October Revolution did not add anything new to this situation, simply confirming that all peoples of the former Russian Empire enjoyed equality of national rights. Many Jews who had taken an active part in the revolutionary movement broke with Jewish tradition and renounced their Jewish nationality.[4] Subsequently, when internal passports were introduced in the USSR in 1933, some of these Jews had themslves and their children registered as Russians.

With the growth of antisemitism after the war, many half-Jews and sometimes even pure-blooded Jews (helped by the possibility that documents might have been lost during the war) also tried to become 'Russians' (or to enter some other non-Jewish nationality in their passports, such as 'Byelorussian' or 'Ukrainian'), in some cases changing their surnames and first names, in others keeping their Jewish names. Conversely there were cases, though less frequent, where half-Jews, even when they had non-Jewish first names and surnames, demanded to be registered as Jews as a protest against outbursts of antisemitism.

The entering of a non-Jewish nationality in the passport, even if the Jewish surname was retained, generally made it easier to get into university and find a job, and also to achieve promotion and a responsible post.

It should be noted that the Jews and half-Jews registered as Russians (or some other non-Jewish nationality) in their passports may be divided into various groups. There were those who actively tried to become assimilated and to make a career for themselves. Some succeeded, but others suffered at times a rather tragic fate. As a rule they carefully concealed their Jewish origin, but were held in contempt by Jews and non-Jews alike (as has been the case, it would seem, in every age with such people). Not for nothing are there so many jokes in the Soviet Union about people 'called Ivanov after their mother'.

However, there were many others who did not conceal their Jewishness. Their official 'conversion' to a non-Jewish status in their passport was often fortuitous, brought about either as a result of pressure from parents motivated by a natural desire to make their children's lives easier, or because under Soviet conditions (i.e. complete absence of any Jewish upbringing and complete isolation from world Jewry) they simply did not have at the age of sixteen sufficient understanding of the crucial significance of this step to make a responsible choice. In some cases they subsequently made an official attempt to change the registration in their passport, which, as we have mentioned before, is not allowed by the Soviet authorities.[5]

In this study we have included as Jews those who, on the basis of their first name, surname and patronymic, indisputably seemed to be so, and also those with whom, as mentioned above, we are personally acquainted. All cases which seemed to us doubtful have not been taken into account. Of course, this approach cannot entirely obviate mistakes, as when, for example, a person with a Jewish surname, first name and patronymic is according to his passport a non-Jew and considers himself such (or vice versa). But these mistakes cannot essentially change the general picture.

Thus, according to the criteria we have advanced, of the total of 1,488 Orientalists included in the 'Dictionary', 210 may be considered Jews. In addition, there is a group of Jews and half-Jews (twenty-two in all), officially counted as non-Jews, which has not been taken into consideration in our calculations.

Let us now examine certain statistics derived from an analysis of the material cited in the 'Dictionary'.

By their social origin Jewish Orientalists are generally middle-class: the overwhelming majority (167 out of 210) said they were children of white-collar workers or members of the intelligentsia (teachers, doctors, musicians, barristers, academics). Only fourteen gave their fathers as manual workers, four as servicemen, three as small farmers, twelve as craftsmen, four as small traders, two as merchants, one as a landlord and one as a 'priest' (evidently a rabbi). Here it should be noted that people born before the Revolution might sometimes give not quite correct information about their social origins since, especially in the early years of the Revolution and even in the 1930s, writing in a questionnaire that you were the son of a merchant or a factory-owner meant virtually depriving yourself of any chance of finding work and occasionally putting yourself under threat of arrest or other forms of persecution. The same applied to children of rabbis. Thus the information given by people born before the Revolution indicating that their father was an 'office worker' must be accepted with the reservations we have mentioned.

It is interesting to take note of the birth place of Jewish Orientalists. As might have been expected, before the Revolution most were born in the cities and towns once included in the Pale of Settlement (eighty-six out of 105). Seven were born in St Petersburg-Petrograd, four in other large cities and eight in small provincial towns not in the Pale of Settlement. The complete absence of Moscow from this list is interesting. A different picture emerges after the Revolution: of a total of 105, only forty-eight were born in the former Pale of Settlement, twenty-seven in Moscow, sixteen in Leningrad, seven in other large cities and seven in districts not originally in the Pale of Settlement. This reflects the clearly observable migration of Jews to the large cities, especially Moscow and Leningrad, after the Revolution.[6]

We have already pointed out that in the first years of the Revolution, when restrictions on Jewish entry to universities either as students or as teachers were abolished, there was a big influx of Jews into all spheres of learning and culture. However, Jewish hopes for full participation in all spheres of life, promised them by the Revolution, were in the end not justified. From the 1930s onwards Jewish participation in public and cultural life began to be suppressed, and during and after the Second World War there was a rapid growth of antisemitism, encouraged from above, which reached its apogee in 1949-53. After the death of Stalin in 1953 and the 20th Congress of the CPSU in 1956, which led to some liberalization of public life in the Soviet Union, little was changed as regards the Jewish question, though the bitterest manifestations of antisemitism were at first mitigated. The new upsurge of antisemitism at the end of the 1960s (under the mask of anti-Zionism) now includes a campaign to oust Jews from scholarship.[7] Let us now consider how these general trends have been reflected in the position of Jews in Oriental studies in the USSR.

With this aim in mind, all the Orientalists cited in the 'Dictionary' have been arranged into six age groups, depending on when they started active work in the field of Oriental studies. For this the main criterion taken was their year of graduation from a department or institute of Oriental studies. The first group contains scholars who started their work in Oriental studies before 1920 (i.e. who entered university before the Revolution and graduated not later than 1920); the second group—those who graduated between 1921 and 1930; the third—those graduating between 1931 and 1941; the fourth—1942-51; the fifth—1952-60; and the sixth—those graduating after 1960. In the third group the year 1941 was taken as a terminal point since it was the last year before the war. In the fifth group we had to take 1960 as a terminal point for the following reason. As already indicated (see the quotation from the preface of the 'Dictionary' at the beginning of this work), the 'Dictionary' includes scholars who gained their Candidate of Sciences degrees in the main before 1968. Clearly, only a few of those graduating after 1960 managed to complete their dissertations before 1968: thirty-six in all according to the 'Dictionary' (including four Jews). In view of the unreliability of data derived from such small numbers, this last group has not been taken into account in our work. The appropriate calculations give us the following table:

TABLE I

Age groups (year of graduation)	Total	Jews	%
Before 1920	114	16	14.0
1921-30	186	41	22.0
1931-41	233	44	19.0
1942-51	496	68	13.7
1952-60	423	37	8.7
After 1960	36	4	11.1
	1,488	210	14.1[a]

[a] Average

Let us now analyse these data. The increase in the proportion of Jewish Orientalists in the second age group reflects the already-mentioned influx of Jews into all types of higher education, including Oriental studies, following the Revolution. In the 1942-51 period the war, and especially the growth of expansionist tendencies in Soviet foreign policy in the early post-war years, led to a sharp increase in the intake of students into institutes and departments of Oriental studies. During these years 496 people, about a third of all Orientalists included in the 'Dictionary', entered Oriental studies in the USSR. But the percentage of Jews in this group (less than fourteen percent—sixty-eight people) showed a drop compared with the second and third age groups. An even greater drop in the proportion of Jews is observable in the following group (i.e. in the 1952-60 period), when the admission of Jews to 'prestigious' centres of higher education and to posts involving work abroad or in government offices was increasingly restricted. To make this clear we need only compare the data for this age group (thirty-seven Jews out of a total of 423 graduates, i.e. 8.7 percent) with the number of Jewish Orientalists of the pre-Revolutionary generation (sixteen Jews out of 114 scholars—fourteen percent). It is interesting also to compare certain data for separate years in the fourth and fifth age groups. Thus while there were eleven Jews out of the total of forty-five Orientalists mentioned by the 'Dictionary' as graduating in 1947, in 1952 there were still eleven Jews—but out of a total of ninety-one graduates; and there was not one single Jew amongst the twenty-eight graduates in 1957 and the twenty-nine in 1958 in this field who started to study in 1952 and 1953 respectively).[8]

Thus the quantitative data we have derived fully confirm that from the beginning of the 1950s entry of Jews into the field of Oriental studies was made more difficult.[9]

The same tendency is reflected in the data for the average age of the Orientalists included in the 'Dictionary' and that of Jewish Orientalists. Of the 1,488 Orientalists mentioned by the 'Dictionary', 534 were born before the Revolution and 945 (i.e. almost two-thirds) after it; while for the group of Jewish Orientalists we have selected the ratio is exactly 1:1; 105 were born before the Revolution and 105 after it.

Let us now move on to the distribution of Jewish Orientalists through the various branches of Oriental studies. It seems appropriate to distinguish the following main divisions: (1) History; (2) Archaeology; (3) Ethnography; (4) Geography; (5) Economics; (6) State and Law; (7) History of philosophy; (8) History of religions; (9) History of science; (10) Study of the fine arts; (11) Study of literature; (12) Linguistics; and (13) Study of general problems to do with the contemporary situation of Eastern countries.

Here we must add a *caveat*: any classification of this kind is bound to be somewhat oversimplified. Several scholars publish works in different branches of Oriental studies (e.g history and economics, history and fine arts, literature and linguistics, etc.) or on various historical periods or on several geographical regions. Lastly there are scholars who publish both scholarly works and semi-propagandistic pieces which have little in common with serious scholarship (and it is worth noting here that a very large number of works published in Oriental studies in the USSR are of the latter type; as a rule these are pot-boilers written to Party orders or for easy money). This is why we considered it necessary to distinguish a special group (no. 13) of Orientalists who study general problems of the contemporary situation of Eastern countries, namely questions to do with international relations in the East and the national-liberation, trade-union and labor movements. Most of the published works in this group are semi-propagandistic or openly propagandistic in character.

There are also many works of this type published in the fields of modern and recent history, economics, international relations and modern literature. To cite one example: even such a seemingly natural topic as the state budget can be presented from a 'Party' point of view: at one extreme, works like 'Turkey's state budget—an instrument of the reactionary policy of the Turkish government' (1954),[10] and at the other, 'The part played by financial, monetary and credit operations in developing the economy of the Chinese People's Republic' (1951).[11] There are whole areas of Oriental studies, such as the policy of Western countries towards Eastern states, the national liberation movement, the labor and trade union movement, the so-called Asian 'People's Democracies', the history of religions, 'bourgeois' historical methodology, etc., where under Soviet conditions the very nature of the topic makes an objective approach to the material impossible. To make this clear let us compare, for example, the following titles: 'The failure of British aggression in Afghanistan in the nineteenth and early twentieth centuries' (1959) or 'Yankees in the East in the nineteenth century, or colonialism without an empire' (1966) on the one hand, and 'How Central Asia became united with Russia (1860-1900)' (1965) (all these last three works were written by the same author)[12], and 'The liberating mission of the Soviet Union in the Far East' (1966)[13] on the other hand.

Subjects like 'Lenin and the East' (in the most varied aspects and 'dressings': Lenin and the national liberation movement, Lenin and the literature of the peoples of the East, the image of Lenin in Chinese (Turkish, Persian, etc.) literature), and similarly 'The influence of the revolutions of 1905 and 1917 on the national liberation and labor movement in Eastern countries', can be endlessly exploited. Here we find 'one-subject' authors[14] as well as Orientalists who, side by side with serious scholarly works, carry out what are clearly Party commissions and thereby earn a bit extra.[15] The Soviet leadership also 'diverts' other Orientalists to the 'treatment of topical subjects' which are sometimes very remote from their main academic interests. Thus R.M. Brodsky, the expert on the Far East, recently published two works directed against Zionism (in Ukrainian)—'Zionism: Hypocrisy, Deceit, Betrayal' (Lvov 1972) and 'Zionism and its Class Essence' (Kiev 1973).

Bearing the above remarks in mind, let us now consider the quantitative data on the distribution of Jewish Orientalists in the various branches of Oriental studies according to the scheme we have outlined. This gives us the following table: (1) History—77; (2) Archaeology—4; (3) Ethnography—5; (4) Geography—7; (5) Economics—19; (6) State and Law (general problems)—2; (7) History of philosophy—3; (8) History of religions—4; (9) History of science—3; (10) Study of fine arts—2; (11) Study of literature—31; (12) Linguistics—29; (13) General problems of the contemporary situation of Eastern countries—24; total—210. This list shows that more than a third of all Jewish Orientalists in the USSR are historians (77), of whom 47 specialize in modern and recent history, 16 in ancient history and 11 in medieval history.[16]

According to this list there are many experts (29) on Eastern languages amongst Jewish Orientalists, of whom 10 are Semitologists, broadly speaking (i.e including scholars studying mediaeval Hebrew and Arabic manuscripts, ancient Semitic languages and also modern Arabic languages and dialects). There are 31 specialists in the literature of Eastern countries, 13 of whom deal with modern literature.

The geographical area now covered by Oriental studies has been extended: after the Second World War and especially with the transformation of former colonies into independent states, Oriental studies in the USSR and many other countries began to include not only traditional geographical regions (the Near and Middle East, South-East Asia, the Far East) but also Africa south of the Sahara (the North African states even before this had been treated as part of the Near East and had been studied by Orientalists). In view of this it would seem interesting to single out particularly the scholars working on Africa south of the Sahara from all the Jewish Orientalists arranged according to our schema in the various branches of Oriental studies. Altogether twenty-two Jewish scholars are working in the field of African studies, i.e. about 10 percent of the total number of Jewish Orientalists. When we compare this figure with the total number of Orientalists working in African studies—ninety-eight out of 1,488, i.e. 6.6 percent, we see that Jews form 20 percent of all scholars in the African field. This high degree of participation by Jews in a new field of Oriental studies seems to be partly explained by the generally recognized fact that Jewish scholars concentrate on new, developing branches of learning. On the other hand it is explained by the fact that in the Soviet Union new fields of learning receive more resources when the authorities are for some reason interested in developing them very quickly; this makes entry to academic institutions easier, since the leadership at first, when there is a dearth of experts in the field, of necessity has to be less discriminating and therefore more liberal in the admission of Jews.[17]

It is interesting also to compare the following numerical data. Of the total number of 1,488 scholars included in the 'Dictionary', 326 (i.e about 22 percent) possess the Doctor of Sciences degree; there are 27 full members and 27 corresponding members of the USSR Academy of Sciences, and 25 full members and 13 corresponding members of the Academies of the Union Republics. The corresponding figures for the Jewish Orientalist group are the following: 87 Doctors of Sciences, i.e. 41 percent of the Jewish scholars and 27 percent of the total number of Doctors of Sciences (it should be remembered in this connection that Jewish Orientalists form 14 percent of all the Orientalists included in the 'Dictionary'). However, there are only two Jewish full members (V.M. Zhirmunsky from 1966 and F.A. Rothstein from 1939) and one corresponding member (A.A. Freyman from 1928) of the USSR Academy of Sciences and one corresponding member of the Tadzhik Academy of Sciences (I.S. Braginsky from 1951). This can be explained by the fact that until recently there was no significant discrimination against Jews in the award of the degree of Doctor of Sciences. Therefore the higher percentage of Doctors of Sciences amongst Jewish Orientalists can be explained to some extent by their higher average age. However, elections to the Academy of Sciences, a very exclusive and prestigious organization, in all probability are directly controlled by the Party élite, and admission to it has always been restricted for Jews.[18]

Of the total number of Orientalists included in the 'Dictionary', 127 graduated from two or more universities or institutes, of whom 25 were Jews (i.e. about 20 percent, and more than 25 percent of the total number of Jewish Orientalists). Of the 41 Orientalists who took part in the revolutionary movement in Tsarist Russia and in the Civil War 11 were Jews (27 percent), but of the 105 Orientalists who held important posts in the Party and in the state administration, only 14 were Jews (i.e 13.5 percent). Of the 100 male Jewish Orientalists, who by their age might have taken part in the 1941-45 war, 35 fought on fronts against Nazi Germany and one against Japan. The corresponding figures for the total number of Orientalists included in the 'Dictionary' are 175 out of 499, i.e. 35 percent. Thus, these data, along with many others which have been published in various sources,[19] also refute the antisemitic fabrications, widely current amongst Russian people, that the Jews sat the war out at the rear and did not fight.

The establishment of communist Oriental studies

By the time of the Revolution, Oriental studies in Russia were already highly developed as an academic discipline. They had basically emerged as a complex of historical and philological studies. The overwhelming majority of Orientalists were involved in the study of Eastern languages, the literature and historical monuments of ancient and medieval times, and ancient and mediaeval Eastern history. Practically no attention was paid to modern history or economic problems.

The assumption of power by the Bolsheviks brought about a fundamental break in the tradition of Oriental studies which (like other branches of learning) now had first and foremost to serve the needs of the new regime, connected with the special role assigned to the East by the Bolshevik leadership as the main reserve of 'world revolution'.[20] The Bolsheviks thought that this meant that the main task of Oriental studies should be the study of the contemporary situation and revolutionary movements in

Asian and African countries. Oriental studies should explain the economic, political, social and cultural processes taking place in the East, from the viewpoint of the national-liberation movements, study the influence of the history of these countries on contemporary events and make informed guesses as to their further development. Here, for example, is how L. Karakhan defined these tasks:[21]

> Soviet Orientalists should direct their attention to the study of contemporary social and political life in Eastern countries. We are carrying out a policy in the East which rouses peoples oppressed by imperialism to new life and struggle. We must know about these peoples, their economy, their political life and the social and political moods in these countries . . . . My advice to Orientalists is: don't go on delving into the dead past, but get closer to the living people if you wish to meet the demands of the world-wide mission facing the USSR.[22]

The second task which the Bolshevik leadership set for Orientalists was the training of cadres who would carry out Soviet policy and strengthen the Bolshevik regime on the former Eastern borders of Tsarist Russia; these cadres had to know local conditions and local languages and be devoted to the Soviet regime.

Orientalists of the old school, at that time mostly concentrated in Petersburg, at the Academy of Sciences (Asiatic Museum),[23] the Russian Archaeological Society[24] and the faculty of Oriental languages at Petersburg University could not and did not want to undertake these tasks.[25] The Oriental specialists who were trained at the Lazarev Institute of Oriental Languages in Moscow[26] for practical work in Russia's embassies and trade missions in Eastern countries also did not suit the Soviet leadership, since the majority of them were not inclined to support and carry out the policy of the new regime.

So from the very beginning the Bolsheviks started to form new Oriental studies' institutions to set against the existing traditional academic institutions, which before the Revolution had been relatively independent of the authorities. In November 1917 the People's Commissariat for the Affairs of the Nationalities (*Narkomnats*) was created. It was headed by Stalin, and its task was to carry out the policy of the Bolshevik regime towards the national minorities in Russia. At first it was simultaneously put in charge of the country's Orientalist work, and created new Orientalist institutions and teaching departments. In the autumn of 1921 on Lenin's initiative the All-Russian (subsequently All-Union) Academic Association of Oriental Studies (VNAV) was formed (attached to *Narkomnats*), which existed until 1930, assuming control over academic Oriental studies.

In the traditional Orientalist institutions of Tsarist Russia Jews made an outstanding contribution only in the field of Hebrew studies, as will be shown in greater detail later on. But in the new organizations created by the Bolsheviks they played a prominent part right from the start because of the historical circumstances which we have already described. Thus one of the major figures in the development of Oriental studies in the USSR was M.P. Pavlovich (Mikhail Lazarevich Veltman), who was appointed President of VNAV immediately after its formation. Like most of the Jewish Orientalists of that period, M.L. Veltman (1871-1927; literary pseudonym—M.Pavlovich; Party nick-name—Volunteer) became an academic via the Revolution. He was born in Odessa, the son of an office worker. While still at high school, in his fourth year, he began to take part in the revolutionary movement. In 1892 he was arrested, spent one and a half years in prison in solitary confinement, then five years in exile in Verkhoyansk. During these years he devoted a great deal of time to educating himself, studying history, political economy and philosophy. Between 1901 and 1905 he worked on problems of military organization in the Social Democratic Party, and joined the Mensheviks at the time of the split in the RSDLP. His booklet 'The Tactics of Street Fighting' was used as a practical manual during the Revolutions of 1905 and 1917. In 1907 he escaped to Finland, from where he made his way to France. Whilst in exile M. Pavlovich began his study of the East, seeing in the national-liberation movement of the Eastern peoples a base for the future world revolution. There were constant gathering at Pavlovich's Paris flat of political exiles from India, Iran, China and Turkey, with whom he discussed plans for revolutionary action. He edited leaflets for them and contributed to their journals and newspapers. This was one of the reasons which led to his parting company with the Mensheviks who, of course, considered the working class of capitalist countries to be the main revolutionary force. After breaking with the Mensheviks, Pavlovich returned to Russia just before the October Revolution. At the beginning of 1918 he joined the Bolshevik Party, and immediately after the Revolution and during the Civil War he carried out a number of responsible Party tasks.[27]

As President of the Academic Association of Oriental Studies Pavlovich was one of the initiators of the trend in Oriental studies which was designed to meet the requirements of the Soviet leadership. In his article 'The tasks of the All-Russian Academic Association of Oriental Studies' he wrote, in complete accordance with these requirements, that the Association was to be 'the highest academic body for the study of the East; it should widely popularize knowledge about the East amongst the masses and at the same time help the Soviet regime to determine a correct policy towards the peoples of the East'.[28]

In another article, published on the occasion of the fifth anniversary of VNAV, Pavlovich remarked that 'Soviet Orientalists study the whole of contemporary life in the Eastern world from the viewpoint of the struggle for freedom by the exploited peoples of the yellow and black continents against imperialism'.[29] Soviet Orientalists were seeking for the Eastern world 'paths of revolutionary development, being guided in this task by the theses on the colonial and national questions enunciated by Comrade Lenin in the famous points adopted at the Second Congress of the Comintern, which are nowadays seen by the whole Eastern world as a sort of Tablet of Commandments'.[30]

Pavlovich, a fairly educated man, realized that the knowledge of the Orientalists of the old school should also be used. In particular he tried to recruit them for work in the historical and ethnological department of VNAV, headed by Prof. I.N. Borozdin.[31] Pavlovich tried to unite within the framework of the Association and the journal *Novy Vostok* (The New East) published by it,[32], scholars of the pre-Revolutionary generation and the new specialists—the Soviet Orientalists who put into practice Soviet policy in the East, i.e. mostly political workers who came to Oriental studies as a result of a Party assignment.

There is a considerable amount of evidence to suggest that this co-operation went far from smoothly. For example, Borozdin wrote later that the academic specialists who had been brought up in the old Orientalist traditions 'did not immediately answer the call, taking a mistrustful and wary attitude to the newly formed organization'.[33] S.F. Oldenburg[34] agreed that pre-revolutionary Oriental studies were not able to give the Soviet regime information about the political and economic life of the modern Eastern world, but warned the 'new-style Orientalists', the 'Orientalist-politicians', against an excessive enthusiasm for purely practical, vitally necessary tasks. 'Practical work without the support of theory[35] soon grows sickly and weak', he wrote.

> Economic problems are very difficult and complicated and require a great deal of preliminary preparation for them to be properly investigated; this preparation is especially difficult because of the complete absence or relative inaccessibility of source material. Therefore Oriental studies first of all devoted itself to the languages, history and literature of the East, thereby laying down a firm base for the understanding of Eastern culture; in order thoroughly to understand a people, one must first understand its language.[36]

Pavlovich, who, it is worth noting, himself did not know Eastern languages, gave a sharp reply to Oldenburg in the article quoted above 'The tasks and achievements of Oriental studies in the USSR':

> While completely agreeing with Academician S. Oldenburg on the necessity

> of studying Eastern languages in order to understand the life of the peoples of the East, we must point out that his remark about the importance of theory as a support for practical work is irrelevant to the question of the merits of pre-Revolutionary Oriental studies. It is clear that neither the Academy of Sciences, nor the Asiatic Museum, nor the department of Eastern languages at Petersburg University, nor the Eastern Section of the Russian Archaeological Society, in short not one of the institutions devoted to Oriental studies, the work of which Academician Oldenburg mentioned, despite all their enormous services, achieved anything, nor could they achieve anything, in the elaboration of a theory which might explain to us the political and economic life of the modern Eastern world. The whole past of the old Eastern world, its economic, political and cultural life, the forms of which had crystallized in the course of centuries—all of this can be explained only from the standpoint of the theory of historical materialism.[37]

The literary output of M. Pavlovich was enormous, including hundreds of articles and dozens of books. In 1924 a twelve-volume edition of his works, under the general title of 'World Politics of the Late Nineteenth and Early Twentieth Centuries', started publication (but this ceased after his death). However, the academic worth of these works is not great. Most of his books are either reprints of already-published articles in journals with minor additions, or collections of popular essays on a common theme, in which he basically examined topical international and revolutionary events of that time from a Marxist position. They contain some interesting factual material, but the main predilection of these books is for the denunciation of imperialism and appeals in various forms for the development of national-liberation movements.[38]

Indeed Pavlovich himself, as his contemporaries have testified, had no aspirations towards academic objectivity. Thus the Orientalist A.E. Khodorov wrote of Pavlovich: 'In his opinion academic learning should be a tool for building a new and happy life for the worker and peasant masses . . .;'[39] 'First and foremost articles and essays should comment on urgent and exciting contemporary topics.'[40] To be fair, it should be said that Pavlovich was not exceptional in this: certainly the majority of young Soviet scholars who started their careers at the time of the Revolution or after it shared these views on the role of scholarship. Despite, or rather because of this viewpoint, Pavlovich played a very great part in the formation of Soviet Oriental scholarship. He was among those who laid the foundations for a Soviet Marxist school in Oriental studies, and especially of the branch of it dealing with the contemporary situation of Eastern countries and with their international relations. He applied to Oriental studies the principles of the Bolshevik approach to scholarship, particularly in the social sciences, which Lenin called 'partisanship' as opposed to 'bourgeois objectivism'.[41] These principles comprise: (1) The attempt to examine all the processes of political, public, social and cultural life under the guidance of rigid Marxist schemas (e.g. the well-known dogmas of class struggle, social-economic formations, etc.), rather than by starting from the facts about what was really happening. On the contrary, usually the facts were adjusted to fit these schemas.[42] (2) A harshly negative and disdainful attitude to all the achievements of so-called 'bourgeois' scholarship; a belittling of the professional activity of scholars who held different views. (3) The use of double standards with regard to events occurring in the Soviet area and in free societies. (4) The use of cliché-ridden formulations, employed to this day in the Soviet social sciences.[43]

M. Pavlovich was naturally not the only representative of the Marxist school of Oriental studies. Many other Orientalists of the Soviet school worked with him at VNAV, both non-Jews like V.A. Gurko-Kryazhin (the specialist on modern Turkey), B.N. Melnikov (a member of the editorial board of the journal *Novy Vostok*, the head of the Far East department at the People's Commissariat of Foreign Affairs, who published under the pseudonym of B. Semenov), A.V. Grebenshchikov (the expert on Manchuria and head of the Far Eastern secton of VNAV) and S.K. Iransky (pseudonym of S.K. Pastukhov, a specialist on Persia); and also Jews, such as A.E. Khodorov, G.N. Voytinsky, E.L. Shteynberg and others.

Abram Evseevich Khodorov (1886-1949) was the closest associate of Pavlovich and VNAV with regard to the problems of China and the Far East and the co-author with him of a book published in 1925, 'China's Struggle for Independence'. Like Pavlovich he was a native of Odessa, and had come to Oriental studies via the Revolution. In 1905 he took part in the revolutionary student movement, for which he was exiled to Vologda province. Between 1919 and 1922 he was head of the Peking branch of the Russian Telegraph Agency (ROSTA) and at the same time in 1920-21 was an adviser on China to the so-called Far East Republic (1920-22: a nominally 'bourgeois-democratic' buffer state, in fact controlled from Moscow). Like other Soviet advisers he took part in the Chinese revolution.[44] On the basis of his Chinese experience Khodorov started to work in the field of Oriental studies. His book 'World Imperialism and China', which was the first Soviet book on China, was stylistically very close to Pavlovich's works,[45], although it does contain interesting factual material gathered by the author during his stay in China. Like Pavlovich, Khodorov did not read Chinese and used mainly publications of journals in Western languages. As the modern historiographer of Soviet Sinology, V.N. Nikiforov, admits, the Orientalists of the Marxist school of the 1920s were not outstanding academic historians, but mainly publicists who responded quickly to the needs of the time.[46] He describes Khodorov's book as 'a cross between a scholarly reference book and a journalistic essay'.[47] He remarks that Khodorov, like other Orientalists of that school who had an inadequate command of the material, made factual errors and handled his sources carelessly.[48]

Like Pavlovich, A.E. Khodorov was a figure typical of the Soviet Orientalists of the first half of the 1920s, and his fate was still more typical. In 1925 Khodorov was sharply attacked by A. Ivin.[49] Some of his criticisms were well founded, in particular his charges of inaccuracy and of rather unscholarly work, etc. But in addition to all this he accused Khodorov of 'ignorance of the basic foundations of Marxism'. This started a polemic in which each author tried to 'shout down' the other in making political accusations. This polemic formed the start of a discussion about forms of society in the Eastern world which had far-reaching consequences for the fortunes of a number of Orientalists.[50] In particular A.E. Khodorov became a constant butt for crushing criticism; after 1930 he was first prevented from publishing and later from any research work. Till 1935 he still taught at the Institute of Oriental Studies, but then was even dismissed from there and was arrested in 1936. What happened to him after that is related by V.N. Nikiforov: 'A.E. Khodorov had great vitality and managed in the Far North [obviously in a camp] to apply his knowledge of geobotany; his manuscripts 'The vegetation resources of the coast of the Sea of Okhotsk' and 'Fodder resources and reindeer pastures' were handed over to the department of reindeer-breeding at the Chief Administration of Construction of the Far North. At the end of his five-year sentence A.E. Khodorov worked in the Kolyma Education Department, and then tought foreign languages at a secondary school in Magadan. In 1944 his conviction was expunged and he returned to Moscow. One can only admire the energy and vitality with which this elderly man, after a ten-year break, struggled to get back to academic life. In 1945 he became a teacher of English at the Lenin State Pedagogical Institute in Moscow, and first started work on a dissertation on 'English Synonyms and Idioms'. Then he tried to get the chance to write a dissertation on a historical subject, and passed the necessary examinations. In June 1947 the Academic Council of the Pedagogical Institute awarded A.E. Khodorov the degree of Candidate of Historical Sciences. After completing his thesis he started work at Moscow State University. But his return to academic life never took place. His fortunes took a tragic turn. At the start of the 1947 academic year he was dismissed from his post, and in March 1948 he was once more subjected to illegal repression. Even such a hardened warrior as A.E. Khodorov could not endure this second blow; in 1949 his relatives were informed that he had died. A.E. Khodorov was posthumously rehabilitated and his name was restored to the annals of scholarship.'[51]

We must now turn to another group of Orientalists of the Soviet school in which Jews played an important part. These were the, so to speak, practical Orientalists. They also came into Oriental studies through their participation in the Revolution, and continued to devote themselves to practical revolutionary activity in Eastern countries while working in Soviet embassies and trade missions and also as military and political advisers (for example for the revolutionary government of the Kuomintang, 1925-1927), were members of the central committees of communist parties in the East and worked in the Comintern and Profintern. In the first place we will mention here (of the Jews in this group) the head of the Soviet mission in China M. Borodin (Mikhail Markovich Gruzenberg), M. Volin (Semen Natanovich Belenky), L. Madyar (L.I. Milgorf, Milhofer), P.A. Mif (Mikhail Aleksandrovich Fortus), M.I. Kazanin, A.Ya. Kantorovich, E.M. Abramson. All these shared the fate of A.E. Khodorov, with individual variations. Their contribution to academic Oriental studies was not great, but together with popular Marxist pamphlets on the national-liberation movement and the fight against imperialism, and also their part in discussions on the role of the Chinese Communist Party in the Chinese revolution of 1925-27, they published frequently interesting factual material gathered by themselves in articles and dispatches sent direct from the scene of revolutionary events, written, as it were, when the tracks were still fresh.

We will give short biographies of some of these people. Mikhail Markovich Gruzenberg (M. Borodin, 1884-1951), a professional revolutionary and Party worker, took part in the revolutionary movement from the beginning of the century. He was a member of the Bund and then in 1903 joined the Bolsheviks. Between 1919 and 1923 as a Comintern agent he went to Mexico, Spain, Turkey and Britain (in Glasgow he was arrested and sentenced to six months in prison with subsequent expulsion). From 1923 to 1927 he was the main political adviser to the Central Executive Committee of the Kuomintang and the head of the legation of Soviet military and political advisers in the Chinese revolution.[52] After his return from China he was Deputy People's Commissar for Labor, Deputy Director of TASS, from 1932 onwards the editor-in-chief of the newspaper *Moscow News*, and also from 1941-49 editor-in-chief of the Soviet Information Bureau. In 1949 he was arrested and died in detention. He also participated in the discussion about the policy of Ch'en Tu-hsiu in the Chinese revolution.[53]

Semen Natanovich Belenky (revolutionary and literary pseudonym —M. Volin) served between 1925 and 1927 in Borodin's legation in China. After returning to the Soviet Union he was appointed head of the newly formed Academic Research Institute for the Study of China.[54] He studied the agrarian question and the peasant movement in China and participated in discussions concerning the nature of China's social system and the Chinese revolution. In 1929 in the course of the discussion about the policy of Ch'en Tu-hsiu he was accused of over-estimating the role of the Chinese bourgeoisie in the revolution ('right-wing deviation') and dismissed from his directorship of the Chinese research institute.[55] There is no mention of his subsequent fate in Soviet publications. All the indications are that he was arrested and perished in detention.

Lyudvig Ignatevich Madyar (Lajos Milgorf, Milhofer) was born in Hungary in 1891, the son of a Jewish small tradesman. He studied in the law faculty of Pécs University, but because of financial difficulties did not graduate. In 1909-10 he was a member of the Hungarian Social Democratic Party; then he joined the left radicals. During the Hungarian revolution he was a member of the National Council, the highest revolutionary body. After the defeat of the revolution he was tried on the accusation of participating in the murder of the dictator of pre-revolutionary Hungary, Count Tisza. Two years later he was exchanged for some Hungarian participants in the White movement arrested in Soviet Russia. From 1922 he was a member of the Russian Communist Party (Bolshevik), in 1923-24 the correspondent of ROSTA in Germany and in 1924-26 headed the foreign department of *Pravda*. In 1926 he was sent to China as a press attaché of the Soviet legation and then headed the information bureau of the General Consulate in Shanghai. On returning from China he was in charge of the Eastern department of the International Agrarian Institute in Moscow. In 1928 his book *Ekonomika selskogo khozyaystva Kitaya* (The Economics of Chinese Agriculture) came out, followed in 1930 by *Ocherki po ekonomike Kitaya* (An Outline of the Chinese Economy). From 1929 to 1934 he worked on the staff of the Comintern, heading the Eastern Secretariat of the Executive Committee of the Comintern. In 1934 he was arrested and apparently perished in detention.[56]

Mikhail Aleksandrovich Fortus (Pavel Mif, 1901-) was in 1917 the Komsomol organizer in Kherson province (Ukraine), took part in the Civil War and worked both in the Party and Government apparatus. After graduating from the Ya. M. Sverdlov Communist University[57] in 1921 he worked as a research assistant in economics and as a lecturer in the same university (1922-23) and also lectured at the Communist University of the Toilers of the East (KUTV)[58] and at the Institute of Red Professors (IKP).[59] From 1926 he was the Pro-Rector and then Rector (1927-29) of the Sun Yat-sen Communist University.[60] After March 1928 Mif's main work was on the staff of the Comintern; from 1936 till his arrest in 1937 he was Rector of KUTV and Director of both the Academic Research Institute for the Study of National and Colonial Problems and of the Academic Research Institute for the Study of China. Mif participated in the organizational preparation for the Fifth Congress of the Chinese Communist Party (for that purpose making a journey to China in February-March 1927) and for its Sixth Congress (held in June-July 1928 near Moscow). He played a prominent part in the formulation and execution of the policy of the Comintern in China and was the organizer of Soviet Sinology (although he himself did not know Chinese). He travelled to China several times on various secret missions: in 1926 for the organization of Party schools in China; in late 1930 and early 1931 he turned up clandestinely in Shanghai to prepare the 'palace revolution' in the leadership of the Chinese Communist Party.[61] In his books and pamphlets on the recent history of China he cited a large amount of factual material, making use of Comintern data and also of material he himself had collected during his stay in China.[62] He edited and published a number of collections of documents[63] and took part in the discussions of the late 1920s and early 1930s about the revolution in China.[64] In particular at the 7th Plenum of the Executive Committee of the Comintern in November-December 1926 Stalin criticized him for supporting the immediate formation in China of peasant councils, calling this 'rushing on ahead'.[65] It may be assumed that this criticism played a large part in Mif's arrest. It is interesting to note that in the late 1960s and early 1970s, with the exacerbation of the polemic between the Soviet and Chinese leaders, the names of many Party workers, including Mif, consigned to oblivion for more than thirty years, once more appeared in the Soviet academic and popular press.[66] In an article on Mif, V.N. Nikiforov writes: 'The Sinologists who worked with and under P.A. Mif speak with respect of his work in the field of Chinese studies. He is amicably remembered by the Chinese comrades who worked with him.'[67] But one of the students of Sun Yat-sen University recalls Mif thus:

> Mif was young, inexperienced and generally unpopular. While he was vice-rector most of the students did not like him, for he seldom mingled with them. He maintained contact only with a handful of students who spoke fluent Russian and who were among those who later became known as the 28 Bolsheviks.[68] He did not even teach a course at the university, and only occasionally delivered speeches to us....[69] While Mif was a man of little personal substance, one should not overlook the important historical role he played....With the backing of Stalin and the Comintern, he played an important role in trying to shape the Chinese revolution and CCP affairs at a time when Russia had many men that were more able than he.[70]

In the late 1920s and early 1930s there appeared fairly frequently in the journal *Novy Vostok* articles, dispatches and reviews under the name of Mokhtadir Sendzhabi. This was the pseudonym of Viktor Arkadevich May (1897-1946). He took part in the revolutionary movement and the Civil

War, and between 1924 and 1927 worked in Iran as the head of an economics department. He was the author of several books and articles[71] on the economic situation in Iran which were based on statistical and other material gathered by him in the course of his work there and which displayed a good knowledge of local circumstances. It is a curious fact that in a collection of essays called *Iran. Ocherki noveyshey istorii* (Iran. An Outline of Recent History), which was published by 'Nauka' in Moscow in 1976, the authors of the section 'Iran in the period of the monarchy of Reza-Shah (1925-1941)', A.I. Demin and V.V. Trubetskoy, refer to the works of Sendzhabi and, apparently considering them to be translations, attribute them to the 'bourgeois press'.[72]

Despite all the revolutionary mood of M. Pavlovich and his like-minded colleagues, the Academic Association of Oriental Studies headed by them and also its journal *Novy Vostok* left some place too for traditional Oriental studies. Thus approximately a quarter (from 60 to 100 pages out of a total 300-400) of each number of the journal was taken up by the so-called historical-ethnological section headed by I.N. Borozdin. In it were published articles by Orientalists of the old school—V. Bartold, V. Gordlevsky, N. Nikolsky, B. Denike, A. Samoylovich and others. Their papers were read at meetings of the section. The reviews section of *Novy Vostok* continued to have a mainly informational and scholarly character, in contrast to the journal *Revolyutsionny Vostok* (The Revolutionary East),[73] where most articles and reviews were directed at annihilating their ideological opponents and were notable for their aggressive tone.

These attempts by VNAV to give some opportunities for the development of traditional Oriental studies as well, and also Pavlovich's statements about recruiting Orientalists of the pre-Revolutionary generation for work in the Association brought forth harsh attacks on him from those of his 'Marxist comrades' more inclined to extremes, who were concentrated round the Communist University of the Toilers of the East (KUTV). In 1927 the academic research group at KUTV which had been functioning since 1925 was transformed into an Academic Research Association for the study of the social and economic problems of the Soviet and non-Soviet Eastern world and of national and colonial problems (NIANKP), which proclaimed as its main task the creation of 'a Marxist school of Oriental studies in the USSR and the delimitation of Marxist from bourgeois and pseudo-Marxist Oriental studies'.[74] The epithet 'pseudo-Marxist' was clearly a reference to the work of VNAV, so from the very start of its existence the KUTV Academic Research Association's declared aim was the abolition of VNAV. In the Association's journal *Revolyutsionny Vostok* there appeared harsh reviews of works published by VNAV,[75] in which authors were generally accused of opportunism, right or left deviations, etc.

The group of Marxist Orientalists centred round VNAV was predominantly of the Pavlovich or Khodorov type, i.e. they had some general and partly Orientalist education and at any rate knew Western, if not Eastern languages. But the people who worked at the Academic Research Association at KUTV and contributed to *Revolyutsionny Vostok* were mainly Party workers with inadequate qualifications in Oriental studies and often without any proper education at all. Many of them were professional revolutionaries, working for the Comintern or Profintern. They published under their Party pseudonyms, often Eastern names, thus making themselves out to be representatives of the exploited and colonial peoples who were writing 'from the provinces' (e.g. Irandust, Nadab, Ali, Sinani, etc.).[76] Many of them were Jews. Thus the well-known Soviet specialist on Japan and international affairs, Khaim Tevelevich Eydus (1896-1972), also one of the Soviet Marxist school of Orientalists, wrote under the 'Japanese' pseudonym of U. Khayama.

Another author who contributed to *Revolyutsionny Vostok* was A. Shami,[77] who dealt with the contemporary situation in Palestine and the Arab countries. As an example of his work, which was typical of the general style of *Revolyutsionny Vostok*, we may cite his article 'The Palestinian revolt and the Arab East'.[78] Taking the Marxist dogma of class struggle as his starting point, he explains the events of August 1929 in Palestine (religious clashes in the Old Town and the subsequent attacks by Arabs on Jewish settlements) as the struggle of the oppressed Arab fellahs against the 'Jewish expropriators'. Moreover, he accuses the Jewish Zionist Organizations (which he calls 'social-fascist', an accepted term in the Soviet press at that time) together with the British administration and the 'Islamic priesthood' of incitement to national-religious slaughter. 'The Palestinian August uprising is one link in the whole chain of the development of the Revolution . . . ',[79] 'The starting-point of a new powerful revolutionary upsurge in the Arab East.' 'The revolutionary situation in the Near East is maturing', he declares. Shami makes a harshly critical attack on 'world social-democracy' and also on the leaders of the Palestinian Communist Party for what in his opinion was an incorrect appraisal of the August events, accusing them of 'rightist errors'. Like many other articles on revolutionary movements in Eastern countries, published in *Revolyutsionny Vostok*, his article contains direct instructions to the Palestinian Communists:

> The communist parties of the Arab countries are faced with enormous tasks—winning the leadership of this movement, clearly formulating the tasks of the Arab proletariat and peasantry, and organizing the Arab masses for anti-imperialist and class battles. In order to fulfil this mission the com-

> munist parties must become stronger both in their organization and their ideology, and become genuine mass Arab proletarian parties.'[80]

After the publication of Shami's article in *Revolyutsionny Vostok*, a polemic started between him and a member of the Central Committee of the Palestinian Communist Party who wrote under the pseudonym of 'Nadab'.[81] Whilst repenting of his own 'right-opportunist errors', Nadab at the same time accuses Shami of leaps from rightism to ultra-leftism.[82] In the final analysis, the articles of both authors boil down to mutual accusations of distorting Marxism; moreover, the commonest method adopted by both authors is juggling with quotations and ascribing to the opponent 'heretical' pronouncements, which are there and then devastatingly torn to shreds. It is worth noting that this method was in general very typical of the style of the 'Marxist discussions' of that period. In a postscript to Nadab's article 'Against rightist—ultra-leftist confusion in the colonial question' the editors accuse both Nadab and Shami of 'mistakes of a right-opportunist character'. Nadab's article also provides interesting material about the part played by Jews in the Central Committee of the Palestinian Communist Party. Nadab says that the old leadership of the Central Committee of the Palestinian Communist Party did not recognize that the 'main danger within the Party is not Arab, but Jewish nationalism', and indicated that the Central Committee of the Party had followed 'the wrong line on the main question facing the Party—the Arabization of the Party'. He maintained that in Palestine, a country

> where the Jewish minority is the main instrument of exploitation in the hands of the imperialists . . . , the Communist Party will only be able to fulfil its revolutionary obligations when it consists of a majority of Arab comrades (both in the composition of the Party as a whole and that of its leadership). The Arabization of the Party from bottom to top and top to bottom is the central task of the Party; unless this problem is solved the Party is doomed to remain a sectarian group.[83]

This short extract shows the part played by Jewish Communists in Palestine at that time in working virtually for the destruction of the Jewish national home.[84]

It should be noted that the 'practical' Orientalists, who worked in the Comintern and Profintern and in the various organizations abroad of the People's Commissariats of Foreign Affairs and External Trade, were always to a greater or lesser degree connected with the Soviet secret service, which is known to have been concentrated in two places: the foreign department of the GPU (NKVD) and in the Chief Intelligence Directorate (the Fourth Directorate) of the Red Army. Some of them were professional intelligence officers. In this aspect the fortunes of Moisey Markovich Akselrod (1898-1940?) were typical. He came from a middle-class Jewish family and as a child received a traditional Jewish upbringing: he went to a *kheder* (Jewish school) and completed his secondary education at a Russian high school in Smolensk. Fascinated by revolutionary ideas he became a member of the Bund and later joined the Bolsheviks. During the Civil War he served in the political unit of a regiment. In 1923 he graduated from the Law Faculty of Moscow State University. While still a student there he simultaneously entered the Arabic department of the Moscow Institute of Oriental Studies, from which he graduated in 1924. After graduating he was sent out first as an interpreter and later as a secretary to the Soviet General Consulate in Jidda (Saudi Arabia). After returning to the Soviet Union he moved to the foreign department of the GPU (from 1934—the NKVD).[85] He worked as an intelligence officer in Turkey (1928-30),[86] then in Europe, mainly in Italy (1934-37), where he lived with his family. Returning to Moscow in the fall of 1937, he lectured in the Intelligence School of the NKVD in Malakhovka, near Moscow. In October 1938 he was arrested (about this time, after the mysterious death on 17 February 1938 of A.A. Slutsky,[87] head of the department in which Akselrod worked, in the office of the Deputy People's Commissar for Internal Affairs Frinovsky, almost all the officials in this department—some 200 people—were arrested). In February 1939 the family of Akselrod was told that he had been sentenced by the military board of the Supreme Court under Article 58 of the Criminal Code (which included counter-revolutionary activities and 'betrayal of the motherland') to 10 years in remote camps without the right of correspondence. Only later did it become known that this meant a death sentence. After the 20th CPSU Congress Akselrod was rehabilitated 'in absence of any *corpus delicti*' and the sentence of the military board of 20 February 1939 was 'revoked in view of newly discovered circumstances'. His family was given a death certificate dated 18 April 1940, on which the headings for the place and cause of death had not been filled in. While he was working in Saudi Arabia, Akselrod wrote several dispatches and articles notable for their lively exposition and good knowledge of local conditions.[88] He also published several articles and reviews on the contemporary situation in Arab countries.[89] In Moscow, during the breaks between his foreign assignments, he delivered courses of lectures on the modern and recent history of the Arab countries at the Universities of Leningrad and of Central Asia and gave papers at meetings of the Association of Arabic Scholars. In 1937 he participated in the work on Kh.K. Baranov's Arabic-Russian Dictionary. The material he prepared was used in the second edition of the dictionary which came out in 1957.[90] He also wrote the section 'The Arab Caliphate' for school and university history textbooks, which was printed without any mention of his name.

We would like to deal with one more interesting Jewish figure in Oriental studies in the USSR in the late 1920s and early 1930s: Semen Markovich Dimanshteyn (1886-1937) He grew up in a poor Jewish family, in a traditional religious atmosphere. At the age of 12 he started to study at a *yeshiva* (talmudical college) and soon became an adherent of the so-called *Musar* movement,[91] but later became a Hassid and moved to a *yeshiva* in Lyubavich. By the early 1900s he had already qualified to become a rabbi, but his spiritual quest did not end there, and in 1904 he entered a Russian high school in Vilna. There he became acquainted with the activity of illegal Marxist groups and joined the Bolshevik Party. He was an active participant in the Bolshevik underground movement, was arrested several times, was sentenced to exile in Siberia and from there escaped to Paris. In 1917 he returned to Russia. During and after the Revolution he held a series of major Party and Government posts right up to 1937, when he was arrested and apparently shot. In 1918-19 he headed the Commissariat for Jewish National Affairs (*Evkom*), which was part of the People's Commissariat for the Affairs of the Nationalities (*Narkomnats*), as one of the secretaries of which he was a close associate of Stalin. He is known chiefly for his work in this post.[92] At the end of the 1920s after the death of Pavlovich, Dimanshteyn was put in charge of VNAV and the journal *Novy Vostok*. He strongly criticized VNAV for 'not being a sufficiently militant Marxist association'. '. . . We must have a clearly delineated Marxist Association for Oriental Studies, to which there would be no admittance for any doubtful elements in this sphere.'[93] Later in the same article he writes:

> At this time, when there are taking place the most serious revolutionary clashes between imperialism and the worker-peasant masses of the East, when we are becoming engaged in the last and decisive battle between the new and the old world in the most dangerous place, that is in the colonial countries, from which the capitalists try to mobilize all reserves against the fighting proletariat—at such a time it is absolutely inadmissible, in practice worse than any rightist deviation, to devote a considerable amount of time to "delving deeply" into the study of Eastern ornaments, vases, etc., thereby pushing into the background urgent topical questions.[94]

This position essentially aimed at the complete elimination of academic Oriental studies. His assertion that in the field of Oriental studies 'we are required at the present time not to introduce reforms but to carry out a sort of revolution'[95] implied a repudiation of the whole of VNAV's previous work.

It is interesting that, according to Z. Gitelman, in his position as Commissar for Jewish Affairs Dimanshteyn displayed moderation in comparison with other officials of *Evkom*. Thus for example one of the Zionist leaders of that time Benzion Katz later wrote of Dimanshteyn: 'He was not in a hurry to implement the October Revolution on the Jewish street'. Katz believes that Dimanshteyn would not on his own initiative have started persecuting Zionists and closing Hebrew schools had it not been for the pressure of former Bund members and the leaders of the Jewish Section of the Bolshevik Party. Dimanshteyn, apparently, also did not sympathize even with the anti-religious campaign conducted by the Jewish Section. He himself, according to Katz, continued to visit the synagogue on Yom Kippur.[96] Nevertheless, his pronouncements with regard to Oriental studies sound quite aggressive enough. After the 20th Congress of the CPSU Dimanshteyn was rehabilitated. In the February issue (no. 2) of the journal *Sovetish Heymland* for 1965 there was a small notice commemorating the eightieth anniversary of his birth, in which almost no dates are quoted and nothing is said about his work at *Narkomnats*, but it is only mentioned that he 'became a victim of the cult of personality'. The supposition that Dimanshteyn's rehabilitation was, as it were, incomplete, is confirmed by the fact that he is not mentioned in the latest (third) edition of the 'Great Soviet Encyclopaedia'.

At the end of the 1920s there began a new phase of ideological suppression connected with Stalin's gradual usurpation of personal power. In the 1930s he succeeded in completely subjecting scholarship and culture in the USSR to Party control. For this purpose the special communist institutions created in the early 1920s in the social science field were disbanded and amalgamated with the traditional institutions which had managed to survive the Revolution: partly also new ones were formed out of the shattered remains of both earlier types.[97] This re-organization was accompanied by the annihilation both of scholars of the pre-Revolutionary generation and of those Marxist ideologists and social scientists who appeared to Stalin for whatever reason to be untrustworthy, or too independent-minded or too intellectual. In these years many Orientalists were arrested and killed, both those of the old, traditional school (N.A. Nevsky, K. Yu. Shchutsky, A.N. Samoylovich and many others) and the Marxist Orientalists (e.g. the above mentioned A.E. Khodorov, E.M. Abramson, A. Ya. Kantorovich, P.A. Mif, etc.) and administrators and diplomats connected with Oriental studies (S.M. Dimanshteyn, L.M. Karakhan). The reorganization of the social sciences took place against the background of the so-called great discussions, conducted under the slogan of the fight for Marxist purity. Each of the opposing sides insisted on the correctness of its interpretation, accusing its opponents of ignorance and distortion of Marxism. Examples of such discussions in Oriental studies may be found in the above-mentioned discussion on socio-economic formations in the East, started by the polemic between A.E. Khodorov and A. Ivin,[98] and on problems of the Chinese revolution. Since, however, there could not be any free expression of opinions in these discussions, by the end of the 1930s stagnation had set in in Oriental studies as in most social sciences in the USSR. Even the Soviet author V.N. Nikiforov in his work on the history of Sinology in the USSR admits that the revolution in Oriental studies proclaimed by Dimanshteyn at the turn of the 1920s never took place. The Association of Marxist Orientalists (later called the Society of Marxist Orientalists), founded under the auspices of the Communist Academy,[99] did not achieve anything outstanding. After the elimination of *Novy Vostok* there was no journal to equal it in importance right up till the post-war years.[100]

Thus, to sum up what has been described above, it must be stated that in the 1920s and 1930s Jews in Oriental studies in the USSR played more a negative rather than a positive role, since most of them loyally served the interests of the Bolshevik Party in founding, along with other Soviet scholars, the so-called Marxist school in Oriental studies in the Soviet Union and in hindering the development of traditional academic Oriental studies. However, it would be wrong to draw the conclusion from this that there were no real scholars at all amongst the Jewish Orientalists of that time.

The scholars

In the previous section we tried to trace the role of Jewish Orientalists in creating the new Marxist school in Oriental Studies in the Soviet Union. Now we would like to throw some light on the scholarly achievements of the Soviet Jewish Orientalists not connected with ideological commitment.

In the already mentioned Sinological discussions a fairly prominent part was played by Mikhail Davidovich Kokin (1906-1937),[101] who together with G.K. Papayan wrote a monograph on the social system of China in the Chou period (eleventh to third centuries BC),[102] in connection with the discussion on the Asiatic mode of production. For all its faults, this book was of a comparatively high academic standard for that time, with use of source material and a large section on the history of the problem. The section on China written by M.D. Kokin for the collection of essays *Ocherki po istorii Vostoka v epokhu imperializma* (Outlines of Eastern History in the Imperialist Epoch) (Moscow-Leningrad, 1934) stands out to advantage because of its calm scholarly tone and volume of factual material quoted, in comparison with similar works of that time, for example those of A.E. Khodorov. It is difficult now to say in what direction Kokin's scholarly work would have developed. He was arrested in the mid-1930s (apparently in 1937, when he was little more than thirty) and perished in detention.

Another interesting scholar whose work was forcibly cut short during the Stalin terror was Mikhail Izrailovich Tubyansky (1893-1937), who was not only a Tibetologist and Buddhologist but also a specialist on ancient Indian and Bengali literature, an expert on Indian languages and a Mongolist. The pupil of F.I. Shcherbatskoy,[103] Tubyansky graduated from the department of Eastern languages at Petrograd University in 1919. From 1920 to 1927 he worked as a research assistant in the Asiatic Museum and at the same time taught Sanskrit, Bengali and Hindi in the Leningrad Institute for Modern Eastern Languages (LIZhVYa)[104] and in the university. In 1927 he was posted to Mongolia, where he worked till 1936, first as a research assistant for the Tibetology study-group of the Academic Research Committee of the Mongolian People's Republic, then from 1930 as the Academic Secretary of this Committee. Soon after returning from Mongolia, in 1937, Tubyansky was arrested. What happened to him after that is not known. Apparently he perished in detention.

To judge from the essay by M.I. Vorobeva-Desyatovskaya and L.S. Savitsky, 'Tibetology',[105] the only work published in the USSR which mentions the life and work of Tubyansky, 'he was a talented, versatile scholar with a wide range of academic interests.' In the 1920s Tubyansky studied the Buddhist treatise on logic by Nyayapraveśa and the commentaries on it by Sisiyahit. For the *Bibliotheca Buddhica* published by the Academy of Sciences he prepared an examination of that treatise and its Chinese and Tibetan versions with three-language indexes of terms. The work was submitted to the publishing house and partially set up, but was nevertheless never published. The only part published was a preliminary report on the research into the authorship of the treatise.[106] During these years Tubyansky was sorting out and investigating the manuscript archive of V.P. Vasilev.[107]

In their study Vorobeva-Desyatovskaya and Savitsky write:

> In Mongolia Tubyansky gathered material for his dissertation 'Ancient Indian Materialism (According to Tibetan Sources)', which he was not given time to complete. He took part in the work of Mongolian scholars who were compiling a Tibetan-Mongolian dictionary and wrote 10,000 index-cards for it, which remained in Mongolia. On returning home Tubyansky continued this work, and on his initiative the Academy of Sciences accepted the suggestion of an Academic Research Committee of the Mongolian People's Republic for the joint preparation of a large Tibetan-Mongolian dictionary. The dictionary was included in the plans of the USSR Academy of Sciences Institute of Oriental Studies, but in 1938 work on it ceased.[108]

To judge from the information provided by Vorobeva-Desyatovskaya and

Savitsky, many manuscript works by Tubyansky on Tibetology and Buddhology were left in Mongolia and, most probably, lost. The authors of the study mention the following works by Tubyansky as being left by him in Mongolia: 'A Reference Dictionary on Indian and Tibetan Medicine'; an examination of the work *Lam-rim* by Tsonkha-pa (1356-1418), who is considered to be founder of Lamaism, with a translation, commentary and lexical indices; a translation and commentary on the works by a nineteenth-century Tibetan author on the reformation movement in Lamaism; and a translation of the work by Sumpa Khan-po 'The Chronology of Buddhism in India, Tibet and Mongolia'.[109]

After Tubyansky's return from Mongolia a prospectus was produced of a new series of studies on Indian and Tibetan literary texts—*Bibliotheca Indo-Tibetica*—under the direction of Shcherbatskoy. We learn from the prospectus that Tubyansky had to prepare for this series Sanskrit and Tibetan texts of a work by Chatuhstava with a translation, commentary and analysis. Tubyansky managed to discover in Mongolia the Sanskrit text of this work, which had been considered lost. In 1932 this text was sent to the Academy of Sciences publishing-house, but neither the text nor Tubyansky's research on it were ever published. Besides this Tubyansky was commissioned to prepare for this series a volume devoted to a review of the Chinese and Tibetan translations of works by the Vinaya circle based on the manuscripts of V.P. Vasilev; this also was never published. Thus if we compare this information with the list of Tubyansky's published works (twenty-one titles, including translations and editions)[110] it becomes clear that most of what Tubyansky did or might have done perished with him.

Among the younger generation of Jewish Orientalists the works of two specialists in Arabic studies—V. Lutsky and I. Filshtinsky—should be mentioned.

Vladimir Borisovich Lutsky (1906-1962) was born in Berdyansk. In 1930 he graduated from the Arabic Department of the Moscow Oriental Institute (MIV); in 1935 he defended his thesis on the modern history of the Arab countries. From 1931 until his death he was a lecturer and research worker in various Oriental institutions in Moscow and Leningrad. His principal field of interest was the modern and contemporary history of the Middle Eastern, especially Arab, countries, on which theme he published over 200 works. Though most of these works are to a certain extent politically biased, they also contain much factual material which is dealt with in a scholarly manner. Lutsky's main work, 'The National Liberation War in Syria (1925-1927)', on which he began his studies as early as the 1930s and continued until the 1950s, was published posthumously by his pupils in 1964. He contributed chapters on the modern history of Arab countries to many Soviet standard works on the history of the East.[111]

This in particular, as well as his pedagogical activities (at Moscow University, Moscow and Lenningrad Oriental Institutes, etc.) laid the foundations for the new school of Soviet historians of Arab countries.

Isaak Moiseevich Filshtinsky (born 1918) graduated in 1941 from the historical department of the Moscow Institute of Philosophy, Literature and History (MIFLI), and in 1945 from the Military Institute of Foreign Languages, where he specialized in Arabic. He began his scholarly career at the same Institute and in 1948 defended his dissertation: 'The Struggle of the Egyptian People Against the French Occupation Forces during the Bonaparte Expedition'. Shortly afterwards, in the post-war wave of Stalinist repressions, Filshtinsky was arrested and spent seven years in prison camps. Only in 1958 was he accepted as a junior research worker in the Academy of Sciences' Institute of Oriental Studies and this enabled him to return to scholarly work. He continued his research on the Chronicle of the Moslem historian 'Abd al-Rahman al-Djabarti (1753-1825), the most important source for the history of Egypt from the end of the seventeenth century until the beginning of the nineteenth century. In 1962 he published his translation of this Chronicle into Russian with commentaries and introduction.[112] At that time, Filshtinsky's main interest shifted to classical Arabic literature, especialy early Moslem literature and culture (seventh-twelfth centuries). He published a number of works in this field.[113] In the 1960s he lectured (temporarily) at Moscow University on the origins and essence of the Koran and on Moslem religion and culture, his lectures enjoying wide popularity among the students. In 1977-78, as a result of his studies, two volumes on the history of Arabic literature in the Middle Ages appeared.[114] Filshtinsky gives here a comprehensive account of the origins and development of Arabic literature and philosophical and religious thought. In the 1970s he published, with introduction and commentaries, two collections: *Arabskaya poeziya srednikh vekov* (Arabic Poetry of the Middle Ages) (Moscow 1975) and *Arabskaya srednevekovaya literatura i kultura* (Arabic Literature and Culture from the Middle Ages—a collection of articles by Western scholars) (Moscow 1978). A profound knowledge of both Arab sources and modern research in his field is characteristic of his studies. Although in 1978 Filshtinsky retired from the Institute of Oriental Studies, he still works in his field of interest.

The achievements of Jewish Orientalists in the field of Eastern philology and linguistics are also noteworthy. First and foremost we should cite here such major scholars as the Iranian expert A.A. Freyman and the philologist, outstanding linguist and historian of literature Academician V.M. Zhirmunsky.

Aleksandr Arnoldovich Freyman (1879-1968) was born in Warsaw, where he received his secondary education. In 1903 he graduated from the department of Eastern languages at Petersburg University in the Sanskrit-Persian-Armenian section. In 1917 he started work at Petrograd University as a lecturer in ancient Iranian languages, became a professor in 1919 and a corresponding member of the USSR Academy of Sciences in 1928. From 1938 to 1950 he was head of the department of Iranian philology and from 1946 to 1956 inclusive director of the Iranian section of the USSR Academy of Sciences Institute of Oriental Studies. In 1933 Freyman led an expedition of the Tadzhikistan branch of the USSR Academy of Sciences, which discovered in the ruins of a castle on the mountain of Mug (on the upper reaches of the river Zeravshan) unique texts in Sogdian, one of the ancient Iranian languages. His research laid the foundation for the study of the Sogdian language and the culture of Sogdiana and led to a series of new discoveries concerning the history of the ancient peoples who inhabited Central Asia and Iran. In 1936 Freyman began to study another ancient Iranian language—Khorezmian, and the results of his investigations were later published as a separate book,[115] which, in the words of a reviewer, gave back to the living a language which had seemingly disappeared forever and established its cognation with other East-Iranian languages.[116] A.A. Freyman's works gained world-wide recognition for their contribution to the study of the Sogdian and Khorezmian languages. Apart from this research, Freyman studied the Avesta and ancient Persian inscriptions and produced an account and a scholarly edition of Pahlavi texts. He worked also on the history and etymology of Iranian languages and dialects and the links between the Iranian and Slavic languages.[117] In 1918 he published an account of the Jewish-Persian manuscripts in the collection of the Asiatic Museum[118] as a continuation of the work of K.G. Zaleman[119] on the editing of these manuscripts.[120] But the ultimate aim of all these studies was the development of comparative-historical Iranian linguistics, which was the main theme of his sixty years of academic activities. Freyman saw as the most important task of Iranian linguistics the composition of a comparative historical grammar and an etymological dictionary of the Iranian languages, which might be able to show the process of the historical development of this linguistic group as a unified system. Unfortunately, the work on the Iranian dictionary was interrupted by the war and was thus never completed.[121]

Viktor Maksimovich Zhirmunsky (1891-1971) was born in Petersburg, the son of a doctor. In 1912 he graduated from Petersburg University, where he remained at the department of Romano-Germanic philology in order to prepare for professorial status. In 1917 he was appointed Professor at Saratov University, and in 1919 Professor at Petrograd (Leningrad) University, with which he remained connected during the whole of his subsequent life and academic activities. In 1939 he was elected a corresponding member of the USSR Academy of Sciences, and in 1966 a full member.

V.M. Zhirmunsky is primarily known as the founder and head of the Soviet school of Germanic studies, but his fundamental works in the field of Turkic linguistics and also on the theory of literary criticism, in particular on the origin of heroic epics, in connection with which he studied Eastern literatures as well, merit some remarks on his contribution to the development of Oriental studies. Zhirmunsky's first scholarly works, which were published in 1913-1919, were on aspects of German Romanticism. In the 1920s he worked on theoretical problems of prosody and on the interaction between various national literatures; he published a series of brilliant articles and books which have not lost their importance even to this day.[122] At the end of the 1930s Zhirmunsky's research in the field of the theory and history of literature reflected his special interest in the comparative study of literatures. In that period he formulated the theoretical principles of his research which were to dominate his later works, namely the attempt to discover behind a multiplicity of individual forms general typological features, the general principles of typologically parallel, but still independent, processes and phenomena.[123]

Zhirmunsky started work on heroic epic poetry during the war while he was living in Tashkent. From the 1940s to the 1960s he published a large number of classic studies on folk epic (mainly Turkic) and on general and specialized questions of Central Asian folklore; his interests also included the comparative study of Eastern and Western literatures and world folklore.[124] He was attracted by general theoretical problems connected with the specific features of epic composition amongst various peoples. He came to the conclusion that the common features of heroic epic poetry which had been observed by researchers amongst various peoples were the result of the common typological character of this genre and not the consequence of influences of various kinds.[125] Zhirmunsky's research received international recognition: he received honorary doctorates from many universities all over the world; in 1962 he was elected a foreign member of the British Academy. His pupils have remarked on the amazing range of his research.[126] In the course of fifty-seven years of scholarly work he published about 400 studies, of which thirty were monographs. He felt himself equally at home in all the many branches of scholarship in which he worked.[127] 'V.M. Zhirmunsky belongs to that small group of scholars who, in an age of ever increasing academic differentiation, has managed to avoid narrow specialization and to combine in his writing a philologist's wide range of interests with the depth and originality of a theoretician's analytical thought both in the field of linguistics and that of literary studies.'[128]

We would like at this point to make brief mention of the interesting works of Adolf Pavlovich Yushkevich (born 1906) and Boris Abramovich Rozenfeld (born 1917). Both of them were mathematicians by training (Yushkevich graduated from the mathematical-physics department of Moscow University in 1929, Rozenfeld from the mathematical-mechanics department in 1939). They did work on the history of mathematics in Eastern countries in the Middle Ages. Since 1957 Yushkevich has been a member of the International Academy of the History of Science and was its president in the period 1966-69; he has published about 200 books and articles. Some of these works were written jointly by these two authors, mainly as publications with commentaries of the mathematical works of Omar Khayyam, Nasir ad-Din at-Tusi, Biruni, etc.[129]

Hebrew and Semitic studies

Let us now move on to a consideration of the role of Jewish Orientalists in the foundation and development of Hebrew and Semitic studies in the USSR. Here we should mention first of all the scholars who laid the foundations of Hebrew studies in Russia: D.A. Khvolson (1819-1911) and A.Ya. Garkavi (1835-1919), whose work belongs to the pre-Revolutionary period. In a collection of essays published to mark the 150th anniversary of the foundation of the Academy of Sciences Asiatic Museum, K.B. Starkova writes in the section 'Hebrew studies': 'The foremost of the Russian Hebrew and Semitic scholars connected with the Asiatic Museum was Daniel (Joseph) Abramovich Khvolson, whose personality and work determined the future course of development of Hebrew and Semitic studies for many decades, both within the Academy of Sciences and the university.'[130] The work of Abraham (Albert) Yakovlevich Garkavi was connected with Petersburg Public Library (from 1877 till his death), since, being unwilling to convert to Russian Orthodoxy, he was compelled to leave the chair in the history of the Ancient East which had been offered him in 1870 and to give up his university career.[131]

After Garkavi's death, from 1919 to 1921 the keeper of Hebrew manuscripts in the Petrograd Public Library was David Hillelevich Maggid (1862-1942?). He published a whole series of books on the history of the Jews, Jewish literature and bibliography, Jewish art, and also on the history and folklore of the various Jewish ethnic groups in Russia (the Caucasian and Crimean Jews). From 1925 he taught Modern Hebrew and Biblical studies at Leningrad University. He published certain manuscripts in the collection of the Public Library, including some poems by medieval Jewish poets. Right up to the time of his death he was one of the few connecting links between Palestinian scholars and the Hebrew manuscripts in Leningrad. He used to send copied extracts from the manuscripts and also photographs of them to Jewish scholars and writers living in Palestine, and compiled for them lists of manuscripts relating to particular themes. A large number of literary texts were published from copies made by him. In addition he was one of the very few scholars who, while living and working in the Soviet Union, had works published abroad.

In 1892 the Asiatic Museum was presented with the collection of Hebrew books and manuscripts belonging to L.P. Friedland.[132] There were two conditions attached to the presentation: the Asiatic Museum was obliged to produce an inventory and a systematization of the library and publish a catalogue of it; and to carry out this work it had to take on as a part-time staff member the bibliographer and Hebrew scholar Samuel Eremeevich Wiener (1860-1929) who had previously worked for Friedland in the selection of the library's collection.[133] Between 1893 and 1918 as a result of S.E. Wiener's activities there were published seven volumes of the catalogue of Hebrew books of the 'Bibliotheca Friedlandiana', covering the letters Aleph to Kaph.[134] This catalogue contained only printed books, while Friedland's library, according to the information given by Wiener in the Preface to the first volume of the catalogue, included about 10,000 books and more than 300 manuscripts.[135] After Wiener's death the work proceeded by fits and starts (see below). Still, the scholarly importance of Wiener's catalogue can scarcely be exaggerated. In a historical survey of the Hebrew book, published in Jerusalem in 1975, the authors, R. Posner and I. Ta-Shema, write that Wiener's catalogue is 'almost without precedent in his excellent sense of bibliographical discipline . . . His bibliographical annotations, phrased with extreme brevity, are so much to the point that to this day it is generally possible with their aid to identify "difficult" problematic volumes as if Wiener's own copies were lying in front of us'.[136]

Soon after the Revolution a special Hebrew section was formed at the Asiatic Museum, the keeper of which was, after 1924, the Hebrew scholar M.N. Sokolov, a pupil of P.K. Kokovtsov.[137] He continued the work of cataloguing the collection of the 'Bibliotheca Friedlandiana', making a start on an inventory of the manuscripts. After the foundation of the Institute of Oriental Studies in 1930 the Hebrew section was transformed into the Hebrew study group, which was planned not only to systematize and inventorize the book and manuscript collections in Hebrew but also to carry out research both in Hebrew studies and on modern Jewry. The Hebrew study group was abolished in 1937 and in its place was formed the study group on the Ancient Orient headed by V.V. Struve.[138] From that time Hebrew studies ceased to exist independently from an organizational point of view in the structure of the USSR Academy of Sciences, and were included partly in the study group on the Ancient Orient and partly in the Arabic study group headed by I.Yu. Krachkovsky[139] (dealing with Semitic studies).

In 1932 J.G. Bender and Yu.O. Solodukho joined the staff of the Hebrew study group. Joseph Genrikhovich Bender (1900-41) graduated from the department of Eastern languages at Petersburg University, where his teachers had been Kokovtsov, Krachkovsky and Struve. His first published article was devoted to research into Biblical sources.[140] His main work in the Hebrew study group was the preparation of the next volumes of the catalogue of Friedland's library for publication. In 1936 he published the eighth volume (the letter Lamed)[141] and completed the preparation of volumes 9 and 10. But, as K.B. Starkova indicates,[142] the war prevented publication, and they have remained unpublished.[143] After the transformation of the Hebrew study group into the Ancient Orient study group in 1937 Bender worked on the decipherment of the newly discovered Ugaritic texts. Besides this he was gathering material for a book on Judaea in the 7th-5th centuries BC. J.G. Bender was killed during the blockade of Leningrad, without managing to complete his work. K.B. Starkova writes of him: 'He was a born historiographer, and moreover with a very wide range, as is shown by his Candidate of Sciences dissertation, which deals with Azariah dei Rossi, a Jewish historian of the Renaissance period.'[144]

Yudel Orelevich Solodukho (1877-1963) received a traditional Jewish upbringing. In 1907 he passed as an external candidate the examinations for the full course at the Teacher's Institute in Riga. After that he taught in Jewish schools, gave private lessons and contributed to Jewish journals and newspapers. His work in the Hebrew study group concerned problems of the social history and of the early medieval period of Jewish society in Near Eastern countries.[145] He had a fluent command of Hebrew and Aramaic and a thorough knowledge of the Jewish oral tradition, and thus was able to use the Mishnah, Talmud and Midrashim as primary sources for his research. In his works he put forward the idea that codes of Jewish canonical law often reflect the legal norms and social structure of the peoples amongst which the Jews lived at that time, and can therefore be used as sources for the history of these peoples.[146] In 1935 he defended his dissertation on 'Slavery in Jewish Society in Iraq and Syria in the 2nd-5th Centuries AD'.[147] After the war (he worked as a research assistant at the Institute of Oriental Studies till 1950) he published a number of articles, which continued and developed the treatment of the problems of his chosen theme.[148]

The work of listing and systematizing Hebrew manuscripts, which had been started by M.N. Sokolov, was taken up in 1936 by Ionah Iosifovich (Osipovich) Gintsburg (1871-1942). In 1905 he graduated from the department of Oriental languages at Petersburg University and in 1934 started work at the USSR Academy of Sciences Institute of Oriental Studies. Between 1936 and 1941 he compiled a systematic inventory of all the manuscripts in the Hebrew collection of the Institute of Oriental Studies.[149] By the start of the war the catalogue was ready in typescript with indices of authors and works in manuscript.[150] At the same time I.I. Gintsburg published a number of articles relating to certain important copies of Jewish and Jewish-Arabic manuscripts in the collection of the Institute of Oriental Studies.[151] K.B. Starkova says that the most important of Gintsburg's works was his study of the unique Hebrew translation of Boethius's 'On the Consolation of Philosophy'[152] In the spring of 1942 Gintsburg died in besieged Leningrad, unable to withstand the ordeals of the blockade. In his *Ocherki po istorii russkoy arabistiki* (Outline of the History of Arabic Studies in Russia) I.Yu. Krachkovsky wrote of his passing:

> May 1942 took away I.I. Gintsburg (born 1871), one of the oldest of P.K. Kokovtsov's pupils, who had had a very hard and taxing life. He was not conspicuously gifted, but he labored with great enthusiasm and persistence mainly in the field of Jewish-Arabic medieval philosophy; his last major work was his study of the *De Consolatione Philosophiae* by Boethius in relation to little-known Hebrew versions. Even in besieged Leningrad he continued preparing for publication a large catalogue of the Hebrew manuscripts of the Institute of Oriental Studies.[153]

Also worth mention are the works of the talented Leningrad Semitologist who died young—Yakov Solomonovich Vilenchik (1902-39). In his childhood he lost his hearing as a result of serious shell-shock at the start of the First World War. But in spite of this Vilenchik not only managed to complete his secondary school education but also to receive special linguistic education in Leningrad University. He chose Semitology as his specialization; he had long felt that this subject was his vocation, and this helped him overcome all the many obstacles which lay in his path. Academician I.Yu. Krachkovsky in a commemorative notice about his pupil writes about how difficult it was for Vilenchik:

> to overcome the scepticism of scholars in this field, who were nonplussed at this unusual phenomenon and sometimes considered fantastic the very idea of someone stone-deaf going in for linguistics, especially phonetics, which had so fascinated Ya. S. Vilenchik from his first year at university. It was not easy to fight against this scepticism: only the results of his work gradually broke it down and won him the right to work in his beloved field.[154]

The main work of Vilenchik's life was a dictionary of the living conversational Arabic language of Syria and Palestine, compiled from the published records of Western Arabist dialectologists. I.Yu. Krachkovsky said of it:

> This dictionary attempts to sum up the whole lexical stock of the living Arabic language of Syria and Palestine, while drawing on linguistic material from other Arab countries of the Near East. In its exhaustive coverage of all available records and publications of the data of linguistic usage it has no predecessors in this field.[155]

The death of Ya. S. Vilenchik cut short work on the dictionary, and it has never been published. However in the course of his studies, whilst making use of the material he had collected, Vilenchik managed to publish a large number of articles on the phonetics, historical grammar and vocabulary of the proto-Semitic and Arabic languages and their dialects.[156] Unfortunately, his fundamental study of the origin of the Arabic article, which was completed just before his death and was prepared for publication by Krachkovsky, has remained in manuscript form.

One of the outstanding scholars and teachers of Semitic studies was Bentsion Meerovich Grande (1891-1974). In 1910 he entered the medical faculty of Moscow University; as a doctor he took part in the First World War. After graduating from the university in 1918, he served in the Red Army for three years as a doctor. Whilst still a medical student he had become fascinated by Oriental culture and studied Arabic as an external student at the Lazarev Institute of Oriental Languages in Moscow. After passing in 1922 the examinations for the full course at that institute (by that time called the Moscow Institute of Oriental Studies), he began his teaching career there. From 1928 to 1944 he worked as a research fellow at the Institute of Ethnic and National Cultures, which was subsequently reorganized as the Institute of Spoken and Written Language of the USSR Academy of Sciences. At that time he was taking an active part in the work on the reform of the alphabets and the elaboration of new systems of written language for a number of languages of the national minorities in the USSR. In 1944 he was invited to join the department of Arabic, formed in 1943 in the philological faculty of Moscow University. In 1947 he became head of the department and in 1957 Professor of Arabic at the Institute of Eastern Languages attached to Moscow University. At the university he lectured on the basic theoretical topics and conducted practical tutorials in classical Arabic, ancient Hebrew and comparative Semitic linguistics. B.M. Grande's scholarly output was considerable: he published more than seventy articles and books. The articles of the pre-war period mainly deal with problems of the reform of the literary languages in the USSR, but his works from the 1950s to the 1970s were connected with the problems of Arabic and Semitic linguistics. After 1960 Grande devoted himself to writing major works which re-cast and generalized the courses of lectures he had given at the university. In 1963 he published his *Kurs arabskoy grammatiki v sravnitelno-istoricheskom osveshchenii* (A Comparative and Historical Course in Arabic Grammar) (published by Moscow University); in 1963 he edited the 'Ivrit-Russian Dictionary', compiled by F.L. Shapiro, which, as G.Sh. Sharbatov puts it in the obituary 'In memory of B.M. Grande',[157] was in the USSR the first 'attempt at a major lexicographical reference-book on modern Ivrit'. Grande had written specially for this dictionary a detailed outline of the grammar of Ivrit, which, as G.Sh. Sharbatov remarks, 'may certainly serve as a teaching manual for students of Semitology in the absence of any appropriate textbooks'.[158] It may be added that Shapiro, the compiler of the dictionary, died during the final stages of preparing it for publication, and B.M. Grande completed this work. In 1972 there appeared Grande's last fundamental work, which sums up his work in the field of Semitology: *Vvedenie v sravnitelnoe izuchenie semitskikh yazykov* (An Introduction to the Comparative Study of the Semitic Languages) (published by 'Nauka' for the USSR Academy of Sciences).

It is obvious from what has been said above that research into written Semitic sources often went hand-in-hand with the study of the ancient history and culture of the Near East. Amongst the eminent pre-war Jewish specialists on the Near East should be mentioned Israel Grigorevich Frank-Kamenetsky (1880-1937) and the major linguist and Assyriologist Aleksandr Pavlovich Riftin (1900-45). Even in his early works Riftin had shown himself to be an impeccably careful philologist.[159] I.Yu. Krachkovsky, in a commemorative article on him, writes that A.P. Riftin 'was not one of those scholars who are in a rush to publish their works; he was not interested in a mere increase in quantity of publications.'[160] He carefully studied the works of his predecessors, made an independent re-examination of the material they cited and was able to shed new light on it. In almost every one of his articles there is material unpublished before, with a painstakingly thought-out commentary. 'When he was bringing forward new material for scholarly use he always tried to give an all-round analysis of it in a concise commentary, not only on the linguistic, but also the cultural and historical aspects.'[161] A.P. Riftin's main work was on the Babylonian tablets in the collection of N.P. Likhachev.[162] The result of more than ten years of systematic work on this collection was his classic study *Starovavilonskie yuridicheskie i administrativnye dokumenty v sobraniyakh SSSR* (Ancient Babylonian Legal and Administrative Documents from Collections in the USSR) (Moscow-Leningrad 1937). In this work Riftin published the texts of 147 cuneiform tablets. The analysis of all these business, procedural and administrative documents required an encyclopaedic knowledge of all questions relating to them; their decipherment and annotation were possible only as a result of many years of persistent and intensive work. Riftin also wrote interesting linguistic studies, mainly on the Akkadian language.[163]

Apart from his scholarly work A.P. Riftin also did much teaching and lecturing. According to Krachkovsky he was no less gifted as a teacher and organizer than as a scholar.[164] In 1944 he took an active part in the re-opening of the Oriental Faculty at Leningrad University after a break of twenty-five years (it had been closed in 1919) and became its first Dean.[165] However, soon afterwards A.P. Riftin died at the age of only forty-five from the after-effects of the blockade of Leningrad.

Israel Grigorevich Frank-Kamenetsky was expelled in 1904 from Kiev University for taking part in student riots. He continued his education in Germany. In the 1920s and 1930s he lectured at Moscow and Leningrad Universities, was a research fellow of the Academy of Sciences Institute of Language and Thought and head of the study group on Semitic and Hamitic languages and of the study group on the oral literature of primitive society in that institute (right up to his sudden death from an accident). From 1911 to 1922 he published a number of studies in the field of the Semitic and ancient Egyptian languages, and also on the cultural history of ancient Egypt.[166] In an article published in 1921, 'The religion of Amon and the Old Testament',[167] Frank-Kamenetsky points out the similarities and differences between Egyptian and Judaic monotheism. In particular the main difference, in his opinion, lies in the fact that the Egyptian religious consciousness was concentrated primarily on the power of God, whereas it was the idea of justice which lay at the centre of the Judaic religion.[168] In 1922 Frank-Kamenetsky got to know the works of N.Ya. Marr[169] and became an enthusiastic follower of the so-called 'new doctrine on language'.[170] It should be noted that Marr's doctrine had an unfavorable effect on the study of ancient Eastern languages as well, since Marr completely rejected the comparative-historical method in linguistics, which he declared to be 'racist' and 'politically unfit for Soviet society'. But in spite of the fact that many of the works of Frank-Kamenetsky of this period were strongly influenced by Marr's ideas, he never went near the extremes (such as the so-called 'four-element analysis') which led Marr and his followers to arbitrary interpretation of the linguistic facts. In those of his works which concern specific observations on linguistic material, Marr's influence is often seen only in the use of his specific terminology. The most important study by Frank-Kamenetsky in the field of Semitology in this period was his work on the ancient Egyptian verb, which was published as two articles and dealt with the origin of the tenses of verbs in the Semitic languages.[171] About the same time he wrote a number of articles on the origin of the mythological and religious views of primitive and ancient peoples, including works on the Bible and the history of early Christianity.[172]

Abram Borisovich Ranovich (Rabinovich, 1885-1948) also investigated the Bible and the Judaic religion from a Marxist position. In his works he recognized the importance of the historical books of the Old Testament as source-material for the history of the ancient Eastern world, but in general his works are notable for their harshly anti-religious tone. He rejects the idea that the Judaic religion had an independent origin, reducing it to the status of 'Biblical fairy-tales borrowed from Babylonian, Assyrian and Egyptian mythology'.[173]

It is worth pointing out that in the pre-Revolutionary period the ancient history of Palestine and the Near East and research in the field of Biblical studies and medieval Jewish-Arabic literature were also given space in purely Jewish publications, for example in the journals and collections of essays published by the Society for the Dissemination of Education amongst Jews in Russia[174] and the Jewish Historical and Ethnographic Society.[175] The work of these societies and of other Jewish publishing-houses was cut short in 1915 because of the war.[176] Publication of the official organ of the Jewish Historical and Ethnographic Society *Evreyskaya starina* (Jewish Antiquities) was renewed only in 1924. At this time there were still glimmers of hope amongst Jewry in the Soviet Union for a revival of Jewish culture. In the Preface the editors of this collection of essays wrote:

> As the Jews have gained more rights and become not so defenseless there has been a marked decline in the keen interest in many phenomena of the recent past which were linked with the Tsarist regime and to which we had to pay excessive attention. The horizon of our academic work is extending. In our historical research we can nowadays move beyond the narrow limits of the history of the Jews in Russia, Poland and Lithuania. We can allow ourselves the luxury of starting to deal with the most varied general and detailed problems of our past in all ages and in all countries where Jews have lived.[177]

In accordance with this programme the three volumes (11, 12, 13) of *Evreyskaya starina* which succeeded in appearing before the final closure of this publication in 1930 contained a number of articles on the ancient history of the Jews, on epigraphy and Biblical studies.[178] The commission for the study of Jewish antiquities which operated under the aegis of the Society was engaged in a classification of Talmudic material on a card-index system which covered the history of medicine and educational theory, Biblical criticism, law and history.[179]

In the 1920s there was also a revival of the work of the Society for the Dissemination of Education amongst Jews. In 1922 and 1926 the Society issued two collections of scholarly and literary works under the title of *Evreyskaya mysl* (Jewish Thought). In these volumes there were also published articles on the ancient history of the Jews and on medieval Jewish literature: 'Unpublished lyric poems by Solomon Gabirol (to mark the 900th anniversary of the poet's birth)', with new translations of the poetry, by S. Zinberg (Tsinberg);[180] 'The doctrine concerning slavery in Biblical-Talmudic and Roman Law (a comparative historical essay)' by M. Ginzburg; 'Survivals of animism in Biblical poetry' by I.G. Frank-Kamenetsky; 'The Biblical account of the period of Jewish residence in Egypt' by S.Ya. Lurye, etc.

In the collection of essays published by the same Society in Leningrad in 1928, called *Evreysky vestnik* (The Jewish Bulletin), it was stated that the Society:

> possesses one of the largest libraries in Europe in the fields of Hebrew and Judaic studies, which also contains a considerable collection of manuscripts . . . . Especially noteworthy is a very valuable collection (over 400 volumes) of Hebrew works which was acquired at the end of 1927 from the heirs of Ya. Kh. Yanovsky. The work of compiling an inventory of the manuscript department of the library has been carried out by S.L. Zinberg. He has already studied, recorded and listed 900 manuscripts and fragments, and a catalogue has been made ready for publication.[181]

The report also mentions that of particular interest amongst the manuscripts are the excerpts from the lyric poetry of Solomon Gabirol, which contain a number of the unpublished poems of Gabirol, parts of the works of Moses ibn Ezra,[182] a Hebrew version of a novel about Alexander the Great, etc. In 1930 the Society was closed down, and its library was transferred to the Institute of Jewish Proletarian Culture in Kiev,[183] which was also abolished not long afterwards. What happened after this to the collection of books and manuscripts and to the catalogue compiled by Zinberg is not known.

In December 1918 the Petrograd Jewish People's University was set up, transformed in 1920 into the Institute of Higher Jewish Studies; a special notice on its work was published in the journal *Vostok*[184] for 1922. There it was stated that the main aim of the Institute was to encourage scholarly research on the history of Jewish culture and the training of academic and teaching personnel by giving them a specialized Jewish historical education.[185] The Institute consisted of two departments: the literary-philological and the social-historical. The course of instruction lasted three years. The main subjects studied were: the history of the Hebrew language and literature, the history of the Jewish religion and cultural tradition, the history of Jewish philosophy and Jewish law, the economic history of the Jews, and the Aramaic and Arabic languages. The first lecturers and teachers included S.M. Dubnov, S.G. Lozinsky, Yu. Brutskus, S. Ginzburg, S. Zinberg, M. Kulisher, etc. I.I. Gintsburg also taught in this Institute between 1922 and 1924. The Institute was apparently closed in 1924.

This is how S.M. Dubnov in his memoirs describes the foundation of the Jewish university:

> The short extracts from extensive notes which are quoted below will suffice to give an account of how we lived in 'Red Petersburg' in that terrible year, cut off from most of Russia and blockaded by foreign powers. Community life was, of course, quite out of the question at a time when savage elemental forces reigned supreme. We, the remains of the Jewish intelligentsia, used to meet only occasionally in the artificially developed Jewish People's University, which had been thought up only to give a crust of bread to a couple of dozen writers and artists. We opened our doors in February 1919 in the abovementioned house on the English Embankment, but by the end of the year had moved to another requisitioned house on Troitskaya Street, near the Nevsky Prospect. Lectures were delivered primarily in Russian, but some lectured in Yiddish.... Many students were attracted there by the bread rations, which were given out upon production of a card from the Commissariat of Education. Sometimes the same kind of 'hand outs' were bestowed on lecturers or 'professors'.[186]

The work of all Jewish organizations and societies was ended in the USSR in the years 1928-30. However, as has been shown above, the academic development of Hebrew studies was possible to a limited extent within the study group on the Ancient Eastern World and also Semitology within the Arabic study group at the USSR Academy of Sciences Institute of Oriental Studies right up to the first post-war years. But from the end of the 1940s the very words 'Jew', 'Jewish' and 'Hebrew' almost completely disappeared even from scholarly usage.[187]

In the last years Meer Natanovich Zislin (born 1916) worked on Jewish-Arabic philology at the Leningrad branch of the Institute of Oriental Studies. The main theme of his research was the study of the works of the medieval grammarian Abu-l-Faradj Harun, using the materials of P.K. Kokovtsov's archive and the manuscripts in the possession of the Leningrad Public Library (the Firkovich collection).[188]

From 1942 to 1953 there worked in the Arabic study group at the Institute of Oriental Studies in Leningrad Isaak Natanovich Vinnikov (1897-1973), a pupil of L. Ya. Sternberg,[189] I. Yu. Krachkovsky and P.K. Kokovtsov. Their influence shaped Vinnikov's academic interests: ethnography, Arabic and Semitic studies. After graduating from university in 1925, Vinnikov stayed there as an assistant lecturer in the department of general ethnography. His first works were concerned with the study of the beliefs of the pre-Islamic Arabs.[190] To the same period also belongs his article 'The legend of Mohammed's divine summons in the light of ethnography', which came out in 1934.[191] During the war he worked on the language and culture of the Central Asian Arabs. His doctoral dissertation[192] on this subject was, in the opinion of I.Yu. Krachkovsky, a major event in Arabic studies in the USSR.[193] This work embodied a rich collection of material on two living Arab dialects which had been discovered in Central Asia in 1936. In a detailed ethnographic introduction Vinnikov gives an analysis of certain questions concerning the everyday life and the folklore of the Central Asian Arabs, which he had studied minutely on his expeditions. The second part of this material related to the dialect of Bukhara and was published by Vinnikov in the 1960s, as 'A Dictionary of the Dialect of the Arabs of Bukhara' (1962) and 'The Language and Folklore of the Arabs of Bukhara' (1969). Of Vinnikov's epigraphic works the most noteworthy are his studies of Phoenician and Aramaic literary texts. It was due to him that there was a revival in the USSR of the traditional study of Phoenician texts,[194] which had been discontinued after the death of B.A. Turaev.[195] The dictionary of Aramaic inscriptions,[196] which Vinnikov started, covered all known Aramaic inscriptions over a period of 1,000 years (from the ninth century BC to the second century AD) and gives an exhaustive treatment of all their lexical and grammatical material, thus forming both a concordance and a grammatical reference book. Using the same method Vinnikov also composed dictionaries of individual literary texts, for example a concordance of Jewish Talmudic literature in Aramaic, amounting to 12,000 items, one alphabetical letter of which (Gimel) he published.[197] I.N. Vinnikov also did much teaching and lecturing. In Leningrad University he delivered lecture courses on the most varied topics: the history of primitive beliefs, Semitic linguistics, Semitic epigraphy, the Phoenician, Aramaic and Ancient Egyptian languages, etc. He introduced for the first time at Leningrad University a course on Arabic dialectology. In the obituary 'In memory of Isaak Natanovich Vinnikov (1897-1973)'[198] it is stated that his research and teaching work had been closely connected with Leningrad University, 'where he worked with only a short interruption from 1925 till the last days of his life'.[199] This obituary does not explain what caused this 'short interruption' (1949-55): at the height of the 'cosmopolitan campaign' the department of Assyrian and Hebrew studies, of which Vinnikov was the head, was closed, and he himself was dismissed from the university. Working without pay, he continued his work till the end of the academic year.[200] In 1951 Vinnikov was dismissed also from the Arabic study group of the USSR Academy of Sciences Institute of Oriental Studies, since it was announced that he 'was not suitable for the post held'. He appealed against this totally groundless decision to the 'very highest' instances and eventually was reinstated in the institute, but he did not return there.[201] After this Vinnikov for several years (till 1955) did not hold any post.

Hebrew scholars in the USSR have done a great deal of work on the Dead Sea manuscripts and documents. Here the most notable figure is Joseph Davidovich Amusin (born 1910). He published over twenty works dealing with the decipherment of individual documents and the problems of the history and ideas of the Qumran sect. He also published the first popularizing monographs on this topic with an original interpretation of a number of complicated problems, which enabled even Soviet readers to gain information on one of the greatest archaelogical discoveries of the twentieth century.[202] For his series of works on the Qumran texts Amusin was awarded the degree of Doctor of Sciences. In 1971 there appeared the first volume of the main Qumran texts in a Russian translation with a commentary, prepared by Amusin and his pupils.[203]

The problems of the ancient history of the Near East, based on North-Western Semitic inscriptions and Hebrew-Phoenician sources and documents in Ancient Hebrew and other Semitic languages, are at the present time being studied at the Leningrad branch of the USSR Academy of Sciences Institute of Oriental Studies by Ilya Sholemovich Shifman (born 1930). The main theme of his works is the social structure of the states of Phoenicia, Syria and Palestine. Since 1960 he has published more than 50 articles on these problems[204] and also monographs on the origin of the Carthaginian state and on the history and culture of Nabatea.[205]

The Semitologist Leyb Khaimovich Vilsker (born 1919), a research assistant at Leningrad Public Library (since 1950), is working on the Samaritan and Syrian languages.[206] He has excellent knowledge of the various genres of Samaritan literature and has made an important contribution to the study and interpretation of the documents found at Nahal Hever.[207] Apart from this research he has translated from the Ivrit several short stories by modern Israeli writers for collections of stories which were published in the USSR in the 1960s, and took part in the compilation of these collections.[208]

Mikhail Lvovich Geltser (Michael Heltzer, born 1928, living in Israel since 1972), a pupil of I.N. Vinnikov, worked in the Soviet Union in the 1950s and 1960s. After graduating from the Oriental Faculty of Leningrad State University in 1950, in the department of the Ancient Eastern World (after the closure of the department of Assyrian and Hebrew studies, in which he had specialized), he was unable to obtain work in his field of interest and until 1958 was forced to teach Russian language and history in secondary schools in Estonia. It was only in 1959 that he succeeded in obtaining casual (hourly-paid) work at Vilnius Pedagogical Institute, where he gave a course of lectures on the history of the Ancient Eastern World in Lithuanian. Only in 1965 was he accepted as a full member of the Institute staff; in 1966 he was made Associate Professor and in 1970 Professor. All this time Heltzer had continued his research work on his chosen topic—the social and economic history and the philology of the ancient states of South Western Asia (2000-1000 BC).[209] In 1969 he defended his doctoral dissertation 'The Society of Ancient Ugarit'. All in all he has published some eighty articles (ten of them after his emigration to Israel) dealing with problems of the agrarian relationships and social structure of the ancient states of Alalah, Ugarit, Phoenicia, Palestine and Syria,[210] and with individual inscriptions. He has also published the book: 'The Rural Community in Ancient Ugarit' (Wiesbaden 1976) (120pp.). At present M. Heltzer is a Professor at the University of Haifa, where he gives courses of lectures and conducts seminars in the history and epigraphy of the Ancient Eastern World.

In June 1977 the talented Leningrad Semitologist Jacob Berkovich Gruntfest[211] (born 1929) emigrated to Israel. After graduating from the Eastern faculty of Leningrad University in 1951 he was unable to find work; he completed a degree at another institute—of Engineering and Construction—and for more than ten years worked in this new field, while at the same time finishing a dissertation on 'The Verb in the Language of Southern Arabia' (defended at Leningrad University in 1966). Apart from the résumé of his thesis and the articles on his thesis topic, he published a number of articles on Sabbeic, Arabic and Ethiopian studies and on comparative Semitology. In 1974 appeared his first major work in the field of Hebrew studies:[212] 'A new document concerning Yemenite-Palestinian connections in the pre-Islamic period'.[213] Gruntfest displayed in this work great erudition in Hebrew scholarship, freely making use of Hebrew texts of various periods and genres from the Bible and Talmud to modern research in the field of Hebrew studies.

Of the younger generation of Hebrew scholars, who worked in Leningrad, we would like to dwell in some detail on the career of Khaim (Vitaly Yudovich) Sheynin (born in 1938), who has lived in Israel since 1972. Sheynin graduated from Leningrad University in 1967. In 1961 he had found it impossible, as a Jew, to be accepted for the department of Semitology, so he became a student at the department of classical philology. At the same time he also attended lectures at the Oriental faculty, and after passing the necessary examinations he managed in his fourth year to change over to the Eastern faculty, specializing in medieval Hebrew poetry. His degree thesis on the thirteenth century poet Joseph ben Tanhum was recommended for publication, but was never published in the Soviet Union. In 1966 he was offered work at the Academy of Sciences Library, at first of a temporary kind, later on the permanent staff, for the purpose of finally systematizing and listing Friedland's collection, which had been in a chaotic state since the war. He completed this work, and the catalogue (on index-cards) is housed in the Academy of Sciences Library in Leningrad. During his student years and while working at the Library Sheynin had written a number of works which were not published and have remained in the Soviet Union, including his article 'The transmission of the mobile *sheva* in Jewish Biblical proper names in the Septuagint', which was written as a student essay and had been highly thought of by those who examined it. In 1969 Sheynin translated into Russian the autobiography of Josephus Flavius, which was recommended for publication in the series 'Literary Texts' published by the USSR Academy of Sciences, and he began publication of the lyric poetry of Joseph ben Tanhum ha-Yerushalmi.[214] In the same year on the invitation of the editors of a collection of essays in honor of the seventieth birthday of Professor I.N. Vinnikov he wrote a detailed descriptive treatise on a newly discovered manuscript of the lyric poetry of Joseph ben Tanhum. The article, when accepted for this volume, was twenty-four typescript pages in length. Following requests from the editors and later the publishers for the shortening of the article, the author re-wrote it more than 20 times (the last version was just six pages long). At the last moment (possibly when the volume was already being printed) the article was withdrawn from the volume without any explanation, although the author had already referred to this publication in other works. At the end of 1971 Sheynin completed his book 'The Sephardic Language' (the first grammar of Ladino in Russian, together with a review of the literature in this language)[215] for the series 'Languages of the Peoples of the East', but because of the author's emigration to Israel in 1972 it was not published and was eliminated from the work-plan of the publishing-house. The same fate befell an article on the first edition of the Hebrew grammar of Moses Kimhi,[216] which was to have appeared in the next (1972) volume of *Knigovedchesky sbornik* (Bibliographical Miscellany). His Candidate of Sciences dissertation on 'The Poetry of Joseph ben Tanhum ha-Yerushalmi', written between 1967 and 1971, remained undefended. Besides this Sheynin had prepared for publication a catalogue of all the Hebrew incunabula contained in the Institute of Oriental Studies in Leningrad and in the Rare Books Department of the Lenin Library in Moscow. Since coming to Israel Sheynin has already published or prepared for publication a number of works,[217] some of which are based on works written whilst he was still in Leningrad, reconstructed from memory, whilst others are new.

Post-war development of Oriental studies

Let us return now to the general development of Oriental studies in the USSR in the post-war years. It is common knowledge that this period has been marked by the still greater centralization of power and extension of Party and State control over scholarship and culture.[218] The indisputable authority of 'Comrade Stalin himself' dominated all branches of scholarship, from biology to linguistics. The campaign against 'Cosmopolitanism' had a ruinous effect on Oriental studies as well. During this period many Orientalists were arrested and spent many years in camps or prisons (e.g. the specialist on African and international affairs A.Z. Zusmanovich); some of these perished in detention (e.g. the above-mentioned A.E. Khodorov). A large number of Jewish scholars were demoted in their work, dismissed from academic and pedagogical institutes in capital cities, and were also slated and persecuted in various ways. Thus for example I.D. Amusin in 1950 had to move from Leningrad University to Ulyanovsky Pedagogical Institute where he worked till 1954; I.N. Vinnikov, as we have noted above, was dismissed from Leningrad University and from the Institute of Oriental Studies; the Hebrew scholar Gita Mendelevna Gluskina (born 1922), dismissed from the university at the same time as Vinnikov, took a degree in the mathematics faculty and worked as a university teacher in mathematics. The young Jewish Orientalists who graduated at this time could not find work. This fact is admitted in some Soviet publications: for example in an obituary by N.V. Gurov and G.A. Zograf devoted to the memory of a talented young linguist and Indologist Semen Gesselevich Rudin (1929-73), who was killed in an accident, it is stated: 'Though one of the best graduates of 1952, he did not at once find a position in keeping with his vocation and his abilities. It was only in February 1954 that he became a part-time, and in the autumn of 1955 a full-time, permanent lecturer in the Eastern faculty.'[219]

When speaking of the development of Oriental studies in the USSR in the post-Stalin period we must point out that young scholars have come into Oriental studies in the 1960s whose method and style of work differ markedly from the style of the works of the pre-war generation of Soviet Orientalists, especially in such branches of Oriental studies as modern and recent history, economics and the history of international relations. This is what an American Sovietologist says about this: 'There emerged during the years of Khrushchev's tenure in power a new, younger generation of social scientists interested in questions pertaining to international relations, who showed a striking propensity, surprising by previous Soviet standards, for methodological and conceptual innovation.'[220] Of the Jewish Orientalists, it is primarily the specialists on the economics of the developing countries

Leonid Abramovich Fridman and Leonid Abramovich Gordon (both born 1930) who belong to this group of scholars. In their works, some of which they have written jointly,[221] much space is given to factual material and the sociological and statistical analysis of it. Alongside these scholars there continue to work to this very day Orientalists who continue the 'glorious traditions' of the Stalin period, such as the head of the section on international problems at the Institute of Oriental Studies Grigory Lvovich Bondarevsky (born 1920), the specialist on international relations and colonialism Naftula Aronovich Khalfin (born 1921), and the philologist Iosif Samoylovich Braginsky (born 1905). As mentioned above, their works are notable for their highly politicized tone and are mainly opportunistic and propagandistic in character.[222] However, it should be noted that the interests of many Jewish Orientalists of the post-war generation are in fields far removed from politics and opportunistic considerations, such as ancient history, philology and linguistics. Here we should mention first the works of the expert on ancient Indian literature P.A. Grintser (born 1928), the linguist and Indologist S.G. Rudin, already mentioned above, the Iranian specialist I.M. Oransky (born 1923), the historians of the ancient East G.M. Bauer (born 1925) and A.G. Lundin (born 1929), the specialist on Malayan literature V.I. Braginsky (born 1945, the son of I.S. Braginsky); in addition there are those scholars who have recently left the USSR, such as the Buddhologist A.M. Pyatigorsky, the linguist A.B. Dolgopolsky, the Semitologist A.M. Gazov-Ginzberg, the expert on ancient Indian literature A. Ya. Syrkin, the Iranian specialist M.I. Zand, the expert on the history of the peoples of Central Asia Yu. E. Bregel, the Sinologist V.A. Rubin, etc. The lives of many of these scholars are very typical of the generation born in the 1920s, which bore the brunt of the tribulations of the war and lived through the dark years of the Stalinist terror and Jewish persecution.

Yury Enokhovich Bregel (born 1925) took part in the war and as early as 1949, whilst still a student at Moscow University, was arrested and sentenced to ten years in the camps. In 1954 he was released and returned to the history faculty at Moscow University, from where he graduated in 1956 in the department of ethnography. In 1957 he started work at the Eastern Literature Publishing House of the USSR Academy of Sciences in the department for the publication of texts. In 1961 he successfully defended as a dissertation a book which he had published that year *Khorezmskie Turkmeny v XIX veke* (The Turkmenians of Khorezm in the Nineteenth Century) (Moscow). In this book Bregel presents a detailed analysis of the geographical distribution, the economic and political changes in the style of life and the social differentiation of the Turkmenian nomadic tribes in the Khiva Khanate in the nineteenth century, and also of their role in the political structure of the Khanate and their insurrection in the years

1855-67. In a review of this book the British Orientalist M.E. Yapp says that Bregel made use of a considerably wider group of sources in his research than the scholars who had previously dealt with these problems. He specially remarks on the precision and care with which Bregel has presented this new material on such a little-known topic as an indisputable merit of the book.[223] In 1962 Bregel moved to the post of junior research worker at the Institute of the Peoples of Asia (The Institute of Oriental Studies) of the USSR Academy of Sciences. In 1973 he emigrated to Israel, where he is at the present time working as a professor at Jerusalem University. Apart from more than 20 articles on the history of the Turkmenians of the Khiva Khanate in the nineteenth century, for which he made use of archival materials, he prepared the enlarged and re-worked edition of the classic biographical survey of Persian literature by C. Storey, a laborious task demanding a most scrupulous approach.[224]

The Sinologist Vitaly Aronovich Rubin (1923-1981), after completing his first year at the historical faculty of Moscow University, went off to the front along with other professors and students as part of a university volunteer corps; his unit was surrounded by the Germans, and he was taken prisoner. After spending three days of captivity in a German unit which was marching victoriously towards Moscow, he managed to escape. After returning to the front, he took part, in the winter of 1941-42, in the battles near Kaluga. But when the special camps for former prisoners-of-war were created, those three days of captivity cost Rubin one and a half years of hard labour in the mines of the coal-fields near Moscow. He was released from the camp in 1944 on grounds of ill-health, and it was only in 1951 that he graduated from the Oriental department of the historical faculty of Moscow University, with specialization in Chinese history. Though he had the qualifications and the right to go on to post-graduate study, he was not accepted, and only with difficulty managed to find work as a teacher of Russian to a group of Chinese students at the Novocherkassk Institute of Engineering and Land Improvement. From 1953 to 1968 he worked as a junior research assistant at the Fundamental Social Sciences Library of the USSR Academy of Sciences, where he was occupied with making abstracts of the Chinese literature there. Only in 1968 did he succeed in moving to work at the USSR Academy of Sciences Institute of Oriental Studies, where he could now completely devote himself to research work. V. Rubin published more than seventy articles and reviews on problems of Chinese history and philosophy. In 1960 he defended his dissertation ' "Tso-chuan" as source-material for the social history of ancient China'. In 1964 he started an intensive study of the philosophical trends in ancient China. In 1967 he published 'The two sources of Chinese political thought',[225] in which for the first time in Soviet

Sinological writing he re-considered the prevailing conception of Confucianism as a conservative state ideology which was preserved unchanged throughout its 2,500-year history. Later he continued the detailed research he had started on early Confucianism and its confrontation and interaction with the three other main trends in ancient Chinese philosophical thought—Legalism, Taoism, and Mohism. In his works he examined the conception of the individual's relation to the state and to culture in these philosophical schools and threw light on the struggle between the early Confucianists and the Legalists.[226] His radical approach to his subject, free from the accepted clichés of Soviet historical scholarship (the 'class essence' of philosophical doctrines, the contrasting of materialism with idealism), provoked the displeasure of orthodox Soviet Sinologists. Following his application to emigrate to Israel, he was forced to leave his job at the Institute of Oriental Studies, and for more than four years, while he was fighting for his right to be repatriated, he could only do research work in snatches. In 1976 Columbia University Press brought out an English translation of his book *Ideologiya i kultura Drevnego Kitaya* (The Ideology and Culture of Ancient China) (Moscow 1970). In his preface to the book the Sinologist W. de Bary, Provost of Columbia University, says:

> What strikes one immediately in Rubin's work is its freedom from ideological preconceptions and sterile typologies. That such an independent standpoint could emerge in an atmosphere heavy with dogmatic definitions and befogged by partisan polemics, takes us quite by surprise—less expectable even than Solzhenitsyn's volcanic eruption from the *Gulag Archipelago*.[227]

After emigration to Israel in June 1976, Rubin became a professor at the Hebrew University of Jerusalem, where he taught the history of Chinese philosophy. In spite of the difficulties he had in mastering a new profession (as a Jew and non-Party member he had not been admitted to a teaching position in the USSR) he succeeded, in the last years of his life, in contributing to research work on ancient Chinese philosophy.[228] A road accident in October 1981 cut short his scholarly career.

The specialist in Iranian philology Mikhail Isaakovich Zand (born 1927, living in Israel since 1971) graduated from the Eastern department of the philological faculty of Moscow University in 1950. Being the son of an 'enemy of the people' (his father, who had taught Western philosophy and dialectical materialism at KUTV, was arrested in 1937 and, apparently, shot) he encountered great difficulties in finding work. After gaining his degree with distinction, he was recommended for post-graduate work simultaneously by the two departments (Iranian and Arabic philology) in which he had specialized at the university, but he was not accepted, and instead was directed to teach at a school in the Orenburg region. He remained in Moscow, and during the year after he graduated he worked for only a few days as the apprentice of a compositor of Arabic type at a printing-works which was printing the works of Stalin in the Uyghur language. At the end of 1950 I.S. Braginsky offered Zand editorial work in connection with the preparation of the re-publication of the 'Short Account of the History of the Tadzhik People', of which Braginsky himself was the official editor. The author of this book, which came out in Russian in 1949,[229] was nominally B.G. Gafurov, at that time First Secretary of the CP of Tadzhikistan and the Director of the USSR Academy of Sciences Institute of Oriental Studies (1956-1977). The first edition had contained many factual inaccuracies, mistakes in the quotations and no scholarly apparatus. These defects were eliminated by Zand, who had to rewrite completely certain parts of the book. As some sort of recompense Braginsky arranged through Gafurov a job for Zand as laboratory assistant at the Institute of Tadzhik Language and Literature of the Academy of Sciences of the Tadzhik Republic in Stalinabad (Dushanbe), where he worked for seven years. Only after the post-humous rehabilitation of his father did Zand manage to return to Moscow, joining the editorial board of the journal *Narody Azii i Afriki* (The Peoples of Asia and Africa), where he headed the literature section. Over all these years Zand had been doing research in the field of Persian literature. All in all he has published about 160 works, including 20 books, amongst which are annotated editions of selected narrative poems by Avicenna (1953) and Rudaki (1957) and of the *Rubaiyyat* of Omar Khayyam (1955). To mark the 550th anniversary of the birth of Abd-ur-Rahman Jami he made the first full Russian translation of Jami's work 'The Spring Garden' with notes and an introductory article.[230] In 1964 appeared his studies in Persian literature.[231] He also took part in the compilation of a catalogue of the Eastern manuscripts in the possession of the Tadzhik Republic's Academy of Sciences, which came out in four volumes between 1960 and 1968. He has written also a number of articles on the Persian language.[232] After 1967 Zand actively participated in the movement of Soviet Jews for repatriation to Israel. After emigrating to Israel he became a professor at Jerusalem University and has published a number of works.[233]

As an example of a relatively 'successful career' we may quote the case of the linguist Aron Borisovich Dolgopolsky (born 1930, living in Israel since the autumn of 1976). After finishing school in 1949 with a gold medal, which gave him the right to enter any higher educational establishment without taking the competitive examination, he was nevertheless not accepted for the philological faculty of Moscow University 'because all the places have been filled'.[234] He entered the Spanish faculty of the Moscow Pedagogical Institute for Foreign Languages, and started to study the history of the Romance languages. By the next year he had received the first prize in the annual competition in linguistics organized by Moscow University. Ironically he was presented with the prize by the very same Dean of Moscow University Philological Faculty, Chemodanov, on whose authority he had been refused entry to the university. In 1954, during the short period of some mitigation in the discriminatory policy towards the Jews after Stalin's death, he succeeded in being admitted for post-graduate work at the institute from which he graduated in the department of general linguistics, but after completing these studies in 1957 it was only with great difficulty that he got a part-time job at the same institute in the translation department, which was far removed from his scholarly interests. It should be said that in all the cases we have quoted of discrimination against Jews in selection for jobs and post-graduate work, 'placement difficulties' arose not because there really were no places: at the same time as Jews were being refused entry, places were being found for non-Jews, often far less able candidates, but who merited the trust of the authorities. In particular there were, for example, frequent cases of the admission to post-graduate study of Komsomol activists who had no academic interests and had sometimes only bare pass marks in their chosen discipline. From 1960 to 1965 Dolgopolsky worked in the department of structural linguistics at the USSR Academy of Sciences Institute of Russian Language, although he was not a specialist in Russian linguistics. It was only in 1965 that he was accepted for the post of junior research assistant in the newly opened African languages section at the USSR Academy of Sciences Institute of Linguistics. Dolgopolsky, being a scholar of outstanding erudition in the most diverse fields of linguistics, at the same time as the work he carried out 'in the performance of his official duties'[235] had continued his studies in the fields which had always interested him—comparative-historical linguistics and the origin of languages, on which topics he published a number of articles,[236] and the book *Sravnitelno-istoricheskaya fonetika kushitskikh yazykov* (A Comparative-Historical Study of the Phonetics of the Cushitic Languages) (Moscow 1973). Since the autumn of 1976 Dolgopolsky has given several courses of lectures at the University of Haifa.

As the concluding example in our survey we will briefly describe the career of a member of the youngest generation of Jewish Orientalists in the Soviet Union—Galya Kellerman (born 1948, in Israel since 1973). While she was still a fourth-year student in the philological faculty of Moscow University she was invited to present a paper before the All-Union Conference on the Ancient Eastern World (March 1971). Her degree thesis, 'A Structural Analysis of the Verb in Ancient Hittite', was recommended for publication. However, in her finals she was given the lowest pass mark possible in Scientific Communism (the only such mark in her year), which disqualified her for post-graduate study (a very common trick practised by Soviet universities and institutes), despite the fact that she had been recommended for research work by the department of linguistics. After spending a long time looking for work she eventually obtained a temporary job as a laboratory assistant at the USSR Academy of Sciences Institute of Oriental Studies. After emigrating to Israel she taught Hittite language at the department of Assyriology at Jerusalem University from February 1974 to August 1975. From November 1975 to June 1977 she held a scholarship awarded by the French Government and wrote a dissertation 'Hittite Construction Rituals' under the supervision of Emanuel Laroche, Professor at the Collège de France. She has published (after emigrating to Israel) five articles on Hittite studies.

Thus, having traced the course of development of Oriental studies in the USSR over a period of 60 years, we may consider the following facts as established: in the first decades of the Revolution Jewish Orientalists actively participated in the organization and creation of a new Soviet school of Oriental studies, and moreover often acted as the champions of Party policy in the academic field (e.g. Pavlovich, Mif); but on the whole in the post-Stalin period it is noticeable that the best Jewish scholars working in the field of Oriental studies have abandoned rigid ideological dogmas and are returning to genuine scholarly traditions. With some of them this coincides with a return to national consciousness and emigration to Israel.

Notes

1 D. Miliband, *Bibliografichesky slovar sovetskikh vostokovedov* (Moscow 1975). Henceforth in this essay referred to as 'Dictionary' . In 1977 the 'Dictionary' was reprinted (a so-called 'additional impression' appeared) in order to eliminate references to some Orientalists who had in the meantime left the Soviet Union (for example, the Indologist A. Syrkin). For details see: I. Rubin, *Approach to Factual Material in Recent Soviet Biographical and Biobibliographical Publications* (Jerusalem 1981), 1; 15-16.

2 There exist the following academic degrees in the Soviet Union. After finishing at university (or a specialized educational institute) a student can do post-graduate studies for three years, in addition to which he defends a dissertation for the degree of Candidate of Sciences (approximately equal to the PhD in the West). The next academic degree is Doctor of Sciences, which requires a greater amount of published works, sufficient experience in research work and defense of a second dissertation. Outside this there exist academic titles connected with the kind of work. In the higher educational system these titles are:

This article was written in 1978 and only minor corrections could be inserted afterwards.

assistant, 'dotsent' (equal to associate professor), professor; in research institutions: junior research worker, senior research worker.

3 On this question see also L. Kochan (ed), *The Jews in Soviet Russia since 1917*, 2nd ed. (London 1972), 126ff.

4 See also S. Baron, *The Russian Jew under Tsars and Soviets* (New York 1964), 203-4.

5 In particular the well-known Soviet Orientalist N.M. Goldberg, who was descended from a Jewish family which had become Christian long before the Revolution, during the antisemitic campaign of 1948 made an unsuccessful request to the appropriate official organizations to change the entry in his passport (personal communication from Professor M. Zand).

6 By 1923 Moscow (86,000 Jews) and Petrograd (52,000) were among the largest Jewish-populated towns after Kiev and Odessa; see Kochan (ed), 131.

7 See in particular Kochan (ed); G. Aronson *et al* (eds), *Russian Jewry 1917-1967* (New York 1969); Baron; S. Schwarz, *The Jews in the Soviet Union* (Syracuse University Press 1951); S. Schwarts, *Evrei v Sovetskom Soyuze s nachala vtoroy mirovoy voyny (1939-1965)* (Jews in the Soviet Union since the Beginning of the Second World War, 1939-1965) (New York 1966).

8 Of course, bearing in mind the fact that the 'Dictionary' includes only some of all those graduating from specialized Orientalist institutions, we cannot and do not intend to maintain that not one single Jew graduated from such institutions in 1957 and 1958. However, the figures we have quoted do show that if some Jews did graduate in these years, they were clearly faced with conditions whereby they were virtually prevented from working in their field of specialization and from publishing their works.

9 S. Schwarz also notes the trend towards lowering the percentage of Jews amongst academic personnel in general. From 1958 to 1964 inclusive, though there was an absolute growth in the number of Jewish scholars, their percentage in relation to the total number of academic personnel in the USSR fell from 10.2 percent in 1958 to 8.3 percent in 1964 (Schwarz, 245).

10 By V.M. Alekseev—see 'Dictionary', 25.

11 By B.G. Boldyrev—ibid., 84.

12 N.A. Khalfin—ibid., 582.

13 A.M. Dubinsky—ibid., 191.

14 For example, A.N. Kheyfets—ibid., 584-5. Of his 14 works cited in the 'Dictionary' nine are on these topics and the rest on related topics. Some specimen titles: 'The Great October and the Exploited Peoples of the East' (Moscow 1959), 194pp.; 'October and the National-Liberation Movement of the Peoples of the East' (Moscow 1967), 32pp.; 'Lenin's ideas—the banner of liberation for the peoples of Asia and Africa', in the book *Lenin i Vostok* (Lenin and the East) (Moscow 1960), 11-66; 'Lenin—the Great Friend of the Peoples of the East' (Moscow 1960), 248pp.

15 For example, L.I. Duman. Alongside a large number of works on the history of ancient and medieval China, he wrote the very tendentious article 'The American imperialists—the bitterest enemies of the Chinese people', in *Uchenye zapiski Instituta vostokovedeniya* (Academic Transactions of the Institute of Oriental Studies), vol. 3 (Moscow 1951), 62-107. See 'Dictionary', 191.

16 There are three scholars who do not fit into these sub-sections: I. Ya. Zlatkin, who works on the history of Mongolia in various periods; L.I. Duman, who

worked on several periods in the history of China; and I. Yu. Perskaya, who works on the historiography of Indonesia.

17 This is also indirectly confirmed by the fact that some scholars moved to African studies from other branches of Oriental studies, e.g. I.A. Khodosh and S.I. Kuznetsova (see 'Dictionary', 587 and 290 respectively), and also from fields not connected with Oriental studies, e.g. F.M. Breskina (ibid., 93).

18 In this connection we would like to quote the following interesting fact which in our opinion very clearly illustrates the situation in the USSR Academy of Sciences in the early 1970s. At this time there was widely circulated in Soviet *samizdat* a 'Declaration' by I.S. Narsky, Doctor of Philosophical Sciences and Professor at Moscow University, addressed to the President of the USSR Academy of Sciences, M.V. Keldysh. Narsky writes: 'Recently I have several times come across allegations spread about me amongst members of the Philosophy and Law section of the USSR Academy of Sciences to the effect that I am concealing my true nationality, since I am allegedly in fact a "Polish Jew". I could have ignored these rumours, had it not been for the fact that they are manifestly connected with my nomination as a candidate for election as a corresponding member of the USSR Academy of Sciences. These allegations and rumours are slanderous in character and in no way correspond to the facts.' He goes on to give detailed biographical information not only about his parents but also about his wife's parents to prove that neither he nor his wife had anything to do with the Jews. Narsky asks Keldysh to circulate this declaration amongst the members of the Philosophy and Law section of the USSR Academy of Sciences, i.e. amongst those of his colleagues who were to elect him to the Academy of Sciences. The instruction appended by M.V. Keldysh to the declaration is: 'Circulate.' The genuineness of the document is beyond doubt: Keldysh's instruction and signature can be clearly seen on the photocopy. One must give Narsky's colleagues their due: in spite of the letter (or perhaps even because of it?) he was rejected in the very first round of voting. (The full text of I.S. Narsky's 'Declaration' is published in the journal *Posev*, March 1973, 61-2.)

19 See e.g. Kochan (ed), 274ff.

20 In the theses on the colonial and national question drawn up by Lenin for the Second Congress of the Comintern (April 1920) it is stated: ' . . . One cannot confine oneself at the present time to the bare recognition or proclamation of the need for closer union between the working people of the various nations; it is necessary to pursue a policy that will achieve the closest alliance of all the national and colonial liberation movements with Soviet Russia . . . ' And further: ' . . . All Communist parties should render direct aid to the revolutionary movements among the dependent and underprivileged nations (for example, Ireland, the Negroes in America, etc.) and in the colonies.' (In *Lenin on Politics and Revolution; Selected Writings*, edited and introduced by J.E. Connor (New York 1968), 316-17.) It is interesting that in the standard collection of Lenin's works published in English translation by the Moscow Foreign Languages Publishing House in 1960 (Khrushchev's era of 'peaceful coexistence with the West') these theses were not included.

21 Lev Mikhailovich Karakhan (1889-1937), Soviet statesman and diplomat; in 1918-20 and 1927-34 Deputy People's Commissar for Foreign Affairs; 1923-26—plenipotentiary in China; 1935-37—Ambassador in Turkey. Arrested and shot in 1937.

22 L. Karakhan, 'The tasks of Oriental studies', in *Novy Vostok* (The New East), Moscow, no. 7, 1925, 3-4.

23 The Asiatic Museum was an academic research institution for Oriental studies which included a collection of Eastern coins and manuscripts in Eastern languages, and also an Oriental studies library. It was founded in 1818. In 1930 it was transformed into the USSR Academy of Sciences Institute of Oriental Studies.

24 The Russian Archaelogical Society (1816-1924) studied ancient momuments, numismatics and epigraphy, organized expeditions and excavations and published edited inscriptions. An Oriental section existed within the framework of the Society from its very beginning.

25 The faculty of Oriental languages at Petersburg University was founded in 1854. In 1919 it was merged with the historical-philological and the law faculties to produce the faculty of social sciences, i.e. it was virtually abolished. In 1920 there emerged within the faculty of social sciences an Association of Orientalists—the College of Orientalists, which in 1921 was put under the jurisdiction of the Asiatic Museum of the USSR Academy of Sciences. In 1925 the faculty of social sciences was transformed into the faculty of language and material culture (*Yamfak*), and in 1930 faculties were replaced by specialized institutes. Out of *Yamfak* was created the Leningrad Historico-Linguistic Institute (LILI) which later on was transformed into the Leningrad Institute of History, Philosophy and Literature (LIFLI). In 1932 the faculties were restored (except for the humanities). In 1934 the historical faculty was reconstituted, in 1937 the philological faculty and in 1944 the faculty of Oriental languages. In the period from 1919 to 1944 Eastern languages, history and culture were taught to a limited extent within the framework of the abovementioned faculties and institutes.

26 The Lazarev Institute of Oriental Languages was founded in 1815 in Moscow as a private 'Armenian college of Lazarev brothers' with the resources of the rich Armenian family Lazaryan. In 1827 it received the official designation and status of an institute and was transferred to the jurisdiction of the Ministry of Education. In 1918 it was re-named the Middle East Institute, and in 1920 it was transformed into the Central Institute of Modern Eastern Languages, on the basis of which in 1921 was founded the Narimanov Institute of Oriental Studies. In 1936 the Institute was re-organized into a sort of higher educational academy, which accepted people only with completed higher education and no less than five years' full Party membership. The Institute trained 'Soviet officials, for the People's Commissariats of Foreign Affairs and Foreign Trade and for TASS'. The period of instruction was fixed at two and a half years. Two foreign languages were studied—an Eastern and a Western one, and courses were held in background-study of a particular country, international law, and the history of the colonial conquests. In 1940 it was again transformed into an educational institute of general range, which existed under the name of The Moscow Institute of Oriental Studies until 1954. In its place in 1956 was opened the Institute of Eastern Languages, which still exists, attached to Moscow State University. Admission to the Institute is restricted: entrants have to have special recommendations and be passed by a Party commission, which in fact means that most of the students are children of senior Party workers and KGB officials. Instruction in the Institute is supervised by the KGB, since the Institute trains chiefly personnel for the Ministry of Foreign Af-

fairs and for the KGB. Needless to say, Jews are not admitted to the Institute.

27 For more details on the life and work of M. Pavlovich see N.A. Kuznetsova and L.M. Kulagina, 'M.P. Pavlovich and Oriental studies in the USSR', in *Vestnik Leningradskogo universiteta* (Bulletin of Leningrad University), no. 20, 1963, *Seriya istorii, yazyka i literatury* (Series on History, Language and Literature), vol. 4, 14-19; and 'M.P. Pavlovich (Veltman) (1871-1927)', in *Narody Azii i Afriki* (The Peoples of Asia and Africa), no. 3, 1963, 189-93. The journal *Novy Vostok*, no. 18, 1927, contains articles in memory of M.P. Pavlovich.

28 *Novy Vostok*, no. 1, 1922, 10.

29 M. Pavlovich, 'The tasks and achievements of Oriental studies in the USSR', ibid., no. 16-17, 1926, iv.

30 Ibid., vi.

31 Ilya Nikolaevich Borozdin (1883-1959), an Orientalist, historian and archaeologist.

32 29 issues of the journal were produced during the existence of VNAV from 1921to 1930 inclusive.

33 I.N. Borozdin, 'M.P. Pavlovich and the All-Union Academic Association of Orientalists', *Novy Vostok*, no. 18, 1927, xxxix.

34 Sergey Fedorovich Oldenburg (1863-1934), a major Orientalist, full member of the Academy of Sciences (from 1908), permanent secretary, acting Vice-President of the Academy of Sciences (1904-29).

35 It should be pointed out that by 'theory', as is clear from what follows, S.F. Oldenburg in this case meant seriously scholarly knowledge in the field of Oriental studies.

36 *Nauchny rabotnik* (Scientific Worker), no. 1, 1925, cited by Pavlovich in 'The tasks and achievements . . . ', vii.

37 Pavlovich in 'The tasks and achievements . . . ' vii.

38 See, e.g., M. Pavlovich, 'The Struggle for Asia and Africa' (Moscow 1923); M. Pavlovich and S. Iransky, 'Persia's Struggle for Independence' (Moscow 1925), etc.

39 A.E. Khodorov, 'The academic and practical work of Pavlovich', in *Novy Vostok*, no. 18, 1927, lxv.

40 Ibid., lxi.

41 Lenin first formulated the idea of *partiynost* in his polemic with P.B. Struve. When speaking of the differences between the 'objectivist' and the materialist scholar, Lenin asserts that in contrast to the objectivists the Marxist does not limit himself to speaking of the necessity of a process, but ascertains exactly what social-economic formation gives the process its content, *exactly what class* [emphasis as in original] determines this necessity . . . Materialism includes partisanship, so to speak, and enjoins the direct and open adoption of the standpoint of a definite social group in any assessment of events' (Lenin, 'Collected Works', vol. I, 1893-1894 (Moscow 1960), 400-1).

42 Thus for instance one reviewer of the late 1920s (presumably M.I. Kazanin) wrote of a book by L.I. Madyar, that he found in it 'on the one hand a notable and keen critical flair for demolishing commonly accepted opinions and ideas, and on the other a readiness to take on trust any facts and figures in order to corroborate propositions which the author believes to be true'; in *Mirovoe khozyaystvo i mirovaya politika* (The World Economy and World Politics), no. 12, 1928, 105, a review of L. Madyar, 'The Economics of Agriculture in China' (Moscow 1928) (cited by V.N. Nikiforov, *Sovetskie istoriki o problemakh*

Kitaya (Soviet Historians on the Problems of China) (Moscow 1970), footnote on p.144).

43 In this connection it is interesting to note that the authors of the article about M. Pavlovich published in 1963, wishing to emphasize his merits, write: 'The influence of M.P. Pavlovich's work has been so considerable that some researchers to this very day unconsciously, willy-nilly use his formulations' (Kuznetsova and Kulagina, 'M.P. Pavlovich (Veltman)...' (see footnote 27 above), 193). In Pavlovich's articles and books we find a plethora of such clichés, as, for example: 'bourgeois Oriental studies have displayed their complete bankruptcy in relation to scholarship'; the colonial journals which are hirelings of the imperialists'; 'foaming at the mouth they criticize the Soviet press'; 'agents of foreign capital', etc.

44 M.I. Kazanin, *Zapiski sekretarya missii. Stranichka istorii pervykh let sovetskoy diplomatii* (Notes of the Secretary of a Trade Mission. A Page in the History of the First years of Soviet Diplomacy) (Moscow 1963), 52-3, 92, 118; V.N. Nikiforov, 'Abram Evseevich Khodorov. (To mark the 80th anniversary of his birth)', in *Narody Azii i Afriki*, no. 5, 1966, 219-23.

45 A.E. Khodorov, *Mirovoy imperializm i Kitay. (Opyt politiko-ekonomicheskogo issledovaniya)* (World Imperialism and China: Politico-Economic Research) (Shanghai 1922). Khodorov writes, for example, about the growth in China of forces 'which are forging the tools of struggle against the remains of feudal power and the "aspirations" of world capital' (ibid., xi).

46 V.N. Nikiforov, *Sovetskie istoriki...*, 97.

47 Ibid., 93.

48 See *Vostok* (The East), no. 3, 1923, 177-8.

49 A. Ivin (Aleksey Alekseevich Ivanov), (1885-1942), participant in the revolutionary movement, Soviet diplomat, specialist on China.

50 For more details on the polemic between A. Ivin and A.E. Khodorov, see Nikiforov, *Sovetskie istoriki...*, 144-51.

51 Nikiforov, 'Abram Evseevich Khodorov...', 222.

52 For more details on the work of M. Borodin and the Soviet legation in China see V.V. Vishnyakova-Akimova, *Dva goda v vosstavshem Kitae 1925-27. Vospominaniya* (Two Years in Revolutionary China, 1925-1927. Reminiscences) (Moscow 1965 — English translation by S. Levine, Cambridge, Mass., 1971); and Kazanin.

53 Ch'en Tu-hsiu (1879-1942), General Secretary of the Central Committee of the Chinese Communist Party and one of the leaders of the revolutionary events of 1925-27 in China. In the late 1920s and early 1930s his policy was strongly criticized in the Soviet press as 'rightist opportunism', 'a mixture of Trotskyism and Menshevism on Chinese soil' (Nikiforov, *Sovetskie istoriki...*, 170-80).

54 The Academic Research Institute for the Study of China was formed in 1928 out of the Sinology study group of the Communist University of the Toilers of China (KUTK). In 1932 it was merged with the Institute of World Economics and World Politics.

55 Nikiforov, *Sovetskie istoriki...*, 178.

56 See also V.N. Nikiforov, 'L. Madyar — revolutionary and scholar', in *Narody Azii i Afriki*, no. 5, 1973, 217-26.

57 The Sverdlov Communist University was the first higher Party educational institution in the USSR which trained Party and Soviet officials for senior posts. It was formed in 1919 out of the courses for agitators and Party instructors

which Sverdlov had started in Moscow in 1918. At first the period of instruction was six to eight months, then it was gradually extended to four years. In its first ten years more than 10,000 people graduated from the university. In 1935 it was transformed into the Higher School of Propagandists attached to the Central Committee of the Bolshevik Party. It subsequently became the present Higher Party School.

58 KUTV was an educational institution of the same type as the Higher Party School. It was formed in 1921 under the aegis of the RSFSR People's Commissariat for Education, but was later transferred to the jurisdiction of the Central Committee of the Bolshevik Party. It trained cadres for the Eastern border-lands of Russia, and its student intake was mainly from the nationalities there. Teaching was conducted in Eastern languages. The University was abolished at the end of the 1930s.

59 IKP was a special higher educational institution which trained lecturers in the social sciences for universities and institutes and also academic-research personnel and officials of the Party and State apparatus. It was formed in 1921 in Moscow. In 1931 it was divided into separate institutes according to departments. It was closed in the mid-1930s.

60 The Sun Yat-sen Communist University was opened in 1925 for the training of Chinese Party political workers and revolutionaries to help in the Chinese revolution. At first not only members of the Chinese Communist Party but also of the Kuomintang Party were admitted. The period of instruction was two years. Apart from Russian and one Western language there were courses in history (mainly the history of revolutionary movements), dialectical and historical materialism, political economy, economic geography, Leninism and military affairs. There were some 200-300 students in each year. In 1928 the university was re-named the Communist University of the Toilers of China (KUTK) and was closed in 1930. For details see Sheng Yueh, *Sun Yat-sen University in Moscow and the Chinese Revolution. A Personal Account* (University of Kansas 1971).

61 For details, see ibid., 40.

62 See, for example, his books: *Uroki Shankhayskikh sobytiy* (Lessons of the Events in Shanghai) (Moscow-Leningrad 1926); *Kitayskaya kommunisticheskaya partiya v kriticheskie dni* (The Chinese Communist Party at a Critical Time) (Moscow-Leningrad 1928); *Kitayskaya revolyutsiya* (The Chinese Revolution) (Moscow 1932), etc.

63 E.g., *Sovety v Kitae. Sbornik materialov i dokumentov* (The Soviets in China. A Collection of Materials and Documents) (Moscow 1933); *Programmnye dokumenty kommunisticheskikh partiy Vostoka* (Programme Documents of the Eastern Communist Parties) (Moscow 1934).

64 For details, see Nikiforov, *Sovetskie istoriki...*, 156-7, 160-5, etc. and 'From the history of Soviet Sinology' in *Voprosy istorii* (Problems of History), no. 2, 1972, 59-66.

65 Stalin, 'Works', vol. 8 (Moscow 1950), 367.

66 See, for example, the collection of essays *Vidnye sovetskie kommunisty-uchastniki kitayskoy revolyutsii* (Prominent Soviet Communists Who Took Part in the Chinese Revolution) (Moscow 1970), and also the reprint of M. Volin's article of 1926 in *Voprosy filosofii* (Problems of Philosophy), no. 6, 1959, 128-36. Not a word is said either in the book or the journal about the arrest and death of these prominent Communists in Stalin's camps. The only

book which appeared at this time and does refer more or less openly to the fate of these people is the book by V. Vishnyakova-Akimova mentioned in footnote 52 above. Recently I was told by reliable sources that in 1969 (i.e. soon after the 'Prague Spring') a secret circular was issued by Party authorities concerning individuals persecuted during Stalin's purges and subsequently rehabilitated. According to this circular, it was permitted to write about such persons, but without mentioning their tragic fate. A comparison of corresponding publications seems to confirm this.

67 Nikiforov, 'From the history of Soviet Sinology', 66.

68 The '28 Bolsheviks' was the nickname of the Chinese students at Sun Yat-sen University who supported Stalin's line in the university in his struggle with Trotsky. For details, see Sheng Yueh, *Sun Yat-sen University...*

69 Sheng Yueh, 38.

70 Ibid., 40.

71 See, e.g., M. Sendzhabi, 'Persian commercial capital and the Persian merchants' in *Torgovlya Rossii s Vostokom* (Russia's Trade with the East), no. 11-12, 1927, 6-7; 'On the Study of the Agrarian Question in Persia' (Baku 1930); 'Persia in Crisis' (Moscow-Tashkent 1931), etc. After returning to the USSR V. A. May worked as a lecturer in Baku and Moscow; he was arrested in 1938, but released a year later during the short-lived halt to the repressions which followed the arrest of the People's Commissar for Internal Affairs Ezhov. He did not continue working after his release, but retired on a pension (personal communication from A.V. May).

72 See p. 54, note 93.

73 *Revolyutsionny Vostok* was the official journal of the Academic Research Association attached to the Communist University of the Working People of the East and was published from 1927 to 1938.

74 *Revolyutsionny Vostok*, no. 8, 1930, 339.

75 See, for example, Z. Frenken's review of V. Gurko-Kryazhin's book 'A History of the Revolution in Turkey': 'How not to write about the history of the revolution in Turkey', in *Revolyutsionny Vostok*, no. 4-5, 1928, 426-34.

76 An interesting account of the activities of VNAV and the professional revolutionary Soviet Orientalists is given by W.Z. Laqueur in his book *The Soviet Union and the Middle East* (New York 1959), 11-17 and 79-85 respectively.

77 A. Shami (Yakov Tepper) was a Comintern emissary to the Middle East in the 1920s, a member of the Secretariat of the Palestine Communist Party and one of the chief organizers of the Communist Party of Egypt. In 1927 he returned to the Soviet Union together with his wife Sonya Roginskaya, also a specialist in the modern history of the Middle East. In 1937 they were both arrested and later perished in detention (for details see J. Hen-Tov, *Communism and Zionism in Palestine. The Comintern and the Political Unrest in the 1920's* (Cambridge, Mass. 1974), 35, 37; Laqueur, 83).

78 *Revolyutsionny Vostok*, no. 8, 1930, 25-52.

79 Ibid., 28.

80 Ibid., 52.

81 Nadab (Nahum Leshchinsky) was one of the PCP leaders and was regarded as the chief theoretician of the Party. In the 1930s he moved to Soviet Russia where he worked at the Communist University of the Toilers of the East. In 1936 he was ousted from the Party, arrested a year after and died on the way to a labor camp. (See also Hen-Tov, 34-5; Laqueur, 83-4.)

82 Nadab, 'Against rightist—ultra-leftist confusion in the colonial question', in *Revolyutsionny Vostok*, nos. 11-12, 1931, 117-37.
83 Ibid., 119.
84 A detailed account of the role of the Palestine Communist Party and the Comintern in the Middle East is given in Hen-Tov.
85 Note that in Miliband's 'Dictionary', 21, in the article on M.M. Akselrod, his intelligence work is designated as 'service in the Soviet Army'.
86 See G.S. Agabekov, *OGPU. The Russian Secret Terror* (New York 1931).
87 See also R. Conquest, *The Great Terror. Stalin's Purge of the Thirties* (London 1968), 437-8.
88 See, e.g., 'At the gates of Abyssinia. The festival of "Mascal". (A letter from Jidda.)', in *Novy Vostok*, no. 16-17, 1927, 329-33; 'The struggle of the parties in Egypt', ibid., no. 15, 1926, 302-10.
89 'Reforms in Hidjaz', in *Mezhdunarodnaya zhizn* (International Life), no. 1, 1928, 44-60; 'Modern Yemen. An economic and political outline', in *Novy Vostok*, no. 28, 1930, 71-98, etc.
90 As reported by Khamdi Selyam, an employee of the Institute of Oriental Studies.
91 The *Musar* movement were the adherents of an ascetic religious and ethical doctrine (opposed to both Hassidism and the Enlightenment), founded in the second half of the nineteenth century by Rabbi Israel (Lipkin) Salanter (1810-83). It was especially widespread amongst the Jews of Lithuania and Byelorussia.
92 For further information on this see the outstanding book, which is rich in detail, by Zvi Y. Gitelman, *Jewish Nationality and Soviet Politics. The Jewish Sections of the CPSU, 1917-1930* (Princeton 1972), especially the chapter 'The establishment of the Jewish Commissariats and Jewish Sections', 105-48.
93 S. Dimanshteyn, 'A turning-point in Oriental studies in the USSR (to mark the All-Union Congress of Orientalists)', in *Novyi Vostok*, no. 28, 1930, xxi.
94 Ibid., xxi. Also interesting here is the purely Party terminology which Dimanshteyn uses. At the beginning of the article he explains that the attack on 'the remains of capitalist elements' and the struggle with 'rightist deviation', proclaimed by Stalin in 1929-30, must be extended also to the field 'of academic work, which was to a considerable extent the monopoly of the ruling classes and served their interests'.
95 Ibid., xxi.
96 Cited by Gitelman, 135, note 77.
97 See also D. Joravsky, 'Parteilichkeit', in the reference book *Sowjetsystem und demokratische Gesellschaft* (Freiburg 1971), Band 4, 1,123-4.
98 See footnote 50.
99 The Communist Academy (before 1924 called the Socialist Academy) was founded in 1918. Its main aim was the study and analysis of the 'problems of the history, theory and practice of socialism', and also 'training scholars for socialism and responsible officials of socialist construction'. Under the aegis of the Communist Academy there functioned a large number of academic-research institutes in the fields of the social and natural sciences. It was abolished in 1936.
100 Nikiforov, *Sovetskie istoriki*..., 131-2.
101 For more detailed biographical data on M.D. Kokin and also on his scholarly activity and published works, see ibid., 290-1.

102 M. Kokin and G. Papayan, *Tsin-T'yan. Agrarny stroy Drevnego Kitaya* (Tsin-Tian. The Agrarian System of Ancient China) (Leningrad 1930).

103 Fedor Ippolitovich Shcherbatskoy (1886-1942), an oustanding Indologist and Buddhologist, from 1918 a full member of the Academy of Sciences.

104 The Leningrad Institute for Modern Eastern Languages was founded in 1919, partly as a replacement for the disbanded faculty of Eastern languages at Petrograd University, in order to train 'practical workers for the East'. In 1927 it was re-named the Enukidze Eastern Institute, and existed till the early 1930s.

105 In the book *Aziatsky muzey—Leningradskoe otdelenie Instituta vostokovedeniya AN SSSR* (The Asiatic Museum—the Leningrad Branch of the Institute of Oriental Studies of the USSR Academy of Sciences) (Moscow 1972), 162-5.

106 M.I. Tubyansky, 'On the authorship of Nyayapravesa', *Izvestiya Akademii nauk SSSR*, series 6, vol. 20, no. 10-11, 975-82.

107 M.I. Tubyansky, 'A preliminary report on the Buddhological manuscripts of V.P. Vasilev and V.V. Gorsky', *Doklady Akademii nauk SSSR* (Papers of the USSR Academy of Sciences), series B, no. 2, 1927, 59-64. Vasily Pavlovich Vasilev (1818-1900) was an outstanding Sinologist and Buddhologist and member of the Petersburg Academy of Sciences from 1886 onwards.

108 *Aziatsky muzey...*, 164.

109 Ibid.

110 *Bibliografiya Indii* (A Bibliography of India) (Moscow 1965), 590.

111 See, for instance: *Novaya istoriya kolonialnykh i zavisimykh stran* (Modern History of the Colonial and Dependent Countries), vol. 1, (Moscow 1940); *Novaya istoriya stran zarubezhnogo Vostoka* (Modern History of the Countries of the Non-Soviet East), vol. 1-2 (Moscow 1952); *Noveyshaya istoriya stran zarubezhnogo Vostoka* (Recent History of the Countries of the Non-Soviet East), vols. 1-4 (Moscow 1954-1960); *Novaya istoriya arabskikh stran* (Modern History of the Arab Countries) (Moscow 1965), repr. in 1966 and 1968 (in English and Arabic).

112 Al-Djabarti, Abd al-Rahman. *Egipet v period ekspeditsii Bonaparta (1798-1801)* (Egypt at the Time of the Bonaparte Expedition 1798-1801), vol. 3, Part 1 (Moscow 1962).

113 For example: 'Problems of periodization of medieval Arabic literature', in: *Narody Azii i Afriki*, no. 4, 1962, 144-56; *Arabskaya klassicheskaya literatura* (Classical Arabic Literature) (Moscow 1965); 'Arabic Literature' (Moscow 1966); *Ocherk arabo-musulmanskoy kultury VII-XII vv.*) (An Outline of Arabic Moslem Culture in the Seventh to the Twelfth Centuries) (Moscow 1971).

114 *Arabskaya literatura v srednie veka* (Arabic Literature in the Middle Ages), vol. 1.: *Slovesnoe iskusstvo arabov v drevnosti i rannem srednevekovye* (Arabic Oral and Written Speech in Ancient Times and the Early Middle Ages) (Moscow 1977); vol. 2: *Arabskaya literatura VIII-IX vv.* (Arabic Literature of the Eighth to Ninth Centuries) (Moscow 1978).

115 A.A. Freyman, *Khorezmiysky yazyk. Materialy i issledovaniya* (The Khorezmian Language. Materials and Research), vol. I (Moscow-Leningrad 1951).

116 See the review by M.N. Bogolyubov in *Voprosy yazykoznaniya* (Problems of Linguistics), no. 6, 1955, 147-51.

117 For a list of A.A. Freyman's ninety-four published works, see *Problemy vostokovedeniya* (Problems of Oriental Studies), no. 4, 1959, 219-22.

118 A.A. Freyman, 'A list of the manuscripts acquired for the Asiatic Museum of the Russian Academy of Sciences by V.A. Ivanov in Bukhara in 1915. Part II. Hebrew-Persian manuscripts', *Izvestiya Rossiyskoy academii nauk* (Proceedings of the Russian Academy of Sciences), vol. 12, 1918, 1,279-82.

119 Karl Germanovich Zaleman (1849-1916), a well-known philologist and Iranian specialist; an academician from 1895 onwards.

120 For more details, see *Ocherki po istorii russkogo vostokovedeniya* (Essays in the History of Russian Oriental Studies), vol. 4 (Moscow 1959), 93-5.

121 *Aziatsky muzey...*, 324.

122 'The composition of lyric poems' (1921); 'The poetry of Alexander Blok' (1922); 'Rhyme, its history and theory' (1923); 'Byron and Pushkin' (1924).

123 See, for example, M. Zhirmunsky, 'On the study of comparative literature'. An Ilchester Lecture delivered in the Taylor Institution, Oxford, on 29 April 1966 (*Oxford Slavonic Papers*, vol. 13, 1967, 1-13).

124 'The Uzbek national heroic epic' (1943); 'On the question of the literary relationships between West and East' (1947); 'An introduction to the study of the Kirgiz epic "Manas" ' (1948); 'The epic of "Alpamysh" and the "Odyssey" of Homer' (1957) (an article in English on the same subject was published in *Proceedings of the British Academy*, vol. 52, 1966, 266-86); 'Alisher Navoi and the problem of the renaissance in Eastern literatures' (1961); 'Epic songs and singers in Central Asia', in N.K. Chadwick and V. Zhirmunsky, *Oral Epics of Central Asia* (London 1969), 269-339, etc. For a list of V.M. Zhirmunsky's published works, see 'Viktor Maksimovich Zhirmunsky' (Moscow 1965).

125 M.M. Gukhman, 'Viktor Maksimovich Zhirmunsky (in honour of his 75th birthday)', *Izvestiya AN SSSR,* Literature and Language series, Moscow, vol. 25, no. 4, 1966, 360-2.

126 L.R. Zinder, T.V. Stroeva, 'V.M. Zhirmunsky as a teacher', *Problemy sravnitelnoy filologii. Sbornik statey k 70-letiyu chlena-korrespondenta AN SSSR* (Problems of Comparative Philology. A Collection of Articles to Mark the 70th Birthday of V.M. Zhirmunsky, Corresponding Member of the USSR Academy of Sciences) (Moscow-Leningrad 1964), 11-16.

127 R. Budagov, 'In memory of Academician V.M. Zhirmunsky (1891-1971)', in *Nauchnye doklady vysshey shkoly* (University Academic Papers), Philological Sciences Series, Moscow, no. 3, 1971, 127.

128 Gukhman, 360.

129 For example, in the book *Istoriko-matematicheskie issledovaniya* (Historico-Mathematical Studies), vol. 13, (Moscow 1960) the articles 'On the treatise on parallel lines by Nasir-ad-Din at-Tusi', 475-82; and 'On the treatise by Kazi-zade ar-Rumi about the determination of the sine of one degree', 533-8; also cf. translation, introductory article and commentary in the book *Omar Khayyam. Traktaty* (Omar Khayyam. Treatises) (Moscow 1961); and 'Mathematics in the Near and Middle Eastern countries in the Middle Ages', in *Sovetskoe vostokovedenie* (Soviet Oriental Studies) (Moscow 1958), no. 3, 101-8 and no. 6, 66-76.

130 *Aziatsky muzey...*, 544.

131 For details on the life and work of D.A. Khvolson and A. Ya. Garkavy, see *Evreyskaya entsiklopediya* (The Jewish Encyclopaedia), vol. 15, Petersburg, 1911, 584-7, and vol. 6, 1910, 180-3 (respectively); and also *Encyclopaedia Judaica* (Jerusalem 1971), vol. 5, 558-9; vol. 7, 1,339-41.

132 Lev (Moishe Arieh Leyb) Friedland (1826-99), philanthropist, public figure,

patron of the arts and collector of Hebrew books and manuscripts.

133 Information supplied by the Hebrew scholar Kh. Sheynin. It should be noted that until then Jews had not been admitted into the Academy of Sciences, so an exception was made for S.E. Wiener.

134 *Catalogus librorum impressorum hebraeorum in Museo Asiatico Imperialis Academiae Scientiarum Petropolitanae asservatorum. Opera et studio Samuelis Wiener.* Fasc. 1-7 (Petropoli, 1893-1918) (*Bibliotheca Friedlandiana*).

135 Ibid., 1.

136 *The Hebrew Book. An Historical Survey*, edited by Raphael Posner and Israel Ta-Shema (Jerusalem 1975), 67-8.

137 Pavel Konstantinovich Kokovtsov (1862-1942), major Russian Semitologist and Hebrew scholar, a pupil of D.A. Khvolson, from 1900 professor at Petersburg University, from 1912 full member of the Academy of Sciences.

138 Vasily Vasilevich (Wilgelm Wilgelmovich) Struve (1889-1965), outstanding specialist on the history of the ancient Eastern world, full member of the USSR Academy of Sciences from 1935.

139 Ignaty Yulianovich Krachkovsky (1883-1951), outstanding Soviet Arabist, author of almost 500 articles and books on Arabic philology; full member of the USSR Academy of Sciences from 1921.

140 J.G. Bender, 'On the problem of classifying the sources for the Book of Genesis', in *Zapiski Kollegii vostokovedov* (Transactions of the College of Orientalists), vol. 3 (Leningrad 1928), 395-416.

141 'Bibliotheca Friedlandiana. A Catalogue of the Hebrew Books (published before 1892) in the Library of the USSR Academy of Sciences Institute of Oriental Studies', vol. 8 (Lamed). Compiled by J.G. Bender, edited by Academician P.K. Kokovtsov (Moscow-Leningrad 1936).

142 K.B. Starkova, in *Aziatsky muzey...*, 551.

143 According to information supplied by Sheynin, after the war the listing of the books in the 'Bibliotheca Friedlandiana' collection proceeded very irregularly, in the form of urgent 'campaigns', usually on the occasion of various meetings or conferences or after specialists had complained at being unable to track down some book or other. Moreover, any suitable people who just happened to be available were recruited for this work, either people working on fixed contracts or staff from the Institute, who knew Hebrew but were not familiar with the rules of bibliographical description, were obliged to take up the work as a compulsory task. Naturally enough, the parts of the catalogue completed in this manner are of a very low standard. Only in 1966-67 was the listing of the books in Friedland's library finished (on index-cards) by V.I. Sheynin. This catalogue is now housed in the Academy of Sciences Library in Leningrad.

144 K.B. Starkova, in *Aziatsky muzey...*, 551. J.G. Bender's defense of his dissertation on 'Azariah dei Rossi (1513-78) as a Researcher in the Field of the Ancient History of the Jews', together with his award of the degree of Candidate of Historical Sciences, took place on 5 June 1935. The theses of the dissertation have been published.

145 See, for example, his article 'The socio-economic structure of Jewish society in Iraq and Syria in the 2nd-5th centuries AD', in *Uchenye zapiski LGU* (Academic Transactions of Leningrad State University), no. 78, Historical Sciences Series, vol. 9, 1941, 49-62.

146 See, for example, his article 'The significance of Hebrew sources of the early

medieval period for the history of the Near East', in *Sovetskoe vostokovedenie*, vol. 2, (Moscow-Leningrad 1941), 36-52.

147 K.B. Starkova, in *Aziatsky muzey...*, 552.

148 See, e.g., his article:'The concentration of land and the dispossession of small landowners in Iraq in the 2nd-5th centuries AD', in *Vestnik drevney istorii* (Bulletin of Ancient History), no. 2, 1947, 40-51; 'On the social structure of Iraq in the 3rd-5th centuries AD', in *Uchenye zapiski Instituta Vostokovedeniya* (AN SSSR), vol. 14, (Moscow 1956), 31-90.

149 I.I. Gintsburg, 'A short survey of the Hebrew collection in the Manuscript Department of the USSR Academy of Sciences Institute of Oriental Studies', in *Bibliografiya Vostoka*, vol. 10, 1936, 125-30.

150 In the 1960s the first part of this catalogue was re-cast and enlarged by the Hebrew scholars K.B. Starkova and A.M. Gazov-Ginzberg, and in 1964 it was submitted to the publishers, with whom it still is (information from Kh. Sheynin). K.B. Starkova, in *Aziatsky muzey...*, 553, has a reference noting that the catalogue 'is being printed'. See on this also Kh. Sheynin, 'Leket shkuha mi-ginzey rusya'. (Forgotten Miscellanea from Russian Repositories) in *Hagut Ivrit Bi-brit Ha-moatsot'* (Studies on Jewish Themes and Contributions to Hebrew Literature by Contemporary Russian-Jewish Scholars and Writers), ed. by Dr M. Zohori, Prof. A. Tartakover, Prof. M. Zand (Jerusalem 1976), 97-122 (in Hebrew).

151 See, e.g., I.I. Gintsburg, 'The manuscript of a Hebrew version of *Mizan* by al-Ghazzali', in *Zapiski Instituta vostokovedeniya AN SSSR*, vol. 6, (Leningrad 1937), 141-68; and 'Arab medicine and the works *Kanun* and *Urdjuza* by Avicenna based on the Hebrew manuscripts in the Institute of Oriental Studies of the Academy of Sciences', in *Trudy vtoroy sessii assotsiatsii arabistov* (Proceedings of the Second Session of the Association of Arabic Scholars) (Moscow-Leningrad 1941) 34-48, 163-73.

152 K.B. Starkova, in *Aziatsky muzey...*, 553. Boethius (480-524 AD), a late-Roman philosopher and major figure at the court of the Ostrogoth emperor Theodoric. Gintsburg wrote a doctoral dissertation 'The Ethical System of Boethius on the Basis of his "De Consolatione Philosophiae" '. The dissertation is kept in the Archive of Orientalists in the USSR Academy of Sciences Institute of Oriental Studies, Leningrad. Posthumously, one small chapter of this dissertation was published in *Kratkie soobshcheniya Instituta narodov Azii* (Brief Reports of the Institute of the Peoples of Asia), no. 69, (Moscow 1965) 116-22.

153 I. Yu. Krachkovsky, *Izbrannye sochineniya* (Selected Works), vol. 5 (Moscow-Leningrad 1958), 169.

154 I. Yu. Krachkovsky, 'An obituary notice on Yu. S. Vilenchik and a list of his works', ibid., vol. 5, 398.

155 I. Yu. Krachkovsky, 'An outline of the history of Arabic studies in Russia', ibid., vol. 5, 152-3.

156 See, for example, his 'Studies in the historical phonetics of the vulgar-Arabic dialects', in *Doklady AN SSSR*, ser. B, 1927, 1-6; 'Arabic gutterals', in *Zapiski Kollegii vostokovedov*, vol. 5, 1930, e.g. 99-107.

157 *Narody Azii i Afriki*, no. 5, 1975, 244-5.

158 Ibid., 245.

159 See, for example, his works: 'Die altsumerischen Wirtschaftstexte', in *Sbornik Egiptologicheskogo kruzhka pri Leningradskom gosud. univ.* (Collected Essays

of the Egyptological Study Group at Leningrad State University), vol. I, 1929, 15-17; 'The Sumerian numerical system', in the collection of essays *Yazykovednye problemy po chislitelnym* (Linguistic Problems Relating to Numerals), vol. 1, 1927, 177-90, etc.

160 I. Yu. Krachkovsky, 'In memory of a pupil', in *Izbrannye sochineniya,* vol. 5, 1958, 436.

161 Ibid.

162 Nikolay Petrovich Likhachev (1862-1936), a major historian and art critic, full member of the USSR Academy of Sciences from 1925. In 1925 he transferred to the Academy of Sciences the unique Museum of Palaeography which he had founded and which contained remarkable collections: stellae and papyri from ancient Egypt; cuneiform tablets from Mesopotamia; Coptic, Greek, Arabic and Roman written texts; incunabula, seals, etc.

163 See, for example, his articles on the Sumerian and Hittite-Cappadocian languages for the first edition of the 'Great Soviet Encyclopaedia' (vols. 62 and 59 respectively), 1933-35, and such works as 'On the two ways of developing a compound sentence in Akkadian', in *Sovetskoe yazykoznanie,* no. 3, (Leningrad 1937) 59f; 'The Origin of the modal forms of the verb in Arabic and Akkadian', in *Trudy vtoroy sessii assotsiatsii arabistov,* 19-23 October 1937 (Moscow-Leningrad 1941), 127-32.

164 I. Yu. Krachkovsky, 'In memory of a pupil', 438.

165 N.M. Postovskaya, *Izuchenie drevney istorii Blizhnego Vostoka v Sovetskom Soyuze (1917-1959)* (The Study of the Ancient History of the Near East in the Soviet Union 1917-1959) (Moscow 1961), 171.

166 See, e.g., his works, 'Egyptian Religious Monuments of the Theban Period' (Moscow 1917); 'The Story of the Decipherment of the Egyptian Hieroglyphs' (Moscow 1922), etc.

167 In the book *Sbornik trudov professorov i prepodavateley Gosudarstvennogo Irkutskogo universiteta* (A Collection of Studies by Professors and Lecturers at Irkutsk State University), Section 1, Humanities, vol. 1 (Irkutsk 1921), 114-40.

168 Ibid., 136-40.

169 Nikolay Yakovlevich Marr (1864-1934), outstanding linguist, Academician from 1912, originator of the so-called 'Japhetic theory' in linguistics ('the new doctrine on language').

170 The 'new doctrine on language' was formulated by Marr in the early 1920s and was soon proclaimed by his supporters as 'the only correct Marxist doctrine on language'. The domination of Marrism in linguistics led in the 1930s to the arrest and death of a number of major philologists who did not agree with this doctrine (e.g. E.D. Polivanov, B.V. Choban-zade, etc.). In 1950 Stalin publicly criticized Marr's doctrine, which led immediately to a complete rejection of this school and to a wave of 'anti-Marrist' articles, speeches, etc. The part played in Soviet linguistics by the 'new doctrine on language' and the discussions connected with it has still to be investigated in detail.

171 G. Frank-Kamenetsky, 'On some survivals of a pre-inflective structure in ancient Hebrew', in *Yazyki i myshlenie* (Language and Thought), vol. 1 (Leningrad 1933), 149-62; and 'The problem of the development of the verb in ancient Hebrew', ibid., vol. 3/4 (Leningrad 1935), 13-46.

172 See, for example, his articles: 'Water and fire in Biblical poetry', in *Yafetichesky sbornik* (Collected Japhetic Studies), vol. 3 (Moscow-Leningrad 1925), 127-64; 'The prophet Jeremiah and the struggle between parties in

Judaea', in the collection of essays, *Religiya i obshchestvo* (Religion and Society) (Leningrad 1926), 60-82; and also his book 'The Testimony of the Miracle-Working Prophets on the Local Origins of the Christ Myth' (Leningrad 1925). For more details on his work on these topics see G.M. Livshits, *Ocherki istoriografii Biblii i rannego khristianstva* (Studies in the Historiography of the Bible and Early Christianity) (Minsk 1970), 76-9.

173 See, e.g., his book *Ocherk istorii drevneevreyskoy religii* (An Outline of the History of the Ancient Jewish Religion) (Moscow 1937).

174 The Society was founded in October 1863 in Petersburg on the initiative and with the financial backing of Baron E. Günzburg. The main aim of the Society was to disseminate the knowledge of the Russian language and of natural science amongst Jews in Russia and to make Jewish and Russian culture accessible to them.

175 The Jewish Historical and Ethnographic Society was founded in 1908 on the basis of the historical and ethnographic commission attached to the Society for the Dissemination of Education amongst Jews in Russia. The Society's main aim was the study of the history and ethnography of the Jews in Russia and Poland. In 1909 the Society started to publish a quarterly *Evreyskaya starina* (Jewish Antiquities), edited by S.M. Dubnov. Ten volumes appeared before the Revolution.

176 In autumn 1915 an order was issued by the military authorities prohibiting all Jewish periodicals in areas affected by military operations. Soon afterwards, even the usage of Hebrew print was prohibited. See I. Yu. Yashunsky, *Evreyskaya periodicheskaya pechat v 1917 i 1918 g.g.* (Jewish Periodicals in 1917 and 1918) (Petrograd 1920), 3-4; *Evreyskaya starina*, vol. 10 (Petrograd 1918), 5; Sh. Ettinger, 'The Jews in Russia at the outbreak of the revolution', in Kochan, (ed), *The Jews in Soviet Russia since 1917*, 26.

177 *Evreyskaya starina*, vol. 11 (Leningrad 1924), 3-4.

178 See, for example, in vol. 11 (1924); V. Struve, 'The history of the period of Jewish residence in Egypt', 45-64; B. Shulman, 'The evolution of the levirate amongst the ancient Jews', 161-75, etc.; in vol. 12 (1928): N. Nikolsky, 'Hittite laws and their influence on the legislation of the Pentateuch', 213-38; B. Shulman, 'The Jewish demos in the first few centuries AD', 239-53, etc.

179 *Evreysky vestnik,* (The Jewish Bulletin) (Leningrad 1928), 224-5. What happened to this material is not known.

180 Sergey (Izrael) Lazarevich Zinberg (1873-1939), Jewish writer; in the first decades of the century he published in Jewish journals articles on Jewish literature and culture in Russia in Yiddish, Russian and Hebrew. He was a member of the editorial board of *Evreyskaya starina* after its revival (1924-30). Arrested in 1938, he died the following year still a prisoner. He was rehabilitated in 1956. See *Encyclopaedia Judaica* (Jerusalem 1971) vol. 16, 1028.

181 *Evreysky vestnik*, 223-4.

182 Moses ibn Ezra (Abu-Harun Musa), a medieval Jewish-Arab philosopher, poet and linguist. Born in Grenada about 1070, died after 1138.

183 *Encyclopaedia Judaica*, vol. 15, 1971, 61.

184 *Vostok* (The East), a journal of literature, learning and art, was published in Petrograd (Leningrad) from 1922 to 1925 (five numbers appeared) by a group of Leningrad professors (V.M. Alekseev, S.F. Oldenburg, B. Ya. Vladimirov, etc.) who apparently did not wish to work for the association VNAV and its

journal *Novy Vostok* (The New East), headed by M.P. Pavlovich (see above in the text).

185 *Vostok*, no. 1, 110.

186 S.M. Dubnov, *Kniga zhizni. Vospominaniya i razmyshleniya. Materialy dlya istorii moego vremeni* (A Book of Life. Reminiscences and Reflections. Source Material for the History of My Time), vol. 2 (1903-22) (Riga 1935), 281.

187 Cf. for example, the titles of works by Yu. O. Solodukho before 1941 and after 1947 (see p.279); the dissertation and published works of G.M. Gluskina, where Alharizi is called a 'Spanish' or simply a 'medieval' poet; and the last works of I.N. Vinnikov, in which the Talmud and Mishna are called 'Palestinian traditional literature'.

188 See, for example, his works: 'Leningrad fragments of "Kitab Al-Kafi" by Abu-l-Faradj Harun ibn al-Faradj (eleventh century) (based on the material in the P.K. Kokovtsov archive and the second Firkovich collection)', in the book *Semitskie yazyki* (The Semitic Languages) (Moscow 1963), 155-66; and 'The Eastern school of Hebrew grammarians in the 10th-13th centuries', ibid., vol. 2 (Part 2) (Moscow 1965), 764-72.

189 Lev Yakovlevich Sternberg (1861-1927), an outstanding ethnographer, journalist and public figure; after the Revolution he revived, and became the head of, the Jewish Historical and Ethnographic Society.

190 See, for example, his articles: 'Widows mourning and the custom of "iftidad" amongst the pre-Islamic Arabs', in *Doklady AN SSSR*, ser. B, no. 3, 1928, 39-43; 'Rain, water and vegetation on the tombs of the pre-Islamic Arabs', in *Zapiski Kollegii vostokovedov pri Aziatskom muzee AN SSSR* (Transactions of the College of Orientalists Under the Aegis of the USSR Academy of Sciences Asiatic Museum), vol. 5, 1930, 367-77. For a list of the published works of I.N. Vinnikov, see *Narody Azii i Afriki*, no. 6, 1967, 157-9; and also in the collection of essays *Voprosy filologii stran Azii i Afriki* (Problems in the Philology of the Countries of Asia and Africa), vol. 1 (Leningrad 1971), 7-14.

191 In the volume *S.F. Oldenburg. Sbornik statey* (A Collection of Articles Dedicated to S.F. Oldenburg) (Leningrad 1934), 125-46.

192 *Araby v SSSR* (The Arabs in the USSR—Ethnography, Folklore, and Language) (Leningrad 1941). The theses of the dissertation were published in Leningrad in 1944.

193 I. Yu. Krachkovsky, 'Essays on the history of Arabic studies in Russia', in his *Izbrannye sochineniya*, vol. 5, 175.

194 See, for example, his articles: 'New Phoenician inscriptions from Cilicia', in *Vestnik drevney istorii* (Moscow 1950), no. 3, 86-97; 'New light on the epitaph of Ahiram from Byblos', ibid., no. 4, 1952, 141-52.

195 Boris Aleksandrovich Turaev (1868-1920), an outstanding specialist on the history of Ancient Orient (in Egyptology, Assyriology and Ethiopian history); a full member of the Academy of Sciences from 1918.

196 *Palestinsky sbornik* (Palestinian Miscellany), vol. 3(66) (Moscow-Leningrad 1958), 171-216; vol. 4(67), 1959, 196-240; vol. 7(70), 1962, 192-237; vol. 9(72), 141-58; vol. 11(74), 1964, 189-232; vol. 13(176), 1965, 217-62.

197 'An experiment in compiling a dictionary and concordance of traditional Palestinian literature (the letter Gimel)', in *Palestinsky sbornik*, vol. 5(68), 1960, 151-228.

198 *Narody Azii i Afriki*, no. 5, 1974, 247-8.

199 Ibid., 247.

200 Information supplied by the Semitologist Professor M. Helzer, I.N. Vinnikov's pupil.

201 Information supplied by the Hebrew scholar Kh. Sheynin. Apparently the story of Vinnikov's dismissal and reinstatement continued till 1953, since in articles about him published in the Soviet press, and also in Miliband's 'Dictionary', the year of the cessation of his work at the Institute of Oriental Studies is given as 1953.

202 J.D. Amusin, *Rukopisi Mertvogo morya* (The Dead Sea Manuscripts) (Moscow 1960-reprint 1961); and *Nakhodki u Mertvogo morya* (The Finds by the Dead Sea) (Moscow 1964).

203 *Teksty Kumrana* (The Qumran Texts). A translation from the ancient Hebrew and Aramaic. Introduction and commentary by J.D. Amusin, vol. 1 (Moscow 1971), 23.

204 See, for example, his articles: 'On the problem of the meaning of the term "BOD" in Punic inscriptions', in *Epigrafika Vostoka* (Eastern Epigraphy), vol. 15 (Moscow 1963), 16-23; 'Social-legal groups in Syrian society of the Hellenistic-Roman period', in *Vestnik drevney istorii*, no. 2, 1971, 119-28, etc.

205 I. Sh. Shifman, *Vozniknovenie Karfagenskoy derzhavy* (The Rise of the Carthaginian State) (Moscow-Leningrad 1963); and *Nabateyskoe gosudarstvo i ego kultura* (The Nabatean State and its Culture) (Moscow 1976).

206 See, for example, his works: 'On the affirmative meaning of the particle a in the Syrian language', in *Kratkie soobshcheniya Instituta narodov Azii AN SSSR*, vol. 86 (Moscow 1965), 25-30; 'Samaritan inscriptions', in the book *Voprosy filologii stran Azii i Afriki*, vol. 1 (Moscow 1971), 152-60.

207 L. Kh. Vilsker, 'New documents discovered at Nahal Hever', in *Vestnik drevney istorii*, no. 1, 1964, 120-30.

208 *Rasskazy izrailskikh pisateley* (Short Stories by Israeli Writers) (Moscow 1965) (translation from the Ivrit and information about the authors); *Iskatel zhemchuga* (The Pearl Diver) (Moscow 1966) (compiled, translated from the Ivrit, and information on the authors given by Vilsker).

209 See, for example, his works: 'Source material for the study of the social structure of Ugarit', in *Vestnik drevney istorii*, no. 4, 1952, 28-37; 'Notes on the history of Phoenicia in the 8th Century BC', in *Palestinsky sbornik*, vol. 3, 1958, 58-70; 'The historical significance of inscriptions on Phoenician and Canaanite spear- and arrow-heads', in *Epigrafika Vostoka*, vol. 16, 1963; 'Royal dependents (bns mlk) and units of the royal estate (gt) in Ugarit', in *Vestnik drevney istorii*, no. 2, 1967, 42-7 (in Russian with English summary).

210 See, for example, M. Heltzer, 'On the Akkadian term "*resu*" in Ugarit', in *Israel Oriental Studies*, vol. 4, 1974, 4-11; 'Mortgage of land property and release from it in Ugarit', in *Journal of the Economic and Social History of the Orient* (Leiden), vol. 19, 1976, 89-91.

211 It should be noted that his name is mistakenly spelt 'Grundfest' in Miliband's 'Dictionary' (p.158).

212 Like other Hebrew scholars in the USSR, Ya. B. Gruntfest because of censorship constraints had to avoid the words 'Hebrew, Jew, Jewish'. Thus he replaces the words 'Hebrew inscription' by 'Yemenite inscription' (after the place where it was found), or by 'P.A. Gryaznevich's inscription' (after the name of the man who discovered and photographed the inscription).

213 In *Palestinsky sbornik*, vol. 25(88), (Moscow 1974), 105-14. Previously these research materials had been published in an abbreviated form under the title

'The inscription "Twenty-four Turns" from Beyt-Hadida' in the collection of essays *Pismennye pamyatniki i problemy istorii kultury narodov Vostoka* (Written Texts and Problems in the History of the Culture of the Peoples of the East), vol. 9 (Leningrad 1973), 71-81.

214 See V.Y. Sheynin, 'Der literarische Nachlass des Josef ben Tanchum haj-Jeruschalmi', *Acta Orientalia Academiae Scientiarum Hungaricae,* Tomus XXII (1969), 245-71.

215 The title of the book was thought up by Sheynin with the censorship in mind and was gladly accepted by the main editorial panel of Eastern literature of the USSR Academy of Sciences Publishers.

216 Moses ben Joseph Kimhi, a Jewish grammarian and compiler of commentaries who lived in France in the twelfth century.

217 See, for example, his above-mentioned article, cited in footnote 150 above.

218 See on this topic, for example, L.R. Graham, *Science and Philosophy in the Soviet Union* (New York 1972), 16-17.

219 *Narody Azii i Afriki,* no. 6, 1973, 238.

220 W. Zimmerman, *Soviet Perspectives on International Relations, 1956-1967* (Princeton 1969), 25.

221 L.A. Gordon, *Iz istorii rabochego klassa Indii. Polozhenie bombeyskogo proletariata v noveyshee vremya* (A Chapter in the History of the Indian Working Class. Status of the Bombay Proletariat in Modern Times) (Moscow 1961); L.A. Fridman, *Kapitalisticheskoe razvitie Egipta* (The Capitalist Development of Egypt) (Moscow 1963); L.A. Gordon and L.A. Fridman, 'The situation of the working class in the economically under-developed countries of Asia and Africa (based on India and the United Arab Republic)', in *Narody Azii i Afriki,* no. 1, 1962, 30-48; and 'The social structure of society and the working class of the developing countries of Asia and Africa', in the book *Rabochy klass stran Azii i Afriki* (The Working Class of the Countries of Asia and Africa) (Moscow 1966), 3-106, etc.

222 See, for example, G.L. Bondarevsky, 'The Portuguese Colonizers—the Enemies of the Peoples of Africa' (Moscow 1962); N.A. Khalfin, 'The Yankees in the East in the Nineteenth Century, or Colonialism Without an Empire' (Moscow 1966); T.S. Braginsky, 'The image of V.I. Lenin in the literatures of the East', in the book 'V.I. Lenin and Non-Soviet Oriental Literature' (Moscow 1971), 267-71, etc. We would like also to mention that I.S. Braginsky was the author of the article 'Class essence of Zionism' published in the Soviet daily *Pravda* (17 March 1970). Here he openly advocated the 'progressive process' of Jewish assimilation as the best and only solution of the 'Jewish question', opposing Zionism, to which he attributed the usual accusations of 'racialism' and 'imperialism' (re-published in English by the Novosti Press Agency in the collection: 'Zionism: Instrument of Imperialist Reaction. Soviet Opinion on Events in the Middle East and the Adventures of International Zionism' (March-May, 1970, Moscow).

223 *Bulletin of the School of Oriental and African Studies,* University of London, vol. 26, 1963, 435-6.

224 C.A. Storey, *Persidskaya literatura. Bio-bibliografichesky obzor v trekh chastyakh* (Persian Literature. A Biographical and Bibliographical Survey in Three Parts). Translated from the English, re-cast and enlarged by Yu. E. Bregel (Moscow 1972), 3 vols.

225 *Voprosy istorii,* no. 3, 1967, 70-81.

226 See, for example, his works: 'Man in ancient Chinese thought', in *Narody Azii i Afriki* no. 6, 1968, 74-85; 'The traditions of Chinese political thought', in *Voprosy filosofii*, no. 5, 1970, 90-101; 'Shen Tao and Fa-Chia', in *The Journal of the American Oriental Society*, 94, no. 3, (July-September 1974), 337-46.

227 V.A. Rubin, *Individual and State in Ancient China. Essays on Four Chinese Philosophers* (New York 1976). Quoted from p.ix.

228 'Values of Confucianism', in *Numen*, vol. 28, no. 1, 1981, 72-80; 'Concepts of Wu-hsing and Yin-yang', in *Journal of Chinese Philosophy*, vol. 9, 1982, 131-157; 'The profound person and power in classical Confucianism', in *Proceedings of the International Conference on Sinology* (Taipei 1981), 339-62 'Ancient Chinese Cosmology and Fa-chia Theory' (in press).

229 B.G. Gafurov, *Istoriya tadzhikskogo naroda v kratkom izlozhenii* (A Short Account of the History of the Tadzhik People), vol. 1: 'From Earliest Times to the Great October Socialist Revolution of 1917' (Moscow 1949). According to information supplied by Professor M. Zand, the original version of this book was written by N. Prokhorov, Gafurov's co-author in a number of works; then this version was translated into Tadzhik and published in 1947 under Gafurov's name with no mention of Prokhorov. The Tadzhik edition was translated into Russian again (partially re-cast and enlarged) by Ershov and published in 1949.

230 Jami, Abd-ur-Rahman ibn Ahmad, *Vesenniy sad 'Bakharistan'* (The Spring Garden 'Baharistan'), translated from the Tadzhik with an introductory article and notes by M. Zand; general editor S. Aini (Dushanbe 1964).

231 M.I. Zand, *Shest vekov slavy* (Six Centuries of Glory). An outline of Persian-Tadzhik literature (Moscow 1964).

232 M. Zand, 'Yiddish as the sub-stratum of modern Ivrit', in *Semitskie yazyki*, vol. 2, 1965.

233 In particular he compiled and published two collections of essays: 'The Prose of the Jews of Bukhara in the Late 19th and Early 20th Centuries' and 'Persian Poetry of the Age of the Samanids' (in Ivrit).

234 It is noteworthy that the interview which is obligatory for university entrants was conducted with Dolgopolsky in German—a very unusual occurrence at Moscow University.

235 Thus while working at the Institute of Russian Language he wrote and prepared for publication, jointly with Sukhotin and Babitsky, the work 'An Algorhythmic Description of Language'. It was, however, not published, because of Babitsky's arrest after taking part in a demonstration in Red Square on 25 August 1968 against the Soviet invasion of Czechoslovakia.

236 See, for example, his articles: 'The hypothesis of the very ancient cognation of the linguistic groups of Northern Eurasia from the viewpoint of probability theory', in *Voprosy yazykoznaniya*, no. 2, 1964, 53-63; 'Methods of reconstructing a proto-Indo-European language and the Siberian-European hypothesis', in the book *Etimologiya. Printsipy rekonstruktsii i metody issledovaniya* (Etymology. The Principles of Reconstruction and Methods of Research) (Moscow 1964), 259-70; 'The structure of the Semitic-Hamitic root in the light of a comparative-historical approach', in the book *Problemy yazykoznaniya* (Moscow 1967), 278-81, etc.

Contributors

JOACHIM BRAUN. Born Riga, 1929. Graduated Latvian Conservatory (violin). In 1964 received postgraduate degree at Moscow Conservatory. Was a leading music critic in USSR. Resident in Israel since 1972. Currently Professor, Department of Musicology, Bar-Ilan University. Has published two books and some 20 studies on Jewish music, Baltic music, and history of musical performance and musical instruments.

SHMUEL ETTINGER. Born Kiev, 1919. Left USSR for Palestine in 1936. Head of Department of the History of the Jewish People, Hebrew University, Jerusalem. Editor, *Zion*, Hebrew quarterly for research in Jewish history. Has written extensively on the modern history of the Jews in Russia and Poland and on modern antisemitism.

ANATOL GOLDBERG. Born St Petersburg, 1910. Left Russia in 1918 for Berlin. With advent of Hitler, settled in Britain. Joined BBC Monitoring Service in 1939 and BBC Russian Service in 1946. Became well known in the USSR for his regular broadcasts to that country. Died 1982.

IGOR GOLOMSTOCK. Born 1929. Graduated Moscow University in the history and theory of art. Was research fellow at the Museum of Fine Arts in Moscow and the All-Union Research Institute of Technical Aesthetics, and lectured in the history of art at Moscow University. Author of books and articles on West European and Russian art. Since 1972 resident in Great Britain.

JACK MILLER. Born Sheffield, UK, 1912. Graduated Sheffield University, 1935. Studied economic planning in Moscow, 1936-37. Lecturer and Senior Lecturer, Institute of Soviet and East European Studies, University of Glasgow, 1945-1977. Editor, *Soviet Studies*, 1949-70 and 1972-77. Editor, *Soviet Jewish Affairs*, 1970-72. Published works on economic and intellectual aspects of present-day Soviet society and on Soviet Jewish subjects.

BENZION MUNITZ. Graduate of Vilnius University in Russian language and literature. Left Vilnius for Israel in 1959. Resident in Great Britain. Engaged in research on early twentieth century Russian literature at University of London School of Slavonic and East European Studies.

INESSA AXELROD-RUBIN. Born 1928, Volsk, Saratov *oblast*, USSR. Graduated 1950 from Institute of Foreign Languages, Moscow. 1951-63 was librarian at Soviet academic institutions. 1963-72 was lecturer in German language at Academy of Sciences. Resident in Israel since 1976. Now librarian in Israeli academic institutions. Widow of Sinologist V. Rubin (1923-81).

EFRAIM SICHER. Born 1954. Former Junior Research Fellow, Wolfson College, Oxford. Now Director, Russian Studies Program and a member of the Research Center for the USSR, Eastern Europe and their Jewish Communities, Ben-Gurion University of the Negev, Beer Sheva, Israel. Published annotated edition of full uncensored texts of Babel's stories in Russian in Jerusalem, 1979.

YEHOSHUA YAKHOT. Born 1919. Graduated from philosophy faculty of Moscow University in 1943, later awarded degree of Doctor of Philosophical Sciences. Veteran of World War Two. 1947-73, Professor, Moscow Finance Institute. Resident in Israel since 1975. Since 1976, Professor, Hebrew University, Jerusalem. Published a number of works on philosophy and history of Soviet philosophy.

Name Index

Abramson, E., 262, 270
Adlivankin, S., 43
Agol, I., 217, 241
Ahad Ha-am, 13, 168
Akhmatova, A., 40, 134
Akhron, I., 67, 69
Akselrod, B., 9
Akselrod, I., 118, 142
Akselrod, L., 118, 142, 215, 217-19
Akselrod, M., 268
Aldanov, M., 177
Aleksandr II, 3, 5
Aleksandr III, 5
Aleksandrov, G., 227
Aleksandrov, V., 119, 142, 143
Aleksandrovich, M., 95-6
Alshvang, A., 85
Altman, I., 118, 142, 143
Altman, N., 27, 29, 30, 31, 34, 36, 37, 38, 39-40, 42, 43, 44, 50
Alyansky, S., 134
Amusin, J., 288, 291
Anders, General, 15
Andreev, L., 7
Andronov, N., 56
Ansky, S., 135
Antokolsky, M., 8, 25, 26-7, 29
Antokolsky, P., 16
Arkin, D., 34, 36
Aronovich, I., 84
Aronshtam, M., 118
Arvatov, V., 34, 38, 114, 118, 141, 153, 154
Asafev, B., 74
Ashkenazi, V., 83
Asmus, V., 118, 153, 155
Auer, L., 8, 68, 69, 76
Auslender, S., 118, 138, 149, 152
Averbakh, L., 15, 118, 145, 146, 147
Aykhenvald, Y., 118, 130, 131, 177
Ayzenshtok, E., 118, 140
Ayzman, D., 7, 13, 177

Babel, I., 14, 167-79
Bagritsky, E., 13, 113, 176
Bakst, I., 78
Bakst, L., 8, 26, 28, 29
Bakunin, M., 133, 148
Bammel, G., 216, 217, 226, 239
Baranov, K., 268
Barenboym, L., 85
Barkauskas, A., 97
Barshay, R., 83
Bartold, V., 265
Basner, V., 79, 90, 92
Batkis, G., 241
Bauer, G., 292

Begun, V., 20
Belenky, S. *See* Volin, M.
Belenson, A., 118, 149, 151
Belinsky, V., 8
Bely, A., 81, 133, 134-5, 136
Bender, J., 279
Benua, A., 26
Berdichever, E., 97
Berdyaev, N., 129, 216
Beregovsky, M., 66, 85-6
Bergelson, D., 13, 173
Berger, J., 56
Berkov, P., 118, 140
Berkov, V., 85
Berkovsky, N., 118, 140
Berlinsky, P., 81
Berlinsky, V., 83
Berman, Y.A., 132
Berman, Y.L., 217
Bernshteyn, S., 118, 149
Bernstein, E., 218
Bialik, H.N., 13, 168, 171
Bikel, T., 98
Birger, B., 56-7
Blanter, M., 78, 79, 80
Bleyman, M., 118
Blok, A., 31, 40, 133, 134-5, 136
Blok, K., 76
Blokh, B., 83
Blumenfeld, F., 76
Blyumfeld, L., 118, 142, 143
Boborykin, P., 4
Bogdanov, A., 112, 218, 233
Boguslavsky, N., 79
Bondarenko, P., 76
Bondarevsky, G., 292
Bondi, S., 118
Borodin (Gruzenberg), M., 262
Borozdin, I., 258, 265
Borshchevsky, S., 118, 140
Boyarskaya, R., 78
Braginsky, A., 84
Braginsky, I., 255, 292, 295
Braginsky, V., 292
Braudo, E., 85
Braudo, I., 76, 83
Braynina, B., 118, 142
Bregel, Y., 292-3
Breytburg, S., 118, 145
Brezhnev, L., 179, 205
Brik, O., 33-4, 36-7, 114, 118, 153
Broder, B., 97
Brodsky, I., 15, 20, 44, 45, 46, 47, 48
Brodsky, N., 118, 140
Brodsky, R., 253
Brovman, G., 118
Bruk, G., 97
Brusilovsky, E., 81
Brutskus, Y., 286
Bruzhenitsky, S., 76
Bubnov, A., 239
Bukharin, N., 188-9, 200, 210-11, 221, 223, 224, 239, 240
Bukhshtab, B., 118, 149
Bulgakov, M., 129
Burlyuk, D., 28, 33, 40, 119, 151
Burlyuk, V., 28, 40
Byadula, Z., 13
Byalik, B., 119
Bykhovsky, B., 215, 234

Calder, A., 41
Chagall, M., 27-9, 38, 41-2, 60
Chaykov, I., 49
Ch'en Tu-hsiu, 262-3
Cherny, S., 177, 178
Chernyak, Y., 119, 142
Chernyshevsky, N., 8
Chuzhak, N., 34, 114, 119, 153, 154
Chwolson, D., *See* Khvolson, D.

Daniel, Y., 20
Danilevsky, Y., 240
Davidov, K., 68
Dayan-Ginzburg, S., 220
De Bary, W., 294
Deborin, A., 215, 216, 217-20, 223, 226-7, 232-6
Demin, A., 265
Denike, B., 265
Derman, A., 119, 140
Der Nister, 13, 173
Descartes, R., 238
Deutsch, L., *See* Deych, L.
Deych, A., 119
Deych (Deutsch), L., 220
Deyneka, A., 46
Dimanshteyn, S., 217, 269-71
Dneprov, V., 119
Dobrolyubov, N., 8
Dobin, E., 119, 145, 146
Dobroven, I., 69
Dobrushin, I., 78, 86
Dobruzhinsky, M., 26
Dolgopolsky, A., 292, 295-6
Dolinin, A., 119, 140
Dostoevsky, F., 4, 132, 133, 187
Drachevsky, General, 67, 78
Drevin, A., 51, 54
Dreyden, S., 119
Druskin, M., 85
Dubinsky, R., 83
Dubnov, S.M., 9, 13, 286
Dumashevsky, A., 7
Dunaevsky, I., 74, 78, 79-80
Dymov, O., 7
Dymshits, A., 55, 119
Dynnik, M., 226

Efimov, B., 49, 55
Efremin, A., 119, 142, 144
Efros, A., 119, 149
Efros, N., 119, 140, 152
Egorshina, N., 56
Ehrenburg, I., 16, 18, 35, 38, 119, 153, 155, 156, 157, 176, 183-213
Einstein, A., 205, 222, 241, 242-3
Eisenstein, S., 15, 46, 114, 119, 153, 155-6
Ekster, V., 40, 42
El Lissitzky. *See* Lisitsky, L.
Eliasberg, K., 84
Elman, M., 8
Elsberg, Y., 119, 145, 146
Enchmen, E., 237-9
Engel, Y., 67, 68, 69
Engelgardt, B., 119, 149
Engels, F., 233
Erberg, K., 119, 134, 135, 136-7
Erdman, N., 119, 149, 152
Erik, M., 13
Erlich, V., 115, 141, 145
Ermilov, V., 201, 206, 209
Esenin, S., 40, 115, 152
Eshpay, A., 80
Eydlin, E., 119
Eydlin, I., 76
Eydus, Kh., 266
Eykhenbaum, B., 119, 149
Eykhengolts, M., 119, 152

Falik, Y., 93
Falk, H., 241, 242
Falk, R., 20, 42, 51-2, 54, 56, 57, 199, 201
Fayer, Y., 69, 84
Fayngold, N., 59, 61
Fefer, I., 86
Feltsman, O., 78, 79
Feuerberg, M., 168
Feygin, L., 93
Feygon, V., 83
Feynberg, I., 119, 140
Feynberg, S., 67, 69, 73, 74, 76

Filonov, P., 40
Filshtinsky, I., 273-4
Fingert, B., 224
Fisher, R., 70
Fokht, B., 226
Fortus, M. *See* Mif, P.
Fradkin, M., 79
Frank, F., 241, 242
Frank, S., 119, 129, 130, 138
Frankfurt, Y., 216
Frank-Kamenetsky, I., 282, 283, 285
Frenkel, A., 220
Frenkel, Y., 79, 99
Freud, S., 222
Freydenberg, O., 120, 149, 150
Freyman, A., 255, 274-5
Frid, Y., 120
Fridland, G., 217
Fridman, A., 241
Fridman, L., 292
Friedland, L., 278
Fritsch, T., 67
Frug, S., 7, 177
Frumkin, L., 14
Fundaminsky-Bunakov, I., 130
Furer, L., 83
Furtseva, E., 89

Gabirol, S. Ibn, 285
Gabo, N., 41, 42, 59, 60
Gabrilovich, L., 131
Gafurov, B., 295
Galich, A., 20
Galperina, E., 120, 140
Gamburg, G., 76
Garkavi (Harkavy), A., 277
Gazov-Ginzberg, A., 292
Gebirtik, M., 97
Gelfanbeyn, I., 76
Gelfand, M., 120, 145, 146, 147
Gerasimov, A., 46, 47, 52, 195, 201
Gerasimov, S., 46
Geringas, D., 82
Gershenzon, M., 8, 120, 135, 137
Gershfeld, D., 81
Gershuni, G., 10
Gertsenshteyn, M., 10
Gessen, B., 216, 217, 241, 242
Gessen, I., 10
Gessen, S., 130, 131
Geyman, B., 120
Gilels, E., 15, 83, 84
Gimelfarb, B., 120, 140
Ginsberg, A. *See* Ahad Ha-am.
Ginsburg, I., 25
Ginsburg, L., 120, 149
Ginsburg, S., 85
Gintsburg, I., 279-80, 286
Ginzburg, G., 83
Ginzburg, L., 84, 85
Ginzburg, M., 285
Ginzburg, M.Y., 34-5, 46
Ginzburg, S., 76
Ginzburg, S., 286
Girinis, S., 239
Gitelman, Z., 269
Glezerman, G., 225
Gluskin, A., 43
Gluskina, G., 291
Gnesin, M., 68, 69-71, 76, 80, 91
Goffenshefer, V., 120
Gofman, V., 120, 149, 152
Gold, M., 176
Goldfaden, A., 11, 78
Goldin, M., 90
Goldshteyn, A., 242
Goldshteyn, B., 84
Goltsman, A., 242-3
Golubeva, R., 95
Goncharova, N., 40, 46
Gonikman, A., 217
Gonikman, S., 224-5

Gopner, S., 217
Gordlevsky, V., 265
Gordon, L., 292
Gordon, M., 95
Gorelov, A., 120, 145, 146, 147
Gorev, B., 240
Gorin, P., 217
Gorky, M., 7, 40, 69
Gornfeld, A., 120, 141, 149, 151
Gorovets, E., 95
Gotlib, A., 83
Gots, M., 10
Grabar, I., 46
Grande, B., 281-2
Granovsky, A., 12, 42
Grebenshchikov, A., 260
Grigorev, A., 44
Grinberg, I., 120, 142
Grinblat, R., 93
Grintser, P., 292
Grobman, Y., 60
Grodburg, G., 83
Gronfeyn, B., 169
Gross, G., 38
Grossman, L., 120, 140
Grossman, V., 16, 205
Grossman-Roshchin, I., 120, 145, 146, 147
Gruber, R., 85
Gruntfest, J., 289
Gruzenberg, M. *See* Borodin, M.
Gruzenberg, O., 7
Guenzburg, I., 8
Gukovsky, G., 120, 141, 149, 150, 153, 154
Guminer, Y., 37
Gurevich, L., 120, 131-2
Gurevich, M., 83
Gurko-Kryazhin, V., 260
Gurov, N., 291
Gurshteyn, A., 120, 142, 144
Gurvich, A., 120, 142, 143
Gurvich, G., 130, 131
Gus, M., 120
Gutman, N., 89
Gutman, T., 83
Guzik, A., 95

Haffkine, V., 7
Harkavy, A. *See* Garkavi, A.
Haykin, B., 84
Hegel, G., 223, 226-7
Heifetz, Y., 8, 68, 69
Heltzer, M., 288-9
Heyfits, I., 15
Hirshhorn, F., 82, 84, 89
Hofshteyn (Hofstein), D., 13, 173, 174
Horovitz, V., 69

Idelson, A., 66
Ignatev, N., 5
Ilf, I., 14, 113
Ilichev, L., 200-2, 206, 209
Ingal, V., 49
Iofan, B., 15
Ioffe, A., 14, 241, 243
Ioffe, I., 34, 37, 120
Ioganson, B., 49
Iransky, S., 260
Isbakh, A., 120, 145, 146
Ivan the Terrible, 115-16
Ivanov, M., 56
Ivanov, V., 129, 132, 134-5, 136, 139
Ivanov-Razumnik, R., 134-5, 136
Ivin, A., 261, 271
Ivnev, R., 31
Izgoev, A., 120, 130, 138

Jabotinsky (Zhabotinsky), V., 13, 168
Jakobson, R., 125, 149, 150
Joravsky, D., 241, 242

Kabakov, I., 59
Kafka, F., 29
Kagan, O., 82, 83
Kamenev, L., 9, 120, 145, 221
Kamensky, V., 33
Kandinsky, V., 36, 42
Kantorovich, A., 262, 270
Kaplan, A., 20, 50
Kaplansky, S., 241
Karakhan, L., 256, 270
Karev, N., 217
Karnaviciane, N., 96
Kassil, L., 177
Kataev, V., 20, 176
Kats, 121, 145, 146
Kats, S., 79
Katsman, E., 15, 44, 45-6, 49, 55
Katsnelson, S., 121
Katz, B., 270
Kaufman, I., 121, 140
Kaverin, V., 14, 120, 140
Kazanin, M., 262
Kellerman, G., 296-7
Kerbel, L., 49
Khabibulin, Z., 70
Khachaturyan, A., 70
Khalfin, N., 292
Khayt, F., 78
Khayt, I., 79
Khmelnitskaya, E., 217
Khodasevich, V., 120, 132, 149, 152
Khodorov, A., 259, 260-1, 270, 271, 291
Khrennikov, T., 70, 91
Khrushchev, N., 17-18, 20, 52, 53-4, 56, 57, 94, 196-7, 198, 199-203, 206, 209-11, 291
Khvolson (Chwolson), D., 277
Kin, D., 217
Kirshon, V., 121, 145, 146, 147
Klausner, J., 13, 168
Kleynbort, L., 121, 142
Kluzner, B., 70
Klyuev, N., 134
Knipper (Kniper), L., 74-5, 80
Knorre, A., 76
Knushevitsky, S., 83
Kochetov, V., 197-8, 203
Kogan, L., 15, 78, 83, 84, 89, 96, 97
Kogan, P., 121, 142, 143
Kokin, M., 271
Kokovtsov, P., 278, 286
Kolman, E., 227, 241, 242-3
Kolmanovsky, E., 79
Koltsov, M., 206
Kompaneets, Z., 74, 79, 81, 93
Kon, A., 217, 224
Konchalovsky, P., 28, 29, 52
Korneev, L., 20
Koussevitzky, S., 8
Kovalson, M., 215
Kovarsky, N., 121, 149
Koygen, D., 131
Kozakov, M., 177
Krachkovsky, I., 279, 280, 281, 282, 283, 287
Kranikhfeld, V., 121, 142, 143
Krasny, Y., 60
Krein, A., 68, 71-2, 74, 80, 91
Krein, D., 72
Krein, G., 72
Krein, Y., 72
Kremer, G., 82, 83, 89
Krestovsky, V., 4
Kriegel, F., 18
Krumm, G., 217
Kulisher (Kulischer), M., 286
Kuperman, Y., 59, 60
Kupershmid, S., 78
Kuprin, A., 174
Kurbsky, Prince, 116
Kushner, B., 33-4, 36, 121, 153-4

Kustodiev, B., 28
Kuzmin, M., 121, 138, 149, 152
Kvitko, D., 216

Landau, L., 14
Lann, E., 121, 140
Lantsman, V., 82, 84, 90
Larionov, M., 28, 40, 59
Lavretsky, A., 121, 140
Lebedeva, S., 51
Lelevich, G., 121, 145, 146, 147
Leman, A., 60
Lenin, V., 40-1, 48, 68, 69, 112, 189, 200, 218, 221, 222, 240, 243, 256, 258, 259
Leningradsky, M., 236
Lenobl, G., 121, 142
Lentulov, A., 29, 52
Leonov, L., 193
Leonov, M., 215
Lerner, N., 121, 140
Lerner, R., 86
Leskov, N., 4
Lesman, I., 83
Levidov, M., 121, 141, 149, 150, 154
Levin, F., 175
Levin, L., 121
Levin, M., 76
Levin, M., 217
Levin, Z., 74, 75, 81
Levit, S., 216, 217, 241
Levitan, I., 8, 24-7, 29, 53
Levitin, Y., 91-2
Levitsky-Tsederbaum, V., 121, 145, 148
Leytes, A., 121, 142
Lezhnev, A., 121, 132, 145, 148
Lezhnev, I., 121, 145, 148
Libedinsky, Y., 121, 145, 146, 147
Liber, I., 83
Lifshits, M., 122
Lifshits, N., 65, 90, 96-8
Likhachev, N., 282
Lilienblum, M., 13
Lipshits, I., 83
Lisitsky, L. (El Lissitzky), 29, 35, 38-9, 41, 42, 46, 50, 53, 155
Litinsky, G., 74, 75, 81, 85
Livshits, B., 122, 147, 149, 151
Livshits, I., 83
Loks, K., 122
Loleyt, A., 35
Lossky, N., 131
Lozinsky, S., 286
Lukács, G., 147
Lukashevsky, A., 76
Lukomsky, I., 241
Lunacharsky, A., 31, 37, 42, 71, 73, 76, 208
Lundberg, E., 122, 129, 134, 135, 136, 137, 142
Lundin, A., 292
Lunts, L., 14, 113, 122, 140
Luppol, E., 217
Lure, A., 73-4
Lurye, S.Y., 122, 140, 285
Lutsky, M., 76
Lutsky, V., 273-4
Lyubimov, S., 95
Lyubimov, V., 82, 83

Mach, E., 112, 132, 242-3
Madyar, L., 262, 263
Maggid, D., 277-8
Magid, D., 66
Maksimov, A., 241-2
Malevich, K., 28, 34, 38, 39, 40, 42
Mandelshtam, L., 14
Mandelshtam, N., 203
Mandelshtam, O., 14, 29, 40, 122, 138, 149, 151-2, 176, 204
Mandelshtam, R., 122, 142, 144

Mandelstamm, M., 7
Mankovsky, L., 217
Margolina, A., 122
Mariengof, A., 115, 122, 149, 152
Markish, P., 13, 173
Markish, S., 177, 178
Markiz, L., 83
Marr, N., 150, 283
Martens, L., 217
Martov, Y., 9, 204-5
Marx, K., 222, 227, 228, 240
Mashbits-Verov, I., 122, 145, 146, 147
Mashkov, I., 28, 29, 52
Matsa, I., 217
May, V. *See* Sendzhabi, M.
Mayakovsky, V., 31, 33, 40, 154, 208
Maydansky, M., 86
Maysky, M., 82
Mayzel, M., 122, 145, 146, 147
Mazel, L., 85
Melnikov, B., 260
Mendele Moykher-Sforim, 13, 168
Mendelson, A., 217
Mendelson, N., 122
Merezhkovsky, D., 129, 132, 137
Messer, R., 122, 145, 146
Messerer, A., 15
Messerer, S., 15
Meyerhold, V., 31, 114, 122, 132, 135, 137, 153, 155, 157, 206
Meylakh, B., 122
Mif, P. (Fortus, M.), 262, 263-4, 270, 297
Mikhaylovskaya, N., 75
Mikhoels, S., 42, 75, 88, 156, 168
Miller, V., 237
Milner, M., 68, 72-3, 96
Milshteyn, Y., 85
Milstein, N., 8, 15, 68, 69
Minin, S., 237
Minkowski, H., 7
Minsky, N., 7, 129, 130, 132, 177
Mints, S., 122, 140
Miron, I., 98
Mitin, M., 216, 217, 221, 225, 227, 235-6, 249
Modzalevsky, B., 122, 140
Modzalevsky, L., 122, 140
Mogilevsky, A., 76
Mordovin, K., 56
Morgalin, M., 77
Müller von Azov, E., 66
Munblit, G., 122
Murphy, A., 175
Mushel, G., 70, 81
Mustangova, E., 122, 145, 146, 147
Myaskovsky, N., 88
Myshkovskaya, L., 122, 140

'Nadab', 266-7
Namizamidze, N., 70
Neivestny, E., 18, 20, 56, 61
Nekrasov, N., 4
Nels, S., 122
Nestev, I., 85
Nevsky, N., 270
Neyman, B., 122
Nikiforov, V., 260, 261, 264, 271
Nikolsky, N., 265
Nikonov, M., 56
Nikulin, L., 14
Nister, Der. *See* Der Nister
Novich, I., 122, 145, 146, 147
Nusberg, L., 59, 61
Nusinov, I., 123, 145, 146, 147
Nyurenberg, A., 43

Oistrakh, D., 15, 76, 83, 84
Oistrakh, I., 83
Oksman, Y., 123
Oldenburg, S., 259

Olesha, Y., 113
Olten, N., 123
Opatoshu, J., 168
Oransky, I., 292
Oyzerman, T., 215

Pakelman, V., 76
Pakentreyger, S., 123, 132, 145, 148
Pantofel-Nechetskaya, D., 84
Papayan, G., 271
Passover, L., 7
Pasternak, B., 14, 16, 51, 114, 123, 138, 149, 151, 176, 198
Pasternak, L., 8
Paustovsky, K., 170
Paverman, M., 84
Pavlovich, M., 257-60, 265, 297
Pazovsky, A., 84
Pekelis, M., 85
Pekker, G., 76
Perelman, V., 44, 46
Pergament, A., 83
Pertsov, V., 123, 153, 154
Perutsky, M., 43
Pervomaysky, L., 13
Pesis, B., 123
Peter the Great, 2
Petrov-Vodkin, K., 28, 136
Pevsner, A., 41, 42, 59, 60
Pikayzen, V., 83
Pikul, V., 20
Pimenov, Y., 46
Pinsky, L., 123
Pisemsky, A., 4
Plekhanov, G., 215, 218, 219, 220-2, 223, 228, 234, 237
Plisetskaya, M., 15
Plotkin, L., 123
Podvolotsky, I., 217
Pokrass, D., 74, 78, 79, 97
Pokrass, S., 74, 78, 79
Poltoratsky, N., 128
Polyak, L., 123, 142, 144
Polyakin, M., 76
Pomerantsev, V., 192, 194, 196
Popova, L., 40
Posner, R., 278
Pozern, B., 217
Pozner, V., 123, 140, 215
Press, I., 68
Pritsker, D., 79
Prokofiev, S., 78, 88
Pulver, L., 75
Pumpyansky, L., 123
Puni, I., 42
Puni, N., 34
Pyatigorsky, A., 292
Pyatigorsky, G., 69, 76

Rabin, O., 20, 58-9, 61
Rabinovich, A. & D., 85
Rabinovich, I., 42, 51
Radek, K., 123, 145
Radimov, P., 44
Radlov, E., 135, 216
Rakhlin, N., 84
Rakhman, B., 236
Raltsevich, V., 217
Ranovich, A., 284
Raukhverger, M., 81
Razumovsky, I., 215, 216, 217, 223
Reentovich, I., 83
Remizov, A., 134-5
Rerikh (Roerich), N., 26
Reshetnikov, F., 4
Reyser, S., 123
Reyzen, M., 84
Reznik, O., 123
Riftin, A., 282-3
Rimsky-Korsakov, N., 67, 75
Risin, I., 84
Riskind, B., 78

Rivkin, A., 76
Rizhkin, I., 85
Rodchenko, A., 35
Rodov, S., 123, 145, 146
Roerich, N. *See* Rerikh, N.
Rogozhina, N., 72
Romm, M., 15
Rosental, M., 215
Rothstein, F., 255
Royzman, L., 83
Rozenberg, V., 123
Rozenfeld, B.A., 277
Rozenfeld, B.L., 123
Rozenfeld, I., 97
Rozhitsyn, V., 219
Rozovsky, S., 68, 69
Rubin, A., 226, 233
Rubin, R., 94
Rubin, V., 292, 293-4
Rubinshteyn, M., 131, 217
Rubinstein, A., 8
Rubinstein, N., 8
Ruderman, M., 123
Rudin, S., 291, 292
Rybak, N., 13
Ryskin, E., 123
Ryzhsky, G., 43

Sabaneev, L., 72
Sabashnikova, M., 135
Saminsky, L., 68, 69
Samosud, S., 84
Samoylovich, A., 265, 270
Sarabyanov, V., 224-5
Saryan, M., 28, 199
Sats, I., 123, 142, 143, 144
Sats, N., 123, 142, 143
Schwartz, B., 87
Selvinsky, I., 13-14, 123, 153, 155
Semashko, N., 241
Semkovsky, S., 241, 242-3
Semkovsky, Y., 216, 217, 223
Sendzhabi, M. (May, V.), 264-5
Serebryakova, G., 200, 202
Serebryansky, M., 123, 145, 146, 147
Serov, V., 52
Seton, M., 155
Shabad, A., 123
Shafran, D., 83
Shakhin, M., 83
Shalit, M., 78
Shalyapin, F., 40, 68
Shami, A., 266-7
Shapiro, F., 282
Sharbatov, G., 282
Shaynin, I., 78
Shcherbakov, A., 15
Shcherbatskoy, F., 272, 273
Shchutsky, K., 270
Shegal, G., 49
Shekhter, B., 81
Shengeli, G., 123, 149, 152
Sher, V., 76
Shershenevich, V., 115, 152
Shestov, L., 124, 130, 131, 132
Shevtsov, I., 20
Sheynin, K., 289-90
Shifman, I., 288
Shifman, L., 83
Shklovsky, V., 124, 141, 149, 153
Shklyar, E., 67, 68, 69
Shkolnik, I., 37
Shilfshteyn, S., 85
Shlikhter, A., 217
Shmit, M., 84
Shneerson, G., 85
Shneerson, M., 124
Shnitke, A., 93
Sholem Aleichem, 168
Sholokhov, M., 202
Shor, E., 76
Shor, R., 124
Shostakovich, D., 74, 87, 88, 92,

93-4
Shtalberg, E., 37
Shterenberg, D., 27, 31, 34, 35-6, 39, 40, 43, 46, 50, 53
Shteynberg (Steinberg), A., 124, 130, 134, 135-6, 138
Shteynberg, E., 59
Shteynberg, E.L., 260
Shteynberg (Steinberg), I., 135-6
Shteynberg, L., 75
Shteynberg, M., 80
Shteynmets, L., 59, 60
Shteynpress, B., 85
Shub, E., 114
Shvarts, L., 79
Sidura, V., 57
Silber, V., 124
Simkin, M., 76
Simonov, K., 194-6
Simsky, B., 76
Sinyavsky, A., 20
Sitkovsky, E., 225
Skuditsky, Z., 86
Slánský, R., 17
Slavin, L., 14, 113
Slivker, B., 226
Slonimsky, A., 124, 140
Slonimsky, Y., 124
Slutsky, A., 268
Slutsky, B., 18
Sobol, A., 177
Sokolov, M., 278, 279
Sollertinsky, I., 93
Solodukho, Y., 279
Sologub, F., 7
Solovev, V., 133
Solzhenitsyn, A., 20, 54, 199, 200, 203, 206
Somov, K., 26, 152
Sorokin, P., 240
Sosnovsky, L., 124, 145, 148
Soutine, C., 27
Spinoza, B., 221, 226, 227-36
Spivakov, V., 82
Stalin, I., 14-18, 53-5, 60, 89, 173-4, 183, 188, 189-90, 191-208, 217, 222, 225, 236, 256, 264, 270, 291
Stanislavsky, K., 12
Starkova, K., 277, 279, 280
Staroselsky, A., 76
Stasov, V., 67
Steinberg, A. *See* Shteynberg, A.
Steinberg, I. *See* Shteynberg, I.
Steklov, Y., 124, 145, 147
Sten, Y., 217
Sternberg, G., 35
Sternberg, V., 35
Stivun-Katsnelson, I., 13
Stolpner, B., 226
Stolyarsky, P., 15, 68
Struve, P., 7, 129, 138
Struve, V., 278
Subotsky, L., 124, 142, 144
Surkov, A., 194
Svirsky, A., 177
Syrkin, A., 292

Tager, E., 124, 142, 144
Tairov, A., 124, 153, 155, 157-8
Targonsky, A., 76
Targonsky, I., 76, 83
Tatlin, V., 28, 38, 40, 41
Telingater, S., 46, 51
Ter, V., 220
Timiryazev, A., 242-3
Tolstoy, L., 6
Tomsky, N., 49, 54
Trakhtenberg, O., 215, 224
Trauberg, L., 124
Tregub, S., 124
Tretyakov, S., 124, 153, 154
Tronskaya, M., 124, 140
Trotsky, L., 9, 113, 116, 124,

130, 145, 147, 218, 221-2, 239
Trubetskoy, V., 265
Tsekhnovitser, O., 124
Tseydman, B., 81
Tseytlin, A., 124, 140, 154, 237
Tseytlin, L., 76, 77, 153
Tsfasman, A., 78, 79
Tsimbalist (Zimbalist), E., 8, 68, 69
Tsiporin, V., 83
Tsirlin, I., 58
Tsukerman, V., 85
Tsvetaeva, M., 204
Tubyansky, M., 272-3
Tugan-Baranovsky, M., 240
Turgenev, I., 6
Tvardovsky, A., 54, 194, 198, 209-11
Tymyansky, G., 216, 217, 223-4, 226, 233
Tynyanov, Y., 124, 149
Tyshler, A., 20, 29, 42, 50, 54

Vaks, I., 76
Valbe, B., 124
Vanshenkin, K., 99
Vantslav, 47
Varias, I., 226
Varshavsky, O., 168
Vasilev, V., 272, 273
Vayl, S., 241
Vayman, M., 89
Vaynberg, M., 88, 90-1, 92
Vaysberg, R., 217
Veksler, I., 124, 142
Veltman, B., 83
Vengerov (Wengeroff), S., 8, 124, 140
Vengerova, Z., 124, 130, 131, 132
Veprik, A., 73, 80
Vergelis, A., 74
Vertov, D., 15, 114, 125, 153, 155, 156
Veshnev, V., 125, 145, 146, 147
Vesnin, A., 46
Vesnin, V., 46
Veysberg, V., 56-7
Vidrevich, V., 83
Vilenchik, Y., 280-1
Vilsker, L., 288
Vinaver (Winawer), M., 10
Viner (Wiener), M., 13, 86
Vinkovetsky, A., 87
Vinnikov, I., 286-8, 291
Vinokur, G., 125, 149, 150
Volf-Israel, E., 76
Volfson, S., 125, 142, 224
Volin, B., 125, 145, 146, 147
Volin, M. (Belenky, S.), 262
Volkenshteyn, V., 125, 140
Volpe, T., 125, 140
Volynsky, A., 8, 125, 131-2
Vorobeva-Desyatovskaya, M., 272
Voronsky, A., 112-13, 147, 148
Voytinsky, G., 260
Voytolovsky, L., 125, 145, 148
Vrubel, M., 26, 53
Vsevolodsky, V., 125
Vygotsky, L., 125, 149, 151
Vysotsky, V., 20

Wengeroff, S. *See* Vengerov, S.
Wiener, M. *See* Viner, M.
Wiener, S., 278
Wieniawski, H., 8
Winawer, M. *See* Vinaver, M.
Witte, S., 6

Yakobson, R., *See* Jakobson, R.
Yakovlev, V., 59
Yakubinsky, L., 125, 149
Yakubovich, L., 95
Yakubovsky, G., 125, 145, 146
Yakulov, G., 35

Yampolsky, A., 76, 82
Yampolsky, I., 85, 125
Yampolsky, L., 78, 96
Yankelevich, I., 76, 84
Yankilevsky, V., 59
Yanovskaya, S., 227
Yanovsky, Y., 285
Yaponchik, M., 172
Yapp, M., 293
Yarkho, B., 125, 149
Yaroslavsky, E., 216, 219
Yudin, M., 76
Yudin, P., 217
Yuditsky, A., 78, 86
Yudovin, S., 51
Yushkevich, A., 277
Yushkevich, P., 132
Yushkevich, S., 7, 13, 177
Yuzovsky, I., 125, 140

Zadkin, O., 27
Zand, M., 292, 294-5
Zarkhi, A., 15
Zarkhi, N., 125, 153, 156
Zaslavsky, D., 125, 145, 148
Zbarsky, L., 60
Zelikhman, F., 76
Zelinsky, K., 155
Zelkina, E., 217
Zernov, N., 128
Zeydel, G., 217
Zhabotinsky, V. *See* Jabotinsky, V.
Zhdanov, A., 88, 177, 188, 192 196-7, 199
Zhirmunsky, V., 125, 149, 150, 254, 274, 275-6
Zhitomirsky, D., 85
Zhuk, I., 83
Zilber, L., 241
Zilbershteyn, I., 125, 140
Zimbalist, E. *See* Tsimbalist, E.
Zimmerman, W., 291
Zinberg, S., 286
Zinoviev, G., 9, 125, 145
Zislin, M., 286
Zisserman, D., 76
Zivelchinskaya, L., 125
Zonin, A., 125, 145, 146, 147
Zundelovich, Y., 125
Zusmanovich, A., 291